SHALL THE RELIGIOUS IN

ERIC KAUFMANN is Reader in Politics at Birkbeck College, University of London. In 2008–9, he was a Fellow at the Belfer Center, Harvard University. He is a frequent contributor to *Prospect* and other publications.

ERIC KAUFMANN

SHALL THE RELIGIOUS INHERIT THE EARTH?

DEMOGRAPHY AND POLITICS IN THE
TWENTY-FIRST CENTURY

P

PROFILE BOOKS

First published in Great Britain in 2010 by
PROFILE BOOKS LTD
3A Exmouth House
Pine Street
Exmouth Market
London ECIR OJH
www.profilebooks.com

Copyright © Eric Kaufmann, 2010

3 5 7 9 10 8 6 4 2

Typeset in Garamond by MacGuru Ltd
info@macguru.org.uk

Printed and bound in Great Britain by
Clays, Bungay, Suffolk

A CIP catalogue record for this book is available from the British Library.

ISBN 978 1 84668 144 8
eISBN 978 1 84765 194 5

The paper this book is printed on is certified by the © 1996 Forest Stewardship Council A.C. (FSC). It is ancient-forest friendly. The printer holds FSC chain of custody SGS-COC-2061

FSC
Mixed Sources
Product group from well-managed
forests and other controlled sources
Cert no. SGS-COC-2061
www.fsc.org
© 1996 Forest Stewardship Council

CONTENTS

For my parents, Steven and Carmen

ACKNOWLEDGEMENTS

I am indebted to many individuals, especially Paul Morland, who read earlier drafts in meticulous detail. My wife Fran provided helpful feedback on earlier drafts and presentations. I also met, exchanged ideas or collaborated with Vegard Skirbekk and Anne Goujon of the World Population Program at the International Institute of Applied Systems Analysis (IIASA), Jack Goldstone, Rich Cincotta, Elliott Green, Monica Toft, Jonathan Githens-Mazer, Rich Sosis, Jonathan Paris, Michael Lind, Chris Caldwell, David Voas, Faissal Hameed, Conrad Hackett, Peter Turchin, Michael Blume, Ehud Eiran, Nelly Lahoud, Shiraz Maher, Jim Guth, Rod Stark, Paul Froese, Byron Johnson, Aviel Roshwald and Mark Rieff. My editor at Profile, Andrew Franklin, has been a constant source of encouragement and constructive criticism. Needless to say, they may not agree with much, if anything, of what I have written.

This work could not have been completed without the generous support of my university, Birkbeck College, University of London. In addition, I was fortunate enough to obtain a grant from the Economic and Social Research Council (ESRC)'s Understanding Population Trends and Processes (UPTAP) programme, which laid the empirical foundations of this research. I benefited from a one-year fellowship from the Belfer Center, Kennedy School of Government, Harvard University, where I greatly deepened my understanding of religion and politics. A Leverhulme Trust grant helped make this possible. Finally, my understanding of religious demography has been greatly enhanced by those at the World Population Program, IIASA, in Laxenburg, Austria.

My website on the political demography of religion contains links to relevant sites and academic articles, papers and presentations of mine which delve into more detail on the data and methodology behind sections of the book: http://www.sneps.net/RD/religdem.html.

INTRODUCTION

A bomb rips apart a commuter train in Madrid. Scores are killed in a suicide attack in a crowded market in Baghdad or Peshawar. Another coalition soldier dies in Afghanistan. As a Canadian resident of London, I'm painfully aware of the steady drip of coalition casualties in both countries. The threat of terrorism is never entirely absent. Behind the scenes, Western societies wring their hands over profound cultural questions which cut to the core of who we are. How much should we bend liberal principles to accommodate religious practices? Is Islam off-limits to comedians and artists? How can we achieve security without trampling on suspects' freedom from detention without trial? Can we attain a measure of unity in the face of growing diversity?

If I am correct, what we have witnessed over the past decade is the thin edge of a rising wedge which transcends Islam. Simply put, this book argues that religious fundamentalists are on course to take over the world through demography. We have embarked on a particularly turbulent phase of history in which the frailty of secular liberalism will become ever more apparent. In contrast to the situation today, the upsurge of fundamentalism will be felt *more* keenly in the secular West than in developing regions. This is because we are witnessing the historic conjunction of religious fundamentalism and demographic revolution.

The world is in the midst of an unprecedented shift from population growth to decline. Europe is leading the way, but East Asia is aging more quickly and may overtake it, while other parts of the world – especially India, Southeast Asia and Latin America – are treading the same path. These changes are driven by rising prosperity, women's education, urbanisation and birth control. Europe's fertility rate – i.e. the number of children the typical woman is expected to bear over her lifetime – has been below the replacement level for four decades. As a result, its native population has begun to fall in absolute terms – a slide which will accelerate over time. World fertility is predicted to sink below the replacement level by 2035. Global population decline will follow several decades later.

It may seem as if the world is in danger of being depopulated and left to the animal kingdom.[1] People are increasingly failing to replace themselves and the openly non-religious among them are displaying the lowest fertility rates ever recorded in human history: sometimes less than one child per woman. However, this demographic transition relies on people's desire to better themselves in this world, not the next one. Those embracing the here and now are spearheading population decline, but individuals who shun this world are relatively immune to it. Everywhere one looks, religious fundamentalists are successfully bucking the trend towards fertility rates below the magic 2.1 children per woman. Even if everyone else died off, homo religiosus would endure. In the West, fundamentalism is also growing because the religion of uprooted immigrants from demographically expanding parts of the world is being radicalised by its collision with Western secularism. Identity politics reinforces and protects faith.

Fundamentalism is a modern response to the threat of secularism. In their quest for religious certainty, Christian, Muslim and Jewish fundamentalists have elevated the most world-denying, illiberal aspects of their traditions to the status of sacred symbols. One badge of fundamentalist belonging is outlandish dress – be this the ultra-Orthodox Jewish sidelock, Salafi burqa or Amish hat. Often these innovations are quite recent. Fundamentalism thumbs its nose at secular modernity in other ways, too, such as by affirming traditional women's roles. Large – sometimes unlimited – family sizes are typically part of the package, as exemplified by America's Quiverfull Protestants. These practices mark out the true believers from the backsliders who have supposedly compromised, to a greater or lesser degree, with secularism.

It is not that fundamentalists have suddenly begun to have more children. It is just that others are having fewer. In the past, when most children died before reaching adulthood, differences in family size had more to do with material factors. Any group trait which lowered infant mortality – African resistance to malaria, Christians tending their sick during plagues, superior Jewish hygiene, the wealthy being able to afford food and shelter – led the group to increase its share of the population. Only around 1900, for example, did European women of lower socio-economic status begin to have larger numbers of surviving offspring than the well-off.[2] Fertility rates were also driven by the need for labour on the farm and insurance in old age, neither of which matters in wealthy societies. Finally, those with access to contraception controlled their fertility better than those without it. Today, however, people – especially in developed countries – are largely able to choose the number of children they have. Why they select as they do depends more than ever on their cultural values and lifestyle choices. This increases the fertility gap between seculars and fundamentalists, paving the way for revolutionary population shifts.

Might secularism's salvation lie in luring away the children of the devout? This may work for the more open fundamentalist sects and cults, such as some American neo-evangelicals or the Jehovah's Witnesses. But strong religions generate powerful motives for people to remain in the fold and powerful disincentives to leave. This makes them more successful than moderate faiths in keeping their flock from straying. Largely endogamous, or in-group marrying, religious fundamentalists such as the ultra-Orthodox Jews or Mormons have been improving their retention rates over the past century. Put high fertility and retention rates together with general population decline and you have a potent formula for change.

The Old Order Amish, for instance, double in population every twenty years. They numbered just 5,000 in 1900, but have close to a quarter million members today. In the period 1997–2003 alone, sixty-six new Amish colonies formed. Only the fastest-growing non-denominational megachurches can match their growth rate. The Amish are still a small group, and they live in the USA, a large country. Might growth and influence lead to moderation? This seems less likely today because fundamentalists have effectively mobilised against the threat of secularism, which helps unify them and prevent moderating splits. Consider the ultra-Orthodox Jews, a larger group who – at least in Israel – occupy a much smaller pond. Once a trace element in the population, they now make up a third of the country's Jewish schoolchildren and are on track to becoming a majority group in the second half of this century. Unless secular Zionists figure out how to arrest their growth in a liberal manner, the outcome is predictable. And it is difficult to see how the rest of the world can avoid succumbing to similar forces as the demographic revolution unfolds.

Even small fertility premiums can lead to impressive gains if maintained over generations. The Mormons should have been a shrinking minority in Utah by now. However, they increased their share of the state's population from 60 per cent in 1920 to 75 per cent by the end of the century in the teeth of considerable non-Mormon immigration. Across the United States, the more numerous evangelicals grew from one-third to two-thirds of white Protestants during the twentieth century. In both cases, fundamentalists enjoyed no more than a one-child advantage over others, but maintained this over a century. Their success has not gone unnoticed and has spawned self-conscious pronatalism. The Quiverfull movement, for instance, which opposes family planning, has formulated a 'two-hundred-year plan' for domination. They may find Islamic fundamentalists in the way: some Islamists envision a demographic conquest of the West and victory 'from below' over the secular regimes of the Muslim world.

Though radical leftist writers assail liberal capitalism, the saga of ever-rising human progress – in science and human virtue – remains the central ideology of Western societies. Yet, as John Gray notes, liberalism is not necessary for modernity, and has largely won by historical accident. Human virtue, unlike science, winds back and forth rather than progressing ever upward. There is no necessary reason why the road ahead will not twist in an illiberal direction, leading to an outcome as violent as anything witnessed during the bloody twentieth century.[3] Religious fundamentalism and demographic transition form a potent cocktail. They will fuel apocalyptic terrorism, but violence is not the main issue. Religious zealots are no more violent than socialists or anarchists. The jihadist revolution even shows signs of having lost its way. The greater threat is cultural: that fundamentalism will replace reason and freedom with moral puritanism. As the recent experience of the Muslim world shows, the violent sting of fundamentalism can only be drawn by trading away secular thinking, women's rights and expressive liberty.

All the same, for many of us, the storm takes place at a distance. We rarely meet a fundamentalist. We don't know any victims of terrorism. We live our lives largely outside religion's orbit. In our world, best-selling New Atheists like Richard Dawkins, Christopher Hitchens, Sam Harris and Daniel Dennett loom larger. The churches and synagogues we know haemorrhage members. We seem on the cusp of a new era of naked atheism. Denmark and Sweden are leading the way, writes Phil Zuckerman: 'Worship of God can wane, prayer can be given up, and the Bible can go unstudied', yet society runs smoothly, with little crime, excellent health and high levels of societal happiness. People in Scandinavia, he writes, live perfectly contented lives knowing that their consciousness will simply expire when they die and that life has no further meaning beyond the here and now.[4]

As Scandinavia shows, there is a strong case to be made that the least religious countries are the most advanced. Pippa Norris and Ron Inglehart draw on decades of worldwide survey data to show that as income, education and equality increase, religiosity declines.[5] Secularisation theorists add that more complex, differentiated societies tear the 'sacred canopy' of religion asunder, reducing its influence and plausibility in modern life.[6] The Enlightenment and secular humanism transformed the consciousness of the West's cultural elite after the mid eighteenth century. Today, nearly all leading scientists and intellectuals in the developed world are non-believers. In Francis Fukuyama's terms, the secular 'last men' of today realise that their inherited religious tradition is simply one among many. Consequently, they no longer believe it to be the truth. Religious authority melts away under the glare of modern cosmopolitanism.[7]

In our politics, the great collective myths are on life support. Political parties now differ only by degree, competing on managerial competence rather than transformative ideology. We witness the 'end of chiliastic hopes' prophesied by ex-Trotskyist Daniel Bell in his *End of*

Ideology (1960). The great secular ideologies – socialism, nationalism and even the liberal anarchism of 1968 – have lost their grip. These ideas once served as surrogate religions, providing a storyline for societies akin to those we invent for ourselves each day. They told us where our societies came from and where we were going, anointing us as the chosen ones who would be gratefully remembered after death.[8] Collective myths and symbols inspired many to sacrifice, helping people achieve a sense of transcendence. In contemplating the Arcadian golden age of our heroic ancestors or the utopia of a socialist tomorrow, we escaped the confines of our profane present.

Secularisation theorists plausibly argue that the lonely, alienated condition of modern society has not stimulated a return to faith in the developed world. In a fascinating model based on recent survey data, David Voas predicts that atheists and agnostics will prevail in Europe, but suggests this process may take a century or two to run its course.[9] Religious revival has arguably succeeded only in the more deprived parts of the world where scepticism has yet to pour cold water on supernatural, enchanted modes of thinking. The upheavals of urbanisation, democracy and capitalism can only spark religious revival when the people remain, in Fukuyaman terms, 'in history'. Failed states, corruption, inequality and civil war generate insecurity, which fuels fundamentalism.

This Whiggish analysis dovetails with a long tradition of thought from Auguste Comte to Friedrich Nietzsche, which says that the triumph of a secular worldview is only a matter of time. Charles Taylor correctly appraises it as an ideological 'subtraction story' that is not susceptible to empirical verification. 'The Positivists,' notes Stuart Hampshire, 'believed that all societies across the globe will gradually discard their traditional attachments because of the need for rational, scientific and experimental modes of thought … there must be a step-by-step convergence on liberal values, on "our values" … We now know that there is no "must" about it and that such theories have a predictive value of zero.'[10] Rodney Stark and Roger Finke go further: 'After nearly three centuries of utterly failed prophecies … it seems time to carry the secularisation doctrine to the graveyard of failed theories, and there to whisper *"requiescat in pace."*'[11]

These sceptics correctly skewer the idea that the end of religion is preordained, but they do not provide solid evidence of what will reverse its current Western free-fall. As Norris and Inglehart rightly remark, 'Were Comte, Durkheim, Weber and Marx completely misled in their beliefs about religious decline? ... Was the predominant sociological view during the twentieth century totally misguided? ... We think not.' They add that critics of secularisation focus largely on marginal anomalies such as the United States while the overall trend is still moving in a secular direction.[12] Even Charles Taylor, who disavows secularisation, has written a fascinating chronicle about how Western thinkers slowly detached their philosophy from its religious training wheels.[13]

Sceptics and proponents alike fail to probe the soft underbelly of secularism: demography. Norris and Inglehart are aware of its power. They observe that less developed countries tend to be more religious than rich ones and have faster growing populations. Population explosion in the developing world creates many more religious people than secularism can digest. The secular West and East Asia are aging and their share of world population declining. This means the world is getting more religious even as people in the rich world shed their faith. Notwithstanding these trends, the authors feel confident that secularism will eventually win out as income and education tame religious fertility in the Third World.[14]

The swift pace of the demographic transition in Asia, Latin America and even the Middle East lends some credence to this prediction. However, I find such hopes to be misplaced. If anything, the developing world is more likely to modernise in an American than European way, retaining its faith as it becomes wealthy. The most perceptive secularisation theorists allow that religion can resist decline when it serves the secular function of maintaining identity. Catholicism distinguished Poland from Orthodox-cum-communist Russia, Brittany from secular Paris. Developing countries cling to their religion as a badge of pride in the face of 'westoxification'. This is most evident in Islam, but the fastgrowing Protestants of the global South also brandish their faith, often as a riposte to their Muslim, Catholic or Hindu neighbours.[15]

As globalisation makes us more similar, we become increasingly sensitive about our differences. This raises the importance of identity politics. The world's tropical denizens are set to increase their share of the world's population and will repopulate an aging West. When non-white religious people encounter the disdain of white secular natives, religion and ethnicity reinforce each other, insulating religion from the assimilating power of secularism. Some rebel by shouting their identities from the rooftops. In Europe, surveys of second-generation minorities confirm that only the children of Christian immigrants are susceptible to the charms of secularity. Muslims resist it almost entirely. Immigration makes Europe more multicultural *and* more religious. Just look at immigration entrepôts such as London and Paris, which – against all expectation – are among the most religious spots in their countries. Imagine a provincial English evangelical of the nineteenth century coming to London to experience the Bible Belt! All of which shows how religious demography can trump secularisation.

Religious demography moves in direct ways as well. All three Abrahamic faiths encourage people to 'go forth and multiply' and extol the virtues of motherhood, marriage and family. This was largely redundant when material necessity compelled everyone to have large families. First, most children died before they reached the age of ten. Second, young hands were needed to work the land and serve as one's old-age pension. Today, by contrast, modern medicine and sanitation have conquered infant mortality. In the city, children are more a burden than a boon. Contraception is readily available to limit fertility. Birth rates are consequently much lower. Under these circumstances, value choices have a bigger impact on fertility, and, by extension, the composition of the population. In other words, those biblical injunctions to reproduce now matter. Across the world, surveys find that the religious – especially fundamentalists – marry earlier and have children sooner and more often than their secular counterparts. This holds even when we narrow our focus to women at identical income and education levels. The difference is most dramatic in modern pluralistic societies, where value choices matter most for family formation.

Fertility rates of the religious may be important in the developed world, but can they keep their kids in the fold? If pious children simply assimilate into the secular mainstream, the radical effect of religious fertility quickly dissipates. This is where fundamentalism enters the picture. It developed in explicit opposition to secularism. Jewish and Christian fundamentalists insisted on the most demanding readings of scripture and tradition as a bulwark against secularism and 'secularised' faiths such as Reform Judaism and Anglicanism. Islamic fundamentalism was born out of resistance to secular ideas of nationalism, socialism and liberalism which were once admired by anti-colonial and post-colonial Muslim elites.

Bracketing immigrant religiosity for the moment, what is fascinating is how well certain fundamentalists have protected their boundaries. Modernity has empowered them to build a parallel world apart from the mainstream, complete with schools and universities, media and even separate beaches, hotels and shopping malls. Of course, joining a fundamentalist American church, Salafi mosque or ultra-Orthodox *kollel* involves sacrifices. Even for those born into the sects, the appeal of the outside world is strong. However, members' social ties are often completely bound up with the sect. Should they choose to exit, they leave behind friends, family and identity – a much bigger step than dropping a moderate religion that forms just one part of a multifaceted life.

Modernity allows institutions to extend their reach, get organised, keep better records and more effectively monitor and communicate with their members. This is why the modern state is so much more effective than pre-modern empires and has well-defined borders. Religious groups also benefit: fundamentalists are increasingly able to sharpen their boundaries and retain members while winning converts from moderate religions. The established, inherited, moderate religions which used to reign unchallenged are being dismembered by secularism and fundamentalism. Once secularism rears its head and fundamentalism responds with a clear alternative, moderate religion strikes many as redundant. Either you believe the stuff or you don't. If you do, it makes sense to go for the real thing, which takes a firm stand against godlessness.

There are several varieties of fundamentalism. Some rely on conversion. In order to proselytise most effectively, their members need to be integrated into the wider society so they can meet as many potential converts as possible. The risk of course is that retention will fall as members interact with the outside world. The open evangelical approach of Pentecostalists or Jehovah's Witnesses is effective in building membership in developing countries but fares poorly in developed societies where the pull of secularism is strong. In the modern West, the most successful groups are what I term *endogenous growth sects* – those that segregate themselves from society and grow their own. The Hutterites, Amish, ultra-Orthodox Jews, Salafist Muslims and American Mormons are the best-known examples. They benefit from the strong communal boundaries and membership retention that ethnic groups possess, but supercharge it with a universalist fervour. This sense of divine mission encourages the sacrifices needed to rear larger families. Because Western populations are flat or declining, all are increasing their share of the population at unprecedented rates.

Nowhere is this amazing growth more evident than in the Jewish world. Ultra-Orthodox, or Haredi, Judaism – which some claim to be no more than a century old – was disproportionately savaged by the Holocaust. At the end of the Second World War, the Haredim looked to be a fading relic. The new state of Israel and the wider Jewish diaspora indulged their needs, largely out of pity and nostalgia. Then, in the 1950s, the Haredim began to cordon themselves off and their fertility advantage over other Jews increased. With increasing retention of members and three times the birth rate of other Jews, their share of world Jewry began to skyrocket. In Britain, they constitute only 17 per cent of Jews but account for 75 per cent of Jewish births. In Israel, they have increased from a few per cent of Jewish schoolchildren in 1950 to a third of all Jewish pupils. In both places, the majority of Jews may be Haredi by 2050 and certainly by 2100.[16]

Fundamentalists have less of an edge in other faiths, but even a small fertility advantage in the presence of high membership retention is enough to ensure compound increase over generations. The early Christians of the Roman Empire grew from forty converts in AD 30 to six million in the year 312. Their growth rate was 40 per cent per decade, somewhat less than the Mormons have enjoyed since 1850. Evangelical Protestants increased – mainly through higher fertility – from a third of American white Protestants born in 1900 to two-thirds of those born in 1975. In all parts of the world, fundamentalist fertility exceeds moderate religious fertility, which in turn outpaces secular fertility. As the world's population levels off and begins to fall with the demographic transition, this throws fundamentalist pronatalism into sharper relief. As they resist population decline, they will begin, like the Haredim, to increase their share of the total.[17]

The most visible aspect of today's demographic revolution is the changing ethnic composition of Western populations. But demography moves in mysterious ways. Ethnic fertility levels are rapidly converging in the West: Muslim family sizes are shrinking swiftly, just as Catholic fertility declined to Protestant levels during the twentieth century. The long-term action therefore lies *within* each faith, where fundamentalists are pulling away from moderates and seculars. Unlike ethnic fertility gaps, the religious–secular divide is, if anything, widening. This makes perfect sense when you contrast secularism's individualistic women's liberation ethos with the pronatalism and traditional gender roles that fundamentalists extol.

Even more remarkable is that fundamentalists are making common cause across lines of faith tradition. In the United States, many white and black conservative Protestants, Mormons, white and Hispanic Catholics, Jews, and, prior to 9/11, Muslims, back the Religious Right's agenda. Their combined effort helped defeat the legalisation of gay marriage in California in 2008. In Europe, interfaith coalitions challenge liberal abortion and blasphemy laws. Inside the bureaucratic corridors of the UN, the Vatican, American Protestant fundamentalists and Islamists are joining hands to fight family planning and women's rights. As Islam grows in Europe, there is a good chance that Europe will follow the American path away from native–immigrant ethnic spats to trans-ethnic 'culture wars' over concerns such as abortion and gay rights.

Where, we might ask, is this process taking us? Marx predicted that the contradictions between labour and capital would result in the inevitable collapse of capitalism. Thesis and antithesis collide in a dialectic of change, and a higher stage of social evolution is reached in socialism. Daniel Bell spotted socialism's weaknesses by the 1930s, and instead offered a culturalist version of Hegel's dialectic. The discipline required to work, save and accumulate capital, which Calvinism first produced, is contradicted by capitalism's hedonistic ethos. The antinomian individualism of capitalism ultimately destroys the system. Yet capitalism seems to have adapted to libertinism rather well. Severe social problems like crime, homelessness, indebtedness and family breakdown have not caused it to fail.

Francis Fukuyama believes that liberal capitalism has outlasted its challengers to emerge as the final form of human organisation. Though Fukuyama is often superficially criticised as a Pollyanna, the idea that liberal capitalism is the apotheosis of human development remains current. As John Gray laments, it 'is still widely believed. It shapes the programmes of mainstream political parties ... guides the policies of agencies.' [18] This contrasts with the classical view that the invasion of advanced societies by more 'vigorous' barbarian ones is a constant of human history. Medieval Arab historian Ibn Khaldun believed that nomadic incursions were a necessary part of a cycle in which the social cohesion of decadent civilisations was renewed. Fukuyama, however, holds that military technology insulates liberal capitalism from that fate.

Does it? Demographic sluggishness was one aspect of decadence which Khaldun, like Cicero and Polybius before him, decried. Hundreds of years later, none other than Adam Smith, paragon of the Scottish Enlightenment, would remark that 'Barrenness, so frequent among women of fashion, is very rare among those of inferior station. Luxury in the fair sex, while it inflames perhaps the passion for enjoyment, seems always to weaken, and frequently to destroy altogether, the powers of generation.' [19] When one considers the demographic deficit of liberalism, it is hard not to conclude that religious demography is its Achilles heel. Religious fundamentalism cannot conquer from the outside with guns blazing, but it can achieve power gradually, over generations, from within. Liberalism's demographic contradiction – individualism leading to the choice not to reproduce – may well be the agent that destroys it. In a sense this is a modification of Bell's argument: individualism is fatal, but its effect is mediated by demography.

This is not the only possibility, of course. If liberalism manages to seduce enough religious children to its message, it could yet prevail. The excess children of the faithful might even complement the demographic deficit of the non-religious. I hope to show that in an age of desiccated secular creeds, the chances of attracting sufficient fundamentalists to secularism are low. And while fundamentalists can be smashed by Soviet or Nazi-style repression, this contradicts liberalism's very own principles. Secular liberalism is on the horns of a dilemma. The secular Zionist attempt to woo the Haredim using the carrots and sticks of integration may not succeed. The Haredim are an extreme case, but in the long run, liberalism will have to face up to the gauntlet that fundamentalists have thrown down. We are all Zionists now.

The stakes are high. Fundamentalist revolution, as in Iran, Sudan or Taliban Afghanistan, is not the primary threat. The authoritarian states of the Muslim world have crushed their Islamist challengers who in turn have lost popularity. Rather, the greatest danger comes from the gradual seepage of puritanical mores into society: restrictions on freedom of expression, science, recreation, the rights of women, minorities, heretics, gays and converts – even a return to barbaric punishments.

Muslim governments have swiftly implemented sharia to defang their jihadi adversaries. In the United States, the religious have a monopoly on the highest public offices and the rising waters of fundamentalism lap against foreign policy, foreign aid, abortion and the curriculum. In Israel, the government yields on yeshiva subsidies and civil marriage, while corporations bend to Haredi boycotts and moral censorship. At least the Zionists have a powerful secular nationalism to deploy against their fundamentalists. Though it has lost some of its shine in recent decades, the Zionist dream becomes relevant with every Palestinian rocket or Iranian nuclear advance. If, or rather when, Europe and North America face similar challenges, seculars will not have the ammunition to respond so robustly. I cannot see a way out.

Evolutionary psychologists marvel at the resources that primitive societies expended on religion. Surely these were extraneous to the process of survival. Some, including Richard Dawkins, maintain that religion served a series of important functions in prehistory. It ensured a high degree of group cooperation for collective goals. Those who were part of hunting and gathering bands that possessed religions had superior survival rates to those who were governed purely by their passions and self-interest. Religious groups passed their genes on more effectively. In the process of natural selection, our ancestors developed a religious sensibility, even a need for it.[20]

The mechanism of natural selection is demography. Demographers Ron Lesthaeghe and Dirk van de Kaa have developed the theory of the second demographic transition (SDT), where values rather than material constraints come to shape fertility and much of society fails to replace itself.[21] Might it be the case that the second demographic transition is a population bottleneck through which only the devout can pass? One would not have to resort to a genetic argument, though twin studies show a significant inherited component to religion.[22] Instead, it may just be that religious ideas, so-called 'memes', are destined to be selected. In Michael Blume's words, when it comes to Creationism vs. Intelligent Design, 'evolutionary theorists brought up far more scientific arguments – but committed believers in supernatural agents brought up far more children'.[23] Scott Atran reminds us that no human culture has survived without some form of religion for more than two generations.[24]

Those who claim that religion is destined to vanquish secularism forever are no more accurate than those who predict that secular reason will eventually smoke out religious 'superstition'. Sixty years ago, when Orthodox Jews were slaughtered like sheep while their more worldly co-ethnics sometimes survived, one would have returned a different verdict. As the social environment – what Dawkins calls a 'memeplex' – changes, so do the criteria of natural selection and therefore the fittest creed.[25] What is today's environment like? We see the collapse of the great secular religions of the twentieth century; the growing importance of values in determining fertility; an uneven demographic transition which is reshaping Western populations; the rise of global identity politics: all this in an atmosphere of multicultural toleration. The confluence of these currents creates a nutrient-rich breeding ground for religious fundamentalism.

In what follows, I hope to show how the demography of fundamentalism is beginning to transform the United States, Europe, Israel and the Muslim world. We are still in the early stages of the process, but once trends are in full swing, population momentum will carry them forward for generations. 'If no solution is found,' warns Philip Longman in *The Empty Cradle* (2004), 'the future will belong to those who reject markets, reject learning, reject modernity, and reject freedom. This will be the fundamentalist moment.'[26] Our social environment is unlikely to change any time soon. Liberals are simply too committed to the ideal of presentist individualism for themselves and tolerance for others. In matters of demography, they insist on a politically correct laissez-faire. This redounds to the advantage of fundamentalists. Yet to do otherwise would be to act against liberal principles, selling one's soul in order to win. Secular liberalism lies hoist on its own petard.

THE CRISIS OF
SECULARISM

The ascent of an outspoken atheism, borne aloft by superstars like Richard Dawkins, Christopher Hitchens, Sam Harris and Daniel Dennett, has re-energised the long-running culture war between religion and secularism.[1] The ferocity of the debate didn't emerge in a vacuum. It was fanned by the global revival of religion. Progressive thinkers of the past two centuries have regularly pronounced faith to be dead, with the proviso that it might take a little time for the news to filter down to the plebs. As socialism and mass consumption spread in the twentieth century, they promised large-scale modernisation, leading many to bring forward the date of religion's demise. Until the 1980s, few intellectuals predicted the rebirth of religion as a social force. Then came the Khomeini and Reagan revolutions of 1979–80, followed by the assassination of Egyptian president Anwar Sadat by Islamist militants in 1981. Ultra-Orthodox Judaism grew sharply in Israel and the diaspora. Pentecostalism exploded in Latin America, Asia and Africa in the early 1970s to become the second largest branch of global Christianity after Catholicism. All of which gave pause to previously unquestioned assumptions. Peter Berger, a leading sociologist of religion who foresaw the inevitable demise of American religion, recanted in the 1980s.[2]

Religion is a belief system which holds that supernatural forces operate in our world. It provides a 'theory of everything' which answers questions about the cosmos, meaning and existence that science cannot.

Strictly speaking, it need not involve more than this, but it invariably does. The supernatural is typically personified by one or more transcendent gods, who exist outside time and space and become the object of devotion. This worship gives rise to rituals, symbols, institutions and monuments. With the advent of writing after 10,000 BC, religions came to be inscribed in holy texts. Clerics penned theological interpretations of scripture which separated sacred objects, practices and texts from profane ones. Their pronouncements underpinned ethical codes such as sharia and Canon law which support the social order. Fundamentalist religious movements uphold the primacy of mores based on holy texts. They argue that these should supersede profane motives such as custom, pragmatism and liberalism. This challenges the legitimacy of the nation state, with its pragmatic policies and reliance on secular nationalism.

Islamist movements are the most dramatic forms of politicised religion. Since the collapse of the Berlin Wall, political Islam has become a leading source of global insecurity. The end of the Cold War and the rise of transnational jihadi terrorism in the 1990s brought religion to the fore as a leading organising principle of international relations. The axis of conflict is not so much Samuel Huntington's 'clash of civilisations' between Christianity and Islam as it is a battle between fundamentalism and secularism. Countries like Pakistan are bribed or cajoled to stand with the West and against transnational Islamist insurgents (and their sponsors) in the global 'War on Terror'. The planet's new religious divisions return us to a state of affairs we haven't witnessed since the Wars of Religion in the 1600s when the Protestant/Catholic cleft organised politics. It takes us back to a time before the Enlightenment, which introduced the liberal, industrial and scientific revolutions of the modern age.

Away from the headlines, a quiet revolution in Islamic practice and theology has shaken the cultural foundations of the Muslim world. Mosque-building is soaring. A new generation of young women is donning the headscarf, often admonishing their more laissez-faire parents. But they are not alone. Young Orthodox Jews in the United States claim the same moral superiority over their less stringent parents. Young American Christians, too, are being drawn into fundamentalist movements which champion traditional women's roles. These trends alarm many secular intellectuals and a wide swathe of the Western populace.

For atheists like Dawkins and Harris, nothing less than the future of human reason and progress, be this in science or ethics, is at stake. The Enlightenment and modernity are imperilled and Western society must act against the new threat. Ironically, this drama is portrayed by secularists in quasi-religious terms: the forces of light are being eclipsed by a veil of ignorance akin to the barbarian invasions which cast classical civilisation into the Dark Ages. In the United States, evangelical Christianity is the villain; in Israel, ultra-Orthodoxy and religious Zionism. Elsewhere, fundamentalist Islam presents the main challenge. Even Hindu, Sikh and Buddhist fundamentalists are riding high, though their moral mantras are saturated with ethnic nationalism.

It is worth considering the story of the barbarians in more detail, because so much of Western liberal culture hinges on the intertwined ideas of progress, civilisation and modernity. From the outset, secular reason set its face against religion. Socrates chose to drink hemlock poison and speak the truth rather than worship the gods of ancient Athens. During the Renaissance, Copernicus shocked the religious sensibilities of his contemporaries by claiming the earth revolved around the sun. Iconoclastic philosophers from Spinoza in the seventeenth century to Hegel in the nineteenth had to tread carefully to avoid raising the hackles of the Church. Charles Darwin went to great lengths to defend the theory of evolution from its outraged religious critics as late as the mid nineteenth century. Those seeking to apply science to society's problems through secular education and health care (including birth control) had to struggle against dogmatic religious opponents. The mid twentieth century saw the overthrow of archaic models of gender relations and repressive sexual mores, a new chapter in the long Whiggish story of human progress. Having won our freedom to reason, say the New Atheists, we must stand on guard against the religious barbarians prowling outside our gates.

There has been no shortage of threats in recent times. On 31 May 2009, anti-abortion activist Scott Roeder assassinated abortion doctor George Tiller inside the Kansas Lutheran church where Tiller was serving as an usher. This was the same state in which the Board of Education tried to introduce Creation Science into the school curriculum. Nationally, successive Republican administrations withdrew funding for global family planning, causing demographic transitions to stall and women's reproductive health to worsen all over the world. Meanwhile, in Taliban Afghanistan, women were forced by the virtue police to cover themselves head to toe (apart from a mesh screen) and walk silently lest their footfalls 'arouse' male passers-by. Arab governments bent over backwards to curtail liquor, television, women's liberties and even hairdressing in an attempt to head off the challenge of Islamist populism. In Israel, ultra-Orthodox Jews stoned vehicles on a major Jerusalem thoroughfare, injuring a child, to protest against driving on the Sabbath. Some of their ostensibly more moderate Modern-Orthodox cousins could be found fanning the flames of conflict with the Palestinians as religious Zionist Settlers or overzealous Israeli Defence Force recruits in the Occupied Territories.

The global revival of religion has been chronicled in a number of important new books.[3] But revivalist accounts must reckon with the claim of sceptics, who rightly point out that the big engines of revival are nearly all in developing countries. Pentecostalism, Seventh-day Adventism, Mormonism and the Jehovah's Witnesses win most of their converts in Latin America, China and sub-Saharan Africa. Islamism is surging mainly in Muslim countries, few of which sport modern differentiated economies. Religious revival can therefore be explained away as the birth pangs of modernisation, not so very different from the Baptist, Methodist and Pietist revivals that took place in the United States and Western Europe in the early-to-mid nineteenth century.[4] One could also make the case that the developing world remains, in Francis Fukuyama's terms, 'in history', or, in Max Weber's phrase, 'enchanted'. That is, susceptible to the charms of heroic storylines and myths in a way we jaded Westerners are not. Many in the Muslim world, for instance, believe in Zionist and American conspiracy theories that would be laughed out of court in the West. The true test of religious revival, therefore, is whether it can thrive in Europe, Japan, North America and Australasia. So far, there is little evidence of genuine revival in these parts of the world.

Does this mean the New Atheists can rest easy? Not quite. For, hidden among the weeds of the global religious revival are some sturdy new growths which are resistant to the charms of Western secularism. The winning formula is not that of the Jehovah's Witnesses, who convert many but suffer from high turnover and have limited appeal in the Western core. Instead, the Enlightenment-resistant strain of religion is that of the Amish, ultra-Orthodox Jews and North American Mormons. All have thrived in the most individualistic, profane Western societies. Their model combines rapid population growth with high membership retention. Like many ethnic groups, they practice endogamy, or in-group marriage, and maintain community boundaries by largely living apart from other groups. Inflow from conversion is limited. Some members are lost to the 'outside', but fertility and immigration are more than sufficient to propel religious expansion in a world of falling fertility. The success of what I term *endogenous growth sects* – religious groups that grow their own – has not gone unnoticed. Mainstream religious fundamentalists already encourage aspects of this strategy. Increasingly, they are coming to understand that the endogenous-growth business model holds the key to success in the 'disenchanted' world. They are, in Daniel Dennett's terms, backward-engineering their faith by learning from religious evolution.[5] This sectarian blueprint has certain features in common with religions-turned-ethnic groups like the Druze, Armenians, Sikhs and Jews. The difference is that unlike ethnic groups, which are content to just be themselves, endogenous growth sects are expansionist, claiming that their truth is the universal one for all humanity. Growth provides proof of chosenness. How did we get to this state of affairs? Ironically, modern secularism helped create the very life form which may come back to haunt it.

Secularisation

To understand religion we need to begin with its opposite, secularism. Secularisation has two dimensions: the *public* separation of religious institutions from those of politics ('church from state') and the decline of *private* piety. The United States exemplifies a society which has high public secularism (the constitutional 'wall of separation') but low private secularism. England is the opposite: the Anglican Church is publicly established, but the piety of the population is very low. Other countries are more uniform: Saudi Arabia, for instance, has little public or private secularism. Personal piety consists of three related but distinct dimensions: affiliation, belief and attendance. Someone might identify their *affiliation* as 'Christian' on a census form, but no longer *believe* in the divinity of Jesus or attend church. They might *affiliate* as Christian and *attend* church for social reasons, but still not *believe* in the Bible. The three dimensions of piety – affiliation, belief and attendance – strongly influence each other, but also remain somewhat independent. Consider the views of Jordan, a tenth-grader from the north of England: 'I don't believe in owt [anything]. I don't believe in any religions ... I'm Christian but I don't believe in owt.' Here the 'Christian' label functions as a largely inherited aspect of identity among those who have been brought up Christian or wish to distinguish themselves from Muslims and other non-Christian groups. Much the same is true of many inner-city French 'Muslims' involved in the 2005 Banlieue Riots, who are loyal to 'Team Islam' but often lead secular lives.[6]

This book considers both private and public secularism, but focuses more on private piety. This is because strong private faith provides a springboard for public religion even in officially secular societies such as America, whereas a weak substratum of piety, as in Europe, undermines the influence of religion in public life. Anglican bishops in the House of Lords do not a religious England make. Secularisation is a word that stirs great passions. The idea of the inevitable decline of religion culminating in its disappearance sticks in the throat of many religious intellectuals. Even secular multiculturalists and radical postmodernists reject secularisation. It is viewed as passé, part of an unquestioning Western belief in progress and reason which is out of step with the times. Charles Taylor derides the idea of secularisation as a misguided 'subtraction story' in which human reason and liberty grow as religion recedes. This notion, he argues, is based not on hard evidence but on a 'master narrative' of progress. José Casanova views secularisation as inseparable from religion: theologians first developed the category of 'secular' time, and only against the backdrop of faith can we discern what belongs in the here and now and what transcends it.[7] Yet while many scholars contest the theory that religion will ultimately disappear, most accept that religious fervour can rise and fall, and that it has been in decline for some time in Western Europe.

Secularisation in the West

One of the most breathtaking developments of the past half-century is the collapse of religious piety in the West. Among advanced Western countries, only the United States seems to have bucked the trend. In 1970, over 40 per cent of the combined population of France, Belgium, the Netherlands, Italy and Germany went to church weekly. In 1998, just 22 per cent did. Across a wider range of ten Western European countries, the numbers fell from 38.4 to 16.6 per cent between 1975 and 1998.[8] Those who remained in the pews were disproportionately elderly and female, raising questions about the future viability of the church. As one devout American serviceman related to me, when he took his family to church in Belgium the congregation consisted of his family and a 'bunch of old people'. Across the continent, churches are dwindling and closing, with many being converted into apartments, homes or even dance bars like 'the Church', a popular London club. Consider the pace of decline in England: in 1957, 20 per cent of English adults attended services weekly. This fell steadily: to 12 per cent by 1979 and 7 per cent in 1998. The 55,000 churches of 1961 declined more gently, to 47,600 by 2005 with another 4,000 projected to go by 2020. And this in spite of generous government grants to maintain them.[9]

Elsewhere, the pews have emptied even faster: Irish attendance plunged by 17 percentage points between 1981 and 2001. Luxembourg's dropped by 21, Portugal's by 17, Spain's by 15, and Belgium and the Netherlands' by 12. Countries with significant Catholic populations experienced the most dramatic collapses.[10] In Eastern Europe, religion imploded for political reasons. Coercive socialist atheism – extending to sanctions, punishment or even murder – was the rod that broke religion's back: a reconstruction of Russian church attendance rates shows a decline from roughly 40–50 per cent attendance in 1920 to 2–3 per cent by 1990. In all Soviet Republics, be they Orthodox, Catholic, Muslim or Protestant, the proportion of people affiliating with their religion fell sharply between 1900 and 1970.[11] These numbers rose slightly after 1989, but generally failed to recover.

In France, where Catholicism was vanquished by the Revolution of 1789, and in Protestant Europe, where attendance peaked around 1850, congregation numbers have stabilised. But regular attenders typically

make up little more than 5 per cent of the population of these countries. Given its current rapid rate of decline, Catholic Europe is set to
catch up with Protestant Europe in a generation or two. Despite this
evidence, scholars such as Grace Davie aver that religion maintains its
power because many who no longer attend continue to 'believe without
belonging'. For instance, across ten European countries in the year 2000
European Values Survey, half claimed to be 'religious', though just 7 per
cent regularly attended services. Europeans also tend to hold a positive
view of religion and are willing to fund it. The British, for example, are
broadly willing to see their tax money go towards restoring churches and
paying for faith schools. In Scandinavia and Germany, the overwhelming majority of Lutherans pay a tax to support the church despite never
attending. They do so in the belief that religion is an important resource
for morality, identity, birth, marriage and death. People do not participate in religious services but imbibe their religion 'vicariously' through
the acts of committed believers and the pronouncements of religious
public figures.[12] The paternalist 'Thought for the Day' from religious
leaders, broadcast on Britain's public BBC Radio 4, may seem horribly
out of place in a secular society but arouses little protest.

Nevertheless, further decline may be in the offing. On a scale of 1 to
10, the proportion from the above ten countries (Scandinavia minus Finland, France, Britain, Holland, Spain, Ireland and Belgium) claiming to
be in the top three most religious categories in the European Social Survey (ESS) in 2004 was more than twice as high among those over 65 than
among those aged 18–24. In England, half the population aged 18–34 say
they identify themselves as non-religious while among those over 55, just
20 per cent do. Patterns across the entire European continent show the
same age-graded pattern of decline encompassing affiliation, belief and
attendance.[13] Even belief in God, the indicator most resistant to erosion,
is starting to fade. Across ten Western countries sampled in 1947 and
2001, those answering 'yes' to the question 'Do you believe in God?' fell
from 85 to 72 per cent.[14] Naturally this varies by country, age and education. Virtually all Irish believe in the deity, but only half of Swedes and
two-thirds of Dutch do. Once again, the drift of the data points towards
decline since the youngest are most prone to defection. For instance, in a
sample of ten West European countries in 2000, the 'God gap' between

those over 60 and under 30 was 20 percentage points. This suggests that as today's young generations age, European societies will become more like Sweden and less like Ireland. We cannot know for sure, because there is some evidence that people return to belief (but not attendance) as they age, but the generational trends all seem to slant in a declining direction.[15]

American secularism?

Many see the United States as the great exception to the rule of secularism.[16] The proportion of Americans claiming to be members of a church, regardless of their attendance, rose steadily after independence, from 17 per cent in 1776 to 69 per cent in 2005. This trajectory wasn't smooth: 'great awakenings' of religion took place during 1725–50 and 1800–1840, and the upward trend was punctuated by occasional declines such as the 'religious depression' of 1925–35, sparked by economic collapse and internal rifts within mainline Protestantism.[17] The trend has stabilised in recent decades, which is verified by detailed post-Second World War survey research. Roughly 40 per cent of the American population report that they attend services weekly, a figure which has held steady for half a century. This has little to do with being an immigrant nation occupying a vast terrain where religion counters rootlessness. Consider how different things look north of the border: in Canada, church attendance in 2004 stood at just half the American rate. Almost 20 per cent of English-speaking Canadians – the spiritual or actual descendants of American Tory settlers – described themselves as having no religious affiliation, up from 12 per cent in 1985.[18]

Though the United States is treated as the great exception to the rule of Western secularism, it has not remained unaffected. The proportion of Americans with no religious affiliation was less than 5 per cent in the early twentieth century. Thus today just five per cent of Americans born before 1925 are unaffiliated and, until about 1992, this was also true of those born during 1925–45. In the early 1990s, the baby boomer generation, born 1946–65, had twice the rate of non-affiliation – 10 per cent – of their parents. But the policy overreach of the Christian Right in the late 1980s and early 1990s struck a serious blow to faith, tugging all generations in a secular direction, especially youth. By 2007, 15 per cent of boomers and 20 per cent of Generation Xers declared their religion as 'none'. Among the youngest, 'Nexter' generation just entering the electorate, rates of non-religion are running at European levels, i.e. in the 35–40 per cent range. Previous work shows that religious identities tend to crystallise in early adulthood and persist through the life course. This suggests that the United States could resemble Western Europe in one or two generations.

Harvard's Robert Putnam, one of the researchers on the above project, told me that he views the post-1992 upswing in non-affiliation as purely political, unrelated to any secularising processes. He considers secularisation a steady, gradual phenomenon, one which by definition cannot account for rapid declines in religious identity. He also mentions that most unaffiliated Americans continue to express high levels of religious belief, and will be lured back to organised religion by astute religious entrepreneurs such as megachurch pastor Rick Warren or liberal evangelical Jim Wallis. Megachurches and modern, hip prayer styles will win the day, but the evangelical message, cautions Putnam, needs to be modified in line with the liberal political preferences of the new generation.[19] Mike Hout and Claude Fischer reached the same conclusion. They show that 60 per cent of Americans who declare themselves to be religious 'nones' pray, two-thirds believe in a higher power and half believe, at least some of the time, in God. One of the strongest predictors of an unaffiliated individual is a liberal political preference.[20] Other studies claim that liberals are exaggerating their non-religiosity on surveys in deference to local norms, just as conservatives overstate their religiosity.[21]

Be that as it may, the evidence for American secularism is too powerful to ignore. Sudden political drivers of religious decline are just as real as the steady drumbeat of economic and cultural change. This is certainly the position of David Martin, one of the most sophisticated secularisation theorists, who shows how religions gain or lose adherents depending upon which secular horses they bet on. Catholicism in Ireland backed the popular cause of Irish nationalism and thrived, while in France it sided with the hated *ancien régime* and sank. In America, religion per se was never closely associated with an unpopular regime, as it was in much of Europe. Religion proved broad enough to offer a brand to everyone – even radicals – across the full 'social geology' of class, region, race and ideology. During bloody strikes, for example, textile workers and mill owners could each count on their clerical allies. Likewise, black churches resisted segregation in the South while white ones backed the existing order.[22] But today, the Religious Right has successfully cloaked itself in the banner of religion, depriving liberals and educated young people of a vocabulary of faith. Obama notwithstanding, they appear to have turned anti-clerical. This resembles what happened in France after 1789 or in Spain after Franco.

That said, there are two caveats. First, secularism can be reversed by religious demography: even if individuals tend to leave religion, society as a whole may become more religious because the religious have more children and benefit more from immigration than seculars. Second, we need to keep the evidence in global perspective. In the rest of the world, only parts of Latin America's southern cone have shown evidence of a decline in popular piety, notably Uruguay, and to a lesser extent Chile and Argentina. These are arguably the most 'European' societies in Latin America.[23] Even Steve Bruce, the leading proponent of secularisation theory, agrees that his theory does not apply outside the Western world because non-European regions lack an Enlightenment heritage.[24] Developments in the West are somewhat distinct. Only in the West have individualism, equality and rationality undermined religion and high birth rates at the same time. In much of the developing world, fertility rates have fallen while religion remains strong – in part because secularism is portrayed as an alien import. In East Asia, religion is weak but has, if anything, gained ground as birth rates have plunged. Whereas social and political shifts undergird the religious revivals of the global South and East, demography drives them in the West. However, Western ideas from nationalism to postmodernism have always influenced the educated strata in the developing world. If young people in anti-Western societies tire of anti-Western tropes, as may be happening in Iran, they could begin to embrace secularism. But the silver cloud will contain a grey lining for secularists. Secularism will breed pluralism, empowering demographic fundamentalism. This will eventually reverse religious decline. Indeed, if we look closely, we can already spot fundamentalist footprints in the religious demography of the Muslim world.

Why secularisation?

Religion arose at some point in human evolution, but can it decline or disappear? The idea of secularisation is as old as social science, and intimately connected with the hopes and dreams of modernity. Most leading Western thinkers of the past two centuries believed that secular ideas and institutions would replace those based on supernatural referents. They pointed to changes which they claimed would erode the connection between church and state and reduce personal piety. All of the 'founding fathers' of modern social theory – Auguste Comte, Henri de St Simon, Karl Marx, Max Weber and Émile Durkheim – believed that secularisation was key to modernity.

In 2008–9, I spent a year as a Fellow in Harvard's Kennedy School of Government. At the north-east edge of campus lies Francis Street, a pleasant row of colonial-style New England homes which begins, fittingly, at Harvard Divinity School. One snowy day, I called at the unassuming home of one of the street's grand old residents, a man who receives few visitors and does not get the attention he deserves: 89-year-old sociologist Daniel Bell. One of the original pre-war ex-Trotskyist 'New York Intellectuals', Bell later taught at Columbia and Harvard, and remains sharp as nails.

He wrote two of the twentieth century's most important books, including my personal favourite, *The Cultural Contradictions of Capitalism* (1976). In the book, Bell sets out his elegant theory of modernity and its relationship to religion. In contrast to the often hyperbolic Marx or abstract Durkheim, Bell's work is both anchored in empirical reality and beautifully written. In our two-hour discussion, Bell's reaction to my thesis was that there must be a cultural cause behind the demographic pattern I was picking up in the data. I agree. In fact, my theory could be read as an extension of Bell's argument that liberal capitalism contains a contradiction between its cultural individualism and its requirement for collective discipline. It's just that I see demography as the intermediate step between cultural individualism and system collapse.

In his work, Bell dissects modernity into three 'axial principles': rationality, individuality and equality.[25] Rationality is the only factor which does not reverse itself, moving ever upwards in linear fashion. We cannot unlearn our times tables. Rationality involves the application of science and human reason to this-worldly problems, and bulks largest in higher learning and the economy. Economic development, specialisation and complexity increase and technology moves relentlessly forward. Governments are imbued with a similar spirit, seeking to justify actions with reference to bureaucratic targets and rules, not theological doctrine. In the process, government appropriates an ever-growing range of functions once provided by religion. Health care, poor relief and schooling are typical targets. In 1905, for example, France established *laïcité*, the institutional separation of church and state, which banned religious symbolism from public schools. Thus we get education for education's sake and health care to improve lives, with performance measured against secular yardsticks like pass rates. Sometimes a religious veneer persists for a while before fading. Who today, for example, knows or cares that the University of Chicago was founded by Baptists and Princeton by Presbyterians? At a broader level, secular law displaces holy law in the name of universality and efficiency. Restrictions on commerce, such as usury or sumptuary laws, not to mention Sunday closing or the prohibition of alcohol, fall away. The interests of the state and its national identity displace religious crusades as the focus of foreign policy, permitting a more flexible set of alliances.

The great avatars of modernity such as St Simon and Marx rested their hopes on economic change as the engine of secularism. Subsequent writers such as Durkheim were inspired by biological analogies. Our highly evolved human biology, Durkheim claims, consists of specialised organs like the heart and brain, which focus on distinct tasks, a far cry from primitive unicellular organisms in which all bodily functions are contained in a single cell, limiting the capability of the whole. In the same way, a highly evolved economy moves beyond the undifferentiated world of the family farm or home workshop. First, home and work are separated. Then specialised occupations emerge, such as doctor, tailor and shoemaker. Specialisms within medicine, academia and light manufacturing take this process to its zenith. Now nobody can be a polymath even if their surname is Da Vinci. A jack of all trades without specialist expertise cannot maintain an affluent lifestyle. Even a survivalist retreating from modernity wouldn't pretend to be able to manufacture his own car and cereal, fix his jet plane and perform surgical operations.

Extend the metaphor to include religion, and you could argue that we have moved away from a monolithic culture where religion permeates everything to a differentiated one. Now there are a wide variety of beliefs and pursuits, of which religion is just one, and a shrinking one at that. Just as religion becomes differentiated from the state, the economy now provides the conviviality and entertainment that churches used to. From bars to sports clubs and movies, church and its associated activities are crowded out. Carrying the argument even further, Robert Putnam cites the general trend towards more in-home and private entertainment, such as TV or the Internet, which has put the squeeze on all forms of face-to-face activities from churches to bowling leagues.[26] Like NBC, ABC and CBS sinking into the morass of a 300-channel universe, religion seems destined to survive as merely one specialism within an increasingly varied mosaic, the hobby of an eccentric few. The jump from biology to the economy makes good sense, and extending the metaphor to the realm of culture doesn't seem that great a stretch. If you travel around Europe, you will find the inhabitants of large industrial cities and towns to be the least religious inhabitants of their countries. Even areas of large-scale agriculture like southern Spain are low-religiosity zones. Break up the tight-knit community and the resulting mobility and specialisation leads to religious decline. Industrialisation explains a good deal of the astounding slide in church attendance across Europe.[27]

Rationalistic explanations for secularisation are important. But reason and economic development constitute just one of Bell's three pincers of modernity. What about liberty and equality? Voltaire, the leading light of the eighteenth-century French Enlightenment, mocked the exclusivity of most religions in his *Treatise on Toleration* (1763): 'Listen to me ... there are nine hundred million little ants like us on the earth, but my ant-hole is the only one dear to God ... all the others will be eternally damned.' Inspired in part by Voltaire's critique, state religions with exclusive truth claims whose elites breathed the intellectual air of the Enlightenment began to accept that other faiths could be tolerated. This is not the whole story: practical considerations of social peace and political unity lay behind England's 1688 Toleration Acts and those of the seventeenth-century Dutch Republic. Still, ideas of toleration increasingly mattered. They made the case for granting the vote to Catholics in Britain in 1829 and enshrining principles of religious toleration in the nineteenth-century constitutions of several Scandinavian countries. Ideals of equality were not the only drivers of change, but bulked ever larger as the nineteenth century progressed. [28]

Charles Taylor makes a similar point. His 874-page tome *A Secular Age* clinched him the £1 million Templeton Prize in 2007. The most lucrative award of its kind, it is granted to 'a living person who has made an exceptional contribution to affirming life's spiritual dimension, whether through insight, discovery, or practical works'. The book offers an intellectual history of secularism, tracing the demise of religious thinking in the Western world. He meticulously documents the way Western philosophers and writers detached their ideas from the supernatural realm. First, monotheistic religions like Christianity and Judaism unmasked the gods of sun, earth and sea. Only the True God was real; others were frauds. Then, the Reformation denuded the rituals and icons from the Catholic Church, disrobing the Pope and his earthly servants in the abbeys and monasteries. The sixteenth-century Wars of Religion and eighteenth-century Enlightenment prompted philosophers to propose new 'rational' forms of ethics based on natural law. Real-world consequences of actions should drive morality, they asserted, not the perfectionist ideals of the Bible. These innovations shoved aside holy law and downgraded the personal God to a backstage role as Grand Designer.

Taylor shows how morality came to be grounded in earthly results like peace and prosperity rather than sacred laws handed down from on high. Nevertheless, he is at pains to stress that reason alone did not kill God. The nineteenth-century Romantic reaction against disengaged reason could have restored faith to its former position atop Europe's intellectual pyramid. Instead, romanticism coincided with religion's last gasp in the Republic of Letters. Friedrich Nietzsche hated reason but despised religion even more. 'God is Dead,' he proclaimed, adding that he felt like washing his hands after shaking those of a believer. Freud, though champion of the unconscious against the rational, wrote that those who remain religious are guilty of failing to shake an infantile belief in their almighty fathers. The solution to this kind of neurosis is to throw off the shackles of childhood, accept that life is unpredictable and grow out of religious beliefs.[29] What decisively pushed Western intellectuals towards secular humanism was therefore not reason, but rather the sense that religion stifled human freedom of expression and reinforced social hierarchies.[30]

Thanks to modern survey research, we can trace the last stages of the intellectual trend Taylor describes. In 1914, American psychologist James Leuba's landmark survey discovered that 58 per cent of a thousand randomly selected American scientists doubted the existence of God, a figure which climbed to almost 70 per cent among the 400 top-ranked scientists in the sample. Nearly twenty years later, the figures had reached 67 and 85 per cent respectively. Clearly, even in the early twentieth century, few intellectual elites believed in God despite the fact that almost everyone else did. Astoundingly, the numbers have continued to dip to the point where the end of academic religion seems nigh: a repeat of Leuba's survey in 1998 found that only 7 per cent of elite American scientists believed in God, less than half the 1933 figure. One wonders if such a survey in Europe would uncover more than a handful of holdouts.[31]

This seems pretty convincing evidence for the secularisation of western elites, but what about the masses? Taylor and Bell both lived through the cultural revolution of the 1960s, and point to that decade as one in which elite secularism was transmitted to a wider population.[32] We noted that the expansion of mass media and higher education led to a whole series of attitude changes in Western populations encompassing childbearing, sex, race and religion. Could it be that secularism will spread within the Western masses as it has among elites? This would certainly correspond with the survey evidence, which finds younger generations to be less pious. Taylor, however, in accord with his own Catholic beliefs and the postmodern spirit of the times, denies this interpretation. At a seminar series on Taylor's book at Harvard, hosted by Taylor and communitarian philosopher Michael Sandel, Taylor repeatedly urged that his argument supported the idea of a 'nova' of increasing spiritual diversity rather than secularisation.[33]

But this postmodern contention cannot conceal the shrinking influence of religion which Taylor presents through 90 per cent of his book. Survey evidence has yet to support the idea of a growth in 'alternative' spirituality among the non-religious. All that can be said is that some move from religion to a spirituality which is inner-centred rather than god-centred while others jump directly to secularism. Once people make the move to secularism, they rarely come back to either religion or spirituality. This explains why many new religious movements like Transcendental Meditation peaked in the 1970s. New Age practices which are growing in popularity, such as yoga and alternative medicine, are typically inspired by earthly desires for health, meaning and wellbeing rather than a connection to the supernatural.[34] In other words, they are not religious. Though I tried to pin Taylor down on this, he is not the most direct interlocutor and managed to skirt his own historical and contemporary evidence. With Sandel in the chair keeping time and calling mainly on his own graduate students, there was little chance for detailed follow-through. Though they were clearly clever, I found Taylor's protestations unconvincing. An employee of the Holy See who went to sleep in 1500 and awoke today would be depressed by what he saw. Spinoza and other freethinkers would be elated.

Taylor astutely chalks secular humanism's success up to its ability to come across as more egalitarian than religion. This is not only because religion gets besmirched as nastier than humanism. At a more mundane level, ideas of equality prompt society to tolerate diversity. Religious diversity, extending to non-religion, leads people to question their faith's claim to exclusive possession of the truth, fostering religious doubt and, eventually, decline. As Francis Fukuyama remarks, modern men 'realise that their horizon is merely a horizon, not solid land but a mirage that disappears as one grows closer, giving way to yet another horizon beyond. That is why modern man is the last man: he has been jaded by the experience of history, and disabused of the possibility of direct experience of values.'[35] Pluralism also results in an increased rate of inter-faith marriage. Parents who follow different religions often fail to agree on which faith to raise the children in, so the default option becomes the secular culture. Pluralism leads, once again, to an erosion of faith. *Ipso facto*, equality breeds a toleration that corrodes religion.

Individualism, the last of Daniel Bell's three arrows of modernity, helps to accelerate the process. Those with individualistic orientations are more likely to leave churches. They join less, participate less, and attend and connect less often with those in their immediate community.[36] They may change their religious clothes frequently, moving denomination or marrying across religious lines. Certainly this has been documented in the late twentieth-century United States as the individualism of the 1960s shaped a new generation. Research finds that many adopt a 'pick 'n' mix' approach to religious symbols: a Christian may combine a cross with punk attire or, if Jewish, tuck into a chocolate matzoh at mealtime.[37] Some make up their own religion entirely, a phenomenon Robert Bellah coined 'Sheilaism' after an interview subject who described herself as an adherent of her own personal religion, though she believed in God: 'My faith has carried me a long way. It's Sheilaism. Just my own little voice,' she says. This is merely the fullest expression of the belief of 80 per cent of Americans – even in 1978 – that 'an individual should arrive at his or her own religious beliefs independent of any churches or synagogues'.[38]

Daniel Bell describes this sensibility as 'antinomianism', a kind of spiritual individualism which refuses to accept any source of truth that does not emanate from within our Self. Charles Taylor coins it the 'ethics of authenticity', the idea that our values should come from self-reflection, while external sources of moral authority such as religion are inauthentic and inimical to the search for selfhood. He adds that this ideal of human individualism presents the number one challenge to religion in our time.[39] Consider the fact that by 1980, less than half of Americans remained members of the same denomination throughout their lifetime. This was confirmed again in a 2007 Pew survey. The end point of individualistic switching is often irreligion. In 2007, nearly 40 per cent of Catholic and a third of Protestant switchers opted to leave faith altogether.[40] In Europe, values surveys find a similar link between expressive individualism and secularity.[41] Western religion, it seems, stands powerless in the face of Bell's three wrecking balls of modernity: rationality, individualism and equality.

Is there a 'need' for religion?

Sociologists who challenge secularisation theory argue that we have an innate desire for religion and that the weakness of faith merely reflects constraints on religious supply. Where there are religious monopolists such as established Churches, protected by restrictions on others' freedom to proselytise, convert and practise, religious fervour wanes. Established clerics become preoccupied with their secular status, split hairs over arcane theological questions and otherwise ignore people's spiritual needs. Just like communist economies, religious monopolies such as those in Europe are less innovative and poorer than religious free markets such as the United States.[42]

Although there may be something to this argument, comparative research has yet to support it.[43] But do religious market theorists have their finger on an important weak spot in secularisation theory? The weakest link in the secular account of human nature is that it fails to account for people's powerful desire to seek immortality for themselves and their loved ones. 'Human beings will no more cease to be religious than they will stop being sexual, playful or violent,' John Gray admonishes.[44] People will probably always pray for good fortune. Hence the maxim 'there are no atheists in foxholes'. But what if such feelings remain beneath the surface? Most of us no longer experience foxholes. We rarely glimpse death, even among animals, which are killed and sanitised well before they reach our table. Infant mortality is a rarity, average life expectancy is pushing past eighty, and deaths from accidents and war are rare. We may not be able to duck death completely, but it becomes so infrequent that we can easily forget about it. Even if everyone found God on their deathbed, or during freak moments of crisis, society could remain essentially secular.

It is instructive to examine the roots of the modern cultural sensibility. For much of human history, our most inspiring stories came from religious myths. Until the end of the nineteenth century, religious motifs inspired art and architecture, joined by depictions of historical figures and timeless landscapes. Only in the modernist epoch, which stirred in the late nineteenth century and continues to this day, did we fully break with tradition. Futurists, cubists and surrealists focused attention on the immediate, or on the future. Our modernist sensibility is impatient for change, remarks Daniel Bell, and demands immediacy. No longer do we reflect on art and life. Contemplation of a painting, which characterises visual art prior to the modernist period, is replaced by real-time art and 'happenings', which are meant to overpower our senses. Dali and Pollock rudely push Michelangelo and Constable aside. Structure gives way to anti-structure. In the process we forget the past and the dead, spurning the ties that bind the generations. We cease to step back and contemplate our lives against the infinity of time and space. Instead, we focus on the present and forget about our own mortality.[45]

As in art, so in life. Our routines are uprooted from the rhythms of communities, our appetites unrestrained by communal regulators. Though we cannot satisfy our soaring appetites, leading to what Durkheim called *anomie*, we attempt to cram ever more – experience, activity, achievement – into every minute.[46] This frenetic activity helps to limit our time for reflection and concentrates us on the present. The so-called 'big questions' of life are forced into the background, only to return at moments of crisis. Anthony Giddens argues that such moments – the death of a loved one, or a disaster – can lead to a 'return of the repressed' existential questions. Daniel Bell foresees a 'great instauration' of religion in response to the existential insecurities of modernity. However, none of this has come to pass and modernism has shown itself to be tougher than we imagined. One of its tools is secular psychotherapy, which has shaped our culture. Psychotherapy seeks to get our race cars back on the speedway of modern life, to enable us to become 'well-adjusted' once again.[47] There is simply no non-religious way to deal with disturbing existential questions like 'Why are we here?' or 'What will happen after death?' other than to forget about them. Consider the following advice from a British bereavement website, whose message is so typical that few of us notice its modernist philosophy:

> It's alright to cry and feel sad when someone you love dies. It hurts – just like when you hurt yourself if you fall over. At first it hurts very much but the pain will go away after a while. It takes time for your knee to heal, and it hurts less and less each day. It is the same when somebody dies ... No one knows what happens when you die. All we know for sure is that it will happen one day – to all of us. *Don't worry or think about it for very long*, as there are a lot more interesting and wonderful experiences to look forward to.[48]

Repressing disturbing questions through psychotherapeutic 'adjustment' successfully defends a secular order from people's 'need' for religion. Freud has written that all societies have taboos. In all places and times, society must work against the grain of some of our biological drives, permitting certain desires to be satisfied while repressing others. Restraint of nature happens every time a red-blooded male sees a beautiful woman walk down the street. As far as his animal nature is concerned, social taboos mean she might as well be wearing a burqa. The same is true when said gentleman passes a store displaying gold watches. Repressing humans' desire to be tribal, or immortal, can be justified by the same principle: social harmony. Hence John Lennon's anarchist vision in 'Imagine' of banishing God and religion, ethnic group and nation.

Whatever the moral case for or against God, the point is that religious demand can be successfully suppressed, perhaps indefinitely. Atheism need not take the coercive form favoured by the Soviet Union, which closed places of worship, hounded believers and executed priests.[49] Instead, it can flow through the soft power of secular norms and modern art, which urge us to forget and limit the depth of our reflection so that we can experience and achieve in this world, right now. Secularism's rise and fall is therefore determined by changes in society and politics, not in the responses of human nature to stimuli.

Liberal religion

The first openly non-religious political philosophers wrote in the late eighteenth century. At that time, leading secular and religious thinkers often moved in similar circles. In fact, prior to the twentieth century, Christianity and the Enlightenment formed part of a unified Western *mission civilatrice*, because Christianity was viewed as more progressive than its 'primitive' competitors. Consequently, the response of many within established religion was to accommodate the new Enlightenment ideas. Deism and Unitarianism depersonalised God, installing Him in his new role of abstract cosmic architect. Once He set the Newtonian universe in motion, its laws became the province of secular science.[50] Meanwhile, the new 'Higher Criticism' of German scholars such as Friedrich Schleiermacher used historical records from the Middle East to refute the literal approach to the Bible and argue for a more allegorical interpretation of scripture. David Strauss's *The Life of Jesus* (1846) and Ludwig Feuerbach's *The Essence of Christianity* (1854) were especially influential. When, in 1860, liberal Anglican theologians tried to incorporate Higher

Criticism into Christian doctrine, they aroused a firestorm and were defrocked. However, they were reinstated just two years later, suggesting that liberal religion had come of age in England. Something similar took place in the Jewish world, where the Reform movement sought to reconcile Judaism with the Enlightenment values prevailing in France, the German-speaking world, Britain and the United States.

The ecumenical movement, which dominated the upper echelons of organised Protestantism in the Anglo-Saxon world after 1900, moved in step with the most advanced secular currents. Ecumenists advanced the scope of liberal religion so far that they questioned the idea that their religion was the only true one, i.e. exclusivism, the idea which forms the basis of all monotheistic religions. Equality was a key impetus for ecumenists. Fearing that missionary activity was culturally imperialist, liberal Protestants pulled out of the missionary business altogether. Writing in the 1925 issue of *The Life* (a Christian Fellowship journal), John L. Childs of the YMCA offered what was to become the general view within liberal Protestantism:

> It is one thing to say that Christianity has its important contribution to make to the progress of the human race, and it is quite another thing to assert that the values which are found in Christianity are so unique, and completely satisfying, that it possesses the obvious and inherent right to displace all other religions.[51]

In 1929, the Reverend Robert A. Ashworth of Yonkers, New York, reiterated the same point with respect to evangelism in general:

> Christianity is in essence a missionizing religion. It seeks to propagate itself. I do not see how Christianity can relinquish that element without irreparable loss. On the other hand, missionary effort which results in ill-will rather than goodwill defeats it own aims. I know of no gain great enough to compensate for the loss or destruction of goodwill.[52]

Catholicism held out against modernist values somewhat longer, but in 1943, Pope Pius XII gave his assent to the new biblical scholarship.

Later, after turbulent debate, the second Vatican Encyclical (1968) was issued by Pope Paul VI and the new liturgy went into effect on 18 October 1969.[53] This muddied the previously hard distinction between sacred and profane, reduced the hierarchical nature of rituals and helped bring Church policy on contraception and birth control into line with the liberal practice of many modern Catholics. Modern ideas also revolutionised Islam. Nineteenth-century Islamic reformers such as Jamal al-din al-Afghani and Muhammad Abduh urged a greater role for *ijtihad*, or reasoning, in making Islamic religious judgements. In so doing, they sought to render Islam compatible with Western rationalism, a view that found concrete expression in the Tanzimat Reforms (1839–76) of the Ottoman Empire.[54] Liberal religion tried to reduce the hierarchical nature of faith and align it with the latest developments in secular thought. In narrowing the scope of the sacred and introducing relativistic tolerance, these innovations can be seen as secularising religion. The ordination of women in many Protestant denominations – up to the level of bishops within Anglicanism – shows how far modernism has progressed. Anglicans in Britain and their Episcopal cousins in the United States even went so far as to ordain homosexuals.[55]

The fundamentalist response

Secularism, like DDT, wiped out much of its opposition but also gave rise to new, resistant strains of religion. The erosion of identity often leads to counter-mobilisations designed to restore the *status quo ante*. New challenges can transform passive cultures into active identities which defend those cultures. This is as true of religions as it is of other forms of culture. When the Irish and Welsh languages were losing out to English in the early nineteenth century, Irish and Welsh cultural nationalism blossomed. The culture of Ireland and Wales appeared threatened, and native intellectuals responded with a self-conscious identity project.[56] When the third-generation descendants of European immigrants in the United States had lost touch with their language, they responded with ethnic revival. The third generation had to consciously *choose* to identify as Italian, whereas their grandparents simply *were* Italian without thinking about it.[57] If stamp collectors were persecuted, philatelists would develop a self-conscious political identity. If the celebration of Christmas was attacked by a large faction of 'anti-ribbonmen', this time-honoured but largely unconscious ritual would become a self-conscious statement of identity. Shopping malls would be politicised as never before. This may be less fanciful than you think: the growing neo-Calvinist fundamentalists in the US forbid the celebration of Christmas, viewing it as a pagan festival.

Religion has now woken up to the fact that it is under threat from secularism. Until the eighteenth century, with the exception of heretics, religion remained largely traditional. Within Christianity, the main battle lines pitted Protestants against Catholics, but daily faith was, like Christmas today, a communal affair that was largely taken for granted. With the advent of the Enlightenment and modernist faith, people's religious assumptions were called into question. In Europe and the United States, many pastors and ordinary parishioners listened with disquiet to the increasingly relativistic tone of the Protestant elite of the Federal Council of Churches. Jewish rabbis found their colleagues and communities gravitating towards Reform Judaism or even secular creeds such as socialism. In the Islamic world, secular nationalism, later joined by socialism, diluted the authority of traditional Islam.

Disgruntled clerics who sought a return to tradition demurred against the modernising drift of their churches, synagogues or, in the Muslim world, official mosques. Monotheistic religions are based around core texts such as the Torah, Qur'an or Bible as well as ancillary commentaries such as the Talmud, sharia and canon law. In order to safeguard 'tradition', these new fundamentalists sifted through their vast storehouse of religious resources to select elements that distinguished the true faith from the Milquetoast fare served up by the modernisers. Given the enormous array of injunctions, parables and interpretations, this was no simple task, so fundamentalists needed certain selection criteria. Ultra-Orthodox Jews, traditionalist Catholics, and Protestant and Islamic Fundamentalists responded by elevating the most demanding, world-denying doctrines to the status of non-negotiables. In so doing, they established clear boundaries between true believers and those who claimed the mantle of religion while being carried along by secular currents.

Fundamentalist teachings picked out passages which stressed traditional women's roles, time-consuming rituals, strange dress and the wickedness of carnal pleasures. Doctrines that collided most squarely with materialistic individualism were upgraded. Fundamentalist critics struck at the weak spots of modernity: drunkenness, crime, illegitimacy and greed. More lenient traditions were ignored, even if they stemmed directly from scripture rather than subsequent human commentaries such as sharia in Islam or Kabbalah in Judaism.[58] In their zeal to return to an idealised past, fundamentalists realised that the highest religious authorities were complicit in their faith's 'secular' drift. Traditional clerical hierarchies were therefore no longer sacred. Instead, doctrine was the pivot around which everything would rotate. Ironically, this was a very modern position to take, reflecting the influence of Enlightenment ideas of equality and religious freedom. The new fundamentalists were not liberals, but, like the Protestant reformers of sixteenth-century Europe, needed to invoke toleration in order to escape the clutches of established religious elites whom they viewed as corrupt.

In the first phase, many fundamentalist movements went underground, withdrawing from the world into enclaves of 'true believers'. These individuals styled themselves the morally superior 'saved', 'defenders of the faith' or 'saints'. They held a Manichean view of the world, seeing themselves as performing God's work against the forces of darkness. Fundamentalists complained of living in a sea of unbelief, a label which encompassed moderate believers. They compared their time to previous ages of depravity, such as the earth prior to the Flood of the Old Testament or the pagan Mecca that had persecuted Muhammad. Often this was backed by an apocalyptic cosmology in which the fundamentalists were assured a chosen place as God's special servants. For American premillennial Protestant fundamentalists, this meant that they, and only they, would ascend to heaven during the 'Rapture' which would precede the End Times. Ultra-Orthodox Jews awaited the coming of the Messiah, and Twelver Shiites the return of the Twelfth Imam and the re-establishment of the House of Ali. Sunni Muslim Salafis and Wahhabis, along with postmillennial Christian fundamentalists, were more optimistic. From the safety of their new enclaves, they would rebuild godly societies. For Sunni *takfiri* militants, the true faith would have to be imposed by force on the backsliding masses and their treasonous religious elites.[59]

Fundamentalists begin by building a counterculture that sets up an oppositional, 'high tension' stance to society.[60] Initially, this may involve worshipping apart; later it can extend to endogamy and residential segregation. Material pleasures are sacrificed for heavenly rewards, individual desires subordinated to collective ones. Fundamentalist communities first try to control education, hence the proliferation of Protestant academies and Bible Colleges, Islamist madrasas and Jewish yeshivas and kollelim. They create a parallel media, making use of modern technologies such as radio, cassette tapes, television and the Internet. They develop marks of distinction. The Muslim beard or ultra-Orthodox Jewish black hat and sidelocks can form the butt of jokes and harassment, increasing tension with the surrounding society. Unusual languages like Yiddish for the Haredim, Hutterite High German or classical Arabic among Salafists help to erect boundaries against the profane world outside.[61]

Endogamy is encouraged by some groups, especially the ultra-Orthodox and Amish. In civil society, these groups form religious associations such as the Islamic *jama'at*, Jewish rabbinic community and Independent Protestant sect. Finally, fundamentalists from each religious tradition approach politics in a different way. Some, like Sunni fundamentalists and religious Zionists, actively seek to implement the Kingdom of God on earth. Ultra-Orthodox Jews, Protestant premillennialists and Shia fundamentalists, on the other hand, initially withdrew from politics.[62] As quietist movements grow, however, they often sprout activist wings and enter politics. Though usually peaceful, the Manichean, eschatological and perfectionist worldview of fundamentalists can be harnessed for political violence.[63] Indeed, none of the Abrahamic faiths has proven immune to the appeal of fundamentalist violence.

Ethnic dynamics are a useful way of approaching religious fundamentalisms, because ethnic groups share many features with the endogenous growth sects that have succeeded so well in the West. Ethnic groups are often shaped by specific opponents: Greeks and Turks, English and French, Serbs and Croats. Within an ethnic group, those who seek to accommodate the enemy are typically smeared as traitors. Congress supporters in India are deemed insufficiently Hindu by the BJP; in Northern Ireland, liberal Unionists such as David Trimble are accused of being 'Lundies' in reference to a famous Protestant turncoat. For religious fundamentalists, the external foes are mainly foreign occupiers while the internal traitors are the regimes which cooperate with the infidel. This is especially characteristic of Islamist thinking in relation to the West, but also shapes the attitude of Orthodox Jews to their 'gentile' neighbours, whether Christians in Europe or Muslims in the Middle East. Even so, xenophobia is not enough to drive fundamentalism, because you don't need to be religious to despise foreigners. Islamist Hamas can never completely differentiate itself from the secular PLO simply by being anti-Israel. More important, therefore, are fundamentalists' internal targets: the religious establishment, the secular state, lax and liberal believers and a decadent consumer society.[64]

Building fundamentalism

The leading theory of nationalism holds that ethnic groups and nations are modern phenomena which first arose after 1789. On this reading, communities used to be so localised that people could not imagine their nation in relation to others. In an era before easy long-distance travel, prior to labour migration and the spread of a common historical consciousness through mass literacy, schooling and media, where the reach of political institutions was weak and mass militaries were non-existent, a sense of ethnicity and nationhood could not exist. A village is real: a pre-modern person could meet all of her fellow villagers and know it intimately. In multicultural cities such as Alexandria, Egypt or Tallinn, Estonia, linguistic groups understood they were different from each other, but lacked the ability to imagine their homeland and links with co-ethnics elsewhere. A Russian speaker in Tallinn could have no grasp of the breadth of Russia and its history, and would share little mental space with a Russian speaker from Omsk.[65] This view undoubtedly exaggerates the sharpness of the break between the pre-modern and modern periods: writings of medieval and early modern European elites shows that a sense of ethnicity existed among them in many places before the advent of modernity. Bede's *Ecclesiastical History of the English People* or the Swiss *White Book of Sarnen* are prime examples. Occasional mass 'nationalist' mobilisations of people did take place before the modern period, notably in ancient Israel.

Yet whatever their leanings, few nationalism theorists dispute that modernising processes deepened, straightened and sharpened ethnic boundaries.[66] Languages such as Italian and French were standardised from a welter of dialects, codified in dictionaries and taught in centralised new school systems; ethnic and national territories were demarcated on maps while government officials manned new customs and border posts; populations were tabulated in state records and censuses, and often assigned to official ethnic categories whether they liked it or not. Militaries changed from mercenary forces to mass citizen armies after the example set by the French *levée en masse* of the Napoleonic era. Modern bureaucracies and economies broke down local monopolies and sucked people around, stretching the horizons of identity towards the national. In many places, democracy and mass parties gave individuals the right to vote and participate in a political process that had once been the preserve of the landed few. In so many ways, modernity truly 'ushered the masses into history'.

Secessionists benefited alongside the state. Modern newspapers and roads helped them to organise ethnic associations, publish separatist tracts, form ethnic parties and coordinate paramilitary activity. Overall, the formerly hazy line between ethnic insiders and outsiders hardened as modern rationality structured society.[67] Religious fundamentalists copied these tactics. They boiled religious doctrines down to a set of fundamentals and standardised the faith to remove local variations. Orthodox Judaism was once part of the fabric of local Jewish life in Eastern Europe, its doctrine varying with the patchwork quilt of dialects in the Pale of Settlement. After 1802, however, the Volozhin yeshiva began drawing scholars from across Europe into a central location in what is now Belarus, where Talmudic study could be rationalised and formalised.[68] In the United States, the Moody Bible Institute was founded in 1886 as a hub of premillennialist Protestant thought. Bible conferences, fundamentalist newspapers and, later, radio and television ministries helped institutionalise a new subculture. The Scofield Reference Bible of 1909 standardised its dispensationalist theology.[69] American fundamentalism is now situated within a modern 'evangelical' Protestant world of megachurches, religious shopping malls, publishing houses, Christian pop culture and parachurch organisations, all facilitated by modern communications.[70]

Modern technology helps to solidify symbolic boundaries. Long-distance communication allows Shiite imams in Iran to instruct their followers in Iraq, who in turn keep their leaders informed about events there.[71] It permits Mormon elites to meticulously track the pace of conversion and defection, enabling them to experiment with methods of improving success rates. It helps Haredi Jews to chart their group's demographic rise and political weight with a high degree of precision. It affords the Haredi masses an opportunity to follow the vicissitudes of their community's dealings with the outside world in real time, reinforcing the boundaries of identity. Small wonder that formerly loose boundaries between religious fundamentalists and the wider community are beginning to harden. Membership retention rates among the Amish and Orthodox Jews have risen sharply over the past generation. Those of American Protestant fundamentalists are noticeably higher than in more liberal sects. Communication between masses and elites has improved and the supply of religious services has risen to absorb demand. Among Utah Mormons for instance, church membership rates rose from roughly 15 per cent in 1900 to nearly 70 per cent by the end of the century.[72] As parachurch activities and media expand, communicants are drawn into an increasingly self-contained fundamentalist world. Like the nation state, religious fundamentalists have become an institutional fixture of modern life.

The crisis of liberal religion

Mainstream religious bodies were caught off-guard by fundamentalist efficiency. Today, moderate religion is in decline, squeezed between the Scylla of secularism and the Charybdis of fundamentalism. What we see is a final reckoning between religion and the Enlightenment, with individuals forced to choose between the two. Liberal Christians watered down their Christianity to minimise dissonance with Enlightenment liberalism, but their children failed to see the point of staying, often opting out of religion entirely. In today's America, just 7 per cent of ultra-liberal Unitarians attend services weekly, compared with 54 per cent of conservative Protestants and 85 per cent of Mormons. In Britain and the United States, liberal denominations such as the Anglicans and their Episcopal cousins suffer disproportionate losses to non-religion, while evangelical Churches such as the Seventh-day Adventist or Pentecostal Holiness expand. Between 1960 and 2000, liberal Protestant denominations saw their share of the American religious market cut in half from 16 to 8 per cent, while conservative Protestants doubled in size from 7 to 16 per cent.[73] Evangelicals also gained ground against the relatively liberal Protestant established Churches of north-western Europe (Lutheran, Anglican, Presbyterian). In the Judaic world, Reform and Conservative Jewry lost out to Orthodoxy.

Elsewhere the traditional religions were grounded in time-honoured folk rituals. These had been passed from parents to children with little attention paid to doctrinal fundamentals. The Catholic Church in Latin America, Buddhism and Shintoism in East Asia and Animism in sub-Saharan Africa lost heavily to Pentecostalism during the late twentieth century. In Islam, both Sufism and traditional folk Islam, which blend religion with pagan practices, are waning. The mushy middle between fundamentalist religion and irreligion seems to be haemorrhaging as people either choose unalloyed secularism or full-orbed faith. Even if moderate religion can hang on, its atheist detractors are as determined as religious fundamentalists to kick it in the teeth. While fundamentalists attack moderates as near-heretics, atheists suggest that moderates legitimise an intellectual subservience and suspension of reason which blazes a path for extremism. In giving credence to religion, the New Atheists argue, theological moderates safeguard the explosive recipe for another 9/11.[74] Moderate religions which base their appeal on custom or their connection to mainstream society are polarising between fundamentalism and secularism. In Marxist terms, the religious-secular contradictions of moderate religion are tearing it apart.

Endogenous growth versus conversion
No religion can grow without first enlisting converts from the wider society. Later, the two strategies for fundamentalist expansion are external proselytisation and endogenous growth. External proselytisation is quicker, but rapid conversion is often accompanied by rapid exit. Endogenous growth is often more enduring. Consider the endogenous growth sects which have thrived in secular environments. The archetype is Mormonism. Its endogenous power is often overlooked because of its proselytising nature. To be sure, the Mormons have done a remarkable job of winning converts. Founded in 1830, the vision of Joseph

Smith, the prophet of Mormonism, has spread so successfully that it may soon become a major world religion. The 200-strong frontier mob which shot Smith dead as he fled a jail in Carthage, Illinois, in 1844 had their eventual comeuppance: Smith's acolyte Brigham Young led his followers west to the wilds of Utah in 1847 and established a thriving Mormon theocracy. By 2003, there were approximately 12 million Mormons – officially known as the Church of Jesus Christ of Latter-Day Saints (LDS) – worldwide, with over half the membership living outside the United States. Mormons believe in the Bible, but add a completely innovative Book of Mormon as revealed by their prophet Smith. They further hold that the presidents of the Mormon Church can experience fresh revelations.

Like all endogenous growth sects, Mormon social values are conservative and communitarian. Since 1830, they have averaged over 40 per cent growth per decade, maintaining this pace in all five post-Second World War decades. Rodney Stark projects that at conservative growth rates of 30 per cent per decade, there will be 63 million Mormons in 2080. At rates of 50 per cent per decade, 267 million Mormons will stride the earth. By 2100, using the same low and high growth rates, Mormons will constitute between 1 and 6 per cent of the earth's population. This gives them an even chance of surpassing Buddhists and Chinese folk religionists (both currently around 6 per cent) in size.[75]

It has happened before. Stark argues that the rise of Christianity in the Roman Empire owed a great deal to demography. He asks how a tiny despised band of forty Christians in AD 30, the 'Jesus movement', could become a 6-million-strong subculture by AD 300. Conversion was certainly important, but demographic forces were arguably more vital. Christianity's family-centred ethos sharply contrasted with the more macho, promiscuous ethos of pagan Hellenism. This had two effects. The first was to boost the Christian birth rate above that of the pagans, the second to attract a disproportionate number of female converts. Women's role in socialising the next generation means that a female-dominated sex ratio leads to a disproportionate number of Christian children. In addition, Christians cared for their sick during plagues, dramatically reducing mortality. Higher fertility, lower mortality and a female skew in the childbearing age ranges endowed Christians with a significant demographic advantage over pagans. Even a small edge can rapidly increase a group's share of the population over several generations. This happens through compounding, as more children beget more mothers, and so on in exponential fashion. Over several centuries, this has impressive social consequences. A Mormon-like rate of increase of 40 per cent per decade, sustained over the period AD 30–300, is all that was needed to create 6 million Christians from forty original converts. In the year 312, the Emperor Constantine adopted Christianity as the official religion of the Roman Empire. This political act prompted a massive expansion of Christianity, but it is unlikely that Christianity would have been adopted if it had remained the creed of a tiny band.[76]

To be sure, conversion is a more important part of the global LDS story than demography, since there are 2.4 converts for every baptised Mormon.[77] However, in the Mormon heartland of Utah and its surrounding states, demographic expansion is vastly more important than conversion. Moreover, Mormon participation and membership retention is far higher in this 'ethnic' heartland than in the rest of the United States and, especially, in the rest of the world. Some estimates suggest that Mormon membership retention outside the United States is as low as 20–30 per cent, with just a third of worldwide LDS members active in church programmes. This may set limits to future LDS growth.[78] One reason for the ceiling is the absence of a Mormon atmosphere outside the heartland: a study of American Mormons in the 1960s found that the chance of a Mormon child becoming Orthodox in belief is three to five times higher if both parents are Orthodox than if just one parent is. Intermarriage obviously eliminates the chances of having two Orthodox Mormon parents. Yet in most of the world there are few LDS marriage partners, so intermarriage rates are much higher than in the LDS-rich Mountain West. In the same study, just 10 per cent of Mormons in Salt Lake City, Utah, were intermarried, compared with 40–60 per cent in the San Francisco Bay area.[79] In recognition of this, American Mormons living outside Utah send their children to university there to improve their chances of finding a Mormon mate.[80]

Mormonism may still be a small fish, but in small ponds it becomes a big one. Twenty countries are now over 1 per cent Mormon, with the leading lights being South Pacific Island states whose residents are considered descendants of the fabled Lamanites of the Book of Mormon. No wonder a third of Tongans and a quarter of Samoans are LDS members. Over eight South Pacific island states are at least 4 per cent Mormon. Even so, the largest collection of Mormons, and the majority of active ones, are in the United States, where 4.9 million LDS members reside. Almost 2 per cent of Americans are Mormons, and among Americans born after the Second World War there are more Mormons than Jews. Utah is of course the Mormon epicentre: 72 per cent of the population is LDS. But in neighbouring states, numbers are also high: Idaho is 27 per cent LDS, Wyoming 10 per cent, Nevada 7.4 per cent and Arizona 5.5 per cent. Many non-Utah Mormons inhabit contiguous areas in a slowly spreading 'Pale of Settlement'. Six counties in nearby Idaho are more than 70 per cent Mormon, and eleven counties outside Idaho and Utah are over 20 per cent LDS. In some western towns, there have been clashes between non-Mormon residents and newly arrived populations of polygamous dissident Mormons.[81]

Demographic forces have been key to Mormon growth from the outset, when Brigham Young and the original LDS pioneers settled in Utah to escape persecution. Throughout their history, Mormon fertility has tracked the American total fertility rate (TFR), but at a rate of one to two children above the national average.[82] Since American fertility has declined greatly due to the demographic transition, a one-child edge means more in percentage terms than it used to. Mormon fertility is not the result of poverty and low education. In fact, Mormons are better educated and wealthier than the average American. Curiously, wealthy Mormons have more children than poorer ones and the education levels of women (and men) do not affect the number of offspring they have. These patterns are the reverse of those noted among other Americans, and indeed, across much of the world.[83] Reflecting second demographic transition (SDT) theory, the fertility advantage of Mormons is most pronounced in developed countries such as Britain and the US.[84]

This has been vital for the maintenance of their position in Utah. Barely ten years after Young's Mormons settled the territory, the federal government was breathing down their necks. In 1857, President Buchanan sent in troops to occupy the Salt Lake Valley and crush dreams of an independent Mormon theocracy. First, American authorities replaced

Young with a non-Mormon territorial governor. The Utah territory was opened up to settlement and in 1867 Protestant churches started setting up shop. Miners and commercial interests poured in. By 1890, non-Mormons formed 16.8 per cent of Salt Lake City's population, rising to 30 per cent by 1906. The government pressured Utah to ban polygamy and curtail the power of Mormon ecclesiastical courts. It forced the territory to jettison its ethnic party system in which the People's Party, representing Mormons, squared off against the non-Mormon Liberal Party. The Mormon hierarchy complied on all counts in 1890 and statehood followed in 1896. No doubt the American government hoped to Americanise Utah through immigration, just as the British tried to anglicise French Canada after the Durham Report of 1840. The French Catholic clerical response in Quebec was '*la revanche des berceaux*' (the revenge of the cradle). Consciously or otherwise, the result was that French-Canadians held their own in the face of massive British immigration. Utah Mormons benefited likewise. Despite continuing immigration, the non-Mormon population of Utah peaked at 40 per cent in 1920. By 1997–8, it had dropped to a mere quarter.[85] This affects both state and national politics. Mormons gave the Republicans 94 per cent of their votes in 2000 and fully 97 per cent in 2004, a more partisan voting record than any other ethnic or religious group.[86]

We find further examples of endogenous growth in recent times among religious groups which trace their lineage to the Anabaptists of southern Germany and Switzerland. Once radical reformers impatient with the slow pace of the Reformation, Anabaptists came to be marked by strong conservative tendencies. They endured harsh persecution in the sixteenth century, and many were beheaded, burned, starved or drowned. The memory of the early martyrs and their communal holocaust persists among their descendants today. The principal Anabaptist groups are the Mennonites, Hutterites, Amish and Brethren. They number more than half a million in the contemporary United States. Of these, only a third can be considered 'Old Order' traditionalists. All Old Order groups have high fertility rates coupled with strong membership retention. The Hutterites, the most conservative of the Old Order groups, averaged almost ten children per family in the first half of the twentieth century. This has declined to between five and six today, but the fertility of their neighbours has tumbled faster. In 1950, for instance, Hutterites had twice the birth rate of other South Dakotans. By 1990, Hutterites held a threefold advantage in spite of having fewer children. Hutterites do not proselytise, but make a strenuous effort to retain children in the faith. As a consequence, losses to switching are estimated at less than 5 per cent of total membership.[87]

The net result has been phenomenal population growth: the North American Hutterite population has expanded from roughly 400 individuals in 1880 to some 50,000 today. These changes were accompanied by somewhat slower population growth rates, but since surrounding populations have declined faster, the proportion of Hutterites in the population has increased. Between 1951 and 1981, for instance, the Hutterite population on the Canadian prairies nearly tripled, from 6,200 to 16,200, but its share of the prairie farm population jumped nearly five times, from 0.7 per cent to 3.3 per cent.[88] This sparked occasional tensions with non-Hutterite neighbours over land, though the surrounding rural population's move to the cities has probably eased these pressures since. The population of Canadian prairie farm operators has declined by 20 per cent since 1981 while the number of Hutterites has nearly doubled, so the Hutterite share of the prairie farm population may now be as high as 7 or 8 per cent.[89] Population growth rates among Hutterites have slipped in the past generation, but are well above those of the surrounding population. Critically, this has occurred against the backdrop of rapidly falling North American fertility, so the Hutterites are poised to emerge as a more visible ethno-religious presence in rural western Canada and South Dakota in coming generations.

A less isolated, larger and more easterly Old Order group are the Amish. Today they number around a quarter of a million, not bad for a community which consisted of just 5,000 souls in 1900. Conversion is basically non-existent, so expansion has been driven by the Amish fertility rate. In 1979, the Amish total fertility rate was estimated at around 7, and a 1996 study shows that this has fallen to roughly 5.3. However, once again, we must bear in mind that absolute declines can coexist with relative growth. If a group's TFR – in terms of surviving offspring – is 6 while others bear an average of 4, this represents a 50 per cent advantage. If the figures sink to 4 and 2 respectively, this becomes a 100 per cent advantage.

The past generation of Amish have experienced a wholesale occupational shift out of agriculture: three-quarters of the previous generation worked the land, but among today's generation of adults, just 10–15 per cent remain on the farm. Amish non-farm families were found to contain just 4.7 children per family as against 6.2 for farm families, so the occupational shift probably explains the overall decrease. Conservative 'Andy Weaver' Amish were predictably more fertile (6.2) than more modern 'New Order' Amish, at 4.8.

Retention is also critical. When the Amish first settled in North America, their horse-based, agricultural lifestyle differed little from that of their neighbours. Population densities were low and the Amish relied more heavily on their non-Amish neighbours to survive on the frontier. Intermarriage and defection were common. By the twentieth century, this had changed. Amish began purchasing land within horse-carriage distance of their churches, forming more contiguous communities. As modern technology transformed their neighbours' lives, the Amish resisted, retaining horses and rejecting the tractor, radio, telephone and automobile. The gap between the Amish and what they call the 'English' grew, slowing defection. Retention of children was a respectable 70 per cent for the generation born before 1945, and has increased with every subsequent generation. Among those born during 1966–75, retention rises to 85 per cent.[90] 'Strict church' theory predicts that the density of social ties in demanding religious communities makes it much more costly and difficult for members to leave. Those who depart lose their entire world, not just one part of it, and may even be refused access to their parents. It is therefore not surprising that Conservative Amish groups keep 95 per cent of their children in the fold while the more progressive New Order Amish retain only 57 per cent. Many who leave enter the mainstream Mennonite community.[91] A small number join evangelical churches.[92]

Like the Hutterites, Amish 'mother' communities spawn 'daughter' colonies when they reach a critical mass of around one hundred. Mother communities help purchase land and finance new ones. Population growth has compounded the rate at which these communities proliferate. Between 1950 and 1970, thirty-seven new Amish communities were founded. This sounds substantial until you consider the current rate of expansion – in just six years between 1997 and 2003, sixty-six new communities formed, and have begun to push out beyond the traditional Amish heartlands in the Midwest and Pennsylvania.[93] Over 2007–8, they grew from 218,000 to 231,000: the equivalent of about 130 colonies. The same is true for the Hutterites, whose three colonies in 1870 now number approximately 450.[94]

The phenomenal rate of Old Order Anabaptist growth is achieved by communal separation from modern secular society. Hutterites seek out isolated locations on the Canadian prairies and American high plains, which reduce assimilative pressures. They are distinguished, like all Old Order peoples, by their distinctive dress as well as a German dialect which is unintelligible to their neighbours. Women dress plainly and men wear beards.[95] They hold property in common and their communities are largely self-sufficient. The Amish, unlike the Hutterites, have frequent contact with outsiders, including growing numbers of tourists. Lacking geographic isolation, they place more emphasis on social barriers. The Amish are thus more apt than Hutterites to 'shun' wayward members of the community, who must sit outside church services in shame as people shuffle in or out. Offenders take their meals alone in basement rooms rather than at the communal table. Only a repentance ceremony returns the shamed member to equal standing. The Amish are also the most anti-technology of all Old Order groups. They use limited electricity and remain opposed to the automobile, tractor and computer, whereas other Old Order groups accept their use for productive – as opposed to leisure – purposes.[96]

Old Order groups elevate the community over the individual. Their faith is traditional and austere rather than expressive and evangelical. Schooling takes place within the community for most groups and often ends before the eighth grade. Children are raised to be obedient, and the 'breaking' of individual wills towards the common good is considered the central task of child-rearing. 'What makes Amish children so nice is the spanking,' commented one mother. 'The more you spank, the better the result.' 'If you spank them a lot,' added another, 'you break their will and they become like you want them.'[97] All Old Order groups are traditionalist, but adopt technology selectively if it benefits the community. After all, the groups must find funds to purchase new land, pay taxes and take care of the health and welfare of the community. In general, Old Order groups have made their peace with technologies of production while limiting technologies of consumption and, especially, communication. Private radios, stereos and televisions are banned by all groups, while computers, cameras and phones are outlawed by all but the most liberal.[98] Old Order pacifism has led to periodic conflict with the state: the communal Hutterites have collided with the government over taxation, which is assessed on the earnings of individuals rather than the community, as the Hutterites would have it. Amish have faced problems because they use slow-moving horse-drawn buggies on major highways, and both Hutterites and Amish have locked horns with officials over the content of the education served up in their schools.[99]

Inward-looking Anabaptists outperform their outward-oriented cousins. The typical North American Mennonite uses modern technology, accepts intermarriage with outsiders, speaks English at home and has an average fertility rate. In other words, they can be considered just another species of white Protestant. Modern Mennonites have adopted an evangelical growth strategy, enabling them to expand internationally through conversion to the point where there are now over 300,000 African Mennonites, a third of the million-strong world communion. However, in the highly secular societies of North America and Europe, these evangelical Mennonites have fared poorly. In Europe, their membership fell 32 per cent between 1984 and 1998.[100] In the United States, the mainstream Mennonite Church Assembly grew just 0.71 per cent per annum between 1970 and 2000. Conversely, despite a lack of converts, Old Order Mennonites grew four times quicker and Old Order Amish eight times faster.[101]

I experienced the two Mennonite worlds first hand when I worked for a year in the forest industry in the small community of Peace River, in north-western Alberta, Canada. The reprocessing plant we used in the city of Edmonton six hours to the south was owned by a modern Mennonite multi-millionaire who identified more broadly with evangelical Protestanism and had just three children. On the other hand, in certain northern mills, most of the employees were traditional Mennonites, some of whom spoke heavily accented English. As with Mormon growth in Utah, sectarian population increase can significantly alter the composition of local political units. The traditionalist Mennonite settlement of La Crete, in the north-west corner of the region, was the fastest growing community in the province. Needless to say, this is not because its semi-arctic wildness attracted other Albertans. This demographic dynamism has spillover effects on the entire North-west Alberta region. Lacking conventional economic pulls, the region's official website emphasises its 'Young, growing population – average age of residents is 23 years, compared to the Canadian average of 37 years! The region experienced 13% growth between 2001–2003 and it keeps on growing.'[102]

Endogenous growth sects are poised to grow substantially in the secular West (including Israel), while evangelistic creeds like Pentecostalism and the Jehovah's Witnesses perform better in more 'enchanted' developing countries where social norms are congenial to religiosity and conversion. Even in the United States, where religious switching is common and faith considered normal, demographically driven religions tend to outperform those which rely on conversion. Looking at the period between 1970 and 2005, mainline Protestants, lacking any demographic boost, experienced decline. Catholicism, though losing many members through conversion, was buoyed by Hispanic population growth. It increased 1.2 per cent per annum, about the same rate as the relatively fertile Southern Baptist Convention (SBC). The most fertile large denominations, Independent Protestants and Mormons, grew 3.1 per cent per annum. But the corresponding Old Order Amish growth rate was 5.3 per cent, rising to 5.5 per cent for Hutterites. Only the most successful independents, such as the high-profile Willow Creek network of megachurches and some Pentecostals, grew faster.[103]

In Europe, the roughly 100,000 Conservative Laestadian Lutherans of Finland and more than 1 million Dutch Orthodox Calvinists have both bucked secularising trends. These high fertility endogenous growth sects are starting to make an impact: there are now more Orthodox Calvinist church attenders than those of its liberal parent, the Dutch Reformed Church, whose parishioners once outnumbered them six to one.[104] These lessons are not lost on other fundamentalists. 'Let's outbreed the Mormons,' urges Russell Moore, Dean of the School of Theology at the Southern Baptist seminary in Louisville, Kentucky. The Quiverfull Protestant fundamentalist movement, like the Laestadians, espouses 'natural' fertility and disdains contraception. It has now caught the attention of leading American fundamentalist intellectuals: 'Probably the most subversive and effective strategy we might undertake,' argues conservative theologian David Bentley Hart, is 'one of militant fecundity: abundant, relentless, exuberant, and defiant'.[105] Dominion theologian Gary North adds that ultra-Orthodox Jewish endogamy is the model for Protestant fundamentalists to follow if they wish to survive.[106]

Why today's fundamentalists won't moderate

Sceptics may counter that high fertility and exclusivity have already been tried by many failed sects. 'Almost every day, somewhere in the world, a new religion appears,' Rodney Stark reminds us. Almost all of these new movements crumble soon after they form.[107] We might fairly ask, 'What is so special about today's endogenous growth sects? Surely they too will rapidly disintegrate?' Religions that break away from established denominations but stay within their parent religion are known as sects in the literature, while completely new faiths are referred to as cults. Cults such as the Jehovah's Witnesses tend to recruit from isolated or alienated individuals, while sects such as the Pentecostalists poach from closely related denominations of a religion. Cults are especially fragile, and 90 per cent of new recruits leave in the first few years.[108] There are only so many socially isolated people to tap, and the clash of egos among these idiosyncratic individuals often proves their undoing.[109] Of course, the longevity of today's world religions, especially Christianity, Islam, Hinduism, Buddhism and Judaism, suggests that a few lucky cults survive and prosper. The revelations of Jesus and Muhammad may have been tender shoots when they began, but have mushroomed into stable, growing faiths. Mormonism, the Witnesses and Seventh-day Adventism, all founded in the nineteenth century, seem well established.

Yet these are the rare exceptions. One study of eighty-three American communes formed in the nineteenth century, including thirty religious ones, found that the Hutterites were the only group to have survived into the present.[110] A high fertility rate was a major reason for Hutterite success. On the other hand, celibate groups such as the Shakers withered when flows of converts failed to materialise. Today, Arnold Hadd (aged forty-nine), Wayne Smith (forty-three), June Carpenter (sixty-seven) and Frances Carr (seventy-nine) are the last remaining adherents, living plainly among the forests, orchards and clapboard houses of Sabbath-day Lake Shaker village in southern Maine.[111] The Cathars, a medieval French heretical movement, were crushed by persecution and papal edict. However, the celibacy of its higher orders did not help it.

Zoroastrians may suffer a similar fate. In India, Zoroastrian Parsees, descendants of Persians who fled the Muslim conquest of Sassanid Persia in 640, are now dwindling. From a peak of 114,000 in 1941, there are now a mere 69,601 Zoroastrians in India, which is the epicentre of the faith. Heavily urbanised and westernised, the mean age at marriage for these 'Jews of India' has long been about ten years higher than the Indian average. Parsee women are highly educated and career-oriented. Their fertility has been well below replacement level for more than half a century: in 1982, in their Mumbai hub, they managed a TFR of just 1.12, compared with 5.2 for Indian women as a whole. With such a small pool of adherents, endogamy is difficult and intermarriage inevitable, but conversion remains prohibited. By 2050, the community is projected to fall to just half its current size. Meanwhile, in Iran, Zoroastrians have shrunk from 60,000 in 1970 to 30,000 today, besieged on all sides by persecution, emigration and outmarriage. 'Many Zoroastrians have emigrated,' bemoans Mehraban Firouzgary, Zoroastrian priest of Tehran. 'Nowadays the younger generation in Iran marry later and have fewer children ... We have therefore become an aging community.' As Zoroastrian-American lawyer Dina McIntyre admits, 'Survival has become a community obsession.' The net result of weak demography may be the extinction of one of the world's great monotheistic religions – a world faith which influenced Islam and Christianity and stretched from Greece and Rome to India and Russia.[112]

Christian Science has succumbed to a related fate. One of the more successful cults, it amassed 140,000 American members by 1926, but later went into steady decline. All social movements age unless recruitment is even across age and sex groups. This makes recruitment-driven cults more risky than birth-driven ones. Christian Science, for instance, attracted disproportionate numbers of older, well-heeled women, and had low overall fertility. This resulted in poor rates of endogenous growth and turned off prospective young converts.[113] Fertility on its own is not enough, however. The Children of God and the Family are two cults with exceptionally high fertility. The Family, surely the alter ego of the Shakers, subscribe to the idea that God's love takes erotic form and practise ritualised communal sex. One study of this cult found that 11 per cent of those over thirty had six children, and 40 per cent had more than seven. However, its free-love ethos and lack of clear boundaries with the rest of society proved its undoing. The second generation deserted in droves.[114] A period of conversion and consolidation, perhaps aided by geographic isolation, is needed to incubate a cult. High fertility coupled with geographic and social segregation from society is vital to improve retention and sow the seeds of growth.[115]

As with cults, so too with sects. The prevailing scholarly view is that sects recruit among lower-status members of a mainstream church – those least likely to succeed in this world. Fundamentalists such as the early Methodists or contemporary Pentecostals promise strong otherworldly rewards to compensate for the lack of goodies in this one. The fundamentalist message is therefore that those who deny themselves the earthly pleasures of sex, status and wealth will be richer in the next one. Since the poor consume relatively little anyway and cannot catch up with the wealthy, this austere creed is appealing, enabling them to transform their misery into a virtue. Fundamentalist practices such as plain dressing or residential segregation deliberately increase tension with mainstream society, raising walls between sect and society which reinforce members' commitment to the group. We see this most clearly among Haredi Jews and the Amish, but also among Salafists and some Protestant fundamentalists.[116]

The flipside of this is that high-status members of a puritanical sect stand to benefit from connections to successful outsiders and their secular reputations suffer, so they agitate for a 'church' movement which can reduce tension with the rest of society. These are the moderating movements which tamed the sectarian zeal of nineteenth-century dissenters such as the Methodists and Baptists, and even led many Mormons and Mennonites to mainstream respectability in the twentieth century. Given this dynamic, can we not expect fast-growing, high-tension sects like the Haredim or Old Order Amish to splinter, spawning moderate 'church' movements that seek to integrate into the mainstream? In this way, a natural process of religious schism could release tension, blunting the radical potential of fast-growing fundamentalist sects.

The problem is that church-sect theory was always too reductionist, failing to appreciate the powerful independent appeal of strong religion. More importantly, the rules of the status game have now changed, with religious identities self-consciously mobilising against secularism and liberal religion. As recently as the 1960s, there was a powerful correspondence in American religion between social status and denomination. The joke was that the successful barefoot Baptist became a respectable Methodist and his son an Episcopalian. Today, that relationship has broken down: just 71 per cent of mainline Protestants born in the years 1960–73 remain in a mainline denomination, compared with 81 per cent among those born during 1900–1909. For conservative Protestants, we find the reverse: 21 per cent of conservative Protestants born in the decade 1900–1909 switched to mainline denominations, but this plummets to just 9 per cent among those born between 1960 and 1973.

During the second half of the twentieth century, a period of rapid upward mobility and growing secularisation, the old religious status escalator stalled.[117] Evangelical Protestants retained their fundamentalist ethos as they ascended the social ladder, spawning a new slick middle-class culture of suburban megachurches, campus ministries, prayer breakfasts and Bible-thumping CEOs. New fundamentalist identities and organisations had arisen which erected barriers against the 'secular' world, including mainline denominations. The new fundamentalist web could better retain the upwardly mobile. Now those who leave fundamentalist sects must say goodbye to their entire social milieu. This makes them think twice, reducing defection.

We find similar trends among the Mormons, who are wealthier and better educated than the average American but shifted decisively towards higher tension with mainstream society after the 1960s. After a period of accommodating to American norms and building theological bridges with Protestants, the Mormon leadership – encouraged by growing American toleration for diversity and alarmed at secularism – began to stress Mormon distinctiveness. Their King James Bible was Mormonised and more attention paid to the Book of Mormon. Temple work, genealogy, family renewal, missionary work and religious schooling took off.

Mormons increased their oddness in the eyes of other Americans.[118] This helped to stanch assimilation. In a reversal of trends in the rest of the Western world, wealthier, better-educated Mormons have higher church participation than the less well off.[119] This doesn't mean that nothing changes. The Amish, Mennonites and Hutterites have all experienced powerful splits between groups based on their degree of modernity. However, many of the modernising movements occurred long ago. Even the most recent modernist breakaways, those of the Beachy (1927) and New Order (1960) Amish, are over a half-century old and pre-date the secular revolution of the sixties.[120]

In American Protestant fundamentalism, neo-evangelical, or 'prosperity gospel' churches are sometimes viewed as accommodationist.[121] But this is a superficial form of modernism. It has not prodded evangelicals to adopt a metaphorical reading of the Bible and their creed is a far cry from the doctrine espoused by mainline churches. Likewise, we find few modernising 'church' movements among the Haredim, and, with small but high-profile exceptions such as Tariq Ramadan's 'Euro-Islam', few in fundamentalist Islam. Certainly fundamentalists are riven by splits as charismatic preachers or rebbes battle for followers and engage in serious infighting. Yet while Jones may villify Graham as the anti-Christ, Shach and Yosef's acolytes may beat each other up and al-Sadr's and al-Hakim's may kill each other, this competition leaves the broader fundamentalist cause unaffected. Competition may even be a sign of strength. Everyone in the fundamentalist tent agrees that whatever their differences, secularism and its moderate religious cat's paw are powerful enemies that must be resisted above all else. Moderating movements are therefore unlikely to answer to fundamentalism's rising tide.

Two species of religious demography
We have followed the trail of religion from secularisation to liberal religion to religious fundamentalist reaction. The most successful species of fundamentalism in secular, low fertility Western environments is the endogenous growth sect. Such sects are flourishing because of their rising fertility premium over the rest of society. Mainstream fundamentalists are paying more attention to the endogenous growth model as one to emulate. Their rise undercuts the widely held notion that religion

can only succeed in insecure, poor or enchanted contexts.[122] However, ours has been very much a Western story. We should not forget that in other parts of the world where the principles of the Enlightenment are not second nature, things work differently. Few non-Western societies, even in secular East Asia, embrace expressive individualism. Norms of liberty, equality and democracy have shallower roots. Religious revival consequently tends to have social and political, rather than demographic causes.

The problem for our Western-centred theory is that while the 'West' (including Russia and Eastern Europe) accounted for 35 per cent of humanity in 1900, this has fallen to 17 per cent today and will tumble to around 10 per cent by 2050. Half of Americans and a quarter of Western Europeans will probably be of non-European ancestry by then, most from places where secularisation has little history of success. Demography therefore matters, not because of fundamentalist pronatalism, but due to indirect growth. The poor tend to be religious and have large families, increasing the world's religiosity. As Pippa Norris and Ron Inglehart write, 'rich nations are becoming more secular, but the world as a whole is becoming more religious.' [123]

This has knock-on effects in the West as the global religious poor migrate to the rich secular West in search of a better life. In short, religion expands indirectly through underdevelopment. It is certainly the case that religion in the global South is often moderate and inherited rather than consciously fundamentalist. Over time, the developing world may follow the Asian 'tiger' economies and catch up with the West. Norris and Inglehart suggest it will secularise as it develops. In the West, the children of non-European immigrants should undergo the same process. But such an account fails to capture the identity dynamics caused by long-distance cultural contact. Non-Western secularisation will be limited, as it is today, by an identity politics in which the religious non-white poor identify with their faith to distinguish themselves from the secular white rich. Even if secularism overcomes identity barriers, its triumph, as we shall see, produces demographic effects that hasten the fundamentalist 'revenge of the cradle'.

2

THE HIDDEN HAND OF
HISTORY: DEMOGRAPHY
AND SOCIETY

The world is in the early stages of demographic revolution. This contrasts with the stable state of humanity since we evolved into our current form around 40,000 years ago. In *stationary* populations, birth rates
match death rates. Imagine peering at our planet from the cockpit of a
spacecraft. If the earth's population wasn't stationary over time, humanity
would either expand to suffocate the planet, obscuring the globe you are
looking at from space like a grotesque biological eclipse, or else disappear
altogether. However, things are different in the short run of decades or
centuries where history is made. In any given period, the balance between
births and deaths determines population change. These rates are often out
of phase, causing the world's population to grow or shrink.

Throughout almost all of human history, population has been stable
and world population changed very little. Variations in death rates rather
than fertility differences drove evolution through nearly all of mankind's existence. It explains why humans displaced Neanderthals, whites
replaced Amerindians and Bantus elbowed aside the San and Pygmies in
Africa. Furthermore, until almost 1900, the better educated had a fertility advantage over poorly educated populations, tending to have larger
numbers of surviving offspring. This is what evolutionary theory would
predict: the wealthy and educated should displace the rest because they
have better access to resources. It is therefore remarkable to reflect on
the fact that the normal pattern of human evolution has reversed itself:

after 1900, those with lower incomes and education began to have larger numbers of children than their social 'betters'.[1]

We do not have to accept the alarmist tropes of eugenicists to see that this has demographic implications both within the developed world and between the wealthy West and poor global South. Instead of the West's wealth advantage continuing to power its demographic conquest of the planet after 1900, it has produced the obverse. In the West and East Asia, we are living through a phase of population decline, with deaths outstripping births (or shortly to do so). Much of the developing world, by contrast, is on a demographic upslope, with births outweighing deaths. It is only a question of how steep the curves of change, and how long the change persists. If growth goes unchecked, there will come a time when death and starvation readjust the world's population to its carrying capacity. At any given place on earth, the relationship between birth and death rates determines population change. Decline in Europe, for example, contrasts with growth in the global South.

Demographically pressured populations are not free to move, but will fight to do so, whether to greener pastures next door, to the next region, or across borders to another country. Differences in population trends between places at any given time are therefore pregnant with political implications. Migratory pressure is only one aspect of this relationship. We live in a world of competing states with well-defined territorial boundaries. Nation states enclose demography, so when demography changes within nation states, so does the relative size of these states.

Most countries have mass-conscript militaries, and 'boots on the ground' still counts for a great deal in warfare. This is especially true of the asymmetric civil wars that convulse the planet today. Numbers also increase the tax base from which income is raised to acquire military hardware. This means that demographic trends lead certain states to grow in strength against their rivals. Naturally economic productivity, geopolitical location, cultural affinities and ideology also determine military might. Yet population is one of the most important drivers of a state's hard power, and may become even more vital in the decades ahead as developing countries close the GDP gap with the West.

This may explain why patriots from Thucydides to Putin have pushed for higher birth rates. From the ancient Greeks to Oswald

Spengler, many view history through a cyclical lens in which youthful growth contrasts with mature decadence and demographic decline. Polybius in ancient Athens held to this view. So did Cicero and Tacitus in late Rome and Ibn Khaldun in the medieval Arab world. All decried the selfishness they felt was leading to demographic decline and weakness on the battlefield in the face of more fecund enemies. Citing the low fertility rates and consequent succession problems within the Roman senatorial elite, Charles Darwin's grandson wondered, 'Must civilisation always lead to the limitation of families and consequent decay and then replacement from barbaric sources which in turn will go through the same experience?' [2]

As Richard Jackson and Neil Howe write, leading powers tend to be demographically expanding:

> In the ancient world, this was true for the Persians, the Greeks, the Macedonians, and the Romans. In the Middle Ages, it was true for the Norse and the Mongols. In modern Western history, it has been true for Portugal in the fifteenth century, the Netherlands in the sixteenth, Russia in the seventeenth, Great Britain in the eighteenth, Germany in the nineteenth, and the United States in the twentieth. On the other hand, it is difficult to find any major instance of a state whose regional or global stature has risen while its share of the regional or global population has declined. [3]

Superpowers tend to be demographic heavyweights: today, 100 million could be considered a threshold, and Russia's decline below that during the twenty-first century may hasten its demise.

Over the course of history, populations have often been stationary, kept in check by natural limits which in turn informed birth spacing and other population control measures. War, plague, natural disasters and migration altered the calculus at times. Sometimes population explosions pushed Vikings, Turks, Berbers and others to sweep out in waves of conquest. At other times, an overproduction of heirs among the elite fuelled revolution and conquest. [4] Nonetheless, enduring transitions only occurred with major technological change.

The shift from hunting and gathering to agriculture after 11000

BC was one such transition. It enabled more people to live off a given piece of land, though life was generally no longer, and, for most, harder. Agriculture (including herding) also brought resistance to disease, social stratification, political organisation, and mobilisation for war. Cultivators such as the Europeans, armed with their 'guns and germs', soon displaced hunter-gatherers like the Amerindians and Aborigines. Bantu cattle-herding tribes in Africa likewise pushed aside the Pygmies and San hunter-gatherers of that continent. Meeting in South Africa, the two colonisers collided in bloody battles after displacing the placid San.[5]

More important for our discussion are the steady technological changes after 1750 which ushered in the modern age. Medical advances cut infant mortality while birth rates remained high. Higher pay, in societies which frowned on sex before marriage, allowed people to marry sooner, start families earlier and therefore have more children. The result was a European population boom that continued into the twentieth century. In 1750, Europe and its settlement offshoots contained around 19 per cent of the world's population, but by 1900 had expanded to more than a third. This helped Western countries to raise taxes, settlers and soldiers to conquer and colonise other lands.[6]

In the euphoria of expansion, however, were sown the seeds of future population decline. Europeans and Anglo-Americans began having fewer children as more survived. High birth rates and death rates produce stationary populations, as do low birth rates and death rates. The shift from the first equilibrium to the second is known as the demographic transition. France experienced its transition soon after 1750. This caused its population to lag behind its German and British rivals in an age when militaries were quickly evolving from professional mercenary forces into mass-conscript armies.

While Britain and Germany exported people to the New World, France began to import them from Catholic countries such as Belgium, Italy, Spain and Poland.[7] The crisis reached its zenith during the interwar period, exacerbated by the wartime loss of 10 per cent of France's able-bodied men:

> France's losses, unlike Germany's, were suffered against a demographic background which was already causing concern before 1914.

Moreover, the war, by keeping couples apart for four years, and by eliminating so many men of reproductive age, caused a heavy deficit in births. After the very short-lived baby boom of the early 1920s, the birth rate resumed its decline, reaching an all peace-time low in the late 1930s.[8]

France responded with an all-out effort to raise its population. Anti-birth-control measures were introduced in 1920, followed by the family allowance incentives of the *Code de Famille* of 1938–9. All this was backed by alarmist state propaganda and pronatalist associations whose membership ran into the hundreds of thousands. Pronatalist policies did raise the birth rate by 1942, though scholars disagree on the magnitude of the effect.[9]

High octane pronatalism was also championed in, among others, Hitler's Germany, Stalin's Soviet Union and Ceauşescu's Romania. Currently, most pronatalist policies are based less on repressive measures such as banning abortion and contraception than on financial incentives such as baby bonuses, tax breaks or free daycare. In an age of plunging fertility rates, no fewer than forty-four countries have adopted such policies.[10] Singapore's Malthusian 'Two Is Enough' has now morphed into 'Three Children or More If You Can Afford It'. China is bound to follow suit: its One Child policy is now under review and cannot persist much longer. By 2030 it will be an older nation than America and the pace of its population-aging will vastly exceed what is taking place in Europe.[11]

The second demographic transition

Most Western societies rebounded nicely from their interwar fertility doldrums, giving rise to the famous 'baby boom' of the 1940s, 50s and early 60s. This fuelled an optimistic theory of population equilibrium based on the magic replacement-level total fertility rate (TFR) of 2.1 children per woman. Henceforth, fertility would rise and fall in cyclical fashion in response to economic opportunities. Large birth cohorts would have to squeeze themselves into tight labour markets adapted to the previous small cohort. The end result would be an older age of marriage and reduced fertility. Smaller generations would behave in the opposite manner, having larger families in response to the roomy structural opportunities they inherit from their parents' large generation, correcting for its baby bust.[12]

Needless to say, the smoothly choreographed script didn't quite work out. Fertility in many Western countries dipped below two children per woman in the late 1960s and early 70s. Most demographers foresaw a rebound, but, as we now know, the anticipated 'correction' never took place, despite evidence of a partial uptick in certain countries. Total fertility rates (TFRs), which measure the number of children that women in the 15–45 age range will bear over their lifetime, seem stuck at low levels in most of the developed world.[13] The stubborn downward trends took most demographers by surprise. Some argued that TFR would rebound because women in countries with below-replacement fertility actually desire larger families but cannot actualise their intentions. Ultimately, proponents of this theory base their views on evolutionary drives which have allowed the human species to survive for millennia. However, this may rest more on blind faith than demographic reality, argue Wolfgang Lutz and his collaborators:

> There is a strong counterargument, namely, that through the introduction of modern contraception, the evolutionary link between the drive for sex and procreation has been broken and now reproduction is merely a function of individual preferences and culturally determined norms.[14]

Lutz, Skirbekk and Testa, failing to see any signs of a rebound in Europe's fertility statistics, advance the contrarian view that lower fertility makes smaller families more acceptable, thereby lowering even *desired* fertility rates below the replacement level. They point to evidence that shows that in countries such as Germany, women now no longer even want that magic number, 2.1 children. The authors hypothesise a self-reinforcing 'low fertility trap' in which low fertility begets lower desired fertility, which in turn drives fertility ever lower, and so on, creating a spiral from which societies will find it very difficult to escape.

Already, in 2005, thirty-four countries had TFRs below 1.5, a figure set to increase in the years ahead.[15] At TFRs above 1.6 children per woman, population decline is gradual. A country with a TFR of 1.8 will be 80 per cent as large after a century of decline, whereas one with a TFR of 1.3 – as in much of southern and eastern Europe and among the Asian 'tigers' – will collapse to a mere quarter of its size by the end of the twenty-first century.[16] The spread of below-replacement fertility to developing countries such as Iran, Burma, Kazakhstan and parts of India has led some to warn of a global birth dearth by the end of the twenty-first century. Indeed, the UN's medium variant projects a world with below-replacement fertility levels by 2035–40, while the low variant envisions this level being attained as early as 2015.[17]

Developments in the industrialised world over the past few decades lead some to consider the possibility that we have entered an entirely new demographic era in human history, known as the second demographic transition (SDT). The first demographic transition was driven by urbanisation and medical advances which cut infant mortality. This reduced the economic advantage of having large families. These materialistic mechanisms continue to operate, but, add SDT theorists, are reinforced by new dynamics linked to cultural individualism and gender equality which began in the 1960s and have since been consolidated.[18]

The 1960s produced a cultural earthquake whose shock waves continue to reverberate through modern societies. Attitudes toward race, religion, sexuality, gender roles, self-expression and the family became markedly more liberal in this period and have remained so ever since. Liberal values and expressive individualism were already well established among secular intellectuals by the mid eighteenth century.[19] Drug and alcohol use, psychotherapy, unconventional relationships, as well as a fondness for jazz and experimental art were staples of the bohemian intellectual scene on both sides of the Atlantic by 1914.[20] Yet these were sports practised by a tiny minority. How did they spread?

Technology provides part of the answer. In 1950, just 9 per cent of American households owned TV sets, but by 1965, fully 93 per cent did.[21] Education is arguably more important. The number of 18- to 24-year-olds in higher education in the US more than doubled in two decades, from 15 per cent in 1950 to nearly a third by 1970, while the average years of education in the population jumped from 10.6 to 12.1 between 1960 and 1970. This increase in educational status was mirrored by a shift in class identity. In the mid 1950s, two Americans identified themselves as working class for every middle-class respondent. Two decades later, the proportions were nearly reversed. Though this took place against the backdrop of steadily rising prosperity and post-industrialisation, surveys confirm that rising education is more strongly linked to class consciousness than economic changes. The new middle classes neatly combined countercultural individualism with the materialistic values of capitalism. Some even argue that the hedonism of the counterculture was necessary to liberate consumer capitalism. Today's bourgeois-bohemian elite ideal, lampooned by David Brooks as 'the rise of the Bobo', is the net result.[22]

The explosion of higher education is critical, since university education is strongly associated with liberal attitudes.[23] Burgeoning universities and a centralised television media acted as a conveyor belt for expressive individualism from a small coterie of intellectual elites to the mass public.[24] Across North America, Western Europe and Japan, a broadly similar value change could be observed, leaving its footsteps in successive Eurobarometer and World Values surveys between 1970 and 1988.[25] Contemporary observers were stunned by the rapidity of the change: 'The life-style once practiced by a small *cenacle*,' remarked Daniel Bell, a leading New York Intellectual of the 1940s and 50s, 'is now copied by many ... [and] this change of scale gave the culture of the 1960s its special surge, coupled with the fact that a bohemian lifestyle once limited to a tiny elite is now acted out on the giant screen of the mass media.'[26]

The shift in sensibility that Robert Bellah terms *expressive individualism* struck community life like a neutron splitting an atom. At the interpersonal level, individuals increasingly opted out of associations and reduced connections with neighbours or others in their community. Gender roles rapidly became more egalitarian.[27] In combination, these forces transformed the family, a cornerstone of demographic behaviour. Divorce and out-of-wedlock birth rates soared, and people embarked on a general shift towards more independent living. This is reflected in the dramatic rise in the proportion of one-person households in the United States, from 11 per cent in 1950 to 24 per cent in 1987.[28] Alex Shoumatoff describes the phenomenon as it appeared in New York:

The greatest concentration of single people in the world, the world capital of rampant individualism, is New York City. In 1980 ... thirty-four percent of the city's entire population fifteen years old or older had never married, and 349,373 of the 706,015 households in Manhattan had only one person in them. Manhattan actually had even more 'singles' than that, because many of those counted had roommates who were also single but who didn't appear on the census rolls; and some 'never-marrieds,' as well as some of the divorced and the widowed who had not remarried, were living with their parents or with other kin.[29]

In all cases, the changes were strongly generational, which resulted in a pattern of slow but steady change as younger generations entered adulthood and older cohorts progressively died off. For example, while more than half of those over sixty-five in developed countries in 1981 claimed that a woman needs children to be fulfilled, just 35 per cent of those aged fifteen to twenty-four agreed.[30] Value changes were linked to the well-educated, liberal baby boomer generation which began to enter adulthood in the late sixties. Three decades on, they were attaining positions of leadership, as with Bill Clinton in the United States or Tony Blair in Britain. By the 1990s, this liberal generation and its successors constituted a majority of the population of the West.

The social upheaval of the sixties had an enormous impact on fertility. Divorce and illegitimacy rose as birth rates fell. These trends all spring from expressive individualism. In Ron Inglehart's words, 'post-materialists place more emphasis on self-fulfillment through careers, rather than through ensuring the survival of the species.' Post-materialism, adds Inglehart, shifts the focus of life 'out of the family toward broader social and leisure activities' in pursuit of individuality.[31] The value changes of the 1960s have proven exceptionally enduring: cultural shifts have been consolidated by subsequent generations along with sub-replacement fertility. Though the attitude changes of the 1960s flattened out by the 1990s, they had reached a liberal plateau far removed from the situation in 1960.

Inglehart's survey evidence sparked the work of Ron Lesthaeghe and other leading demographers of the Second Demographic Transition

(SDT) school, who convincingly protested to the demography establishment that economic changes and the availability of contraception were only one side of the low-fertility coin. Value changes had to be factored in: not only were they important, they might even hold the key to fertility change.[32] The first demographic transition was accompanied by family norms which emphasised a bourgeois moral structure characterised by marriage and religiosity. Fertility – even in France – only ever dipped below replacement after large wars or serious economic crises. The post-1960s second demographic transition, by contrast, involves a loosening of society's normative structure and a concomitant shift to below-replacement fertility.[33] If below-replacement fertility is tied to individualism, then the scope for public policy to raise fertility back to replacement levels is limited. Indeed, a good deal of demographic research suggests that pronatalist incentives have been surprisingly ineffective in raising birth rates.[34]

Of course, cultural shifts do not explain everything. Fertility in France declined more slowly than in the rest of Europe and rose somewhat after 1993, so today its TFR is quite similar to what it was in the 1930s. This makes it the most fertile country in the European Union. Together with Scandinavia, France has the highest fertility rates in Western Europe, but is no less individualistic than fertility laggards like Germany, Croatia or Italy. Meanwhile, Hong Kong, Macau, Japan and South Korea have not been as revolutionised as the West by the value changes of the 1960s, yet have exceptionally low fertility. Low-cost childcare and fewer obstacles to young women combining work and family seem to explain Nordic and French success in maintaining near-replacement fertility levels.[35]

This doesn't mean that Michelle Goldberg is correct in her assessment that 'feminism is the new pronatalism'.[36] Helping women combine work and family is a step in the right direction, but is no silver bullet. Feminist-friendly social policies cannot explain why those of religious bent, in almost all Western societies, bear significantly more children than the non-religious. This is the case even when we account for their education, income, age and other characteristics. In France, for instance, white women who practise their religion have a half-child fertility advantage over non-religious women, and this has been increasing over time.[37]

One reason for the secular-religious fertility gap is that religion's pronatalist message contrasts with the culture of low fertility now prevalent in the secular-individualistic West and secular-materialistic East Asia.[38] Once material circumstances free people to choose their fertility levels, values come to matter more in determining individual fertility. 'One of the most central injunctions of virtually all traditional religions,' remark Pippa Norris and Ron Inglehart, 'is to strengthen the family, to encourage people to have children, to encourage women to stay home and raise children, and to forbid abortion, divorce, or anything that interferes with high rates of reproduction.'[39]

In relatively religious societies, the relationship may also work the other way: those who start families may be drawn into the arms of religion because taking their children to services is the done thing.[40] Economic explanations for fertility gaps such as differences in social provision between Scandinavia and southern Europe provide little insight into why relatively religious Israel, the United States and Ireland – North and South – have markedly higher fertility rates than the more social democratic but secular Austria and Germany.

Geopolitical implications of the second demographic transition

The developing world lags well behind the First World's population curve. In some places, such as Yemen or most of sub-Saharan Africa, the first demographic transition is in its infancy. Uneven transition will shift the centre of gravity of the world's population from temperate to tropical climes. This will inevitably reduce Western power. Consider the following: in 1950, Europe (including the USSR), North America and Australasia constituted about 30 per cent of the world's population. In this sense, the pre-eminence of these countries in world politics, the international economy and global culture was backed by demographic heft. This in turn served to justify their domination of the UN Security Council, Warsaw Pact, G8, World Bank and other global power 'clubs'.[41]

Now look ahead to 2050. According to the latest UN projections, Europe and North America will account for just 12 per cent of the world's population. In 1950, Europe alone had two and a half times the population of Africa; by 2050, the UN projects that Africa will have more than four times Europe's population.[42] This is not about reading tea leaves. By looking at the structure of the world's under-fifteen population in 2005, we *know now* who will be the fifty and sixtysomethings of 2050. The future is already alive today, which makes demography such a powerful predictive tool. What we find is that just 11 per cent of the world's under-fifteens currently live in Europe (including Russia) and North America. That is the future, pure and simple. Elsewhere on the planet, we find two distinct paths. In non-Muslim Asia, populations are aging and fertility rates have swiftly declined. China, Vietnam and southern India, for instance, have below-replacement fertility levels and surging productivity. They are rapidly developing. In sub-Saharan Africa and much of the Muslim world, by contrast, demography is a coiled spring whose explosive potential is only just being released.

In 2050, population superpowers Pakistan (305m.), Nigeria (258m.), Bangladesh (243m.), Congo (177m.), Ethiopia (170m.) and Uganda (127m.) will be larger than Japan and Russia. Indeed, the only developed country with a secure footing in the nineteen-member club of 100 million-plus countries will be the United States.[43] In the words of Hedley Bull, a leading international relations theorist, a population of over 100 million is not sufficient to guarantee great power status, 'but it is widely thought to be necessary for this status'.[44] Neorealism, the leading school in international relations, posits that a large population is a *sine qua non* of state power.[45] In the new world order of 2050, the West will be a minnow whose only source of strength may be its 'soft power' of persuasion.[46]

These changes will be compounded by shifts in the age structure of the world's powers. Currently, 20–25 per cent of Japan and Europe's population is over sixty, but that figure is set to approach 40 per cent by 2050. Greyer populations tend to shy away from sacrificing their precious sons in battle, and more of the national product has to be diverted away from productive and military uses to care for the elderly. Gunnar Heinsohn argues that the excess sons of Europe, who inherited nothing, became the West's explorers, warriors and conquistadors. Fewer surplus sons means fewer men willing to risk their lives in battle. Heinsohn adds that the more advanced age structure of Lebanon in 2006 meant it had more to lose in a war. This restrained the country from sacrificing its sons to civil war – as it did in 1975 when its population was much younger.[47]

The flipside of this equation is that scholars have found a link between the relative share of the population aged fifteen to thirty and violent conflict. A large 'youth bulge' in this age group can spell trouble. Young men are more risk-taking and aggressive than other population segments and find it difficult to enter labour markets designed for smaller cohorts. Large numbers of unemployed men between the ages of fifteen and thirty can thereby serve as tinder for violent movements based around ethnicity, nationalism, religion or class.[48]

Intervention by Western forces into young societies in sub-Saharan Africa and the Muslim world will become increasingly problematic from a demographic standpoint unless foreign troops compromise an ever-growing component of Western military forces. Already, recruitment is one of the biggest problems faced by the American, British and Russian militaries. Personnel and retirement costs are escalating at the expense of weapons procurement, and this problem will worsen in the future.[49] All told, a grey, shrinking Europe will find it difficult to command the same power it does today. Conversely, sub-Saharan Africa and much of the Muslim world will have young, fast-growing populations. These could fuel insurgent movements that Western armies will find impossible to contain.[50] One day our descendants will marvel at the extent of Western troop commitments in Afghanistan and Iraq, just as we do when looking back at the demographically dynamic Victorians, who were willing to accept large casualties to hold colonies such as India and South Africa.

On the move: global migration

The differential population growth rates of the world can be viewed geologically, with a sharp gradient forming between countries in close proximity who possess vastly different age structures. This global demographic topography features high tablelands in sub-Saharan Africa, easing gently to rolling hills in the Maghreb, plunging off a cliff into Europe, a land lying below sea level protected by dykes. If these landforms disintegrated, population would 'migrate' from regions of higher elevation to low-lying (i.e. aged) areas. Economists would predict that in a free market, excess supply of labour in one region of the world coupled with excess demand elsewhere should lead to the increased movement of people. Ideally, labour is a factor of production which should flow across borders until its productivity equals its price. The mountains, to paraphrase Led Zeppelin, should crumble to the sea.

In reality, labour migration is heavily controlled. But the developed world may not be able to keep immigrants out even if it wants to. William Durch suggests that US border control is 91 per cent effective in apprehending Mexican illegals, yet this has failed to stem a tide of some 600,000 to 800,000 illegal immigrants a year. The need to cross water makes it more difficult to get to Europe from Africa, but those who make it across are often successful in evading the authorities. Spain is just 45 per cent and Italy only 30 per cent effective against illegals from North Africa. Russia, whose immigrant population stock is second only to that of the United States in size, is just 2 per cent effective in policing its vast southern border.[51] In one dramatic incident in 2005, on the Spanish enclave of Melilla on the Moroccan coast, 500 sub-Saharan African migrants charged the border. One hundred and thirty made it, their hands torn and bleeding from barbed wire. Meanwhile, in the Canary Islands, 30,000 West African 'boat people' had arrived by 2005–6. Tragically, not all completed the journey: 'boats that drifted off course had been found months later, loaded with cadavers, as far away as Barbados.'[52]

In the five years from 2000 to 2005, roughly 17 million people successfully moved from developing to developed countries. By 2006, 191 million people in the world were immigrants, up from 76 million in 1960.[53] Differential population growth between world regions will increase pressure to decant excess population from the South to an aging North. This new human cargo may shore up Western power by slowing population decline, but it carries highly unpredictable social and political effects. In this sense, the West may have to choose between international power or inter-ethnic strife as migration transfers the theatre of demographic conflict from the international to the domestic sphere.

Ethnic change within nations

The coexistence of demographic haves and have-nots is set to realign the globe's geopolitical axis. But nations are not monolithic: they contain their own internal demographic winners and losers, which often correspond to the source countries from which such populations migrated. We know that fertility differences between developing and developed nations are leading to growth in the share of the world's population of tropical origin. This will be reproduced in microcosm within those developed countries that are open to immigration.

This basically means the West. The growing proportion of native-stock elderly will track the rise in ethnic-minority young people. We can read the future in the youngest part of the population. In the United States, for instance, the population in 1960 essentially consisted of a traditional African-American minority of 12 per cent and a white majority of over 85 per cent. Today, those of non-Hispanic white origin constitute just two-thirds of the total, while Hispanics, at 14 per cent of the population, have overtaken African-Americans as the largest minority. By the 2020s, half the under-fives will be minorities. In 2042, the US Census Bureau projects the US will reach the 'majority minority' point. Hence the well-accepted view that the 'browning of America' is an unalterable reality. Texas, California, Hawaii and New Mexico are already there. Since a white majority was a de facto condition of statehood, it is interesting to speculate whether these states would have passed muster with Congress in the nineteenth century.

Ethnic changes are especially pronounced in gateway immigration states such as Florida, Illinois, New York and California. It is often remarked that California is a trendsetter for America as a whole, from movies and computer technology to the 1960s counterculture and fitness craze. The same is true of demography, since the ethnic composition of the US population is trailing that of California by about fifty years. Consider the breathtaking pace of ethnic change there: in 1960, the golden state was about 85–90 per cent white, roughly the same percentage as in the 1880s, when ugly race riots put a stop to Chinese immigration. In 2006, less than fifty years later, immigration, largely from Mexico, had transformed its population: it was now just 44 per cent non-Hispanic white.[54] In Western Europe, minority populations have historically been small. Even today, those of non-European extraction constitute just 3–4 per cent of the European total. Change is on its way, however. We can expect these numbers to triple in the next fifty years – a faster rate of change than in the United States.[55]

Once upon a time, when politics was a game played by elites and their mercenaries, demographic change mattered less. But demography becomes increasingly important as modernity unfolds. This may seem counterintuitive, since demography is the mechanism behind evolution and we presume that our cultural development permits us to circumvent such 'animal' processes. Sure enough, technology reduces the power of demography by enabling less populous countries to hide behind advanced weapons systems while better controlling migration flows. However, while this safeguards countries from predators in the international arena, it does not impact relations between ethnic groups *within* states. Meanwhile, all the other outriders of modernity – liberty, equality, democracy, nationalism and globalisation – magnify the power of demography within states.

The American and French Revolutions of the eighteenth century completely altered the relationship between demography and power. When a foreign monarch like the Habsburg emperor in the Czech lands or Ottoman sultan in Egypt could legitimately rule, the uneven growth of various populations in the kingdom was immaterial. Once power was vested in the nation, however, and popular sovereignty replaced the principle of the divine right of kings, the stage was set for demography to shape history.

All of a sudden, the legal distinction between nationals and foreigners effaced status distinctions between the aristocracy, bourgeoisie and peasantry. Native soldiers replaced foreign mercenaries, foreign rulers and non-citizens were expelled or marginalised, and shared nationality rather than the persona of the monarch became the fount of sovereignty.[56] Democracy hands power to the demographic majority, unseating elite minorities such as the Arabs of Zanzibar, Baltic Russians or, more recently, Iraq's Sunnis. Where there is no clear majority, as in Lebanon or Kenya, battles for domination emerge. If the other side cannot be disenfranchised, then one must exhort one's own to reproduce for the group.[57]

The principle of equality, by which all individuals lay claim to rights and resources, is a further aspect of modernity that raises the demographic stakes. Under a regime of social welfare provision combined with one person one vote, changes in population composition imply a shift of resources from one group to another. This is especially marked when one ethnic (typically native) group is aging and declining while immigrant groups are younger and growing. The difficulty in getting wealthy, taxpaying whites in many US districts to pay for public schooling and welfare facilities for younger populations of African-Americans or immigrant Hispanics has resulted in the problem of 'white flight', impoverishing certain municipalities. Even where this doesn't occur, elderly white voters tend to vote for lower levels of welfare-state spending in more diverse places. Hence a growing body of political and economic research concludes that the policy aims of ethnic diversity and social provision conflict.[58] In cases where minorities have the money, such as Malaysia or Zimbabwe, the opposite problem applies. In these instances a poor majority uses its political muscle to wrest resources away from wealthy minorities, sometimes deploying the rhetoric of affirmative action.[59]

Liberalism is the third of the French Revolutionary trinity, and a pillar of Western modernity. Like nationalism and democracy, it is also a handmaiden of demography. Global demographic change cannot affect states unless they open themselves up to it. Kuwait and Singapore, which rigidly police the inflows into their countries, will remain unaffected by global demographic storms even if their share of the world population plummets. By contrast, when liberalism extends to immigration and naturalisation – which largely occurred after the 1950s in most Western countries – it opens states up to global demography.

Liberalism unlocks the doors of the nation, removing its insulation from the demographic inequality outside. Historically, poor global communications meant that large-scale, long-distance migration was uncommon. Most migration within Europe took place between regions of a country, i.e. from Andalusia to Catalonia within Spain or south to north in the United States. Rich European countries also received migration from surrounding European societies, as with Polish or Italian immigration to France. Once upon a time, these flows proved socially and politically traumatic. Their place has been taken by long-distance migration, which brings together people who are more distant in culture and physical appearance.

Notwithstanding the involuntary mass transport of slaves from Africa to the Americas, major immigration flows to the New World were similarly European in origin. The Chinese and Japanese participated in these flows in small numbers, but were excluded by racially discriminatory legislation after 1882 in the USA and later in Canada and Australia. After the Second World War, these countries repealed Oriental Exclusion acts. In the 1960s, they removed ethnic selection criteria in their immigration policies.[60]

None of this had anything to do with Western population-aging. European populations were young and growing. The liberalisation of immigration was a purely cultural and political phenomenon, reflecting internal ideological changes which emerged in the wake of the Holocaust and Civil Rights era. It is only by coincidence that the opening up to non-white immigration coincided with the demographic revolution. This great churning of population spawned South–North migration flows into Western nations whose doors had been unlocked in advance by liberal reformers. By the 1970s, non-European immigrants were becoming a permanent and recognised part of Western populations.

Ethnic change and violence

Does ethnic change lead to conflict and violence? In many cases the answer is a resounding yes. Where assimilation is rare and endogamy (marriage within the group) prevails, ethnic boundaries become rigid. Changes in ethnic composition result in a zero-sum game which translates directly into conflict. Migration, in or out, along with fertility differences underlie many modern civil wars. In Northern Ireland, Protestants entered the demographic transition more than half a century before Catholics, but Catholics emigrated at higher rates, offsetting the difference. When Catholic emigration slowed after 1945, the growing Catholic population raised fears among the two-thirds Protestant majority that they would be bred out of power. This spurred the Protestant-dominated Stormont regime to reject electoral and housing reforms in the hope of making life so miserable for Catholics that they would leave. Instead, Catholics rebelled, setting in motion the Troubles of 1969–94.[61]

Protestants dominated by a ratio of 65:35 when the province of Northern Ireland was created in 1921. Today, the balance is 53:47 and Gerry Adams of the Irish republican Sinn Féin Party stakes his long-term strategy on the demographic ascent of the Catholics to majority status. Already, Belfast has switched from a Protestant-run to a

Catholic-controlled city and a majority of schoolchildren attend Catholic schools. When they reach adulthood, this Catholic majority could, according to the provisions of the 1998 Good Friday Agreement, vote for a reunification of Ireland against the wishes of the future Protestant minority.

Protestant anxiety manifests itself in many ways. Unionists who harassed the Catholic parents and schoolchildren attending the Holy Cross school in the Ardoyne area of Belfast in 2001 were venting their anger at a rerouting of their Orange Order's parade, but also at the incursion of Catholics into demographically declining Protestant areas. Conflicts between Protestant Orangemen and Catholic residents is often caused by the expansion of the Catholic population into formerly Protestant or previously uninhabited areas adjacent to marching routes, such as Portadown's Garvaghy Road, the scene of violent confrontations in 1985–7 and 1995–2001.[62]

Lebanon, like Northern Ireland, was carved out of a larger entity – Syria rather than Ireland – with a two-thirds ethnic majority. The French intended it to be a Christian-dominated state. Over time, however, Christian emigration and higher Muslim fertility altered the population balance to the point where Christians now form little more than a quarter of the population. Hezbollah, linked to the demographically buoyant Shia, are the mightiest force, not Christian militias.

Lebanon's early ethnic make-up was frozen into its constitution and the demographic changes since 1932 have proven so contentious that no census has taken place since. The arrival of large numbers of Palestinian refugees from Israel after wars in 1948–9, 1967 and 1973 further upset the finely balanced demographic picture, leading to instability. The Lebanese Civil War of 1975–1990 was not a purely ethnic affair, but much of the fighting saw Christian militias square off against Muslim ones. Today's divisions pit the youthful Shia against the demographically mature Sunnis and Christians, both of whom have an advantageous constitutional position over the traditionally less developed Shia, who in turn resent this.[63]

Across Lebanon's southern border, in Israel-Palestine, one finds some of the highest levels of fertility ever recorded in modern societies. In 1998, Palestinian women in Gaza had a fertility rate of 7.41 children per woman. Ultra-Orthodox Jewish fertility in Israel was similar. Demographer Philippe Fargues convincingly argues that ethnic conflict props up fertility rates among Jewish and Palestinian women whose education level suggests that they should be having far fewer children.[64] Arabs have markedly increased their share of the population of both Israel-Palestine and Israel proper since 1967.

The Israeli withdrawal from settlements in Gaza forms part of a wider policy of demographic retrenchment initiated by Ariel Sharon's advisors, since Jews will be a minority in greater Israel-Palestine within a decade.[65] Radical proposals from secular nationalist Avigdor Lieberman aim to surgically remove the effects of demography by trading Arab bits of Israel for Jewish-settled parts of Palestinian territory while disenfranchising Israeli Arabs through loyalty oaths.[66] This may not be necessary: the stratospheric ultra-Orthodox Jewish birth rate is coinciding with an Arab transition to lower fertility rates. So much so that Jews have overtaken Arabs within the youngest Israeli age cohorts. Between 2001 and 2008 alone, the Arab share of Israeli births fell from 30 to 25 per cent, and is on course to reach 20 per cent, their current share of the Israeli population.[67] This may relax Israeli anxieties and contribute to peace.

In the former Yugoslavia, differential rates of ethnic population growth increased the likelihood of conflict. Between 1961 and 1991, the proportion of Muslims in Bosnia increased from around a quarter to almost 45 per cent, while Serbs dropped from 43 to 32 per cent. Part of the change involved the semantics of census categories, but much could be explained by a younger Bosnian Muslim age structure and higher fertility, combined with Bosnian Serb outmigration. Serbs in districts where ethnic change was most rapid were most sympathetic to anti-Muslim genocide during the 1992–4 war. Bosnian Serbs in areas with comfortable Serb majorities and small Muslim minorities were much less active in aiding the ethnic cleansing campaign.[68]

Similar dynamics were at play in Kosovo several years later. Between 1945 and 1961, Serbs and Albanians in Kosovo had roughly similar rates of population growth. Over the next thirty years, however, the proportion of Serbs dropped from 23.6 per cent to just 9.9 per cent owing to higher Albanian fertility and further Serb outmigration. Milosevic's 'Greater Serbia' nationalist ideology motivated his campaign of ethnic

cleansing in 1999. Even so, his path was eased by local Serbs, partly radicalised by their demographic decline, who stoked the fires of violence.[69]

In Asia, a prominent example of immigration-driven ethnic change
is taking place in the north-eastern Indian state of Assam. A Hindu-
majority tongue of Indian territory lying north of Muslim Bangladesh,
Assam has long been host to large-scale illegal, but peaceful, Bengali
immigration. Bengali Muslims grew 30 to 50 per cent over the period
1971 to 1991. They now constitute more than 30 per cent of Assam's population and are believed to control the electoral verdict in 60 of Assam's
126 Assembly constituencies. Numerous battles have taken place over
whether large numbers of Muslims have the legal status necessary to add
their name to the electoral rolls.[70]

Muslim growth has been the catalyst for ugly Assamese attacks
against unarmed Bengali workers since the 1980s, and an Assamese political movement demands the deportation of illegal immigrants.[71] This
conflict is regional, but on the wider Indian level, the growth of the
Muslim population through higher fertility and an often exaggerated
degree of illegal immigration has been a red flag for Hindu nationalism.
The Muslim population's fertility advantage over Hindus was 10 per cent
at partition in 1947, but is now 25–35 per cent. Only a fraction of this
gap can be explained by relative Muslim poverty. Muslims grew from
roughly 8 per cent of the Indian total in 1947 to 14 per cent today, and are
projected to rise to 17 per cent by 2050. These are not staggering numbers, yet have proven useful tinder for Hindu nationalists and sparked
sporadic violent reprisals against Indian Muslims.[72]

In sub-Saharan Africa, we see analogous trends. Labour migration
was initially encouraged by colonial rulers seeking to open up new lands
for plantation agriculture in sparsely settled areas. These movements
often continued or intensified after independence. Unfortunately, these
areas of settlement lay in other tribes' traditional territory, so migration was deemed an illegitimate invasion by the native people. In Côte
D'Ivoire, northern ethnic settlers – Dioula, Senoufo, Malinké – were
encouraged by the French to move south from what is now Burkina Faso
in the colonial period. They continued to immigrate after independence
to the point where more than a quarter of Côte D'Ivoire's population
consists of non-citizens, mainly Muslims. In many southern towns they

are now a majority. In 1998–99, Laurent Ggabo, a southern political entrepreneur, mobilised his FPI Party on a violently anti-immigrant, anti-Muslim pro-'autochthon' ticket. His victory in 2000 was marked by outbreaks of anti-northerner paramilitary violence which marred the electoral landscape in this once-peaceful society.[73]

In Uganda, anti-migrant violence is largely focused in the south-western Kibaale district, where the considerable movement of ethnic Bakiga into Bunyoro territory underpinned 'autochthonous' violence there.[74] 'Sons of the soil' wars between natives and settlers are one of the most common forms of civil war today.[75] But major metropolitan areas are not immune. In Kampala, Uganda, in September 2009, members of the dominant Baganda group rioted because their title to the greater Kampala area remained unrecognised and they felt dispossessed in their homeland by other groups. The Kenyan electoral violence of January 2008 has a similar origin. It fed on anti-Kikuyu nativist sentiment which had festered ever since the advanced Kikuyu had migrated to occupy formerly white-held lands in the ethnically Maasai or Kalenjin Rift Valley province. Whether ethnic 'others' hail from another country or merely another region within the same country, rapid ethnic demographic change often leads to conflict.

Ethnic change in the West

With regard to the demographic processes which are changing Europe, demographer David Coleman recently remarked, 'low fertility combined with high immigration [is] … changing the composition of national populations and thereby the culture, physical appearance, social experiences, and self-perceived identity of the inhabitants of European nations.' [76] Will such changes spark ethnic violence in Western Europe and North America along the lines of what has taken place in the former Yugoslavia, Ivory Coast, Assam or Lebanon? Much depends on the tightness of ethnic boundaries.

It is noteworthy that the nations of the West have not experienced English politician Enoch Powell's prophesied 'Rivers of Blood', largely avoiding serious 'sons of the soil' violence between natives and immigrants. This could not always have been predicted. In California in the 1880s, a Chinese population of less than 10 per cent was enough to ignite anti-Chinese pogroms and rioting.[77] In the north-eastern US, anti-Catholic violence was common until the early twentieth century. The arrival of non-Europeans to Europe after 1950 sparked native responses early on, as with the 1958 Notting Hill riots, directed against West Indian immigrants to London. However, subsequent incidents were more immigrant-driven, as with the 1981 Toxteth Riots near Liverpool, the 2001 Mill Town Riots in northern England or the 2005 Banlieue Riots in France. The exceptions have mainly been isolated attacks perpetrated by a neo-Nazi fringe.

The waning of systematic anti-immigrant violence is connected to the more robust egalitarian individualism which spread widely in the 1960s as part of a wave of liberal attitude change. Overtly racist attitudes declined and inter-racial marriage became more accepted. Identities among members of dominant majorities shifted somewhat, from national identity to lifestyle subcultures. The increasingly fragmented, 'loose-bounded' nature of society helped to soften ethnic boundaries. Liberalism therefore has a double-edged effect. On the one hand, it opens states to demographic change and empowers demographic forces, but on the other, it promotes a tolerant individualism which erodes the rigidity of ethnic boundaries. This mitigates conflict. The ultimate question is whether the ethnic change introduced by immigration and uneven fertility can be dissipated rapidly enough by assimilation or ethnic boundary expansion to prevent violence.

The rapid jump in inter-racial marriage in the West is remarkable. There are now almost as many babies born in the UK to one black Caribbean and one white parent as there are to two black Caribbean parents. In the United States, a third of Hispanic Americans and half of Asians marry out. Even black Americans, who were legally and socially barred from marrying whites in many states until the 1960s and remain highly segregated, have begun to break down traditional barriers. Ten per cent now choose non-black partners. By contrast, in 1960, less than a fifth of a per cent of American marriages were interracial.[78] Barry Edmonston claims that mixed-race Americans will make up 20 per cent of the total in 2050, and David Coleman adds that the largest racial category in the UK in 2100 will be mixed race.[79]

These statistics are encouraging, but fail to consider the possibility that certain groups may choose not to accept the offer of assimilation. In that event, it is difficult to see how conflict can be avoided as whites decline and others grow. Only if non-white groups intermarry and the 'white' category expands to include those of mixed race will ethnic competition be avoided. Another possibility is for the dominant group to lose its sense of identity entirely to lifestyle individualism while minorities remain ethnically motivated. To some extent this has taken place.

Still, it is hard to imagine how cohesive minorities can continually expand without awakening an ethnic response among a declining majority. Indeed, we already see signs of majority retrenchment in the post-1986 tripling of support for the European Far Right and the imposition of tighter immigration measures. In one Western European sample of seven states, the Far Right garnered an average of 14 per cent of the vote, and the figure has reached 35 per cent in Austria, and over 20 per cent in France and Switzerland.[80] Though society has become more individualistic, the ethnic identities of European majorities have acquired salience. Rapid demographic change has not produced significant violence, but it has reintroduced ethnic conflict at a time when older Protestant-Catholic-Jewish faultlines were fading away.[81]

The long experience of the United States with immigration suggests that the balance between immigration and assimilation mediates the political impact of demographic change. Assimilation helped de-ethnicise immigrants, promote intermarriage and expand the boundaries of the white majority to include Catholics and Jews.[82] Across the broad sweep of American history, swift demographic changes stoked ethnic tension. The rapid rise of the Catholic population from 2 per cent in 1790 to more than 25 per cent by 1924 raised the temperature of ethnic relations. When the economy soured, wars increased insecurity, cross-cutting issues faded or religious issues mapped on to ethnic ones, intergroup conflict took place.

This can be seen in the two major waves of American ethno-nationalism of 1840–60 and 1885–1925, which coincided with large-scale immigration from non-traditional sources. In the 1840s and 50s, priests were regularly attacked and Catholic churches burned to the ground. It took the Civil War of 1860–65 to distract American anti-Catholicism. The second great immigration wave culminated in Prohibition and the rise of a 6-million-member Ku Klux Klan in the mid 1920s. In response, immigration was controlled from 1924 to 1965 by the ethnically discriminatory 'National Origins' scheme, which reduced ethnic tension.[83] This can be seen in polls from the 1945–65 period, which chart a steady growth in positive attitudes towards immigration within the American population.[84]

The period since 1965 is more complex. On the one hand, immigration and ethnic change in the United States rose dramatically, to levels similar to those of 1885–1925. Opposition to immigration has risen to almost 80 per cent among the American public, in step with ethnic change. Yet despite their opposition, immigration consistently ranks low on American voters' list of priorities. Public debate frowns on raising the issue of legal immigration. Even illegal immigration is a touchy subject, and opponents take care to highlight their opposition to it on the grounds of legality and security. In Canada, a similar increase in immigration, which boosted the proportion of non-whites from 2 to 13 per cent during 1970–2000, produced only a small rise in anti-immigration sentiment.[85] This is connected to the consolidation of 1960s tolerance and individualism, which has dampened the popular backlash.

Political expressions of anti-immigrant hostility in America are muted in comparison with 1885–1925 and are dwarfed by what is happening in Europe today. We can trace this to liberal attitude changes and a cosmopolitan elite consensus which even encompasses traditionally restrictionist lobbies such as the unions and patriotic societies.[86] The Republican Party elite has strenuously tried to keep immigration restriction off the party's political agenda, and came out against controversial anti-immigrant measures – even when popular – such as California's Proposition 187 in 1994. Under George W. Bush, the party battled its grassroots to promote an amnesty for the nearly 12 million illegal immigrants in the country. This is partly driven by the Republicans' laissez-faire economic agenda and partly by a pragmatic fear of alienating the growing Hispanic electorate, which handed Bush 40 per cent of their vote in 2004. So long as whites care less about restricting immigration than non-whites do about promoting it, more votes will be gained from liberalisation than restriction.

On balance, does liberty, democracy and equality lead to ethnic conflict? The answer in the West seems to be yes, but to a much smaller degree than would be predicted from the experience of more 'tight-bounded' societies. Opening doors to immigration leads to pressures which make ethnic conflict more likely. Liberal attitude changes within the dominant ethnic group inhibit violent responses and anti-immigrant politics, dissipating some of the effects of demography. Not all members of the ethnic majority are open to mixing, as 'white flight' and far-right voting show. But the degree of tolerance is high enough to blur racial and ethnic boundaries, resulting in rapid assimilation of groups such as the Afro-Caribbeans and East Asians of Europe.

All the same, the rosy past may prove a poor guide to the future because it takes two to tango, not just a willing majority. What if a minority doesn't want to dance? The renowned sociologist Ernest Gellner developed a theory of nationalism which foresaw the mass assimilation of diverse populations into the official culture of the new nations of post-1789 Europe. He did, however, note the possibility of some groups remaining apart due to 'counter-entropic' traits. These are characteristics which allow ethnic groups to resist assimilation into the dominant culture. Gellner viewed religion as the counter-entropic trait par excellence.[87] In the absence of separate political structures or majority persecution, a group's best chance of survival comes from religion. The Jews of central Europe or the Armenian diaspora are two cases in point. A distinct set of religious institutions and symbols helped them to resist assimilation. Today, Gellner's observations would apply to ultra-Orthodox Jews, and also to most Western Muslims.

European Muslims are particularly resistant to assimilation, despite the fact that Arabs and Turks in continental Europe are more similar in appearance to their host populations than the more 'assimilable' Afro-Caribbeans and East Asians. Only time will tell if this trend will persist: should the War on Terror abate, Islamic theology shift or a Western-oriented third generation emerge, Muslim assimilation could start to soar. At this point, however, there is little evidence of Muslim intermarriage, the acid test of assimilation. In the absence of intermarriage, the higher fertility and immigration rates of European Muslims translates directly into a larger population. This portends increasing conflict with dominant European majorities.

In the United States, by contrast, the small Muslim minority and continuing high rates of inter-racial marriage point towards more of a 'melting-pot' scenario, in which overt conflict is limited. Canada, where the Muslim population is increasing rapidly due to high immigration, may come to resemble Europe in the long run. This is especially true in Quebec, where Muslims are a more significant group and the French-Canadian majority has a strong sense of self-consciousness. The success of the populist Action Démocratique du Quebec (ADQ) in 2007–8 proved a wake-up call to many in the Quebec political establishment and followed a period of intense debate over the degree to which Muslim demands should be accommodated.[88]

From ethnicity to religion

Ethnic change often brings religious change. This either emerges through immigration or on the back of decades of differential fertility, as in Northern Ireland and Lebanon. Many Americans are at ease with the idea that their country will become 'browner'. European liberals likewise accept the idea that immigrants and their descendants will replace native ethnic groups. I recall an Australian professor of migration studies in the 1990s who proudly claimed that most of his students said they wouldn't mind if future Australians looked different from themselves. However, how many *bien-pensant* Western elites are willing to celebrate the transgressive idea that seculars will be replaced by religious people? What if carriers of the ideals of the European Enlightenment are gradually displaced by committed Christians, Jews and Muslims?

In the United States, the ethnic division between Anglo-Protestants, Catholics and Jews was superseded by a religious divide separating the godly from the secular. What if religious Muslims and Christians join forces to defeat secularism in the West? This may seem far-fetched, but who on the eve of John F. Kennedy's election would have predicted that in less than fifty years most religious American Catholics would vote against a Catholic presidential candidate, John Kerry, in favour of George W. Bush, an evangelical WASP. Simply put, God displaced Tribe as the main cultural faultline. A similar change could happen in Europe.

There is an optimistic tendency among both neoconservatives and liberals which assumes that the power of ideas always triumphs over 'dumb' biology. This is as naive as the obverse idea that demography is destiny. The cultural character of Kosovo, Quebec and Utah was produced by high native birth rates which confounded assimilation. England lost its Celtic character with the Anglo-Saxon invasions of the sixth century.[89] Palestine similarly suffered both changes. It shifted from an Arab to a Jewish land after 1900 as Jewish immigrants poured in. Turkey only became Turkish between 1000 and 1453 when migrants from central Asia displaced or absorbed the Byzantine Christians of Anatolia. Aboriginal Australia and the Americas turned European, while Bantu speakers displaced San and Pygmies throughout Africa.[90]

On the other hand, the power of ideas sometimes tames demography. The Normans did not turn England and Ireland into Normandy but went native. The descendants of pre-Reformation English landlords in Ireland became Irish Catholics. Germanic invaders of the Roman Empire were Latinised, and their descendants are Portuguese, Spanish and Italians. The Slavs who moved en masse into Greece during the Byzantine period did not displace the Greeks but were absorbed into them. Most immigrants to the US have become Anglo-American in culture, and unhyphenated 'American' is now the most popular ethnic option among whites.

But let's keep things in perspective. The assimilation of the children of many immigrants into the English mother tongue in the Anglo-Saxon world has not been sufficient to match Chinese population growth. Mandarin is the mother tongue of over a billion people, while only half as many are native English speakers. This is a victory for demography. Even if we assume that ethnic minorities will assimilate into the dominant culture and secular ideas prevail over religious ones – two big ifs – the question remains: how can we be sure that religious demography won't simply overwhelm secularism much as waves of nomadic Turks erased the lettered Byzantines?

3

'A FULL QUIVER':
FERTILITY AND THE
RISE OF AMERICAN
FUNDAMENTALISM

Shortly after the 9/11 attack on the World Trade Center, the Reverend
Jerry Falwell declared on the Christian television programme *The 700
Club*, 'The pagans, and the abortionists, and the feminists, and the gays
and the lesbians ... all of them who have tried to secularise America ...
caused God to lift the veil of protection which has allowed no one to
attack America on our soil since 1812.' Later in the show, Falwell's Christian Right successor Pat Robertson, former candidate for the Republican nomination and founder of the Christian Coalition, concurred that
9/11 was divine punishment: 'We have sinned against Almighty God ...
The Supreme Court has insulted you over and over again, Lord. They've
taken your Bible away from the schools. They've forbidden little children to pray. They've taken the knowledge of God as best they can, and
organisations have come into court to take the knowledge of God out of
the public square of America.' [1]

Falwell and Robertson became the godfathers of the Christian Right
movement, cropping up on the national, state and local political scene.
Today, Christian public policies are on the agenda in ways no one could
have imagined before the late 1970s. Christian symbolism and 'god talk'
pervades American politics. In short, religion has crashed the secular
party that was the American public sphere. This wasn't in the script of
American modernisation. For a long time, American scholars prophesied
that religion's days were numbered. The future lay with secularism, the

next stage in the development process. This supposedly began with the great twentieth-century move to the cities and culminated in the expressive revolution, post-industrialism and the rise of television. One of the few who admits getting it wrong is Peter Berger, a leading sociologist of religion who wrote in 1967 that American religion stood on the cusp of decline, but had recanted by the 1980s.[2] Not only had church attendance and religious belief remained stable, but the constitutional 'wall of separation' between church and state was under assault.

The origins of American Christian fundamentalism

The story of American Christian fundamentalism shares much with its Jewish and Islamic cousins. The rise of secularism and liberal theology proved a foil for early fundamentalists. Modern institutions and modes of communication helped the movement marshal its resources and limit membership loss. The perceived excesses of post-industrial modernity – women's liberation, consumer hedonism and the retreat of the sacred from public life – added fuel to the fire. In their quest, fundamentalists drew on a rich set of religious memories. Religion has long been more vital in America than in Western Europe. The religious zeal of the initial wave of seventeenth-century Puritan settlers in Massachusetts first established a theocracy, then a moralistic political culture. In the eighteenth and nineteenth centuries, New England writers, educators and theologians set the intellectual tone of the country. Though many leading moneymen and politicians hailed from New York and Pennsylvania, the top universities and intellectuals were dominated by those of New England stock. Harvard was basically a New England enclave in which those from other regions – especially the South – were outsiders. The writing of American history was so thoroughly a New England enterprise that Woodrow Wilson, a Southerner who got his Ph.D. in 1886, reacted to their dominance much as African-Americans would approach whites several generations later.[3]

Back then, secular learning and religious thought were heavily intertwined. It is therefore no coincidence that New England intellectuals spearheaded the 'Great Awakenings' of 1725–50 and 1800–30 in which large portions of the country were evangelised and brought into church membership. The South, once the least religious region, was swept up in revival, first Methodist, later Baptist. By 1850, a third of American churchgoers were Methodist, up from just 3 per cent in 1776. American diversity – sectarian more than ethnic – was also critical. After independence, the new country contained a great diversity of Protestant sects, which helped reinforce the separation of church and state and prevent the establishment of a national Church, as in England.[4] The large number of competing sects created a fluid religious market in which religious innovators hit upon emotion-grabbing techniques such as using popular songs, preaching simple sermons and hosting tent revivals.[5]

Geographic mobility and social dislocation created a demand for certainty and community. This was nowhere more evident than in upstate New York's vast 'burned-over district'. Here migrant workers from New England constructed the Erie Canal in 1825, linking the Atlantic to the Great Lakes. The fertile, wooded region, characterised by its New-England-influenced neoclassical architecture and place names (like Utica and Rome), also served as a staging area for the settlement of the West. Its transient atmosphere bred social ills such as alcoholism and poverty. This, combined with the moralistic New England heritage of the population, formed a potent perfectionist cocktail. Western New York became an epicentre of religious experimentation and revival, spawning Mormonism, Seventh-day Adventism and numerous other sects.[6]

After the Second Great Awakening, a new challenger appeared which reduced sectarian squabbles to a sideshow: Catholicism. After 1830, Catholic immigrants from Ireland and Germany poured into the northern states. Protestants, who formed 98 per cent of the population in 1776, became a minority in the urban North during the second half of the nineteenth century. The Protestant–Catholic divide solidified into the principal determinant of vote choice among white northerners, with Protestants opting for the Republicans and Catholic immigrants going solidly Democratic. In the South, race predominated, with white southerners backing the Democrats while blacks, where allowed to vote, chose the Republicans. Religious issues were therefore completely shot through with ethnic, racial and regional concerns. Even moral crusades like Prohibition in the 1920s turned into a largely Protestant (dry) versus Catholic (wet) contest.[7]

The East Coast 'Protestant Establishment' in the form of the

Federal Council of Churches (FCC), the Vatican of American main-line Protestantism, set the tone for American Protestants. Each summer, FCC leaders such as Robert Speer and John R. Mott would meet with political elites and captains of industry such as Henry Ford or John D. Rockefeller at Mount Desert Island, off the Maine Coast. Some, like John Foster Dulles, were active in both the FCC and the highest echelons of government. But beneath this chummy elite, many rank-and-file American Protestants were growing restive. The FCC was determined to move in step with the leading secular ideas. Its Social Christianity and modernist interpretation of scripture proved too much for many conservative Protestants, who harked after the old-time religion. Nor could the FCC appeal to its anti-Catholic roots to placate fundamentalists. Once a fierce critic of Catholicism, the FCC had turned ecumenical by 1910, weakening the Anglo-Protestant ethnic unity that had papered over the modernist–fundamentalist divide.[8] At the same time, secular writers such as H. L. Mencken and Sinclair Lewis mocked fundamentalists as never before. The 1925 Scopes 'Monkey' trial in which Clarence Darrow defended the teaching of evolution against populist Democratic presidential candidate William Jennings Bryan proved a public relations disaster for biblical literalism. These developments dramatically revealed to conservative Protestants just how far the nation's cultural centre had drifted away from them. In effect, literalist Protestants were waking up to the realisation that they were not the country, and would have to fall back on their own resources to preserve their culture.[9]

Slowly, fundamentalists began to organise. There were some loose precedents. A summer Bible Conference in 1875 brought conservative preachers together and became an established feature on the clerical calendar thereafter. The first Bible institute, the Moody Institute, was established in Chicago in 1886. The Bible Institute of Los Angeles, founded in 1908, emerged as a leading producer of fundamentalist pastors. An influential series of pamphlets, 'The Fundamentals of the Faith', were published in the 1910s to define the boundaries beyond which conservative Protestants would not go. Foremost among these was the idea of the inerrancy of scripture – the Bible was the infallible word of God and not a human document subject to historical criticism. Bible colleges helped to develop and standardise the fundamentalist critique of modernism, while Bible institutes trained pastors and missionaries. By 1930, more than fifty 'true faith' Protestant Bible institutions were operating – well outside the orbit of the established liberal-Protestant mainstream.

One revolutionary idea promoted by the new fundamentalist world was premillennial dispensationalism, which marks American evangelicalism to the present day. This cosmology claims that those who commit themselves to Christ will be saved during the 'Rapture', a seven-year period of turmoil in which the earth succumbs to the End Times. In the words of St Paul, 'the dead in Christ shall rise first, and then we [saved] which are alive and remain shall be caught up together with them in the clouds, to meet the Lord in the air.' At the Armageddon, Jesus defeats the Antichrist to usher in a new millennium of peace and righteousness on earth. According to dispensationalist writers, we are living in the sixth of seven historical periods, or 'dispensations', before the End of Days. During this time, wickedness, war and natural disaster befall the earth, and the faithful must detach themselves from it to be 'Rapture-ready'. Needless to say, modernist or nominal Christians will not be among the saved. To avoid their fellow men being vaporised during the Rapture, evangelicals must seek to 'save' them – a transformation also known as 'finding Jesus', or being 'born again'. [10]

Premillennialism was introduced to America by Anglo-Irish evangelist John Darby in the mid nineteenth century, but not codified until 1909. In that year, James Scofield set down the tenets of premillennial dispensationalism in his landmark Scofield Reference Bible, a leading fundamentalist text of today. His work pays close attention to the apocalyptic pronouncements of the Book of Daniel in the Old Testament and the Book of Revelation in the New. More recently, these ideas were popularised by Hal Lindsey, whose *The Late Great Planet Earth* (1973) connected dispensationalist theology to the world events of the twentieth century and went on to sell over 40 million copies. Two decades on, Tim LaHaye's *Left Behind* series of fifteen apocalyptic novels sported titles such as *Armageddon* and *The Rapture*. In little over a decade they have sold 65 million copies. Today, fully two-thirds of those in conservative Protestant denominations report having had a 'born-again' experience in which they fully committed themselves to Christ. [11]

American fundamentalists built networks and institutions, but their pastors and parishioners remained within the denominational structures of the Protestant establishment. In the South there were few modernists so little controversy, but in the North, modernists and fundamentalists battled for control in the 1910s and 1920s. 'Shall the fundamentalists win?' the liberal New York City Presbyterian clergyman Harry Emerson Fosdick asked his audience. 'Shall Unbelief Win?' retorted his conservative adversaries. In the end, Fosdick and the modernists won the day among Baptists, Presbyterians, Methodists and Congregationalists. Many disgruntled conservatives opted to leave to form their own separatist denominations such as the General Association of Regular Baptists (1932).

On campus, universities were rapidly shedding their religious roots in favour of secular science. In leading seminaries such as Princeton or Harvard, the study of scripture in its historical-critical context pushed aside a literal approach to the Bible. This was too much for noted Princeton divine J. Gresham Machen, who left the venerable Presbyterian institution to form his conservative Westminster Theological Seminary in 1929. Machen's fellow Westminsterite Carl McIntire struck a further blow for fundamentalism with his American Council of Christian Churches (ACCC) in 1941. The Baptist Bible Fellowship (BBF) moved in a similar direction in the 1930s. Fundamentalists had established a whole network of parallel countercultural institutions between the wars – Bible colleges and institutes, universities and colleges, day schools and publishing houses, missionary boards and radio ministries – a remarkable achievement.[12]

In the 1970s, television ministries joined the chorus, while the 'God Business' expanded to encompass Christian-themed shopping malls, amusement parks and rock music. These are modern in form, but their content resounds with 'the Lord' and 'Jesus'. At the Holy Land Experience theme park near Disney World in Orlando, visitors are invited to experience 'A living, biblical museum that takes you 7000 miles away and 2000 years back in time to the land of the Bible. Its combination of sights, sounds, and tastes will stimulate your senses and blend together to create a spectacular new experience.' There is also a serious side: 'Above all, beyond the fun and excitement, we hope that you will see God and His Word exalted and that you will be encouraged in your search for enduring truth and the ultimate meaning of life.' Along with Orlando, Nashville and Colorado Springs emerged as centres of fundamentalist Christian production and distribution.[13]

There has always been a division within fundamentalist religion between the emotional and the doctrinal, the mystical and the scriptural. Typically, emotional and mystical religion predominates among the less well-off, while the educated middle class demands a more puritanical, text-based faith. Ernest Gellner remarked upon this distinction in Moroccan Islam, where rural holy men and their magical creed contrasted sharply with the demanding scriptural puritanism of the learned ulama in the urban centres. In Protestant fundamentalism, Pentecostalism, with its emphasis on miracles, experiencing the Holy Spirit and speaking in tongues, exemplifies the emotional side of Protestantism. Calvinism, by contrast, stresses ascetic self-denial and obedience to doctrine.[14]

You can spot the difference in the career of two American evangelists, Billy Graham and Bob Jones, Sr. Jones, born in 1883, was a contemporary of the legendary radio preacher Billy Sunday and emphasised a neo-Calvinistic 'fundamentalism' which excluded Catholics. His son, Bob Jr., followed in his father's footsteps. Graham, the father of 'neo-evangelicalism', attended Bob Jones College in 1936 but found its teachings too legalistic. In the 1960s, he emphasised evangelism over doctrinal purity, and reached out to Catholics. He termed Kennedy a 'Baptist president' after his assassination, spoke warmly of the Pope and attracted many Catholics to his revivalistic 'crusades'.[15] Future Pope John Paul II later helped Graham to establish the Campus Crusade for Christ in Poland and allowed Graham to guest-preach from the Pope's Krakow church on the day of his coronation.[16] By contrast, Bob Jones, Jr's fiery pal, Northern Ireland's Reverend Ian Paisley, a Member of the European Parliament, once interrupted a speech by Pope John Paul on the floor of that Catholic-majority body to denounce him as the Antichrist. Jones Jr. shared Paisley's view, but drew his circle even tighter, assailing Billy Graham as the Antichrist for his 'spiritual fornication' with Catholics.

The fundamentalist–'neo-evangelical' divide remains important today. Neo-evangelicalism lies behind the freewheeling, this-worldly message of many conservative Protestant evangelists. According to Alan

Wolfe, mainstream evangelical churches, fearful of losing members to rivals, have distanced themselves from their 'hellfire and damnation' roots. Forced to compete with other churches for the fleeting attentions of fickle, spoiled consumers, evangelical churches now offer 'theology-lite' fare. Preachers spoon-feed parishioners with simple, easily grasped bits of scripture, and drown it in feel-good homilies about rewards, not punishments. Billy Sunday and Carl McIntire must be turning over in their graves at such therapeutic, non-judgemental cotton candy. More-over, Protestant hymns and prayerbooks have been replaced in many large churches with Christian rock and high-tech presentations. The idea of women working outside the home has been subtly digested, with little fanfare, by most evangelical churches and parachurch organisations. In a competitive market, you don't want to offend your core customers.[17] The lengths to which some are going is truly astounding. Women's Aglow, a Pentecostally inspired parachurch movement, emphasises that faith in Jesus and improving one's appearance go hand in hand. Books on Christianity and dieting, such as Don Colbert's *What Would Jesus Eat?*, complement the message of those like the pastor of Parkview Free Church in Houston, who tells his flock that sex (within marriage) 'is a beautiful thing. You should anticipate it and you should enjoy it.'[18]

In Latin America and Africa, Pentecostalism's prosperity gospel – that faith will improve one's fortunes in this world – is part of its appeal. The same is true in the United States, where parishioners pray for success in real estate, money and health rather than repressing these desires as earthly sins. Exemplifying this self-centred spirituality is Bruce Wilkinson's *The Prayer of Jabez* (2000), which has sold 9 million copies. It urges children and adults alike to pray for God's blessings in their business and personal lives, and to notice the difference when they do so. The only thing missing seems to be the money-back guarantee.[19] Churches are also not shy about borrowing ideas from management and psychotherapy, and harnessing the latest fruits of modern technology. Megachurches, defined as churches with over 2,000 members, exemplify this approach. Many have flourished in recent decades, often under the aegis of a star preacher, or 'pastorpreneur'.[20] The largest, such as Lakewood church in Houston, Willow Creek in South Barrington, Illinois, or Saddleback, in Orange County, California, have 20,000 to 40,000 in attendance each week. The religious entrepreneurs who run these churches, such as Rick Warren of Saddleback, often sit astride a vast religious empire, including religious publishing and media. At Willow Creek, the amenities range 'from food courts to basketball courts, from cafes to video screens'. It employs a management team, two MBAs and a consulting arm and has 'even been given the ultimate business accolade: A Harvard Business School case study'.[21] The number of megachurches has leapt tenfold since 1980, though this needs to be kept in perspective: less than 10 per cent of the houses of worship in most denominations are megachurches, and there has also been growth among small churches of less than a hundred.[22]

Evangelicalism's world-affirming focus is reflected in the lifestyles of the rank and file. Eighty per cent of unmarried Conservative Protestants report having had sex in the past year – no different from other Protestants. Evangelicals cohabit and divorce at about the same rate as others.[23] In terms of social attitudes, evangelicals are more conservative than other groups, but more centrist than their Christian Right spokespeople. Half disapprove of premarital sex (despite the fact that most practise it), but so do a quarter of mainline Protestants and nearly 40 per cent of Afro-American Protestants. When it comes to beliefs about sex, drink and smoking within marriage, it is hard to fit a paper clip between evangelicals, white Catholics and mainline Protestants. Most evangelicals prefer traditional families, but over 80 per cent support the idea of women working, very similar to other groups in the population.[24] One might add that white evangelicals are not even remotely residentially segregated the way Hutterites, Amish or even Utah Mormons are.

From quietism to activism

The mainstream of American conservative Protestantism is clearly more neo-evangelical than fundamentalist. On the other hand, evangelicals differ from mainline Protestants in some key areas. Only 28 per cent of evangelicals, compared with 45 per cent of mainline Protestants, approve of abortion if the mother is too poor or does not want any more children. There is a significant 15–20 per cent gap on attitudes to homosexuality and a 20–30 per cent difference when it comes to voting for the Republicans.[25] In effect, while evangelicals have average personal mores, they are more politically conservative than other groups. Moving rightwards, we can also identify a significant minority of fundamentalists who are doctrinaire neo-Calvinists. They are inerrantist – the Bible is God's literal truth – and ascetically deny themselves the pleasures of this world. Bob Jones University in Greenville, South Carolina, is a centre of such purist thought. Jones Jr. has opposed both Billy Graham and Jerry Falwell for their more inclusive approach to denominations like the Lutherans and Catholics. Instead, he prefers the company of anti-Catholics such as the Reverend Ian Paisley of Northern Ireland, who, together with Jones, hosted the grandly titled 'World Congress of Fundamentalists', which consisted only of Jones, Paisley and their followers.

A more activist variant of old-time Calvinist fundamentalism is Dominion theology, the main branch of which is known as Reconstructionism. Adherents of these ideas seek to rebuild God's Kingdom on earth with the same theocratic spirit that animated Calvin's Geneva and Puritan New England. Premillennial dispensationalism, the main American evangelical tradition, is inherently quietist. If society is going to hell, why bother to change it? Personal faith and saving souls is more important than social activism or politics. Reconstructionists, on the other hand, chastise the premillennialist evangelical mainstream for their 'rapture fever', and cite the Book of Genesis, which urges mankind to 'take dominion' of the earth. Their view is postmillennialist: that man cannot retreat from the world, but has a duty to remake society into a godly one before the Messiah can return. R. J. Rushdoony and his son-in-law Gary North refined postmillennialism in the 1960s and 70s, pointing to the precedent set by New England Puritans, with their dream of creating a divine 'City Upon a Hill' in the New World.

By invoking the Puritans and rekindling the idea of America as a godly nation, Dominion theology legitimates both Christian nationalism and theocracy. More importantly, it clears the way for fundamentalists to get involved in politics. Democratic politics is a messy business of compromise and coalition, so Rushdoony and his Reconstructionists endorse the idea of 'co-belligerence', which – in contrast to Jones's separatism – endorses cooperation with 'wayward' faiths such as Catholicism and Mormonism. In effect, evangelicals are implored to save the country as well as individual souls, and to forge alliances across denominational lines. A political strategist seeking to mobilise evangelicals couldn't wish for more. This accounts for the influence of the Chalcedon Foundation, the main Reconstructionist think tank, based in California. As the Christian Right became increasingly active and built cross-denominational coalitions in the 1980s, Pat Robertson, Jerry Falwell and other Christian Right political leaders eagerly lapped up the Reconstructionist message.[26]

There were few precedents for the entry of Protestant fundamentalism on to the political scene. True, many who supported successful political crusades like the prohibition of alcohol in 1920 were biblical literalists. The multi-million-member Ku Klux Klan of the 1920s was principally a northern, anti-Catholic organisation, but conservative moral politics formed a subsidiary part of its platform.[27] On the clerical side of the ledger, Carl McIntire and Billy Sunday broadened their preaching to bang the drum against communism, Catholicism and 'wets' in the interwar period.[28] Anticommunism's campaign against 'godlessness' proved particularly appealing in the 1950s and 60s. But looking across the sweep of fundamentalist institutions, clerics and parishioners, most remained disengaged from the political process, content in their premillennial separatist bliss.

During the first six decades of the twentieth century, the mainline 'Protestant establishment' and Federal Council of Churches (FCC) – now turned National Council of Churches (NCC) – set the tone of American religious life. Mainline Protestant intellectuals such as Reinhold Niebuhr and Paul Tillich were mainstream figures, featured in *Time* and *Life* magazines.[29] Mainline Protestants enjoyed a comfortable numerical advantage over their literalist country cousins and felt themselves to be in the driver's seat of American culture. Furthermore, many believed that theological conservatism was linked to class. As late as the 1960s, barefoot Southern Baptists and Pentecostals tended to convert to moderate mainline churches like the Episcopalians when they worked or married their way up the social ladder.[30] Maybe a bit of spiritual upward mobility was all that was needed to maintain mainline Protestant dominance.

But change was afloat, stimulated by the social upheavals of the 1960s. In the South, race was delegitimated as a political ideology after the Voting Rights Act of 1965. Evangelical Protestant politics swept into the vacuum like a hurricane. In the North, John F. Kennedy's election in 1960 brought the long chapter of anti-Catholicism towards a close. Catholics and evangelical Protestants could now make common cause on issues like abortion. It was not always thus. Consider abortion and contraception. These were once viewed as largely Catholic concerns in a Protestant America. The 'Sanger Incident' in 1940 in Holyoke, Massachusetts, a Catholic-majority town, illustrates how the Protestant–Catholic divide overwhelmed religious issues. Local Catholic leaders pressured a Protestant church into reneging on its speaking invitation to Margaret Sanger, a prominent birth-control advocate, prompting nationwide Protestant angst. Many Protestants wondered if Holyoke was a harbinger of what might happen when Catholics took over their country.[31] A decade later, Paul Blanshard's *American Freedom and Catholic Power* denounced Catholic teachings on birth control, gender equality, abortion and more, becoming a runaway best-seller among the wary Protestant majority. Conservative Protestant clerics unselfconsciously used birth control while abortion remained low on their list of priorities.[32]

This changed rapidly when the demise of segregation and sectarianism opened the door to fundamentalist politics. The landmark Roe *v.* Wade Supreme Court decision of 1973 threw down the gauntlet which united conservative Catholics and Protestants. Conservative religion appeared like a vision in the night for the Republicans, a cipher to unlock the power of southern evangelicals and mobilise them behind the Grand Old Party (GOP). Sensing an opportunity, Republicans Richard Viguerie and Paul Weyrich, both Catholic, and Howard Phillips, a Jewish convert to evangelical Protestantism, forged links with Southern Baptist clergyman Jerry Falwell. Their marriage led to the Moral Majority, the first Christian Right political coalition.[33] Once a quietist voting bloc whose votes were as likely to go to Democrats like Jimmy Carter as the Republicans, evangelicals rapidly emerged as the backbone of the GOP. Together with local Christian Right organisations, the Moral Majority opposed abortion and same-sex marriage while advocating school prayer and family values. Their energy redefined American politics. Falwell's movement ran out of steam in the 1980s, but Virginia televangelist Pat Robertson picked up the torch in the 1990s under the aegis of the Christian Coalition. Charles Dobson's Focus on the Family emerged as another major parachurch pressure group in this period.

The Christian Coalition claimed over a million members at its peak, dwarfing virtually all other political pressure groups. It effectively mobilised large numbers of volunteers who had never been involved in politics. Much of its activity focused on the local level. Social movement theory emphasises the importance of prior networks for movement success.[34] The Coalition was perfectly situated in this respect since it could tap into a vast evangelical network of clerical and lay activists. Pentecostalists and evangelically minded Protestants within established denominations formed the backbone of the Coalition, which worked at precinct level to distribute millions of voter guides ranking candidates on their religious voting record. The loose, decentralised nature of the American polity makes it easy for a committed group to seize power at state and local levels, especially in the short term. The strategy of the Christian Right was to shape the nation's cultural agenda from the grassroots up by targeting low-profile institutions which few voters cared about. These included state school boards and Republican Party branches.[35]

In South Carolina, Texas and Kansas, to take just three examples, school boards quickly fell to the Christian Right, which mobilised its voters while most others stayed home. Their goals: to reinstitute school prayer, teach 'Creation Science', pare back sex education and end the toleration of homosexuality in the curriculum. In Kansas, the Christian Right-controlled board of education voted to withdraw evolution from the list of required subjects on state tests. In Texas, the state board of education voted 8–4 in 1998 to sell its stock in the Disney corporation. According to the American Family Association of Texas, which led the campaign, the company 'Allowed homosexual celebrations in its objectionable films; allowed a convicted child molester to direct a Disney movie; published a book aimed at homosexuals; and promoted numerous other anti-family policies and activities.'[36]

The other pincer of the Christian Right attack targeted the Republican Party. Most states followed federal practice in abandoning local party branches in favour of primaries. The languishing party branches proved easy prey for the Christian Right, which packed their membership rolls with evangelical activists. Next, the Christian Right mobilised to control state party primaries. Here they ran up against a process which more people cared about, stopping the Christian Right's march. Though the

Christian Right fell short of becoming a kingmaker, it wielded disproportionate influence in, and heavily shaped the agenda of, state politics. In virtually all states, and at the federal level, it moved from a fringe social movement to an institutionalised Republican faction. It refashioned white evangelicals, a once dormant segment of the electorate, into a cohesive group with above average political participation and a near-80 per cent Republican presidential voting record. Along the way, it boosted the careers of state politicians such as George Allen in Virginia and national ones such as George W. Bush.

Working through independent state movements and larger organisations like the Christian Coalition and Focus on the Family, the Christian Right pushed its policy agenda through state ballot initiatives. These referenda permit legislation to be put to a plebiscite if activists collect enough signatures. This form of Christian Right activism contributed to the defeat of the feminist Equal Rights Amendment in the 1970s, even in northern states such as Maine and Iowa. Later, the Christian Right helped repeal or block same-sex marriage initiatives (or sponsored anti-same-sex marriage ballots) in many states. It successfully fought for laws compelling minors seeking abortions in many states to notify their parents.[37] The Christian Right even notched up some successes at the federal level, as when President George W. Bush signed into law a ban on a late-term procedure known as 'partial-birth' abortion.

Bush also endorsed an unsuccessful amendment opposing same-sex marriage and created the Office of Faith-Based Initiatives. The latter helped to funnel a billion dollars of federal money to religious charities during Bush's first term of office.[38] Paying religious organisations rather than federal employees to deliver social welfare services represented a rollback of public secularisation: since the New Deal, the state had appropriated the job of providing food, housing and other welfare functions from churches, but now religion was getting these functions back. Barack Obama, burnishing his religious credentials, has reaffirmed the Office. So much for the inevitable progress of secularisation.

In foreign policy, the so-called 'Bush Doctrine' rose from the ashes of 9/11. The administration of George W. Bush proclaimed a willingness to take pre-emptive military action, and backed this up by invading Iraq. It unequivocally supported Israel against the Palestinians and spurned international institutions, animated by the belief that the United States has a special role to play on the global stage. This approach chimed with secular neoconservatism, but drew its most important support from premillennial dispensationalists. Evangelicals had written about the prophetic implications of Jewish settlement in Palestine as early as 1839. Somewhat later, John Darby expanded upon this vision, arguing that the Jews will resettle the Holy Land and rebuild a Third Temple on the site of the Dome of the Rock where the al-Aqsa mosque now sits. These Zionists would be resisted tooth and nail, but in the end they would succeed, come to recognise Christ and greet him as the Messiah at the Second Coming. Writing in 1967, Hal Lindsey considered Israel's conquest of the West Bank (biblical Judea and Samaria) and Jerusalem to be an 'electrifying' sign of impending prophecy.[39]

Premillennialist views find an echo in the wider evangelical population, which is significantly more likely to support the Bush Doctrine and Israel than other Christian Americans.[40] So much so that Kevin Phillips, who once helped to organise conservative Christian voters into the Republican camp, warns that conservative Christians have hijacked the Republican Party and push an apocalyptic agenda that threatens the country's health and its time-honoured separation of church and state.[41] Some complain that Christian Zionist support for the Israeli right has exacerbated the conflict by emboldening Jewish settlement of the Occupied Territories while discouraging the Israelis from making the territorial compromises necessary for peace. Critics charge that Christian Zionism whips up Muslim resentment against the US, damaging its foreign policy interests. It even hurts Israel by endorsing reckless policies that endanger Israel's security and possibly its very existence. At home and abroad, the rollback of American secularisation is not just personal but political, and is beginning to resacralise the state.[42]

The rise of the Christian Right in demographic perspective

Where did the Christian Right come from? The conventional wisdom maintains that it is a purely social phenomenon, the child of cultural responses and political events. But the elephant in the room is surely demography. To illustrate, compare the strength of the Christian Right in South Carolina, where a near-majority of residents are white evangelicals, to Maine or Washington, where evangelicals are only half as thick on the ground. Nationwide, a drop in the proportion of white evangelicals from their current 25 per cent to 10 per cent could reduce Christian Right influence to Canadian-style insignificance. Conversely, a doubling of white evangelicals' share would make the US look like Texas or South Carolina, where the Christian Right has pushed the boundaries of policy up hard against the restraints of the courts and federal laws.[43]

The explosive growth of the Amish and Mormons can inform our understanding of the rise of evangelical Protestantism. Liberal and moderate Protestants made up nearly two-thirds of white American Protestants born in 1900, but constituted little more than a third of those born in 1975. Evangelicals had become the majority. Why? Conversion of mainline Protestants to evangelical denominations is part of the story, and represents an important change from previous eras, when the cachet of mainline Protestant churches attracted converts from humbler fundamentalist sects. In 2003, according to the General Social Survey (GSS), the rate of conservative Protestant retention of members between childhood and adulthood was 67 per cent, compared with 58 per cent for liberal and moderate Protestants. The flow of converts therefore favours conservatives: 21 per cent leave liberal and moderate denominations for evangelical ones, while just 15 per cent go the other way. Yet differential fertility is far more important. Conservative Protestant women born in 1900 enjoyed a one-child fertility advantage over mainline Protestant women from the same cohort. Though the lead narrowed over the next seven decades, cumulative fertility differences explain three-quarters of the growth of conservative Protestant denominations during the twentieth century.[44] As with the early Christians, political power – this time in the guise of the Christian Right rather than Constantine's edicts – followed demographic expansion.

The end of evangelical growth?

Not so fast, some say. The demography of evangelical growth and mainline decline can be explained by the late modernisation of conservative Protestants. The sunbelt has been experiencing an economic boom for decades. Air conditioning has lured Yankee capital and immigrants to the heavily evangelical Deep South. This has narrowed the education and wealth gap between evangelicals and mainliners, reducing fertility differences.[45] There is a great deal of truth in this, and evangelical fertility is converging towards the national norm. In 2003, according to the GSS, the total fertility rate of white conservative Protestants stood at 2.13 children per couple, not much higher than that for moderate Protestants (2.01) or liberal Protestants (1.84). The combination of conservative gains from switching and a higher fertility rate will continue to increase the evangelical share of the white Protestant total. But conservatives will only gain a few percentage points from mainliners in the next fifty years – a much smaller change than that which took place over the previous half-century. Given the projected growth of the secular and non-white populations, white evangelicals will barely manage to hang on to their 26 per cent share of the white population, and will decline as a proportion of the American total.[46]

It is interesting to peer at the American religious landscape in 2050. Since the Americans being born today will be the median Americans of 2050, we can speak with a high degree of confidence about this. It says something about the US that its census asks detailed questions on race and makes racial projections to 2050, but does not do the same for religion. To fill this gap in our knowledge, I teamed up with demographers based at the International Institute for Applied Systems Analysis (IIASA). Located in a charming former Habsburg palace near Vienna, IIASA was set up during the Cold War to bring Western and Eastern scientists together. Today, it continues to bridge international divides in the name of science. We used GSS data and immigration statistics on the top eleven religious groups in the country to make our projections. Survey questions enabled us to determine the fertility of religious groups and their gains or losses from switching groups. Some of the eleven groups, such as Muslims or Hispanic Catholics, have a very young age structure, while others, such as Jews or Liberal Protestants, are much older. Total fertility rates vary a great deal: Muslims (2.84) and Hispanic Catholics (2.75) are the most fertile, Jews (1.43) and seculars (1.64) the least. Finally, immigration disproportionately benefits Hispanic Catholics and non-Chistian religions.

We found that ethnic religions retain their members best between age sixteen and adulthood: 87 per cent of black Protestants and 81 per cent of Jews and Hispanic Catholics stayed with their religious group into adulthood. By contrast, those with no religion, i.e. seculars (56 per cent) along with Mainline Protestants (57–8 per cent) retained fewest, losing many to switching. White Catholics and Muslims (71 per cent) and evangelical Protestants (67 per cent) occupy a middle ground. It is worth bearing in mind, however, that evangelical Protestants pick up far more converts, two to three times as many, from other religions than do Catholics. Seculars do best of all, creaming off between 7 and 19 per cent of the membership of every other group. On balance, therefore, seculars and evangelical Protestant denominations gain most from switching. Most of the rest – especially Catholics and mainline Protestants – are net losers.

Looking ahead, we find that on current trends, the biggest single change will be the rise of Hispanic Catholics, who will grow entirely through demography despite losing many to secularism and Protestantism. They are projected to increase from 10 per cent of the total today to 19 per cent in 2050 and 27 per cent in 2100. Even if immigration were cut off and their fertility dropped to the national average, Hispanic Catholics would more than double their population by 2100, increasing to over 13 per cent in 2050 and 15 per cent by 2100. This surge puts all other religious groups in the shade.

Muslims are a partial exception. Their demography resembles that of the Hispanics, and will propel them from half a per cent today to around 1.3 per cent of the population in 2020, when they will overtake Jews. Five years later, Muslims will gain the edge over Jews in the voting age population. This could alter the pro-Israel slant in American foreign policy. John Mearsheimer and Stephen Walt, in their influential book *The Israel Lobby*, take care to emphasise that the lobby is largely composed of non-Jewish actors on the American Right.[47] That said, there is an important Jewish dimension to the lobby, especially at the elite level. It is hard to imagine it functioning without its main Jewish-American organisation, AIPAC, and the strongly Jewish neoconservative movement.

Jews are among the best educated, wealthiest Americans and have disproportionate – if often exaggerated – media clout in American society.[48] The harmony between the interests and ideology of American and Israeli conservatives is a force multiplier for the lobby. Does this innoculate the lobby from demography? Not quite. Jews' presence within the

American elite explains much of their power. But the Jewish vote also matters. Their high electoral participation levels have enhanced their demographic weight in the electorate, and a shrinking Jewish share in the population will undercut this. The ascent of Islam into third place behind Catholicism will also have a symbolic effect on the 'Protestant-Catholic-Jew' settlement which has defined American civil religion since the Second World War.[49] Indeed, Jews will probably drop to fifth place behind both Muslims and Mormons by the 2020s. In a highly pluralistic society which is sensitive to cries of 'discrimination', American Muslims could begin to use their new-found clout to dislodge the Jews' 'special relationship' with American Christians. Arab-American Christians such as John Zogby, president of the Arab-American Institute, could provide the bridge for American Muslims to challenge the status quo.

More important for our story is what will happen to the secular share of the US population. Demographically, seculars have a young age profile which locks in growth. Young people, who will raise tomorrow's children, are 30–40 per cent secular.[50] Culturally, they benefit most from switching since secularisation is an important force in all denominations. In light of this, it is odd that our projections discovered that seculars will barely grow between now and 2050, increasing half a percentage point to just 17 per cent of the total. After 2030, secularism will enter into steady decline, settling out at 14 to 15 per cent of the population by the end of the century. Why? A low fertility rate (1.64) and only modest immigration provide the answer. Young women, who have the greater influence on children's religious upbringing, are more religious than men, which also affects the results.

Secularism will need to keep the apostates flowing in at the same pace as in the past to maintain their numbers. This presents no easy task: sociologists show that left-wing believers responding to the rise of the Christian Right were behind the spurt in secularism. In private, over half of seculars pray and a majority believe in either God or the existence of a 'higher power', so may be lured back to faith. The rise of a more vocal Religious Left could dry up the flow of apostates.[51] If religious apostasy slows down, to say nothing of religious revival, the population of seculars could peak as early as 2020 and decline to just 10 per cent of the total by the end of the century. These numbers play a tune which is distinctly out of key with the theme of secularisation. They dramatically highlight the way demography constrains cultural change. Secularism can win the battle for individual souls but lose the national war in the same way that secularism has won the West while the world as a whole has become more religious. In effect, secularism must run to stand still and sprint in order to succeed. In America, as in the world, it looks destined to fail in the long term.

The one place where secularism will enjoy its greatest near-term triumph is among white Americans. Seculars are most likely to spring from among the ranks of young whites. Immigrants, even if religious, tend to be non-white, so do not bolster the ranks of religious whites. In combination, these forces will raise the non-religious share of the white population from less than 20 per cent today to 30 per cent by 2050. Yet even among whites, low secular fertility will cause the rise to plateau after mid-century and begin a gentle decline beyond 2070. And this assumes that the strong inflows of religious apostates of the 1990s – which shaped the survey respondents of 2003 – can be maintained. Closer scrutiny of the white population also reveals that the middle is being hollowed out. As white secularism grows, evangelical Protestants will maintain their position while mainline Protestants, Jews and Catholics decline. But, as we shall see, this is not the only reason why those who remain religious will become more fundamentalist in composition.

Quiverfull: demographic radicalism in the heartland
Conservative Protestants' fertility advantage over mainline Protestants in the twentieth century was largely responsible for evangelical growth. Today, more than a quarter of Americans are white evangelicals. But this growth has largely come to a close. Our medium-term religious projections point to stability in the future. If anything, white seculars will surpass white evangelicals in number over the next two decades. On the other hand, Latino, Asian and Muslim immigration, and these groups' relatively high fertility rates, are reshaping America and coun-terbalancing the growth of secularism. The new immigrant groups will keep America more religious and socially conservative in the future than would otherwise be the case. For twentieth-century white evangelicals and Catholics, as with twenty-first-century Hispanics and Muslims,

demography operated indirectly. Church teachings on contraception may have slowed things down, but by and large, religious ideology did not directly shape reproductive choices. White evangelicals and Catholics lost most of their fertility advantage as they ascended the social ladder, gained access to contraception and attended college. The children of Latino and Muslim immigrants have smaller families than their parents, higher incomes and better education. This will lower their fertility even more. Surely the era of religious demography is nearing its end?

There are several important reasons why this is unlikely. First, it is far from clear that Hispanics will pull even with whites in the economic pecking order. Hispanics' lower social status and their minority consciousness in an age of identity politics will keep their fertility above the national average. Immigration from poor countries, which tends to be religiously traditionalist, is unlikely to abate. Furthermore, even if ethno-religious growth comes to an end, pronatalist religious growth is just beginning. Its most dramatic outrider is a Protestant fundamentalist movement which resembles endogenous growth sects like the ultra-Orthodox Jews and Amish. Known as Quiverfull, it emphasises patriarchal gender roles, biblical inerrancy, endogamy, large families and separation from the wider world – including the wider evangelical world. The phenomenon is still small – adherents number only in the tens of thousands – but numerous others in the growing 1–3 million-strong evangelical homeschool movement are influenced by its teachings.

Quiverfull's doyen is Doug Phillips, son of converted Jewish Christian Right activist Howard Phillips. Doug Phillips's Vision Forum is the star around which a lively subculture of churches, websites, conferences and publishing ventures orbits. The foundation texts are Rick and Jan Hess's *A Full Quiver: Family Planning and the Lordship of Christ* (1989) and Charles Provan's *The Bible and Birth Control* (1989). Influenced by anti-feminist homeschool advocate Mary Pride, the Hesses urge women to relinquish their wombs to God, who will determine how many children they should bear. On this reading, contraception is a step on the road to abortion. Even the rhythm method represents undue human control over God's Plan.[52] According to Provan, three biblical sources underlie the movement: the Genesis command to be 'fruitful and multiply'; the fable of Onan, slain by God for spilling his seed on the ground;

and Psalm 127, which reads, 'Like arrows in the hands of a warrior are sons born on one's youth. Blessed is the man whose quiver is full of them.' Martin Luther's opposition to birth control provides extra-scriptural backing.

The movement seems to have emerged from many taproots, spread within a neo-Calvinist grassroots network which has stolen the clothes of pre-Vatican II Catholicism. In many ways, the rise of anti-contraceptive 'natural family' ideas represents a logical development of the post-1960s anti-abortion and anti-feminist movements in American fundamentalism. A generation ago, few conservative Protestant pastors had large families, but now, fundamentalist pastors with self-consciously large broods are emerging. Doug Phillips has eight children, and preaches a 'two-hundred-year plan' for fundamentalist dominion based on high fertility and membership retention. Men who father many children who in turn do the same, counsels Phillips, will preside over a 'dynasty' of thousands in four generations. Phillips's Vision Forum counterpart Geoffrey Botkin has even produced a spreadsheet which predicts that he will be the patriarch of 186,000 male descendants within two centuries. At the birth of his latest addition, Anna Sofia, Botkin passed his hand over the abdomen of the sleeping newborn, praying for her to be the 'future mother of tens of millions'. Large families are increasingly common in Quiverfull families. In the Gospel Community Church of Coxsackie, New York, the pastor has eight children, the assistant pastor eleven and parishioner Wendy Dufkin, to take just one example, thirteen. In fact, in Quiverfull circles, women with just three or four children have been known to break down and cry, despairing of their chosenness because the Lord has not granted them a 'full quiver'.[53]

Large families complicate daily life. How do you fit them into a car, feed them or pay for health care? What can you do about the scorn of the general public? Thank goodness for Quiverfull websites and support groups. As with ultra-Orthodox Jews, outside prejudice helps to reinforce communal boundaries and deepen clerical influence over the community. Phillips and other Quiverfull leaders speak of family-integrated churches, which tie family and church life ever more closely together. In common with Islamic Salafists, Quiverfull churches provide scriptural guidance across a wide range of spheres of daily life. Like the Amish, whom some movement activists openly emulate, corporal punishment is encouraged and non-compliant members may be shunned by the congregation.[54] Quiverfull adherents keep their distance from secular society – including mainstream evangelicals – by homeschooling and even home-churching. Vision Forum and other fundamentalist media outlets provide approved books, CDs, teaching materials and even doll sets which emphasise home economics. Some members live 'off-grid', generating their own electricity and water. Endogamy is developing through the idea of courtship, whereby dating is replaced by potential suitors approaching the parents of the daughter whose hand they seek in marriage. In this way, families can prevent children from slipping away from the movement through intermarriage.

Quiverfull families are not yet as insulated as ultra-Orthodox Jews, Amish or even Utah Mormons from the wider culture. Though their women dress modestly, Quiverfull fundamentalists appear less distinct than their Anabaptist counterparts and lack a shared language, territorial base or distinct symbols. But early signs are that Quiverfull is emulating the successful retention record of Anabaptists and Mormons.[55] Infused with a sense of mission and divine election, Quiverfull children have been raised in opposition to the secular, and even evangelical, mainstream. Phillips's daughters are among the poster-girls of the movement, exemplifying a more modest, Victorian style of submissive beauty. What's more, Quiverfull networks intersect just enough with those of the wider evangelical world to offer avenues for rapid growth through conversion. Phillips, of course, is the son of a major Christian Right figure with numerous connections. Lutheran economist Allan Carlson and his Mormon colleague Paul Mero have written *The Natural Family: A Manifesto*, which supports Quiverfull movement aims. Carlson is particularly influential, having served as Ronald Reagan's appointee to the National Commission on Children and advised Senator Tom Brownback of Kansas.

Quiverfull wields influence beyond its membership because its concerns resonate with wider Western fears of population decline. Mainstream religious intellectuals are also beginning to climb aboard the pronatalist bandwagon. The respected Catholic journal *First Things*, for example, publishes numerous articles against contraception, motivated by pronatalist arguments against Western decline. Theologian David Bentley Hart has written in the magazine that 'probably the most subversive and effective strategy we might undertake would be one of militant fecundity: abundant, relentless, exuberant, and defiant child-bearing. Given the reluctance of modern men and women to be fruitful and multiply, it would not be difficult, surely, for the devout to accomplish – in no more than a generation or two – a demographic revolution.'[56] Even Centrist Democrat Philip Longman urges policy action to avert the West's 'Demographic Winter', to paraphrase the title of a recent Christian Right film. Longman has endorsed Carlson and Mero's *The Natural Family* and envisions the return of patriarchy as a natural correction to excessive individualism in decadent societies from ancient Greece to contemporary Europe.[57]

Quiverfull is a new movement whose ideas have yet to hit their peak, so it is difficult to know what its ultimate impact will be. One possibility is that it will morph into an Amish-like sect. Another is that it will drag the theological right wing of evangelicalism towards higher fertility. To date, one can discern little pronatalist impact on liberal churches, some of whom discourage large families as ecologically irresponsible. Katharine Jefferts Schori, Presiding Bishop of the Episcopal Church in the United States, when asked in an interview whether Episcopalians are being encouraged to have children to shore up declining numbers, replied, 'No. It's probably the opposite. We encourage people to pay attention to the stewardship of the earth and not use more than their portion.' But mainstream evangelicals differ considerably from liberal Protestants on this question. The evangelical flagship journal *Christianity Today*, for instance, emphasises traditional gender roles and discourages childlessness, though it stops short of criticising family planning. Southern Baptist Theological Seminary, which nominally represents 16 million evangelicals, is positively pronatalist.

Richard Land and Albert Mohler, two prominent Southern Baptist leaders, have both criticised the environmental argument against smaller families. This attitude, claims Mohler, is 'rooted in an elitist distaste for larger families and an ambition to control the reproductive destiny of others'. 'The far larger issue,' he added, is 'the glory of God in the birth and maturation of godly progeny. Children are to be received – and

conceived – as gifts, not as threats of environmental disaster.' An awareness of the competition also spurs evangelicals towards larger families.
'Let's outbreed the Mormons,' urges Russell Moore, Dean of the School
of Theology at the Southern Baptist Theological Seminary. As with
Quiverfull, it is much too early to tell what effect such pronouncements
may have. Southern Baptist fertility rates are no higher than the national
average, and Mohler himself has only two children, but this may reflect
the past rather than the future.[58] Indeed, there are impressive trends in
the data which suggest that religious conservatism directly influences
fertility.

Religiosity and fertility

According to second demographic transition (SDT) demographers, the
low fertility rate of secular Americans should come as no surprise. Secular
individualism emphasises self-fulfilment and gender equality, frowning
upon obligations to group and tradition. Postponing family formation
to further a career, travel, widen one's set of experiences or simply find
the right mate is encouraged, but these practices lower fertility rates.
Moral traditionalists, by contrast, tend to get married earlier and bear
more children. According to Ron Lesthaeghe, a leading SDT theorist,
when you graph a state's 2004 Republican share of the presidential vote
against its white fertility rate, you find a 78 per cent correlation. This
means that for every point increase in a state's white total fertility rate
(TFR), the share of the vote for Bush increases by almost eight-tenths of
a point.[59] Fertile, Republican Utah contrasts sharply with Democratic,
below-replacement New England. In other words, conservative religious
people don't simply have larger families than seculars as a byproduct
of their being uneducated, poor or immigrants. Their beliefs encourage
them to have larger families than the non-religious.

Conservative pundits have taken considerable comfort from these
facts. As Arthur Brooks, president of the right-wing AEI think tank put
it, 'Liberals have a big baby problem: they're not having enough of them,
they haven't for a long time, and their pool of potential new voters is suffering as a result.' Unsurprisingly, conservatives foresee an ultimate victory arising from religious fertility. In Mark Steyn's words, 'By 2050, there
will be 100 million fewer Europeans [and] 100 million more Americans

– and mostly red-state Americans.' Those outside the conservative fold have also remarked upon the differences, often to raise the alarm. 'Among white Americans fertility differences reflect a gulf between the religious and the secular,' writes Michael Lind. 'In largely Mormon Utah, there are 90 children for every 1,000 women of child-bearing age, compared to only 49 in the socially liberal Vermont of Howard Dean.' 'In [secular] Seattle,' adds Philip Longman of the non-partisan New America Foundation, 'there are nearly 45% more dogs than children. In [conservative, Mormon] Salt Lake City, there are nearly 19% more kids than dogs.' [60]

Recent scholarship illuminates the demographic distinctiveness of core fundamentalists within the wider evangelical family. Evangelical fertility numbers look quite different when we subtract the giant Southern Baptist Convention, whose 16.2 million members make up the largest Protestant denomination. Fundamentalists orchestrated a takeover of the SBC in 1979, and SBC central agencies such as the Southern Baptist Theological Seminary purged moderates from their ranks after 1987. The action was carefully planned by fundamentalist leaders like Texas judge Paul Pressler. He recognised that the Convention chairman's position, once seen as honorary, held the key to power. Working behind the scenes at the local level with his Texas lieutenant Paige Patterson, he held meetings and rallies designed to ensure the maximum fundamentalist turnout at the 1979 Houston convention. They never looked back.

Fundamentalists soon conquered the SBC's agencies, where health and education initiatives yielded to church expansion and missionary work. Abortion, school prayer and the Christian Right agenda displaced liberal concerns such as hunger and poverty. At Southern Baptist Theological Seminary, the president was forced from office and professors who chafed at the new doctrinal restrictions left. Yet central decrees have not dramatically affected the SBC tradition of congregational independence. Today, a higher proportion of lay SBC members identify themselves as theologically liberal than conservative. Jimmy Carter is a case in point. Similar divisions characterise the 2.4 million-strong Lutheran Church Missouri Synod (LCMS), which was captured by biblical inerrantists in the 1969–74 period but remains ideologically diverse.[61]

Removing the more moderate SBC and LCMS from the evangelical picture yields a more accurate portrait of the relationship between

American fundamentalism and fertility. Thus the National Survey of Family Growth (NSFG), which considers the SBC as mainstream rather than evangelical, discovered that evangelical Protestant women aged thirty-five to forty-nine averaged 2.5 children per couple in 2002, against 2 for mainline Protestants and 1.5 for those without religion. These symmetrical figures should give us pause. Based on these rates, in a population evenly divided between seculars and evangelical Protestants, with no net conversions, the proportion of evangelicals would increase from 50 to 62.5 per cent in one generation. The following generation would be 73.5 per cent evangelical, rising to 99.4 per cent by the tenth generation, fulfilling Doug Phillips's 200-year plan. It sounds far-fetched until you realise that this is how the early Christians and contemporary Mormons did it.[62] In actual fact, demographic radicalism is concentrated among a small slice of evangelicals who average more than 2.5 children per couple. Women in mainstream evangelical churches may have the same number of children as those in other denominations, but the smaller, fast-growing ones such as independent Baptists, Foursquare Gospel or the Anderson Church of God have Mormon-like fertility.[63]

The same is true in other faith traditions. Increasingly, 'ethnic' fertility differences *between* religions such as Protestantism, Catholicism and Judaism are fading while those *within* each, based on the secularism–fundamentalist axis, are growing. This reflects the same trans-ethnic 'religious restructuring' logic that is changing American voting behaviour. Jews, for example, have the lowest total fertility rate of any American religious group, 1.43, which is well below the 2.08 average. Yet *Orthodox* Jewish fertility is above the national average, and *ultra-Orthodox* Jewish fertility is two to three times the average.[64] The Catholic fertility rate was once as legendary as the Catholic Democratic vote. Catholics had more kids because they were poor immigrants and because enough of them obeyed their priests' ban on contraception. Since the Vatican II reforms of 1968, however, fertility differences between Protestant and Catholic have disappeared. In the 2003 GSS, white Catholics had a total fertility rate of 2.11, compared with 2.13 for fundamentalist Protestants and 2.01 for moderate Protestants.

But as the culture gap narrowed, the fundamentalist one widened. During 1972–85, 44 per cent of American women between the ages of forty and sixty believed the Bible to be the word of God. They bore 3.3 children on average, compared with 2.86 for modernists who considered the Bible to be merely the 'inspired' word of God or a book of fables. This gave fundamentalists of all religions a 15 per cent fertility advantage over the rest. In the period 1986–95, the fundamentalist edge climbed to 21 per cent over modernists. In 1996–2006, it reached 25 per cent (2.33 vs. 1.86). Fundamentalist fertility actually fell over time, but that of modernists, affected more deeply by the second demographic transition, tumbled further. Likewise, women aged forty to sixty who believed that 'homosexuality is always wrong' enjoyed a fertility advantage over gay-tolerant women that climbed from 11 to 16 to 21 per cent over the same period. For abortion, the figures are 22, rising to 28 and now up to 38 per cent. That's worth a second look. In the period 1996–2006, the 46 per cent of American women aged forty to sixty who endorsed abortion if a woman did not want a larger family averaged just 1.69 children. Their traditionalist sisters who opposed granting abortion on these grounds bore 2.35 children during the same period. It doesn't sound like much, but if these distinctions are maintained over several generations, the impact will be nothing short of revolutionary.

We find identical fertility gaps between political conservatives and liberals. Every two years, the GSS asks whether Americans consider themselves liberal, moderate or conservative. In the 1970s, conservative women in their forties (assumed to have completed their fertility) had fewer children than liberal women, perhaps reflecting the higher class position of low-fertility fiscal conservatives. By the 1980s, however, conservative women had acquired a 13 per cent fertility edge over liberals, increasing to 19 per cent in the 1990s and 28 per cent in the 2000s. Part of this was due to the rise of the culture wars, which brought higher-fertility, low-status Americans into the conservative fold while pushing some low-fertility fiscal conservatives into the liberal camp. It also polarised the population: in the 1970s, less than half of Americans knew which of the two major parties was liberal and which conservative. Three decades later, two-thirds did.[65]

Polarisation has also recast the partisan fertility gap. Recall the strong relationship between white fertility in a state and the vote for Bush in 2004. This kind of advantage had been offset by the large families of

Democratic-leaning Hispanics, African-Americans and low-income whites. However, times are changing as ideology – which is increasingly linked to religious traditionalism – lines up with partisanship. Accordingly, in the 1972–84 period, Democratic women over the age of forty bore 2.85 children compared with 2.59 for Republican women, a ten-point lead. During 2001–6, however, Republican women pulled even with Democrats, and among women over seventeen, Republicans opened up a seven-point advantage. The American National Election Study, a separate survey which has run for over fifty years, confirms the GSS trends.

What does this tell us about the future? It's much trickier to project the size of attitudinal entities like traditionalists and modernists than concrete denominations. Catholic parents are more likely to have Catholic children than liberal parents are to have liberal children. Still, for the period 1948–2004, almost three-quarters of Americans whose mothers were Democrats became Democrats as adults, and ideology is now nearly as stable an attitude as partisanship. So, political demographers can credibly speak of liberal and conservative 'populations', each with their own demography.[66] Is the population of pro-life Americans like the population of Southern Baptists? Much depends on whether religious traditionalism resides at the congregational or individual levels. If the congregation is the key ideological unit, then we can expect traditionalist or modernist attitudes to be passed down from parent to child, reinforced by the community. If traditionalism varies within congregations those projections will be less accurate, but if parent-child trends in partisanship are any indication, most kids will inherit their parents' beliefs.

Assuming this, we find that the proportion of Americans who oppose abortion will rise from 60 per cent today to 64 per cent by mid-century. The proportion of biblical literalists will remain flat at about a third of the total. Finally, those who oppose homosexuality outright will decline modestly, from around 23 per cent today to 20 per cent in 2045. Might the young simply rebel against their parents? These projections already take into account the fact that young people are more liberal than their parents and more likely to 'switch' to a more liberal position in their early lives. But unless these age-related swings exceed those of the past forty years, they will not be enough to alter the results. Altogether, the evidence suggests that America will change little in the next three decades: traditionalists will gain some territory on abortion, tread water on literalism, but lose slightly on homosexuality.

More revolutionary is what will happen if current trends persist for several generations. The rule in demography is that migration has a bigger effect than fertility in the short term, but fertility counts for more over several generations. In the very long run, fertility differences are pivotal. Should traditionalists retain their current natal advantage, they will increase their share of the American population after 2050. Projections over a century are less accurate because migration and fertility are more likely to change. However, if current immigration and fertility trends persist, the United States will be almost three-quarters pro-life by 2100, up from 60 per cent today. Those opposing homosexuality will rise from just over 20 to 30 per cent of the total, reversing the liberal gains of the past few decades. This is entirely a demographic effect driven by traditionalist fertility and immigration.

Of course, large-scale attitude changes of the kind we saw in the 1960s could rapidly reverse traditionalist gains.[67] But major attitude shifts are less likely because the country is more polarised than it was in the 1960s and 70s. Since that time, ideology has increasingly come into alignment with party choice. Conservative Democrats and liberal Republicans are rarer. The proportion of political independents has also declined since the 1980s.[68] Residential segregation has risen too. Conservatives once lived next to liberals while Republicans rubbed shoulders with Democrats in their communities. Long commutes were uncommon. At election time, signs from both parties appeared on local lawns. Americans have always been a mobile people, but previous migration – think of the outflow of southern whites and blacks to the north – was economically driven, prompting cultural mixing.

Then things began to change. Since the 1970s, cultural preferences linked to partisanship have become more important in determining where people choose to live. Certain states tend to vote reliably 'red' (Republican) or 'blue' (Democratic), but this is even more intense at county level. Now that people are no longer solely driven by economic necessity, they are freer to select a locale on the basis of its religiosity and political colouring. In 2004, those leaving a Republican county were two and a half times more likely to settle in another Republican county than in a Democratic one. The proportion of Americans living in 'landslide' Republican or Democratic counties (where one party wins by at least twenty percentage points) has almost doubled since 1976. National elections have been very close in recent decades, but this is not the experience of the roughly half of Americans who inhabit landslide counties. These almost never change hands.[69]

As Americans increasingly inhabit ideological monocultures, majority norms dominate, reproducing local political cultures that cannot relate to the other half of the country. I was living in Arlington, a suburb of Boston, during the 2008 presidential election, and only once spotted that rare species, the McCain-Palin sign. Though a small minority had voted for Bush in 2004, their effect on the local political culture was effectively zero. Across the country, secular, multicultural, college-educated Democratic cities on the coasts contrast with highly religious Republican towns and provincial cities in the interior. The combination of ideological mobilisation, growing partisanship and residential segregation locks in political stasis. In a polarised country, few are converted to the other side of the culture war, so the game becomes a demographic one of growing your own.

Interfaith fundamentalism
America is 'browning', but racial diversity does not entail ideological diversity. Many make the common error of assuming that religious and racial conservatism go together just because liberals endorse secular diversity. In fact, cultural conservatives are divided: secular social conservatives lean towards white nationalism while religious conservatives tend to be liberal on questions of immigration. This is true of both the Christian Right leadership and the evangelical rank and file.[70] This makes sense because religion is a culture-transcending ideology while ethno-nationalism seeks to maintain ethnic boundaries. Some find it hard to believe that the Christian Right can act ecumenically and reach beyond its white evangelical base. Christian Right social movement organisations such as the Christian Coalition or Focus on the Family recruit few outside the white evangelical fold, and both Catholic and African-American Protestant leaders have spurned the Christian Right's advances

in many states. While such chasms seem too wide to bridge, the eclipse of racial differences symbolised by Obama's election may, paradoxically, enable the Christian Right to build bridges. As minorities gain in confidence and acculturate, they begin to privilege their social conservatism over their colour.[71]

The precedents are certainly there. Originally, the Christian Right struggled to unite Pentecostals and charismatics (largely Robertson supporters) with Southern Baptists (Falwell's base).[72] The logical next step, in post-Kennedy America, was to reach out to conservative Catholics. Soon after, the Christian Right courted Orthodox Jews, who responded eagerly to Republican school voucher proposals for private Jewish religious schooling. Republicans' faith-based initiatives and support for Israel didn't hurt either. As the Christian Coalition mission statement proclaimed, 'The Christian Coalition is leading a growing new alliance of evangelicals, Roman Catholics, Greek Orthodox, Jews, African-Americans and Hispanics who are working hard for common-sense legislation that will strengthen families.' Prior to 9/11, conservative Muslims readily meshed with this coalition. At a large conference of American Muslims in 2000, right-wing presidential hopeful Pat Buchanan enjoyed an easy rapport with his audience. 'American Muslims are sometimes described as Patriarchal-Authoritarian, believers in large families,' he began. 'It sounds to me very much like my own father.' As one former staffer recalls, this went over very well.[73]

This was not just empty talk. The Coalition has consistently opposed immigration-restrictionist measures such as California's Proposition 187 as well as proposals to curtail family reunification in favour of more selective immigration. As Robertson's successor, Ralph Reed, wrote, 'It was the religious values of our people that made this nation a refuge for the poor, the outcast, and the downtrodden. America has lifted its lamp beside the golden door of entry to all immigrant groups, particularly Jews, and to victims of persecution the world over. We are part of that legacy. Let me be clear: the Christian Coalition believes in a nation that is not officially Christian, Jewish, or Muslim.'[74]

The strategy worked. Mormons, though castigated as un-Christian by evangelicals, now eagerly back Christian Right measures. White Catholics have been moving rightward for decades and first played their part in conservative Christian politics in 2000 and 2004. In Oregon and Washington, for example, Catholic leaders worked with evangelicals to oppose assisted suicide laws. What of Latino Catholics, the fastest-growing group? Though they tend to vote Democratic (two-thirds backed Obama in 2008), many have simultaneously expressed their social conservatism in ballot initiatives such as California Propositions 22 (2000) and 8 (2008) opposing same-sex marriage. Hispanics supported Proposition 22 more strongly than non-Latinos and much more so than whites: while 31 per cent of California's Hispanics, 23 per cent of African-Americans and 17 per cent of Asians described themselves as part of the 'conservative Christian political movement', just 13 per cent of whites did. In Texas, Latinos and African-Americans gave similar support to initiatives opposing homosexual and abortion rights.[75]

The changes are not lost on scholars, who in the 1980s began to observe that religious denominations mattered less than the traditionalist-modernist or 'culture war' divide which cross-cuts them.[76] Charismatic congregations within supposedly mainline denominations were often highly conservative, while certain evangelical churches were in fact quite liberal. James Guth and his co-authors call this cross-cutting process 'religious restructuring'.[77] Religious restructuring helped to erode the walls between Catholic and Protestant, North and South, which defined American society between the 1830s and the mid 1960s. In effect, traditionalist Catholics have more in common with like-minded evangelicals and Jews than they do with their own moderate coreligionists.

The career of Billy Graham exemplifies the change: once a staunch opponent of the Vatican and John F. Kennedy, he came to embrace Catholics and they in turn made their peace with him. In the 1980s, Graham held a crusade at the Catholic Notre Dame University and met Pope John Paul II. The new mood transformed voting patterns. In 1960, 86 per cent of practising Catholics under the age of forty voted for the Catholic candidate John F. Kennedy, while less than 20 per cent of practising Protestants from the same age group did so. The sectarian divide was clear. Note the difference in 2004: once again, a Catholic (John Kerry) squared off against a Protestant opponent (Bush), but this time just 26 per cent of young practising Catholics voted for their coreligionist. This was actually a *lower* figure than the 31 per cent of practising Protestants from the same age group who voted for Kerry. In effect, committed Catholics and Protestants had become more attached to religious conservatism than to their own sect. The less religious, on the other hand, gravitated to the more liberal candidate regardless of sectarian affiliation.[78]

In four presidential contests between 1992 and 2004, the cross-cutting modernist-traditionalist divide sharpened while sectarian divisions faded. Consider the two-party vote (i.e. excluding independents). In 1992, 53 per cent of traditionalist Catholics backed the Republicans while 47 per cent chose the Democrats. The Republican share of the traditionalist Catholic vote rose steadily, from 54 per cent in 1996 to 61 per cent in 2000 to 74 per cent in 2004. On the other side of the ledger, the proportion of modernist Catholics supporting Bush in 2004 was a mere 38 per cent of the two-party vote. Ethno-religious categories still matter, with 90 per cent of blacks and 70 per cent of Jews opting for Kerry in 2004. Yet two-thirds of the young, fast-growing Orthodox Jewish population voted for Bush, while elderly Jews – few of whom are Orthodox – backed the Democrats to the tune of 90 per cent. Seculars of all stripes are as Democratic as Jews, and statistical analyses confirm that the modern-traditional axis matters more than religious affiliation in determining voting outcomes. In 2008, the growing Orthodox share of the Jewish population may have affected national trends for the first time: Jews were the only ethno-religious group to swing against Obama.[79]

Residential segregation poses no barrier to interfaith fundamentalism because of the decentralised nature of American parties and political movements. This facilitates the rise of non-partisan fronts uniting traditionalists of all races and religions against their secular opponents. Ballot initiatives such as California's Proposition 8, opposing gay marriage, are one medium through which this front expresses itself. Single-issue lobbies and political action committees (PACs) another. American parties, which tend to be big tents, are a further bridging force. The Republican Party will increasingly attempt to mobilise a diverse range of religious traditionalists, containing racial differences within diverse party structures. Both sides have done it. The Democratic Party, for example, managed the contradictions between southern white Protestants and northern Catholics for over a century. Each wing subsumed its narrow agenda in a common cause. Today, the party juggles the contradictions between its culturally liberal activists – teachers, feminists, secularists, gays and Jews – and its socially conservative base of working-class whites, blacks and Hispanics. The feel of the Democratic Party in San Francisco has little in common with its counterpart in blue-collar north-east Minnesota, but both can agree to mobilise against some aspect of Republican Party policy. Among Republicans, rural white evangelicals have a hard time sharing a convention dinner table with 'country club' conservatives, yet both make common cause against the Democrats. At its extreme, decentralisation leads to a 'franchise' model of party organisation, where local branches may hold opposing views on many issues, but subscribe to the same party brand.[80]

Interfaith fundamentalism has even vaulted into the international arena. The Family First Foundation (FFF), an alliance of Mormon, Catholic and evangelical activists linked to a smattering of Jewish and Muslim allies, is taking the fight against abortion and family planning to the UN and the European Union. Allan Carlson is a leading light at the FFF, and also co-founder of the World Congress of Families (WCF), which holds international, interfaith conferences to push a traditional values agenda. At its summits, evangelical Christians rub shoulders with dignitaries from the Vatican and conservative Islamists. WCF co-founder Richard Wilkins has linked hands with Muslim fundamentalists to build the Doha International Institute for Family Studies and Development in Qatar. One of his principal contacts was Sheikh Yusuf al-Qaradawi, Dean of the College of Shariah and Islamic Studies in Qatar and host of a popular Islamist talk show on Al-Jazeera. This is the same al-Qaradawi who caused a storm of controversy on a visit to Britain when he endorsed executing sodomites and approved of wife-beating, albeit as a 'last resort'.[81]

Muslim fundamentalists have been extremely receptive to Christian Right overtures, though 9/11 forced some of these links into the background. In 1994, Iranian deputy foreign minister Mohammed Hashemi Rafsanjani, in talks with the Vatican, enthusiastically declared that 'The future war is between the religious and the materialists. Collaboration between religious governments in support of outlawing abortion is a fine beginning.' Allan Carlson returns the favour, citing the mutual values of

Christian and Muslim fundamentalists who 'share a common foe, which is a radical secular individualism that has turned against a common value system resting on the Abrahamic traditions'. Another champion of the movement is Austin Ruse, whose Catholic Family and Human Rights Institute (C-FAM) lobbies the UN and the EU. Ruse's group also engages in direct action, as when C-FAM sent representatives dressed as monks to pray for the souls of feminist NGO workers. In 2000, Ruse sent around a memo at the UN calling for representatives of the Abrahamic faiths to 'rise up together' against feminism. He waxes optimistically about the global pro-family movement as the most important international development since the Reformation and promises that his group will make 'mayhem' among the women's rights and family planning advocates of the UN.[82]

An early fruit of such efforts was the 'Global Gag Rule' for American aid. First tabled under the Reagan administration in 1984, the policy cut off aid to any foreign organisation which used funds – whether American or otherwise – to perform abortions or even provide information to women about abortion. This implicated the many family planning clinics which advised on abortion, contraception and reproductive health, with dire consequences. The policy rapidly turned into a political football: abandoned by Clinton in 1993, reinstated with vigour by Bush in 2001 and dropped once more by Obama in 2008. When the political winds blew in their favour, evangelical pro-family activists harassed American family planning officials, engineering the exit of career bureaucrats such as Richard Benedick, long-time coordinator for Population Affairs at the State Department. The American Life Lobby, one militant anti-abortion group, went so far as to pen a memo to Muslim delegates at a family planning conference entitled 'Special Warning to all Islamic Pro-Lifers: These men [USAID Population delegates] are dangerous to your health.' Under Reagan and Bush, pro-life groups received generous funding from USAID to run global anti-abortion conferences and promote abstinence over contraception in the fight against AIDS. Reagan and especially Bush realised that packing delegations with evangelical pro-life activists was an easy way to placate the Christian Right without advancing the CR's more contentious domestic agenda.[83]

American women could afford to ignore a few million dollars

switched from one foreign aid track to another, since their abortion rights under Roe *v.* Wade remained untouched. Overseas it was a different story: the policy change reverberated for years, producing fatal results. As the largest donor to family planning and women's reproductive health clinics in the developing world, USAID affects the lives of millions. The withdrawal of US funds to two major organisations, International Planned Parenthood Federation (IPPF) and the Marie Stopes Foundation, was devastating since they form the backbone of the women's reproductive health infrastructure of many Third World countries. IPPF and Marie Stopes are mainly in the family planning business, but also provide counselling and assistance to women about safe abortion in countries where abortion is legal. This reduces the number of unsafe abortions in developing countries, which currently kill approximately 70,000 women a year. In addition, IPPF and Marie Stopes address the maternal health issues which cause half a million women annually to die in childbirth.

Meanwhile, the Christian Right worked with the Vatican and Muslim allies to advance a pro-life agenda. The Vatican was especially active in persuading Muslim delegates not to attend the UN Conference on Population and Development at Cairo in 1994. At a follow-up UN conference in Bangkok in 2002, Bush's Assistant Secretary of State, Arthur E. Dewey, declared that his country 'supports the sanctity of life from conception to natural death ... [T]here has been a concerted effort to create a gulf by pushing the United States to violate its principle and accept language that promotes abortion. We have been asked to reaffirm the entirety of the ICPD [1994 Cairo conference] ... even though we have repeatedly stated that to do so would constitute endorsement of abortion.' The pro-life American delegation tried to strong-arm Asian delegates to water down the 1994 provisions, but were unsuccessful. They achieved more foreign policy success in the Muslim world – where alliances were forged with Iran and Sudan – as well as in Latin America. In 2004, New Jersey Congressman Chris Smith faxed a letter to Uruguay, co-signed by other pro-life congressmen attempting to forestall that country's legalisation of abortion. In Nicaragua and El Salvador, the Christian Right and the Vatican supported successful anti-abortion campaigns.[84]

These Central American countries' policies do not permit abortion, even to save the mother's life. As Michelle Goldberg relates:

> Eighteen year-old Jazmina Bojorge, already the mother of a four-year-old boy, was five months pregnant when she arrived at Managua's Fernando Velez Paiz hospital, and she'd started having contractions. She was miscarrying, and under the circumstances the doctors should have given her a drug to speed the process. [But] ... Just a week earlier, Nicaragua's Asamblea Nacional voted to ban all abortions, even those meant to save a woman's life. In Bojorge's case, an ultrasound showed that her fetus was alive, and her doctors, ignoring medical protocols in order to try to rescue the pregnancy, gave Bojorge a drug to stop her contractions. She was kept on the medicine until tests a day later showed the fetus had died at which point she was allowed to deliver. By then, though, her placenta had detached and her uterus had filled with blood. She went into shock and died.

These abortion policies were in accord with Vatican policy under Pope John Paul II, as when he posthumously canonised Italian paediatrician Gianna Beretta Molla, a mother of three who died when she refused an operation to remove a tumor in her uterus that would have killed the fetus but saved her life.[85]

The global pro-family movement has succeeded in stanching the advance of women's rights, but at least women's rights advocates can count on a vociferous feminist lobby. The same cannot be said for family planning programmes. Radical feminists, marching in the name of women's 'reproductive rights' and Third World solidarity, urged the UN to empower women to have as many children as they desire rather than 'push' family planning. Birth control, claimed radicals like Bella Bazug and her Women's Environment and Development Organization (WEDO), smacks of white elites forcing sterilisation on the black and brown masses. Feminist icon Germaine Greer, hardly the steadiest compass on such matters, intoned against Western imperialist contraception, defending the chador, chastity and traditional motherhood. This was music to the ears of many on the anti-colonial left and traditionalist right in the developing world, some of whom continue to see family planning as a Western imperialist plot to reduce non-white growth. It also dignified the cheap arguments of radicals who raised the spectre of Indian sterilisation, the Chinese 'One Child' policy and Nazi eugenics.

Caught in the crossfire of both religious fundamentalists and radical multicultural feminists, family planning languished.[86] Between 1995 and 2003, for instance, American policies caused international support for family planning to plummet from 560 to 460 million dollars. Clinics closed and the supply of contraceptives, which had been distributed by the clinics, contracted. In Kenya, to take one example, the proportion of unwanted births doubled from 11 to 21 per cent, stalling its once-promising demographic transition. In Ethiopia, the number of unsafe abortions rose. In Uganda, American pressure forced the country to abandon its successful, contraception-driven campaign against HIV. In many countries, the family planning infrastructure was inferior to what existed in the 1970s. [87]

It is certainly the case that moderate feminists won out at Cairo in 1994 over fundamentalists and radical feminists. Yet even moderate feminists, in shifting the UN's emphasis from family planning to 'reproductive rights', diverted attention and resources away from contraception. Though poor women may initially wish for large families, there is also a societal imperative to champion (not coerce) contraceptive practices which can reduce developing-world population growth. Excess population growth in developing regions not only condemns millions to lives of suffering and death, but generates 'youth bulges' which delay democratisation and development and increase the incidence of violent conflict. Such intransigence will add hundreds of millions of people to countries least equipped to feed them. How, in 2050, will the 180 million in both Congo and Ethiopia, and the 127 million in Uganda, fend for themselves? Shifts in the American culture wars therefore spell life and death for many in the developing world.[88]

Christian fundamentalist violence

Religious terrorism is much less common among American Christian fundamentalists than it is among their Middle Eastern Islamist counterparts, but is far from absent. Much pivots around the anti-abortion crusade. Michael Bray, pastor of a radical breakaway Lutheran church and publisher of the militant *Capitol Area Christian News*, regularly harangued the Clinton administration on homosexuality, abuse of power and abortion. He was also involved in seven attacks on abortion clinics in the Middle Atlantic region. On 29 July 1994, this reached tragic proportions when Bray's friend Paul Hill killed abortion doctor John Britton and his volunteer escort James Barrett as they drove up to the Ladies Center, a clinic in Pensacola, Florida. Many radical anti-abortion activists are inspired by Dominion theology, notably the Reconstructionism espoused by R. J. Rushdoony and Gary North. North's quibble with Hill and Bray is not simply that they had committed murder. Indeed, North places his ideal of theocracy above loyalty to an American government he views as corrupt. Rather, North believed that Bray and Hill had not obtained sufficient 'covenantal authority' to act on God's behalf.

Another story in this saga concerns abortion doctor George Tiller. Tiller was gunned down by another member of the Bray circle, Shelly Shannon, as he drove away from his clinic in Wichita, Kansas, in 1993. Tiller survived the attack, but was seriously wounded.[89] Sadly, this was not the end of the story. On 31 May 2009, Tiller, the *bête noire* of the anti-abortion movement, was shot in the head by Scott Roeder at point-blank range in Reformation Lutheran Church in Wichita, where he was serving as an usher. Roeder was an anti-abortion militant who subscribed to a radical pro-life newsletter advocating 'justifiable homicide'. Tiller's murder was roundly condemned by mainstream pro-life advocates such as the Reverend David Osteen, but there were exceptions. Randall Terry of the mainstream anti-abortion group Operation Rescue, for instance, merely expressed regret that he had not converted Tiller to Christ before he was shot.

Pro-life radicals, meanwhile, were jubilant, reflecting a significant reservoir of sympathy for the murderer. 'If you honestly believe abortion is the murder of helpless children,' proclaimed columnist Jacob Sullum, 'it's hard to see why using deadly force against those who carry it out is immoral, especially since the government refuses to act.' Southern Baptist minister and radio host Wiley Drake simply quipped, 'I am glad that he is dead.' Altogether, anti-abortion terrorists have killed nine people since 1993, and are responsible for between 10,000 and 15,000 violent incidents a year. These range from assaults and anthrax attacks to threatening phone calls and vandalism.[90]

The dawn of liberal America?

On 5 November 2008, Barack Obama defeated John McCain to become the first African-American president of the United States. Two-thirds of Latinos and those under thirty plumped for Obama. A highly educated, urbane young senator with a liberal voting record, Obama seemed to represent a new chapter in American history; a tipping point when young, highly educated, multicultural 'metro' America triumphed over the aging white Christian 'retro' America of George W. Bush's Republicans. Non-white immigrants and secular voters, both of whom are disproportionately young and Democratic, seemed to symbolise the new order. Liberal writers now look forward to the day when the Democrats can not only win, but do so on an openly liberal platform. Chris Bowers of *The Nation* triumphantly celebrated the 'End of Bubba dominance' as swing voters ceased to be dominated by socially conservative blue-collar whites. From 2008 on, he remarked, 'liberal elite' Democratic candidates like Obama can succeed by courting the young, non-white and non-religious. Political demographer Ruy Texeira added that Hispanics, professionals, youth, non-traditional families and 'urbanizing suburbanites' – all currently Democratic leaning – will replace white working-class voters in the electorate.[91]

The Christian Right seemed to crumple along with Bush, their Great White Hope. Since the late 1990s, the Christian Right's surge has abated. Many of the policy gains of its local 'stealth' campaigns and ballot initiatives were repealed or defeated in the courts. Even in its southern heartland, the Christian Right lost control of school boards and failed to institute school prayer, teach Creationism and restrict abortion. Newly mobilised anti-fundamentalist Democrats and outraged socially liberal 'country club' Republicans forced the Christian Right to moderate its policy agenda in the late 1990s. Its attempt to influence the Republican Party's presidential nomination in 2000 was partially successful, in that George W. Bush proved more willing to tip his hat to the Christian Right than previous presidents. However, Bush's fundamentalism was largely symbolic, a far cry from Pat Robertson's. Bush prioritised economic and foreign policy over cultural issues during both his terms of office. Even if he had been inclined to push the Christian Coalition's agenda, Bush faced stiff opposition from both Democrats and moderate Republicans in Congress. As a consequence, religious initiatives languished under his presidency. Even the Bush Supreme Court, containing seven Republican nominees, turned out to be more interested in strictly interpreting the secular constitution than advancing Christian Right aims.[92] To top it all off, in 2008, the California and Connecticut supreme courts ruled in favour of same-sex marriage.

Nevertheless, behind the headlines, only the most optimistic secularist can deny that religion is a bigger presence in the American public square than it was a quarter century ago. And this at a time when Europe has moved in the sharply secular direction that St Simon, Marx and their heirs predicted. Today, no candidate for the Republican Party can be nominated in a presidential or state primary without acknowledging the Christian Right and at least symbolically adopting part of its platform. Pro-choice candidates have no chance of success. In all but a handful of states, Christian Right activists have established themselves as a faction – sometimes the dominant faction – within the Republican Party. This is not only true of the South but also of Midwestern states like Michigan or Minnesota and liberal coastal ones like California and Maine. Though most Christian policy gains have failed to materialise, their efforts have changed the symbolic nature of politics. The situation in Florida, a swing state, is typical: 'Wherever one now looks in Florida,' remark two scholars of the Christian Right's rise in the Sunshine State, 'religious phrasing and concerns permeate the political environment.'[93]

Though Democratic candidates need not run the gauntlet of the Christian Right, they must demonstrate their personal piety before being pronounced electable. After all, half the population would not vote for an atheist. Vermont's secular Howard Dean was described by the left-leaning *New Republic* as having a 'religion problem' which helped sink his Democratic presidential bid. John Kerry, though a nominal Catholic, was blasted by conservative Catholic publications for his liberal views on abortion and other religious issues, swaying Catholic swing voters and dealing a fatal blow to his candidacy. Barack Obama likewise had to go out of his way to trumpet his Christian faith in the face of rumours that he was Muslim, or worse, a faithless academic. His selection of Rick Warren, pastor of the giant Saddleback megachurch in California, to deliver his invocation angered gay and liberal groups, but was viewed as a political necessity. Indeed, it is unlikely that deist presidents like Thomas Jefferson or George Washington would pass muster with many of today's voters.

As is so often the case, the nation's future is a vista that can be glimpsed from Mount California. In 2008, Barack Obama soundly won the state, thumping McCain 61 per cent to 39 per cent in popular votes. But even in this Democratic bastion, Obama had to share the winner's podium with the Christian Right, which successfully sponsored a ballot initiative, Proposition 8, seeking to overturn the California Supreme Court's same-sex marriage law. The amendment passed 53–47 on the strength of a rainbow coalition of white evangelicals and traditionalist white Catholics, African-Americans and Latinos. In an impressive display of interfaith mobilisation, Prop 8 proponents featured Mexican television star José Eduardo Verástegui in Spanish-language commercials urging Latinos to support the measure. The California Catholic Church also backed Prop 8. Among voters, Californian whites proved the most liberal, with a clear majority in exit polls opposing the measure. However, Latinos split and a solid majority of African-Americans supported Prop 8, enabling it to pass. In the words of African-American student Christopher Miracle of Oakland, 'Look at the Bible': marriage 'is not [between] a man and a man'.[94]

In Florida, which also went for Obama, opponents of same-sex marriage triumphed 63–37, and a similar measure passed 56–44 in Arizona. Class divisions prevent the Republican Party from mobilising this diverse conservative coalition at election time, but lightning-rod initiatives on 'culture war' themes are capable of doing so. Unencumbered by Republican economic elitism, the Religious Right may become adept at honing an ecumenical, post-ethnic religious message. The new suburban megachurches may lead the way. Martin Luther King once observed that eleven o'clock on Sunday morning is the most segregated hour in America. This remains true, but a glance inside non-denominational megachurches such as Lakewood in Houston shows them to be far more polyglot than traditional ones. Asian and Latino Protestants also help breach racial boundaries: 90 per cent of the Yale chapter of the Campus Crusade for Christ is now of Asian descent.[95] Evangelical cooperation with conservative Latino Catholics on issues such as abortion, same-sex marriage and assisted suicide in diverse states like Texas and California is surely a portent of things to come.

High evangelical fertility rates more than compensated for losses to liberal Protestant sects during the twentieth century. In recent decades, white secularism has surged, but Latino and Asian religious immigration has taken up the slack, keeping secularism at bay. Across denominations, the fertility advantage of religious fundamentalists of all colours is significant and growing. After 2020, their demographic weight will begin to tip the balance in the culture wars towards the conservative side, ramping up pressure on hot-button issues such as abortion. By the end of the century, three quarters of America may be pro-life. Their activism will leap over the borders of the 'Redeemer Nation' to evangelise the world. Already, the rise of the World Congress of Families has launched a global Religious Right, its arms stretching across the bloody battle lines of the War on Terror to embrace the entire Abrahamic family.

4

THE DEMOGRAPHY
OF ISLAMISM IN THE
MUSLIM WORLD

In the Western world and Israel, religious conservatives are in the minority. Fundamentalists may score occasional policy successes, but for the most part they do not affect the lives of those who don't share their beliefs. They cannot, as yet, challenge the secular mainstream. On the other hand, religious fundamentalism now dominates the public culture in a wide range of Islamic countries. While Islamists only hold power in Sudan, Iran and parts of Somalia and Pakistan, they have successfully set the tone of the mass culture and limited the freedom of seculars and minorities.

Most Westerners, if forced to trade places with their Abrahamic cousins in much of the Muslim world, would find life intolerable. There, all must live with restrictions on freedom of expression and consumption, tip their cap to religion in debate and law, and obey the dictates of a puritanical moral code. Life is particularly gruelling for women, religious minorities, converts and gays, who have limited rights and often suffer persecution or worse. Some argue that fundamentalism is merely another wonderful colour in the multicultural rainbow of liberal society. In the West, they are largely correct, but the argument only holds as long as fundamentalists do not become a plurality or a majority that can restrict the liberties of others. If they do, then we need look no further than vast reaches of the Muslim world to see what we are in for.

The rise of fundamentalism in the Muslim world is a fait accompli.

Its ascent is primarily a social and political phenomenon, but could not have taken place without the demographic boost provided by a population explosion among poor, pious Muslims – who gravitated to fundamentalism when they moved to the cities. They increased because they were poor and rural, not because they were religious, but the net result was the same. This represents an amplified version of the population boom of the twentieth-century American South, which eventually brought fundamentalist Protestantism into the Oval Office. Had it not been for the deluge of religious demography, secular nationalists in major Muslim cities could have altered the self-consciousness of the Muslim masses. This is precisely what took place in Germany and Italy in the half-century after the 1860s when nationalists vanquished the Catholic anti-nationalism of the peasantry. Finally, even if the tide of religious conservatism can somehow be turned, as it may in Iran, this could prove a Sisyphean quest: the resulting pluralism creates conditions which favour the demographic re-emergence of fundamentalism.

The demography of the Muslim world

As in the United States, fundamentalists in the Muslim world have larger families than others. Yet the Muslim world is only part-way through its demographic transition. Thus religious pronatalism and fundamentalist population growth is present only in modern contexts where the second demographic transition has begun; in other words, in places where the shift from material to cultural determinants of fertility has taken place because large numbers of children have become more a burden than a benefit, infant mortality has been conquered and contraception is freely available. The size of the fundamentalist fertility premium is already as big or bigger in the Muslim world than in the US, but considerably smaller than in Israel or among endogenous growth sects like the Amish.

As in the US, the rural poor have inadvertently given religion a boost. As previously noted, pious Muslims, like twentieth-century American Southern Baptists, expanded in numbers because they were disproportionately rural and poor, not because they were religious. But the outcome is the same: religious populations have gained ground against seculars and moderates. In addition, in contrast to Christian and Jewish countries, Islamists in much of the Muslim world have been able to influence state population policies, thereby delaying the implementation of family planning and female emancipation. This has prolonged the population explosion in the more religious Muslim countries, increasing their share of world population. One day, the Salafists, with their high birth rates and relative isolation, may emerge as the Haredim of the Muslim world, though we currently lack the data to be certain. For the most part, however, it is the modest but significant fertility premium wielded by supporters of sharia law and an Islamic state – compounded over generations – which will tilt the balance in the Muslim world away from more moderate voices.

The countryside comes to town

The great migration of the pious masses from the countryside into urban politics is the big demographic story behind the Islamist crescendo. It originated in declining infant mortality, which caused rural population explosion, pushing surplus young people into the disorderly cities where their traditional Muslim worldview made them ripe for fundamentalism. Most people get religion the old-fashioned way: they inherit it. In most Muslim states, secular ideas failed to dent the consciousness of the youth bulge population which swelled the teeming slums of Muslim cities and swept to political prominence.

This happened all over the Muslim world. As a result of this population boom, the Muslim proportion of the world's population surged from 15 per cent in 1970 to nearly 20 per cent by 2000 and is projected to reach 23 per cent by 2025. In the same period, Christianity's world share remained flat at around 34 per cent, where it is predicted to stay for the next two decades. The natural increase of Muslims was nearly *double* that of Christianity, allowing it to outpace Christianity despite the fact that Christianity trumped Islam 3:1 in the market for converts.[1] The Arab world's population alone has grown from 80 million to 320 million in the past fifty years and half its population is under twenty. In Pakistan, 40 per cent of the population is under fourteen. Total fertility rates in Somalia, Afghanistan, Yemen and the Palestinian Territories remain above five children per woman.[2]

At first glance, Muslims seem more resistant to family planning than others. Research on Muslim fertility in India, for instance, concludes that

Indian Muslims have been more reluctant to adopt contraception and family planning than Hindus or Christians, despite equal access. Muslims tend to have an especially large fertility advantage when they are in the minority. In Europe, India, Thailand, Russia, China and the Philippines, the Muslim fertility advantage is greatest. This is particularly true of zones of conflict like Israel–Palestine. One could argue that minorities in general, not merely Muslim ones, tend to have higher fertility rates than majorities. Yet in Muslim-majority Indonesia and Malaysia, Muslims outbirth most Hindu, Christian and Chinese minorities, while in the Arab world, Muslim fertility is higher than that of the minority Christians and Druze. Even in Europe, Bosnia and Albania, the only Muslim-majority regions, had the highest fertility on the continent until very recently.[3]

Even so, these trends largely reflect economic backwardness: where Muslims are better off or more urbanised than non-Muslims, as in much of sub-Saharan Africa, their fertility rates are lower than average. Thus we should expect Muslim fertility to converge with non-Muslim fertility over time, just as Catholic and Protestant fertility drew together in the West. Furthermore, Islamic doctrine is less pronatalist than current Muslim fertility rates suggest. On marriage, the Qur'an is unambiguous, decreeing that only 'those of you who can support a wife and household should marry'. Those who cannot 'should take to fasting which is a means of tempering sexual desires'. The Qur'an also permits men to take up to four wives. Women are directed to breastfeed for two years. Late marriage, polygamy and lactation all reduce fertility.

Qur'anic teachings in the key areas of contraception, family planning and abortion reinforce this position and show that Islamic doctrine is much more flexible than conservative Christianity. The Qur'an does not proscribe birth control or abortion, and a *hadith* (an oral tradition about the Prophet's life) records that the Prophet approved of *azl*, or male birth control. Most Islamic jurists, including the austere Hanbalis, accept birth control for this reason. This extends to abortion. The Qur'an sees life forming through a five-stage process. A *hadith* of the Prophet is unequivocal: 'All of us have been kept as a drop of seed ... for forty days. Then for another forty days it remains in the form of a clot of blood. Then another forty days it remains as a lump of flesh. Then an angel is sent to the foetus who blows spirit [life] into it.' This does not mean there is perfect consensus. Hanbalis permit abortion only up to forty days, and the Twelver Shias not at all. Still, the overwhelming view of Muslim theologians is that abortion is permissible within 120 days. No wonder the Pope and his Christian Right allies experienced difficulty winning Islamists to the pro-life cause at UN population conferences.[4]

While Islamic teachings generally support family planning, they are more restrictive when it comes to women's autonomy. Like the Bible, the Qur'an encourages women to marry and glorifies motherhood. Women's education and employment are the single greatest drivers of fertility decline, but female empowerment loosens the grip of husbands over wives. This means Islam can be invoked by patriarchal fundamentalists to resist female education and work, keeping fertility high.[5] The Qur'an also permits women to marry provided they are of 'sound judgement', and no clear age is spelled out. The fact that the permissible age of marriage for women has been as low as nine in some Muslim countries tends to raise fertility rates. In addition, the Qur'an follows the Bible in actively promoting fertility. 'Marry women who are loving and very prolific,' it tells men, 'for I shall outnumber the peoples by you.' This is backed up by a *hadith* which states that on the day of Resurrection, the Prophet will be proud if his community outnumbers others, thus he admonishes his followers to reproduce and increase in number.[6]

Exploiting the openness of Islamic teachings, government-appointed ulama (clergy) have been able to convincingly provide the fatwas necessary to facilitate family planning in nearly all Muslim countries. This has been given the imprimatur of a number of Islamic family planning conferences, beginning with the Rabat conference of 1971 and including a high-profile 1990 convention in Indonesia sponsored by al-Azhar University.[7] More recently, ninety delegates from almost every school of Islamic thought attended a three-day 'International Ulama Conference on Population and Development' held in the Pakistani capital Islamabad in 2005. The consensus, drawing on the examples of Tunisia, Iran, Indonesia and other low-fertility Muslim countries, was that family planning was in harmony with the tenets of Islam.[8]

There is mounting evidence that Muslim fertility is heading the way of once-famous Catholic fecundity. Iran, Algeria, Lebanon, Tunisia and several Muslim Central Asian, Balkan and Caucasian countries now have below-replacement fertility rates, part of a longer-term demographic transition which emerged in the late twentieth century.[9] Libya, Egypt, Turkey and Indonesia are moving in the same direction. Overall, Muslim average total fertility rates were in the 6–7.5 range in the 1960s and have fallen to about half that level today. With a few exceptions, Muslim Asia and the Middle East/North Africa region has lower fertility than sub-Saharan Africa, and is moving smartly through its demographic transition.[10] The Muslim countries which remain ultra-fertile tend to be in impoverished sub-Saharan Africa, where Muslim and non-Muslim countries share the same high birth rates.

Among the many devout Muslim societies that have embraced family planning, none is more striking than Iran. In the 1960s and 70s, the Shah pursued a westernisation policy focused on getting women outside the home into education and work, and making contraception widely available. Fertility began to decline. Then came the Iranian Revolution of 1979. The mullahs derided family planning clinics as an imperialist plot against Islam and closed them; the sexes were segregated and women's work disparaged. The regime lowered the age of marriage from fourteen to nine, and praised the traditional woman's role as mother. The Iran–Iraq war in the 1980s added steam to the regime's emphasis on higher fertility. Unsurprisingly, fertility rates, which had dropped from 7.7 to 6.3 children per woman between 1966 and 1976, rebounded to around 7 in a few short years after the Revolution.[11] Then the unthinkable occurred. As the population approached 60 million and the burdens of a young population tugged at the seams of the state budget, religion bent to accommodate secular demands. 'Secular' voices came from all directions: up from the street and down from policymakers and intellectuals. These actors lobbied the religious authorities to act. Their efforts were smoothed by the content of Islamic texts, which do not forbid contraception and are unclear on abortion. A fatwa was obtained from a prominent cleric, and within a very short space of time in the late 1980s, family policy in Iran went full circle, from pronatalism to planning:

> The religious authorities saw as their first and primary task to dispel

the myth that the population debate originated in modern Western society. Reviewing debates on the permissibility of fertility control and sponsoring research and republication of medieval Islamic works on population and contraception, they established that concern about population had preoccupied Muslim scholars long before it was discussed in the West. Thus, the authorities were able to celebrate Iran's Islamic heritage, to promote family planning, and to reinforce their independence from the West.[12]

Khomeini's regime poured funds into reopening clinics and training an army of local women as family planning advisors and practitioners. Fertility plummeted from 6 to 2 children per woman in under two decades. Today, Iranian TFR is just 1.71, well below replacement level. Women continue to marry early, in accordance with Islamic law, but combine this with early and effective use of contraception.[13]

Not all were so enlightened. Hardline factions within the regime such as Ayatollah Tehrani battled these developments tooth and nail, airing their complaints in the semi-official *Jumhuri Islami* newspaper.[14] Iranian president Mahmoud Ahmadinejad remains distinctly displeased with the turn of events. Criticising Iran's below-replacement fertility rate, he wants Iran's population to grow from its current 70 million to 120 million. Along the way, he favours scaling back women's participation in the labour force to concentrate on reproduction. 'I am against saying that two children [per woman] are enough,' thundered Ahmadinejad. 'Our country has a lot of capacity. It has the capacity for many children to grow in it. It even has the capacity for 120 million people. Westerners have got problems. Because their population growth is negative, they are worried and fear that if our population increases, we will triumph over them.' Unfortunately for this maverick, Ahmadinejad faces an established opposition, backed by a majority of young Iranians and clerics who can point to Khomeini's fatwas.[15] The repeated victory of reformist candidates such as Mohammad Khatami and Mir-Hossein Mousavi, who sparked the 'green revolution' in June 2009, highlight the strength of popular support that must be overcome for pronatalism to turn back the clock of Iranian policy.

Khomeini's change of heart may be the exception that proves the rule, however. In other parts of the world, conservative Islamists clamour for population growth. In Sunni societies, they continue to castigate family planning. Pakistan is a prime example. There, Abu Ala Mawdudi, founder of the Islamist Jamaat-e-Islami (JI) Party, in his *The Birth Control* (1937) savaged contraception as a Western plot against Islam. Family planning, he maintained, would introduce Western promiscuity, sexually transmitted diseases and women's liberation to Muslim lands. Mawdudi's opposition to abortion derives from a Qur'anic verse which instructs families not to kill children during times of want. He also quotes verses and *hadith*s extolling the virtue of children and marriage. Taking their cue from him, fundamentalists have attacked Pakistan's family planning policies as a Western import linked to decadence, painting it as an imperialist attempt to control Islam. In stark contrast to Iran, no Islamist scholars have come out in support of family planning. In the words of Abdul Hakim, 'the family planning programme in Pakistan works under a severe threat from religiosity ... people are afraid lest they are considered irreligious for advocating family planning ... whereas in Indonesia and Bangladesh the approach has been to convince religious leaders of the importance of this [family planning] programme and its compatibility with religion.' [16]

The contrast between Pakistan and poorer Bangladesh is stark. Pakistan's religious authorities resisted family planning far longer than their counterparts in Bangladesh, who are much less influenced by Mawdudi and the fundamentalist theology of the Deobandis. [17] There was also a close link between Mawdudi and Pakistani military ruler Zia ul-Haq. Zia admired Mawdudi, and co-opted Mawdudi's JI into his administration. Mawdudi was a willing partner, and Zia's long reign between 1977 and 1988 oversaw the progressive implementation of sharia in Pakistan. Nourished by the fat of American aid in support of the Afghan mujahidin, Zia gave the Salafists a free hand in social policy and diverted funds from social services to Deobandi madrasas. The result was sharia in all its glory: education and the economy were Islamised and a new Islamic penal code became law. This included the usual raft of medieval punishments known as *hudud*, such as cutting off the limbs of thieves, stoning women for adultery and whipping drinkers of alcoholic beverages. Though Zia was assassinated in 1988, his Islamisation policies rolled on

– driven by popular demand from Salafists, the devout middle class and Islamised rural migrants.[18]

After 1999, General Pervez Musharraf began to confront the country's Islamists on several fronts. One was family planning. Pakistan's official clerics now offer family planning information at mosques, and agree that Muslim texts support contraception. But they do so against the grain of a powerful Islamist opposition which commands considerable popular support, especially in ethnically Baluchi and Pashtun areas of western Pakistan. Many Pakistani women believe that contraception contravenes Islam, and the rate of contraceptive take-up is just 34 per cent.[19] Pakistan's TFR has fallen in the past two decades and now hovers around four children per woman, but the country's late start in the process means that Pakistan's projected population will be many millions higher than if it had adopted a Bangladeshi-style programme in the 1970s.[20] This will greatly increase child poverty and misery, placing enormous pressure on the country's economy and health-care infrastructure while endangering its fragile political stability.

Next door in Afghanistan, and in north-west Pakistan's tribal areas, local religious leaders exercise enormous influence over people's perceptions of contraception. In Taliban-dominated southern Afghanistan, locals tend to accept the prohibitionist views of their conservative imams.[21] Tragically, Taliban insurgents have taken Islamist opposition to family planning to new heights, or rather depths. A favoured tactic is to assassinate clinicians. Threats, kidnappings and assassinations have brought family planning to its knees in disputed areas. After murdering a female health-care worker in Kandahar, Taliban insurgents wrote to her employer. 'We took up arms against the Infidels in order to bring Islamic law to this land,' they raged in a letter bearing the seal of the Taliban military council. 'But you people are supporting our enemies, the enemies of Islam and Muslims ... Personnel were trained to distribute family planning pills. The aim of this project is to persuade the young girls to commit adultery.'[22]

Occasionally such views dovetail with the secular imperatives of nationalists. Palestinian nationalism has long been pronatalist, with its politicians, journalists and poets singing the praises of their 'demographic weapon' against Israel.[23] Between 1968 and 1995, Palestinian fertility in

Gaza remained flat at around 7.5 children per woman – an astoundingly high level for such an educated population – while it declined by two children to around 5.5 in the West Bank. Since 1995, the respective figures have dropped to 5.2 and 3.3, though these reproduction rates are still sufficient to fuel enormous population growth in one of the most densely populated places on earth. Though both secular and Islamist Palestinians extol the virtues of pronatalism, it is noteworthy that fertility rates are much higher in Gaza, a Hamas bastion and stronghold of the Islamist-inspired second intifada, than in the secular, Fatah-controlled West Bank.[24]

One finds shades of Hamas's pronatalism among radical Islamist factions in virtually all Muslim states, who excoriate the government for endorsing family planning. The story in many Sunni societies is thus a variation on the Pakistani theme. In Saudi Arabia and Iraq, contraception was illegal until the 1990s and throughout most of the Arab world less than half of couples use contraceptive methods.[25] Nationalism is partly to blame. Gulf oil states such as Saudi Arabia, Oman and Kuwait encouraged population growth to limit their reliance on foreign workers. Poorer Arab states such as Egypt, Syria and Jordan believed that their excess population could be exported to the Gulf to provide remittances back home. These two logics are at odds and depend on high oil prices. In the 1980s and 90s, prices fell, putting downward pressure on people's incomes. The high costs of pronatalist policies forced regimes to face their population problem.

Nevertheless, Islamist opposition foreclosed the birth control option until population pressure became too great to bear. In Egypt, private mosques fought the official ulama's endorsement of contraception. In Syria and Jordan, population policy was delayed and implemented in a half-hearted fashion because of fears of rousing Islamist protest. By contrast, Tunisia, with its weaker Salafist movement, was able to implement population policy early and effectively, which partially explains its below-replacement TFR. Women's education, the most important driver of fertility reduction, lagged behind. As a result, Muslim states grew faster than other developing countries. Overall, family planning began two decades later in most Arab states than in the rest of the developing world. Muslim fertility eventually fell substantially, but recent trends show a slowing of this trend. In Syria, Jordan and Egypt, fertility rates barely budged in the 1990s and 2000s. In Afghanistan, Somalia and Yemen they remain sky high. As of 2008, TFRs stood at three or above in a majority of Muslim countries. Islamist resistance is a major factor in prolonging the population explosion. Perhaps the fundamentalists are motivated by reason as well as revelation, since high fertility generates the unemployed young urban migrants who flock to the Islamist banner.[26]

Even in Turkey, where secular nationalism is powerful, the fertility rate is low and Islamists moderate, religious parties fight a rearguard action against family planning. Mindful of the power of nationalism, they marry Islamist opposition with secular reasoning. In the lead-up to the 1994 UN Cairo Population Conference, Turkish Islamists denounced family planning as Western imperialism. In 1994, prime minister-to-be Necmettin Erbakan of the Islamist Welfare Party spoke of the need for a larger Turkish population. 'Would-be westerners [family planners] are trying to reduce our population ... We must have at least four children,' he urged his audience.[27] Erbakan's heir, current prime minister Recep Tayyip Erdogan, leader of the Islamist Justice and Development Party (AKP), cut his teeth by attacking contraception and abortion to woo nationalist and Islamist alike. In 2002, two years before he was elected, Erdogan pulled few punches: 'To recommend to people not to procreate is straight out treason to the state,' Erdogan told a crowd gathered to celebrate the opening of an AKP office in Istanbul. 'It's a means of wanting to erase the history and the surface of the land.' Having played on nationalist registers, he moved to religion: 'Have babies,' he told the crowd. 'Allah wants it.'[28] This message comes across as distinctly off-key to the majority of Turks: surveys find that just 10 to 15 per cent oppose contraception. When asked, only 10 per cent of Turkish women agree that contraception and family planning contravene Islam, and even among these, half admit to having used it.[29]

One day, most Muslim states may succeed in reducing their fertility to replacement levels. This decline, if it takes place, will run against the grain of Islamist pressure. But Islamism may start to exert more sway when the population stabilises. Why? Because fertility, as in the West, may come to reflect people's value choices rather than material constraints. Several decades from now, Islamists may conclude that they are better off encouraging religious fertility among their flock so as to take over from below than trying to change government policy from above. This echoes the political strategy of the Muslim Brotherhood. Governments must be mindful of secular considerations like the high cost of feeding and schooling dependent young populations and providing jobs for them as they grow up. Opposition movements, however, can be more irresponsible.

There are already several straws in the wind. At the individual level, committed Islamists are having larger families than other Muslims. One intriguing study scraped together the fragmentary evidence on the fertility of women who enrol their children in madrasas. Data were only available for four countries in disparate corners of the Muslim world: Indonesia, rural Bangladesh, rural parts of the Indian states of Uttar Pradesh and Bihar, and Côte D'Ivoire in West Africa. In most areas, the authors found that Muslim families who send their children to Islamic schools have higher fertility rates than those that don't, even controlling for education and other factors. However, the difference was always less than 30 per cent, which will be significant over a century but not overwhelming in the near term.[30]

This is probably because, in these largely developing societies, education and material factors matter more than religious values when it comes to determining fertility. In addition, the proportion attending madrasas was small and many may have attended because it was the only schooling in town. The real test will come when these underdeveloped societies modernise and material barriers to birth control disappear. Only then would second demographic transition (SDT) theory predict that Islamists would start having more children than other Muslims, increasing the Salafist share of the population.

We also need to recognise that fundamentalist Islam is a modern movement that fans out from urban centres of learning. Since it acts as a competitor to rural Sufi traditionalism, we should not expect Islamism to be associated with above-average fertility just yet. We see this in Iran, where traditionalist ethnic peripheries of Kurds and Baluchis have high fertility rates while Islamist Persian districts are no more fertile than average.[31] In Turkey as well, religiosity is only weakly related to fertility: more religious, AKP-voting provinces are no more fecund than secular ones.

Traditionalism, as measured by arranged marriage, payment of a dowry, living in an extended family, rural residence and illiteracy, is what spawns larger families. In Turkey, as in Iran, Kurds have higher fertility than others.[32] Only when the significant reservoir of traditionals enters the modern world, as they have in the West, will the second demographic transition kick in. People's family size would then become consciously chosen, with the pious opting for larger broods than seculars and moderates. I therefore expect the religiosity–fertility nexus to strengthen in the Muslim world.

This is already emerging in the World Values Survey (WVS)'s 1999–2000 wave, the only individual-level survey that permits us to focus on Islamist fertility. The WVS asked roughly 8,500 people in seven Islamic countries whether they agreed that the state 'should implement Shari'a only' as the law of the land. The proportion of Muslims favouring sharia was an impressive two-thirds, ranging from over 80 per cent in Egypt and Jordan to around half in Indonesia, Nigeria and Bangladesh. Mapping people's attitudes to sharia on to their fertility patterns, I discovered a strong association between Islamism and fertility, which is statistically significant even when controlling for age, education and income. On the other hand, the small minority who claimed not to be religious had markedly lower fertility.

Religious Muslims bear more children than the non-religious, and Islamist Muslims have more kids than non-Islamists. What is especially intriguing is that the fertility advantage of Islamists over their non-Islamist neighbours increases in more modern contexts, as SDT theory predicts. In urban areas of 100,000 or more, Muslim women most in favour of sharia bear twice as many children as Muslim women who are least in favour. In rural areas of less than 10,000 people, the Islamist advantage is only half as strong. In statistical analysis with data from 1999 to 2008, Muslim religiosity and the belief that sharia should be law are not significant predictors of fertility in cities under 50,000 but are strongly significant in those over 500,000.[33] These results are intimations of the future, and are confirmed in Europe, where Muslims are modern, urbanised and have unfettered access to contraception. The result is that observant Muslim women are 35 per cent more likely than non-observant Muslim women to have more than two children, even when controlling for age, income, education, birthplace *and family values.* Given the link between family values and religiosity, the overall Islamist fertility premium is undoubtedly much higher. Gilles Kepel relates how he is struck by the size of Salafist families, who stand out from other Muslims in Salafist enclaves like those in the vicinity of Paris's Gare du Nord railway station.[34]

No other surveys of Muslim countries tap the connection between fertility and religiosity, but one can enquire into people's attitudes towards population growth. A 2005 ARDA survey of 18- to 25-year-olds in Egypt and Saudi Arabia reveals an impressive connection between Islamism and demographic beliefs. Most young Saudis think 'it would be a good thing for the country' if people had fewer children. However, among those who believe that it is 'very important' that sharia be the law of the land, support for reducing population growth falls to 60 per cent, whereas it rises to 90 per cent among those who think the implementation of sharia is 'less important'. When the Islamist question turns to support for 'an Islamic government, where the religious authorities have absolute power', we find a similar pattern: just 60 per cent of those answering 'very good' to the Islamist statement favour lower national fertility, compared with 90 per cent for those replying that an Islamist government would be 'fairly bad'.[35]

Islamist fertility matters because it could increase fundamentalism's clout in Muslim countries, resisting moderating trends should they appear in the future. Might higher Muslim incomes, education levels and a more mature age structure affect this picture? Not really. Developed Muslim societies in Europe such as Bosnia or Kosovo have lower levels of religiosity and support for sharia, but this seems more a function of their European context and political history than their high per capita incomes. On balance, wealthier Muslim countries, mostly in the Gulf, tend to back religion and sharia to the hilt. Survey data on Muslims shows that wealthier, better-educated, younger and city-dwelling Muslims are no more opposed to sharia than others. This flies in the face of arguments which claim that human development will produce secular outlooks.[36] Far from ushering in a tolerant generation, demography is likely to tilt the balance in the Muslim culture wars in an Islamist direction. Thus far, Islamic revival has taken place with little help from

Islamist fertility. But, like a resistance machine, Salafist fertility will increasingly kick in as Muslim societies modernise. Liberal regimes, should they arise, will then face an uphill struggle in their quest to break the grip of conservative Islam.

The emergence of Islamic fundamentalism

While religious revival in the West is more demographic than social, the reverse is true for Islamic fundamentalism. Indeed, it is hard to deny the power of social and political change in fanning Islamic revival in this part of the world. The story of modern fundamentalism begins with lay preachers rather than the established ulama. In 1949, an introverted Egyptian bachelor named Sayyid Qutb won a scholarship to the United States, pursuing his studies at the Colorado State College for Education at Greeley. Greeley at the time was a dry, God-fearing town, but Qutb still managed to conjure up a nation of whores:

> The American girl is well acquainted with her body's seductive capacity. She knows it lies in the face, and in expressive eyes, and thirsty lips. She knows seductiveness lies in the round breasts, the full buttocks, and in the shapely thighs, sleek legs – and she shows all this and does not hide it. [37]

Qutb went on to become one of the three main architects of radical Islam, alongside Abu Ala Mawdudi and Ayatollah Khomeini, influencing, among others, the assassins of Anwar Sadat, the blood-soaked Algerian GIA and jihadi megastar Osama bin Laden. Qutb's experience demonstrates two things. First, the globalisation of people, culture and goods does not tend to produce cosmopolitan 'last men'. Rather, global encounters can shock and alienate, awakening a sense of difference and cultural self-consciousness. After his American sojourn, Qutb did not lock arms with the League of World Federalists, but returned with a heightened sense of Islamic identity. In the 1950s, he joined the Muslim Brotherhood, a large association dedicated to fundamentalist revival whose call for an Islamic state drew it into bloody conflict with Nasser's secular nationalist regime. In 1966, Qutb was hanged for his activities, earning him the status of martyr (*shahid*) in the eyes of many.

The second lesson of Qutb's life, which is often missed by writers who fixate on Islamist violence, is the centrality of moral puritanism to the Islamist message. For Islamic fundamentalists, Satan is not a bloodthirsty savage or domineering exploiter, but rather a seducer, 'the insidious tempter who whispers in the hearts of men'.[38] The principal jihad, or struggle, to which Muslims are enjoined is an inner, cultural one: the fight against temptation – of sex, liquor or the urge to backslide in their religious beliefs. Fundamentalist Islam began as a movement of cultural defence and moral regeneration. Today that remains its primary goal. While traditional, moderate Muslims – the majority in the Muslim world – take a more rounded view of their faith, Islamists instead focus on the most demanding aspects of their texts and elevate these to the status of a litmus test – which sorts true believers from the impious.

This is not to deny that the other face of Islamism is political. Many Islamists seek to establish an Islamic state which fuses spiritual and temporal power under the guidance of a divine ruler, as the Prophet Mohammed and the first four 'righteous Caliphs' are said to have done. Yet there are immense practical barriers to this project: who is to exercise power on behalf of the divine if humans are imperfect? What happens when disagreements arise in interpreting the holy texts? How to determine succession for Caliphs? Cultural puritanism, by comparison, is far more pleasing to the palate of secular rulers because it does not challenge their authority. Its only victims are women, minorities and secularists, all of whom are politically expendable.

The roots of fundamentalism

Like its Protestant cousin, Islamism is primarily a response to the challenge of secularism. While there is a rich history of pre-modern Islamic fundamentalism which goes back to the Kharijites of the seventh century and Hanbalis of the ninth century, this was a minor chord in Muslim empires. Instead, pragmatism was the order of the day. Only in the nineteenth century, with the Deobandis in India (1867) and Wahhabis of Saud-ruled Najd in Arabia, do we find the first fundamentalist movements. The Deobandis emerged soon after the British conquest of Muslim India in 1857. They sought to purify their faith against Hindu, Christian and secular British influences. The Wahhabis of Arabia arose in the late eighteenth century in the context of Ottoman imperialism. Many of today's key Islamist touchstones, *kuffar* (unbeliever), *takfir* (apostate) and *jahiliya* (pagan ignorance), though grounded in earlier Hanbali ideas, were revivified only in the modern period.[39]

Islamic fundamentalists deemed the ideas of the colonists to be more of a threat than their troops. Chief among these was secular nationalism, which attracted many anti-colonial Muslim intellectuals, beginning in Lebanon and Egypt.[40] Turkey proved most receptive. Following the humiliating defeat of the Ottoman Empire and its dismemberment after the First World War, Ataturk ('Father of the Turks') declared a secular Turkish Republic. In 1924, he abandoned the millennium-long Islamic caliphate to which the Ottoman Empire had been heir. In effect, Istanbul renounced its role as temporal leader of the umma, or community of believers. His secular nationalism charged ahead at breakneck pace, breaking with a millennium-old Islam-centred worldview. He instituted revolutionary social changes: emancipating women, replacing Islamic law with European legal codes and introducing Western dress. He banned the veil and fez, which he considered symbols of weakness and backwardness, and dropped Arabic script in favour of the Latin alphabet. He even tried to compel local imams to change the millennium-old chant 'Allah-u-Akbar' to the Turkish 'Tanri Uludur'.[41]

Inspired by German nationalism, Ataturk sought to displace the Arab-oriented Islamic story with a Turkic-centred 'Turanian' one. This envisaged the Turks as the descendants of Oghuz Khan, speaking an ancient Central Asian language purified of Arab accretions by modern linguists.[42] Ataturk detested the ulama, the classically trained Muslim clergy, accusing them of miring the nation in backwardness. 'For five hundred years these rules and theories of an Arab sheik and the interpretations of generations of lazy, good-for-nothing priests have decided the civil and the criminal law of Turkey,' he complained. 'Islam, this theology of an immoral Arab, is a dead thing.' He is even known to have ordered a local minaret to be cut down when the call of the muezzin interfered with his enjoyment of a dance band in Istanbul's Park Hotel.[43]

In Iran, the secular Reza Shah moved to emasculate the mullahs. Like Ataturk, he reoriented his people to their pre-Islamic Persian past, venerating Cyrus the Great and the Aryan linguistic connection which tied Iran to Europe. He tried to suppress the Shiite Ashura celebration – in honour of Imam Hussein – and forbade Iranians from making the pilgrimage to Mecca. In 1931, he reduced the powers of sharia courts. Like Ataturk, Reza Shah instituted a dress code. Men were required to don Western dress and women were prevented from wearing the veil. Tensions came to a head during Ashura in 1929. Reza Shah's police surrounded the Fayziyah Madrasah in the holy city of Qom. Students wearing traditional clothes were forced to strip and put on 'modern' clothes. In 1935, a protest against the Dress Laws at the shrine of the Eighth Imam in Mashhad was brutally crushed by police, who fired on the crowd, killing and wounding hundreds.[44]

The spirit of the age was modernist. Nationalism, not Islamism, was the pre-eminent idea around which Muslim intellectuals rallied to expel the colonial powers.[45] By the late 1960s, most of the Muslim world had broken free from colonial rule. Their political ambitions took the form of the post-colonial nation state, not the umma. Their guiding philosophies, with the exception of Saudi Arabia, were secular. Those aligned with Moscow included Nasser's Egypt, Baathist Syria and Iraq, Qadaffi's Libya, the Algeria of Boumedienne and Ben Bella, South Yemen, the PLO (after 1968) and Sukarno's Indonesia. On the American side of the fence stood secular Turkey and Tunisia, plus pious Saudi Arabia. Secular Iran under Reza Shah and his son Shah Mohammad Reza Pahlavi backed the US, though Mossadeq's brief interlude in the early 1950s pulled the country out of America's orbit. In all but a small number of monarchies, clerics lost land and power. Islam was recognised as a symbol of nationhood, but the guiding ideology was nationalism, be it pan-Arab or local.

Islam awakens

Though secular nationalists carried the day, national consciousness in the weak states of the Muslim world barely touched the masses. In most countries, including Turkey, the social structure was still rooted in traditional Islam. In the countryside, where most people lived, Islam was often heterodox, incorporating pre-Islamic traditions such as the veneration of shrines. Religious life for the largely illiterate peasant-nomad masses was organised by local holy men, themselves unlettered, who possessed only rudimentary Qur'anic knowledge. Religious practice was lax, tied to tribal rituals.

In urban areas, by contrast, a literate ulama, in touch with pan-Islamic theological currents, espoused a demanding, universalist brand of Islam based on the holy text, not local tradition. Their allies were the traditional urban middle class of artisans and *bazaari* merchants. This group, as with Europe's Calvinists, gravitated to puritanism partly because it reinforced the habits needed for their dull, disciplined working lives. They tended to resent the luxurious hedonism of the courtly elites and identified with the ulama against the idolatrous, lax faith of the countryside.[46] Somewhere in the middle lay the urban Sufi brotherhoods. Lodge members adhered to mystical rituals that could involve drink, song and dance, while otherwise obeying the rigorous tenets of sharia.[47] The traditional middle class was distinct from the Europeanised middle class of bureaucrats, teachers, military men and scientists who initially supported socialism and secular nationalism.

In the face of reform movements, Islamists realised they needed to change if they wished to have a place in the modern world. Reformist theologians like Abduh and al-Afghani in the late nineteenth century championed flexibility, claiming that Islam gave birth to modern science. They prodded Muslims to break the cake of juristic precedent (*fiqh*) to get to the Qur'anic essentials, which could be interpreted using human reason (*ijithad*) as early Muslim scholars had once done.[48] Fundamentalists agreed with stripping away custom, but rejected *ijtihad* as a human innovation which usurped God's authority. Some fundamentalists went further. Like the early Protestant reformers, they questioned the exclusive right of the established clergy to interpret the holy texts on behalf of the people and sought to democratise Qur'anic study.[49] Fundamentalists also realised that nationalists and socialists were better organised. In answer to them, Islamists began the slow work of building national and transnational associations (*jama'at*), schools (madrasas) and mosques, under centralised leadership. In this sense, fundamentalists were modernisers who sought to break the stranglehold of the traditional ulama.

One of their first outlets outside Arabia and India was the Muslim Brotherhood, formed in 1928 in the city of Isma'iliya on the Suez Canal by Hassan al-Banna and several labourers. In 1932, al-Banna moved the

Brotherhood's headquarters to Cairo, a hospitable location where the movement took off. By the time of his assassination in 1949, the Brotherhood could boast half a million members in a population of only 20 million. This made it by far the largest association in the country. Al-Banna was a teacher and, like his acolytes, possessed no religious training. To all intents and purposes, the religious establishment at the prestigious Al-Azhar University in Cairo could have been a million miles away.

At this point, the Brotherhood's aims were predominantly cultural, geared toward Islamic revival. The Brothers lamented the tendency towards secular lifestyles in their country, which they associated with poverty, immorality and colonial domination. They called for censorship of newspapers and radio, clamouring for Islamic history and the Qur'an to be taught in schools. They urged members to abstain from dancing, gambling, drink and sex outside marriage. Unlike the communists, who failed to strike deep roots, the Islamists could count on Egyptians' familiarity with Islamic doctrine and capitalise on their pre-existing ties to their local mosque.[50]

Though referencing the fourteenth-century Hanbali ideas of ibn-Taimiya, the Muslim Brothers were a highly modern, self-conscious movement. Like the nationalists and socialists, they drew much of their membership from the mobile, uprooted part of the Egyptian population, especially university students. Those working as teachers, bureaucrats and scientists were also prominent. Brotherhood strength lay in the modernising urban areas, whereas it failed to penetrate traditional landlord–tenant networks in the countryside. This echoes patterns in nineteenth-century Europe, where minority nationalist associations flourished best in modernising urban contexts with a high density of schools and transport links.[51] National movements like those of the Czechs and Croats in the Habsburg Empire staged plays, competitions and festivals to foster self-consciousness. The Brotherhood focused instead on religious services to achieve the same ends. They built mosques, madrasas and clinics. In so doing, they created a network which could bring thousands on to the streets. This threatened the Egyptian monarchy, which responded by attacking the Brotherhood and killing al-Banna in 1949.[52]

The South Asian counterpart to the Brotherhood took the form of the Jamaat-e-Islami (JI), which controlled a network of mosques and madrasas offering free instruction in the Qur'an. Founded by the legendary fundamentalist preacher Abu Ala Mawdudi in 1941, the JI spread among Urdu-speaking middle-class urban Pakistanis. It later served as an engine of Taliban extremism by helping to indoctrinate detribalised young Afghans in the camps of Peshawar, Pakistan, during the Soviet-Afghan war of 1979–89. It also served as a conduit for Saudi funds and influence. Nonetheless, the JI remained a primarily urban, middle-class movement.

By contrast, the Tablighi Jamaat (TJ), or Society for the Propagation of the Muslim Faith, founded in India in 1927, had a larger rural and working-class following. Linked to established Deobandi clerics, it was set up to resist the perceived encroachment of 'impious' behaviour in Indian Muslim life. The Tabligh condemned traditional practices such as mysticism, shrines and brotherhoods as idolatrous. It vociferously opposed the Sufi Barelwis and Pakistan's 10–20 per cent Shia minority as heretics. Its theology picked the most stringent aspects of Islam, looking beyond the Qur'an to oral traditions about the Prophet (*hadith*s), including his dress, which inspired many Tablighis to don the flowing white jellaba. The Tabligh soon spread to Afghanistan, where it would later join the JI and others in educating recruits for the Taliban.

Clerics entered the political fray relatively late in the day, and traditional mosques were the last to be mobilised. The spirit of the TJ is represented by the Jami'at-i Ulama-i Islam (JUI) party, which emerged only in 1949, representing Deobandi clerics, while the more Sufi (Barelwi) ulama formed the rival Jami'at-i Ulama-i Pakistan (JUP). There are also ethnic aspects to these schools, with Pashtuns and Baluchis backing the JUI, and Mohajirs (Indian immigrant Muslims) the JI, while for many years Sindis were a pillar of the JUP. Meanwhile in Iran, the Shiite network of tens of thousands of mosques, shrines and madrasas benefited from a tax levied by mosques on *bazaari* merchants which made the mullahs financially independent of the Shah's secular government. With theological changes in the 1960s, they, too, entered the modern world of politics.[53]

Whereas traditionalists like the TJ tended to focus on local issues, the transnationally minded fundamentalists of the Muslim Brotherhood were sprouting offshoots beyond their Egyptian home base into Jordan and Palestine, where it eventually took the name Hamas. This ferment paralleled that of the nineteenth-century European cultural nationalists and twentieth-century Christian and Jewish fundamentalists. Like those movements, Islamism was laying a social network which could later be activated for mass politics. At this stage, such movements were quietist, concerned with spiritual and cultural revival. But politics is never far from the surface in Sunni Islam, and this meant that by the 1930s and 40s, sections of the Brothers were caught up in struggles with the Egyptian regime, and against the Jews and British in Palestine.[54]

Religious mobilisation was building at a fortuitous moment. During the colonial period, religion reinforced secular nationalism since both shared a common imperial enemy. Though Islam was adopted as a symbol of nationhood by all Muslim nations – even the Turks – its substantive influence was curtailed. This brought Islamists and nationalists into conflict. Soon after Nasser threw off the yoke of British influence in Egypt, Islamists began agitating for the implementation of sharia and an Islamic state. This exposed their differences with Nasser to the harsh light of day. In response, Nasser cracked down on the Brothers, driving them underground. In 1961, he placed the thousand-year-old al-Azhar University, the leading centre of Muslim theology, under his control. Meanwhile in Iran, Reza Shah Pahlavi and his son Mohammad Reza Shah ruled in a nearly unbroken line from 1925 until 1979. Like Ataturk and Nasser, they introduced modernising reforms which encouraged the spread of radio, television and the unveiling of women. The clergy were increasingly subordinated to the government, their offices absorbed into the state. From Morocco to Indonesia, the script was similar, though the pace of secular reforms varied.[55]

In this atmosphere of secular repression, radical Islamists like Sayyid Qutb railed against the nation state as a man-made idol. True believers should invest their loyalty in God and the umma, not the nation state. Qutb's followers held that Nasser and the leaders of other Arab states were *takfir*, lapsed Muslims. Some even accused the moderate Muslim majority in the country of living in pagan ignorance (*jahiliya*). They also tried to compel ordinary Muslims to fight a holy war against the nation state by obliging people to wage jihad against the regime. Mawdudi in Pakistan was especially clear on this: he believed that the obligations of a Muslim extended beyond the five traditional duties (profession of faith, almsgiving, prayer, fasting at Ramadan, pilgrimage) to compulsory jihad. True Muslims had a duty to sweep away the nation state and realise the Islamic state. Qutb and Mawdudi were lay clerics, but they influenced the thinking of Ayatollah Khomeini, a prominent, classically trained Shia imam.

Prior to Khomeini, Shia were noted for harmlessly flagellating themselves at the annual festival of the Mourning of Muharram in grief at their inability to prevent the death of Hussein, the third imam. Their attitude was one of sorrow and solidarity, and most were content to await the return of the twelfth 'hidden' imam, whom 'Twelver' Shias believe was spirited away by god in the tenth century and remains in a state of occultation. Shiites were even doctrinally permitted to lie about their religion to save themselves. Khomeini and his muse Ali Shariati, influenced by modern ideas of socialism, helped to shake up this quietism. Forced into exile by the Shah in 1964, they reversed centuries of Shiite teaching by endorsing revolution. The entry of Khomeini into the fray marked a turning point in the legitimacy of the Islamist movement. Khomeini was the first established Muslim cleric to endorse radical political Islam. Prior to this point, learned ulama could write off fundamentalist preachers such as Qutb and Mawdudi as ignorant rustics who made it up as they went along. No longer.[56]

This was an opportune moment for Islamism: many post-colonial Muslim states failed to deliver economic benefits to the people and had proven corrupt. This took the shine off progressive nationalism, leading many to question its aura of inevitability. The cataclysm was the disastrous Six-Day War of 1967, when Israel smashed the combined might of the armies of Egypt, Jordan, Syria and other Arab states inside a week. Secular Arab nationalism never recovered.

Not all were implicated in this disaster. The great abstainer from secular nationalism had been Wahhabi Saudi Arabia, where the clergy and sharia remained powerful. Moreover, the Saudis benefited from burgeoning oil production after 1945, buoyed by rising oil prices, which spiked in 1973. Allies of the Americans, they fought for ideological leadership of the Muslim world against the socialist pan-Arabism of Nasser and the Baathists. The Saudis embraced their missionary role with gusto, offering sanctuary to Islamist refugees such as the Egyptian Muslim Brothers of the 1950s and 60s. The Brothers were far better educated than the tribal Saudis and soon occupied high positions managing the kingdom's oil wealth. They also took leading roles in the emerging world of Saudi Islamist NGOs. Convinced that their oil wealth was a sign from God, the Saudis created evangelistic NGOs in the 1960s, such as the Muslim World League (MWL), the World Assembly of Muslim Youth and the Al-Haramain Foundation. This began in earnest with the MWL in 1962. Its aim was to fund mosques and madrasas and otherwise evangelise throughout the Muslim world on behalf of the strict Wahhabi-Taimiyite, or Salafi, brand of Islam. The Americans in their turn considered the Saudis a benign alternative to the Moscow-leaning pan-Arabists.[57]

Saudi religious supply reacted with popular demand – spurred on by the collapse of pan-Arab socialism – to produce Islamic revival. This spread like wildfire across the Muslim world. In the 1970s, formerly leftist university student bodies began falling to the Islamists. Often this was a case of former Marxists and nationalists converting to Islamism.[58] This was not as big a leap as it seems, since local socialist ideology hadn't spurned religion quite the way Marx did. Qur'anic Marxism had recast the Qur'an as a socialist document, while Arab nationalism used Islam as a symbol of identity. Meanwhile, off campus, a drop in infant mortality was powering a Muslim population explosion. By 1970, the 'youth bulge' (aged fifteen to twenty-four) component in the Muslim world was as numerous as the rest of the working age population (twenty-five to sixty-four) combined.[59] Thanks to post-colonial education and mushrooming cities, the rising young population was simultaneously more urban and literate than ever before. This meant that the god-fearing mass of the population were moving to places where they could be easily mobilised. Crowding into the slums of mega-cities like Cairo, Algiers, Jakarta and Istanbul, they entered the modern world of mass politics.[60]

The post-colonial era of elite politics, which favoured secular creeds, had come to a close and the voice of the religious masses was about to speak. Like Catholic anti-nationalism in pre-1930s Sicily, Islam survived because secular nationalism, attached to a weak state, could not break religion's monopoly of moral and spiritual legitimacy among the poor. When the masses emerged from the political wilderness into the glare of modernity, they brought their Muslim worldview with them.[61] The impoverished children of illiterate rural migrants joined what Gilles Kepel calls the 'devout middle classes' of the towns in this entry of the pious majority on to the stage of history.

Islamic revolution

In 1979, Ayatollah Khomeini seized power in Iran. His was the first revolution to weld the pious masses into a powerful agent of change. Khomeini appealed to *bazaari* merchants who had lost out to large industrial enterprises, to clerics bypassed by the shah's reforms, and to the swelling ranks of young poor migrants to the cities. He nominated himself *velayat-e-faqih*, supreme interpreter of the law, which ruffled few feathers among a Shiite population used to following charismatic imams. Religion and the state were declared indivisible in the new constitution. Khomeini imposed the sharia, codified Islamic dress into law, resegregated the sexes and pushed Iranian working women back into the home. These edicts were enforced by the *pasdarans*, Guardians of the Islamic Revolution, who wandered the streets searching for insufficiently veiled, secular middle-class women to harass or molest. This established a pattern: wherever Islamism gained ground, its first targets were symbols of secularism and individualism.[62]

This volatile combination of religious perfectionism and power soon exploded into violence. In the first year of the Islamic Republic, Khomeini denounced America as the 'Great Satan' and 500 of Khomeini's supporters stormed the American embassy, taking US diplomats hostage for over a year. Over the next three years, Khomeini conducted bloody purges to rid himself of secular leftists who had initially welcomed the social radicalism of the Revolution. Around the same time, the Iran–Iraq war began, conveniently providing Khomeini with a safety-valve for his young unemployed poor, whose dreams of social transformation came to nothing under their revolutionary new leader. Poorly equipped young men followed Imam Hussein into martyrdom as part of Iran's 'human wave' attacks, walking unprotected through minefields and machine-gun fire to clear the way for regular troops. Hundreds of thousands perished while many more were tied down in a senseless war that lasted eight years. The regime drew legitimacy from these martyrs, erecting memorials and providing aid to the families of the slaughtered.[63]

Giddy with fervour, the Iranian regime attempted to export its revolution. Sunnis politely declined the offer, but it had better success among its Shia brethren in chaotic South Lebanon. There, it directed funds to the newly formed Hezbollah ('Party of Allah'). The Shia were the poorest and fastest-growing segment of the Lebanese population, and Shiite youth soon gravitated to Hezbollah's revolutionary message. Iranian funds helped Hezbollah build schools, hospitals and mosques. It redistributed land, adding to its popularity in the areas it controlled during the country's long civil war of 1975–90. Iran's prodding quickly launched Hezbollah into the business of political violence. The French, Americans and Italians had contributed troops to South Lebanon to replace the Israelis in response to global condemnation of the Sabra and Shatila massacre of Palestinians by Christian militiamen in 1982. Western troops were rewarded for their generosity by Hezbollah in 1983, which vaulted to worldwide prominence by killing and maiming them in a series of suicide attacks. Hezbollah followed this up with a hostage-taking campaign against Western targets which reached its maximum intensity during 1984–8. Iran and its Hezbollah proxy impressed many and won the plaudits of dispossessed young Muslims throughout the world.[64]

Exporting Salafism

The Saudis and the Americans watched Khomeini's revolutionary Shiism with horror. For the Sunni Saudis, the problem was not the puritanism of Khomeini's regime, with which they wholeheartedly agreed, but rather the revolution, which unseated an established monarchy. Might the House of Saud be next? The Iranians' Shiism added to Saudi revulsion. Worse, the Iranians could now pose as champions of Islam, threatening the Saudis' moral leadership of the Muslim world. Though Shiite, Iran's revolutionary regime could more credibly represent the teeming masses of poor young Muslims than the Saudi sheikhs and their American allies. The Iranians' violent, radical tactics won favour among the same constituency. This emboldened Khomeini. In the 1980s, Iran successfully pressured the Saudis to admit more Iranian pilgrims to Mecca. While there, an aggressive section of the overrepresented 65,000 Iranian contingent waved placards of Khomeini and chanted anti-American slogans in defiance of the Saudis. Saudi police had to act to prevent them taking over the Grand Mosque, and 400 were killed in the ensuing mêlée.

Iran directed an incessant barrage of vitriol against the Saudis and their US allies, portraying itself as the conscience of Islam. Khomeini repeatedly challenged the legitimacy of Saudi-run pan-Islamist organisations such as the Organisation of the Islamic Conference (OIC), established in 1969. During the First Gulf War in 1991, the mullahs even buried the hatchet with their bitter enemy Saddam Hussein, hosting a high-profile *salon des refusés* of Islamist miscreants to counter the OIC. They accused the Saudis of collaborating with the Americans by admitting American troops onto Saudi soil. Though this damaged the Saudi's Islamist credentials, Riyadh deemed it necessary in order to repel Saddam's looming assault on the kingdom from across the border in Iraqi-controlled Kuwait. Osama bin Laden's offer to the Saudis to mobilise Islamists against Saddam was refused in favour of US help, enraging bin Laden and jumpstarting his career as a jihadi outlaw.[65]

The First Gulf War inflicted a serious blow to the Saudis' Islamist credentials. In the meantime, Saudi largesse had sharply increased the supply of fundamentalist Islam in the Muslim world. People forget that even in the United States, it wasn't until the late twentieth century that the supply of church services caught up with popular demand.[66] In the Muslim world, Saudi money helped to service a more pressing excess demand for imams and mosques. In a rare instance of genuine Muslim transnationalism, Saudi funds supported the construction of Salafist mosques in foreign countries, often channelling the money through branches of the Muslim Brotherhood or local Salafist groups such as the Tablighi Jamaat, which operates in eighty countries. They distributed millions of Qur'ans through their emerging networks: the kingdom currently pumps out 30 million a year. The Saudis similarly burnished their Islamist credentials by launching the Islamic banking and finance system, a kind of kosher banking, *sans* interest, which makes money for investors in Qur'an-proof ways. The considerable flow of labour from poor Muslim countries to the oil-rich kingdom generated remittances which became vital for the receiving states, providing yet another conduit for Saudi soft power.[67]

The effects were impressive. In Indonesia, mosque growth outpaced rapid population growth, raising the ratio of mosques to people by 30 per cent between 1986 and 1996.[68] In Egypt, the number of mosques outside formal government control – run by the Muslim Brotherhood and financed by the Saudis and local contributions – rose from 20,000 in 1970 to 46,000 in 1981. By 1991, an estimated 140,000 were operating. The Egyptian government tried to bring these under their wing, but lacked the resources to do so. Legitimacy was another problem. Local sentiment favours the private mosques as untainted by the regime. Entrepreneurial imams go on tours of the Gulf to raise money to build their mosques. Saudi money also buys legitimacy for Islam by funding the charitable activities and social services which are appended to private mosques and run by Salafist organisations. Once again, the Islamists appear as an efficient, fair and incorruptible alternative to a ramshackle government.

The political consequences of Egypt's youth bulge became clear in the poor outskirts of major Egyptian cities, where the *Da'wa*, or 'Call' to Salafi Islam took off in the 1970s. A large contingent of poor students – graduates of swollen, underfunded universities – mixed among the growing local population of urban poor from the countryside. Egyptian universities originated in a period of buoyant government funding and ample civil service jobs, but by the 1970s, graduates had little prospect of finding work or decent housing. Blocked upward mobility translates into frustration: economic, political and even sexual. Lacking income and housing, students are forced into the slums and must delay marriage, which, in a conservative society, means that sexual abstinence can last into the thirties.

In such an atmosphere, the mosque and Brotherhood provide an outlet for anomic energies. Educational overproduction created a highly motivated army of skilled labour for the Islamic sector. They ran countercultural Qur'anic study groups and charities and inculcated a message of resistance. The students who succeeded in finding poorly paid public employment gradually changed the face of government. Brotherhood activists infiltrated Egypt's schools and government agencies, using these positions to criticise the regime and promote their slogan, 'Islam is the solution.' Teachers even instructed their students not to salute the flag, sing the national anthem or mingle with Christian pupils. The goal is multigenerational: to capture society from below, gradually eroding the social base of the regime. In the words of one volunteer, 'when we are 90 per cent of society, then those who I have brought up' will take over.[69]

Jihadist violence, which the majority of Salafists oppose, is but the tip of a vast social iceberg. The quiet revolution of spiritual revival represented by *Da'wa* is the truly revolutionary phenomenon – one that has transformed many Muslim societies since 1970. The new generation is being cast in the Saudi mould of Salafism, a more centralised, rationalised version of the faith. One symbol of the change is the reappearance of the veil among women from Cairo to Beirut, Ankara to Jakarta.[70] Saudi oil has greased the wheels of the Salafi locomotive, but religious demand is arguably more important than Saudi baksheesh. Just because you build mosques does not mean they will come. As in other parts of the world, changes in identity and social norms opened individuals up to Saudi influence.

In the West, we tend to equate conservatism with older generations, imagining that youth are always more liberal than their parents. But Whiggish optimists need to understand that children can be more conservative than their elders when conservatism becomes fashionable. The support base for far-right nationalism in Western Europe, as with hardline sectarianism in Northern Ireland, is disproportionately young.[71] This is because youth are impatient with established parties and demand revolutionary change. Likewise, the anti-establishment status of Islamist groups and the stripped-down, simple nature of their faith appeals to the young. As an added bonus, it casts aspersions on their parents' rural traditions. Salafi Islam is hip.

As with modern Orthodox Jews, many Muslim children admonish their parents for failing to observe the tenets of the faith, or for practising an impure faith based on folk tradition or 'superstitious' practices such as venerating shrines. When secular ideologies lost their lustre, this provided the final push for Islamic revival. In some cases, former atheists repented. In Soviet Central Asia, for example, Islam was actively suppressed by the communists and atheism flourished among an important minority of people. This was also true of the westernised elite of many Muslim states. In those cases, atheists literally had to be born again when the call to revival sounded.[72] The Islamic *Da'wa* is a true religious revival, and demonstrates how people who were sceptics can become believers when fashions change. But for most poor Muslims, there was little need for spiritual rebirth. They never lost faith, and when, after 1967, the winds of ideology began to favour the declassé ulama, the clerics could rely on popular Islam as a springboard to power.

Jihad: the sharp end of Salafism

Population explosion, fuelled by Islamist resistance to family planning, supercharged the global Islamic revival. These population flows will be less powerful in a few decades, but by then Islamist fertility will begin to boost the Salafist share of the population. Strictly speaking, Salafi Islam refers only to the quietist, jellaba-clad Saudi-funded brand of fundamentalism, whose Riyadh-based sheikhs now attack the Muslim Brotherhood as 'Qutbist' and jihadis as innovators.[73] But competing theologies, whether revolutionary or obedient, share much in common and may be subsumed under a wider Salafi label. In Saudi Arabia, many princes continue to bankroll the Brotherhood despite the hostility of Saudi government sheikhs. Salafism is a non-violent social movement, but provides a perfectionist ideological atmosphere which can incubate violent splinter movements. Recall the three constants of Islamic fundamentalism we visited earlier: moral puritanism, theocracy and anti-imperialism. So long as fundamentalists merely seek to reinforce the five pillars of Islam (prayer, fasting, etc.), they can credibly steer clear of politics. But Salafists also insist on blending political and religious authority. Government-appointed imams and religious presidential rhetoric do not satisfy them. Instead they want the government to rule in accordance with sharia and enshrine it into law.

They also place loyalty to Allah and the umma above loyalty to the state. The presence of non-Islamic influences – in the form of military aid or, worse, foreign troops, is considered an outrage against God. The logic of national security and alliances cuts little ice with them, especially if foreign infidels (*kuffar*) are believed to be propping up a regime deemed to be apostate (*takfiri*). The Shah of Iran is the paradigm case of a *takfir*: secular, 'impious' and backed by the American Christian infidel. The Saudis and Pakistanis are reasonably kosher on religious grounds, but sully the honour of Islam by collaborating with foreign troops. Iran fits the bill, but its Shiism is considered heretical. Only revolutionary Sudan and Taliban Afghanistan can truly be considered beyond reproach. What switches a quiet Salafist on to the track of violence is therefore a reinterpretation of jihad as not merely a spiritual quest but a military duty. When an Islamic preacher issues a fatwa imposing a duty on the believer to wage jihad against the infidel in defence of Islam, this can motivate fundamentalist Muslims to engage in violent conflict.[74]

Religion is no more conflict-prone than secular ideologies, and even contains resources which can be used to combat violence. However, religion can add fuel to the fires of civil conflict by sacralising it, elevating the struggle into a cosmic war between the forces of darkness and light. This renders negotiation and compromise more difficult. Consequently, civil conflicts involving religion last longer, recur more often and are bloodier – especially for civilians – than other civil wars. In Israel-Palestine, Sudan and Nigeria, the sacralisation of ethnic conflicts exacerbated the bloodletting and frustrated peace agreements.[75] Since 1940, 90 per cent of the civil wars fought within a religion, and 73 per cent of the thirty-two conflicts in which the parties differ by religion, involved Islam. Fifty-eight per cent of states gripped by religious civil wars had a Muslim majority. Religion has also revolutionised the terrorism industry. As late as 1980, just two of sixty-four terrorist movements were religious. Fifteen years later nearly half were.[76]

The trail of jihad begins in Egypt in the 1950s and 60s. Revolutionary factions of the Muslim Brotherhood were crushed by Nasser and found themselves fleeing to Saudi Arabia. There, they entered a kingdom flush with new oil money and a sense of religious mission. When war came to Afghanistan in 1979, these Egyptian fundamentalist émigrés yoked the energies of Salafism to the struggle against the Soviets. Volunteers poured in from around the Muslim world. The patient work of Abdullah Azzam and Osama bin Laden in publicising the Afghan struggle to the wider Muslim world and creating a network of transnational volunteers launched Al Qaeda. At the war's end, in 1987, veterans of the struggle returned to their Middle Eastern homelands, where they continued the jihad against the authoritarian nationalist regimes that ruled them.

Most regimes, apart from Saudi Arabia, had secular nationalist antecedents, and were thus considered impious. In jihadi eyes, even the Saudis suffered from the taint of corruption because of the presence of American forces on their territory during and after the First Gulf War. As a consequence, numerous Muslim states were targeted by jihadi insurgents. Violence was most severe in Algeria, where over 100,000 were killed in a nasty civil war between 1992 and 1997. Towards the end of the war, religious extremists accused the populace at large of being *takfiri*, or apostates, because they did not support the jihad. This culminated in Islamist massacres of ordinary civilians.

There was further 'blowback' from American military aid, Saudi religious instruction and Pakistani support: Afghan refugees, many of them orphans, were trained in Saudi-funded Salafist madrasas in Peshawar and other parts of border Pakistan. There they coined themselves Taliban, meaning 'students' in Pashto. When the war ended in 1987, many returned to Afghanistan, and their movement bore fruit as the Taliban regime between 1996 and 2001. Elsewhere, the Iranian revolution of 1979 released revolutionary energies that found their way into the Shiite Hezbollah militias of Lebanon – even spreading as far afield as Hamas in Palestine. Iran's revolutionary Shiism challenged Saudi Salafism for leadership of the Islamist movement.

In addition, Al Qaeda emerged as a transnational Salafi-jihadist force opposed to both the Saudis and Iranians, and captained by a wealthy Saudi, Osama bin Laden. In 1983, President Nimeiri took power in an Islamist coup and imposed sharia law in Sudan, sparking off civil war. Osama bin Laden established himself there but was later forced out by American pressure. Luckily, the victory of the Taliban in Afghanistan in 1996 offered him a handy refuge. After the Taliban's demise in 2001, bin Laden fled to Pakistan's Pashtun tribal areas, where he remains to this day. The Afghan war and Iranian revolution helped to globalise Islamic extremism, with tongues of violence reaching the United States by 1993 and Europe by 1995. At home, however, the appetite for insurgency was dampened after the indiscriminate terrorist campaigns of the Afghan jihadi veterans killed innocent Muslim civilians and alienated many. The authoritarian regimes were able to gain the upper hand, and have been relatively successful in containing subsequent insurgencies.[77]

The victory of moral puritanism

Islamist violence divides Muslims, but the Salafi *cultural* message commands wide assent. The authoritarian regimes of the region understand this, and have stolen the clothing of their revolutionary adversaries by 'out-Islamising' the jihadists. In this way, the cultural conservatism of the jihadis has triumphed while the more progressive political aspects of their programme have been neutered. Many Muslims believe that one cannot be moral without being religious.[78] Calls for stronger morality in politics thus translate into an appeal for society to move closer to the tenets of sharia. In seven countries during 1999–2000, the World Values Survey (WVS) asked whether respondents supported sharia as the exclusive law of the land. The proportion of Muslims answering yes ranged from roughly half in Bangladesh and Nigeria, to 61 per cent in Pakistan, 71 per cent in Algeria and over 80 per cent in Egypt and Jordan. A 2009 survey confirms the pattern: 81 per cent of Egyptians and 76 per cent of Pakistanis and Moroccans agreed with the 'strict application of sharia in every Muslim country'. Even half of Indonesians felt the same way. When it came to the proper place for sharia in the 'way the country is governed', 76 per cent of Egyptians, 46 per cent of Pakistanis and 27 per cent of Indonesians wanted it to play a greater role. Among Saudis aged eighteen to twenty-five polled by ARDA in 2005, 98 per cent felt that it was important for government to implement sharia. Sixty-eight per cent of Egyptian youth agreed.[79]

Another aim of Salafi-jihadists is to invest religious authorities with political power. This commands surprisingly strong support in Arab Muslim countries. According to the ARDA youth survey, 94 per cent of the young Saudis approved of a system of government where 'religious authorities have absolute power', though just 60 per cent of young Egyptians did. Does this mean they spurn democracy as an alien form of government? Hardly. Eighty-nine per cent of those favouring sharia on the 1999–2000 WVS approved of democracy, exactly the same proportion as among those who opposed sharia. These results are confirmed in the Arab Barometer survey of 2006, which covered five countries, Morocco, Jordan, Algeria, Palestine and Kuwait. In this sample, 56 per cent favoured 'men of religion' having influence in government, while 44 per cent did not. What is fascinating, however, is the consistently high support given to democracy by those who want more religious influence in government. Eighty-five to 90 per cent of political Islamists back democracy as the best form of government.[80]

The centre of gravity of many Muslim publics favours a conservative Islamic democracy in which the ulama and sharia carry more weight. Most Muslims back Salafi-style moral reform, but oppose violent revolution and have no appetite for losing their national sovereignty to a supranational caliphate. In most societies where Islamists have contested elections, they have failed to win a majority. Yet a core of grassroots support persists, which can approach half the population. In Algeria in 1990, the FIS won 54 per cent of the popular vote. Next door in Tunisia, the banned Ennahda movement, which seeks to steer the law towards harmony with sharia, may command the sympathy of almost half the population. In the Palestinian Authority, Hamas won the 2006 election with 44.5 per cent of the vote in 2006, and in Turkey, the Justice and Development (AKP) Party triumphed with 46.6 per cent support in 2007. In Egypt, the Muslim Brotherhood has attained 38 per cent of the poll, and in Jordan, 33 per cent. In Lebanon in 2006–7, Islamists were the choice of almost 30 per cent of voters, and in Yemen, Islamist party support hovers close to 25 per cent. In most countries, Islamist support is holding steady, but stands well shy of a majority.[81]

Perhaps John Gray is correct when he foresees that 'twenty years from now most of the Middle East looks set to be ruled by Islamist versions of illiberal democracy.' Yet he is too blasé about the human cost of this outcome.[82] Democracy may be safe and revolution a chimera, but from a liberal standpoint, the advance of an Islamist social agenda poses serious risks. Wherever Islamist movements have acquired power, their first targets have been secular liberals. In the Palestinian territories, Hamas activists attacked those selling liquor as agents of Western or Jewish depravity. Unveiled women faced the risk of abuse and had acid thrown in their faces.[83] In Algeria, the rise of the FIS to municipal power in the early 1990s created a whirlwind of censorship and cultural repression. Local government employees were forced to wear the veil; shops selling liquor, videos and other 'immoral' services were shut down; women accused of 'easy morals' were harassed; and coastal municipalities segregated their beaches and banned 'indecent' clothing. The GIA's assassination campaign against secular intellectuals in the 90s dealt Algerian secularism a blow from which it has never truly recovered.[84]

In Iran, seculars were purged or 're-educated' to Islam, the sexes resegregated and morality enforced by roving bands of young *pasdaran* and *basiji* thugs loyal to the Supreme Leader.[85] In Afghanistan after 1996, the Taliban regime pounced with fervour on 'immoral' Dari-speaking Kabul, forcing the burqa – which permits only a mesh-covered slit for vision – on women who had been free of it for fifty years. Women were forbidden to work, reducing those who had lost their husbands to the war to begging with their starving children. Prevented from seeking medical help from male, i.e. most, doctors, women succumbed to disproportionately high rates of illness and death. One remarkable edict forced them to walk silently on the streets lest their footfalls set male testosterone flowing.

All this was enforced by the *mutawa*, or virtue police. In Afghanistan, as in Iran or Algeria, these goons were poor young men who took out their frustrations on the 'immoral' privileged classes. These men relished their role as moral guardians, setting to work with truncheons on women who were insufficiently veiled, and men who lacked long beards – regardless of their genes. Their resentful dragnet snared anyone with the misfortune to be outdoors during prayer time or who otherwise deviated from strict Salafi codes of conduct. Television and music were naturally forbidden, though public entertainment was available in the local stadium on Fridays. There one could watch thieves having their arms cut off, drinkers being whipped and accused murderers being executed by families of the victims, who were given machine guns to make the job easier. When the regime was finally ousted in 2001, the city's residents celebrated by shaving their beards and flying kites.[86] The Taliban spirit lives on, and not only in Afghanistan and Pakistan. Today I read that in rebel-held Somalia, al-Shabaab militants have closed schools and sent out patrols to make sure children attend public executions.

The surge of support for sharia in the Middle East, North Africa and Asia has shifted the cultural centre towards puritanism by forcing secular regimes to co-opt the Islamist message. We have already seen how this slowed the family planning movement, even in Baathist Syria where Islamists are firmly repressed. In Pakistan, Zia's regime implemented sharia, endorsing the harshest of Qur'anic *hudud* punishments while inviting Mawdudi and his Jamaat-e-Islami into the corridors of power. Madrasas were funded and their graduates given posts in the army and government. In Egypt, first Anwar Sadat ('the believer president'), then Hosni Mubarak, elevated Islamism to prominence, reversing Nasserite civil reforms. The state increased television airtime for religious programming, banned alcohol on Egypt Air flights and censured secular intellectuals if they 'brought religion into disrepute'.

Local governors in Islamist areas enacted 'dry' legislation and gave the Muslim Brotherhood and Gamaat Islami a free hand in closing hairdressing, video and liquor shops. The intellectual climate in Egypt was greatly shaped by the assassination of secular intellectuals such as Farag Foda in 1992, a murder subsequently sanctioned by a government cleric who agreed that Foda was an apostate and therefore deserved to die under Islamic law. Episodes like these effectively silenced secular and liberal voices. Those accused of apostasy are now at risk of losing their lives. In Jordan, Islamist elites were absorbed directly into the government, where they shaped the tone of social policy.[87]

Even in Malaysia, Mahathir Mohamad tried to steal the thunder of the rising Malaysian Islamic Party by restricting working hours to accommodate Ramadan, creating halal government eateries and more. Muslim couples were issued identity cards so that police could determine whether they were married and were thereby consorting illegally (*khalwa*). Islamist influence has had less success in secular Turkey, but in 1982, the ruling generals, bending to Refah's Islamist pressure, agreed to make religious education compulsory to reduce the appeal of the party. Beyond this, however, the generals and the Turkish secular majority were not prepared to yield. Turkish Islamists had to content themselves with their enclaves of religious resorts where women are veiled, attired from head to toe and bathe on separate beaches.[88] This doesn't stop self-appointed guardians of faith from taking vigilante action. Even in liberal Istanbul, young couples meeting in local parks risk serious assault: 'Fundamentalist Islamists have attacked, beat, and sometimes pushed them into the sea, claiming they should be separated, when they have merely been sitting together on a bench hand-in-hand.'[89]

In Saudi Arabia and Oman, laws never much deviated from sharia.

In fact, the Taliban's virtue police were modelled on the Saudi *mutawa*. In the kingdom, car ads display headless dummies in the driver's seat to avoid depicting the human form, and liquor and videos are illegal. There is, to be sure, a lively black market in illicit goods which the authorities overlook. Women, however, have no easy option: they cannot drive and are rarely seen in public. Though they make up the majority of University of Riyadh undergraduates, they are forced to attend lectures in segregated halls via video linkup and to carry out tutorials with male lecturers by telephone. Transgression of these norms, as in other Salafi societies, brings down the wrath of the virtue police. There are Islamo-liberals who try to justify liberal reforms by reference to Qur'anic sources, but they are weak. At one point, after the Americans invaded Kuwait and stationed troops on Saudi soil, there was a brief moment of liberal euphoria and seventy women drove cars into Riyadh in protest against restrictions. The clerics and the Salafist majority were not amused, denounced the women as 'communist whores' and had them fired from their jobs. Women have increasingly turned to literature to express their frustrations. Many stories in underground circulation relate tales of depression brought on by limited freedom, coercive arranged marriages or alcoholism.[90]

Yet respect for Islam and tradition mutes open criticism. Broadly speaking, sharia remains popular. In Khaled Hosseini's best-selling novel, *A Thousand Splendid Suns*, the lead character, Mariam, is oppressed more powerfully by her husbands and their patriarchal culture than the Taliban. As the 2009 UN Arab Human Development Report makes clear, women experience widespread oppression and violence in Arab countries from both social norms and the law. Violations of human rights in the name of sharia are extensive: husbands can maim or kill their wives and get off lightly if they claim their 'honour' has been besmirched; they can unilaterally divorce their wives, whereas women generally cannot divorce without the husband's approval; wives have a duty to obey their husbands; women's testimony in Islamic law is worth just half a man's; marriages are often arranged, and so forth.

Some traditional practices are opposed by Salafism, but in other cases, Islamists are complicit through their support for patriarchal norms. Female genital mutilation is a cruel but common practice: over 90 per cent of Egyptian women are estimated to have undergone the procedure.

Arab women's health and education is typically inferior to men's while rapes go unreported. In addition, between a quarter and a half of women in most Arab countries are estimated to be victims of domestic violence, and many accept this to be part of Islam, even if there is no basis for it in scripture. A UN survey found that between 40 and 50 per cent of Moroccan and Palestinian men would beat their wives if they committed an act which 'violated custom and tradition'. Muslim countries circumvent international pressure to ratify women's rights conventions by citing conflict with the sharia. Even if they do sign up, reforms are rarely implemented.[91]

While support for Salafist mores in many Arab countries cannot be underestimated, there are limits to this fervour in more secular areas, notably large cities such as Kabul, Beirut and Tehran, and in much of the Muslim world outside the Middle East. The behaviour of Kabulis after the fall of the Taliban speaks volumes, as does the consistent support of young Iranians for reformist clerics. In Sudan, women have tentatively begun donning Western wear beneath their Islamic dresses, and local journalist Lubna Hussein mounted a high-profile legal challenge to her sentence of forty lashes for wearing a pair of trousers. The Pan-Malaysian Islamic Party (PAS) dropped sharia after its puritanical rhetoric cost it votes in 2004, which led to an improved showing in 2008. In Turkey, many female Islamists back sharia but baulk at the specific restrictions it entails.[92]

Yet we should not imagine that a Muslim sexual revolution is around the corner. Sharia gains stature in many Muslim countries because it is seen as a symbol of incorruptible morality against the backdrop of kleptocratic governments. It reinforces traditional patriarchy. Most importantly, sharia makes a nationalist statement, much as Prohibition did for 1920s Protestant Americans who drank illicitly but wanted to make a point to Catholics and modernists that America was still a Protestant country.[93] Thus Muslim states like Iran and Saudi Arabia and social movements like the Muslim Brotherhood compete to out-Islamise each other, a game in which the secular West is the common reference point and success is measured by the degree of adherence to sharia.

Nationalism can also resist Islamism. Turks, Indonesians and Malays are proud that they are more economically advanced and progressive in their Islam than Middle Easterners. This nationalism keeps the wolf of sharia away from the door. Arab jihadis from the Middle East who came to the aid of Balkan Muslims discovered this when they tried to impose Salafist fundamentalism on the unique Bosnian and Kosovar Muslim cultures. Acting like this was just another theatre of jihad, they broke up the ceremonies of ancient Balkan brotherhoods, imposed the veil and destroyed cafés. They married Bosnian girls in extra-legal sharia ceremonies and smashed priceless Ottoman-era Islamic architecture because these embodied human images – a taboo for Salafists. In the end, even sympathetic Bosnian Islamists had to restrain the zealots and bend to the wishes of the local people to send the disillusioned Middle Easterners packing. Today, the only Arab trace in the region is a remote settlement where some Arab immigrants settled with their Bosnian wives.[94]

Conclusion

Fundamentalist Islam has enjoyed an extraordinary resurgence since the late 1960s, caused by the demise of socialism and secular nationalism. The movement has been carried by competing Islamisms – some state-led, others anti-state – jockeying to outdo each other in fervour. The revival is both cultural and political, but the two cannot be neatly separated. The Salafi 'Call' to Islam, which the Saudis bankrolled from the 1960s, also spawned the Salafi-jihadism of Al Qaeda. Al Qaeda's quest for an Islamic superstate has failed and remains unrealised even at the domestic level because authoritarian regimes have co-opted or crushed the insurgents. But secular liberalism is the lamb that has been sacrificed to appease the Islamists. Governments have given way on cultural policy, curtailing the civil liberties of secular intellectuals, women and minorities, not to mention anyone who just wants to drink, watch television or even fly a kite.

Demography played a backstage role in this drama. Population explosion flooded the cities with poor young people who were receptive to the message of the born-again Islamist intelligentsia. Islamists in turn managed to thwart family planning efforts for two decades, boosting the demographic heft of Islam on the world stage. Paradoxically, as Muslim societies modernise and contraceptives become more widely available, Islamists will open up a growing fertility gap over other Muslims, setting in motion a self-propelling dynamic. Not all Islamists will match Osama bin Laden's twenty-five children (and counting) or his father's fifty-four. But ironically, demographic radicalism will gain momentum if Muslim societies open up. Secularism's triumph, it seems, sows the seeds of its own demise. Heads sharia wins, tails you lose.

5

SACRALISATION BY
STEALTH: RELIGION
RETURNS TO EUROPE

On 7 July 2005, during morning rush hour, a coordinated suicide
bombing attack struck the London transport system. Three devices
exploded on Underground trains and one on a bus, killing 52 commuters
and 4 suicide bombers and injuring more than 700. For me, the jihadis
struck a little too close for comfort. The bus bomb was detonated in
Tavistock Square, in the heart of the University of London precinct, a
stone's throw away from my office. Tragically, the terrorists' handiwork
claimed the life of Benedetta Ciaccia, a thirty-year-old Italian student
taking an Information Technology course at Birkbeck, the University of
London college where I teach. Ironically, she was engaged to a Muslim
Londoner, Fiaz Bhatti, and the two had planned an elaborate wedding
in Rome which would have blended Muslim and Catholic rites. Interviewed soon after the bombing, Fiaz commented, 'We believed in different religions but that was never an issue. Both religions essentially teach
the same thing: you shouldn't kill, you shouldn't steal and you should
treat others with respect.'[1]

All the bombers were raised in Britain, spoke with English accents
and were culturally assimilated. One was a Jamaican-born convert, Germaine Lindsay (twenty-nine). The other three, Hasib Hussain (eighteen),
Mohammad Sidique Khan (thirty), and Shehzad Tanweer (twenty-two),
were British-born Muslims of Pakistani descent from heavily Muslim
Beeston, a suburb of Leeds. Leeds, along with Leicester, Bradford,

Oldham, Burnley and Birmingham, form a belt of English Midland cities with the largest concentration of Muslims in the country.[2] The bombings graphically illustrate how religion has re-entered the politics of 'secular' Europe. As we shall see, they also drive home the importance of hidden demographic forces which are reversing religion's slide into political obscurity.

Europe exemplifies how secularisation and uneven global demography can interact to produce fundamentalism. This is only partly a Muslim story. As we previously saw, there has been a stunning decline of European Christian piety since the 1960s. This has reduced most church congregations to an aging, mainly female, remnant. However, there are important sources of vitality in European Christendom. Younger Christians tend to be more traditionalist in their faith – why else buck the trend set by one's secular peers? Consider the increase in so-called 'charismatics', church members who remain within established denominations but claim to have entered into communion with the Holy Spirit. Since 1970, they have expanded at a rate of roughly 4 per cent a year, in step with Muslims. They are arguably behind the surge in pilgrimages to sites such as Santiago de Compostela in Spain or Lourdes in France.

In the 1950s, Lourdes attracted a million pilgrims a year. Today it draws 6 million. Even on slow days, no fewer than 50,000 pass through the site, and young people make up a disproportionate share of them. Today, evangelicals, Pentecostalists and charismatics make up more than 8 per cent of the European population, twice as numerous as Muslims, and they are increasing at the same rate.[3] Though fundamentalist Christianity is enjoying a global resurgence, its expansion in Europe is more noticeable because of surrounding decline. In effect, Christianity seems to be retrenching: religious decline *is* taking place, but as the loosely attached fall away, they reveal a vital and growing core of fundamentalist energy. As elsewhere, the moderate middle is being squeezed out.

Another commonality with other parts of the Western world is the impressive role of demography in boosting fundamentalism. Religious immigration and fertility are both at work. Several recent studies examine the connection between religiosity – whether defined as attendance, belief or affiliation – and fertility in Europe. Traditionally, education was considered the main determinant of a woman's fertility. Yet in many

European studies, a woman's level of religiosity is as or more important than her education in determining the number of children she will bear. In Spain, women who are practising Catholics have significantly more children than their non-practising sisters – a difference that holds across all income and education levels.

This wasn't the case as recently as 1985, when many still practised for social reasons, thus masking the underlying fertility difference between nominal and true believers.[4] In France, researchers find that fertility rates actually *rose* substantially among generations of practising, native-born Catholic women born after 1950, while rates for non-practising and nominal Catholics remained flat or declined. Among French women born in 1960, there is a half-child difference in fertility between practising and non-practising Catholics. The authors estimate that religious decline in France since the 1960s accounts for 15–18 per cent of fertility declines across French birth cohorts in the past half-century.[5]

If current patterns persist, we should start to see Christianity's demographic revival. Already, there is a flattening of religious decline in countries that began to secularise first. In France and Scandinavia, where secularisation took firm root in the nineteenth and early twentieth centuries, it is only among pre-1945 generations that we see older generations with higher attendance rates than their children. Among those born after the war, younger generations attend no less frequently than their elders. To be sure, just 5 per cent of individuals in these countries attend regularly, but this seems a pretty committed group, largely resistant to further decline. In effect, secularisation in Europe is now largely confined to newly secularising Catholic countries. As the proportion of practising Catholics falls to Scandinavian levels in a generation or so, i.e. 5 per cent attendance, we would expect a similar troughing to occur.[6]

Flattening of secularising trends may well prove the prelude to demographic revival, as seems to be happening among Jews. Jewish women who describe themselves as religious in the combined European Values Surveys (EVS) of 1981, 1990 and 1997 have twice the fertility rate of Jewish women who are non-religious or atheist. The gap is even wider among younger women who have yet to complete their childbearing.[7] Behind the figures lie three distinct populations. The first is the secular, economically successful European Jewish majority with below-average fertility and a strong tendency to marry across religious lines. The second is the relatively deprived ultra-Orthodox community, which has three to four times the fertility rates of other Jews and loses few members to secularism and intermarriage. A final segment are the modern Orthodox, who have intermediate numbers of children and high religious retention, but are also more likely than other groups to emigrate to Israel.

In Britain, 2008 was the first year since the Second World War that Jewish birth rates in Britain exceeded death rates. Between 2005 and 2008, the Jewish population of Britain increased for the first time in living memory. This was certainly not because of secular Jews, who average 1.65 children per couple. Their low fertility rate, high average age and tendency to intermarry or leave the faith explain the plunge in British Jewish numbers from 450,000 in 1950 to a mere 280,000 today. However, ultra-Orthodox women average 6.9 children each and lose few to secularism or intermarriage. Ergo, by some calculations, they now account for three-quarters of all Jewish births in Britain, despite constituting just 17 per cent of the Jewish population. They are thereby on course to become the majority of British Jews by 2050.[8] Patterns are probably similar in the rest of Europe.

Another example of endogenous fundamentalist growth is provided by the Laestadian Lutherans of Finland. Numbering perhaps 80,000 to 150,000, they remain a small community. Since many of them reject contraception, they have an exceptionally high fertility rate compared with other Finnish Lutherans. In the village of Larsmö, where there is an important concentration of Laestadians, their fertility advantage over others has risen as Finland's overall TFR has fallen: their advantage climbed from under 2:1 in the 1940s to nearly 3:1 in the 1960s and almost 4:1 by the late 1980s, neatly demonstrating the power of second demographic transition theory. By 1985–7, the Laestadian and Finnish TFRs stood at 5.47 and 1.45 respectively. Even within the Laestadian TFR of 5.47, there is diversity, with a 'moderate' group preferring to stop at four and practise birth control while a conservative cluster engages in unrestrained reproduction. No research has been done on Laestadians' level of endogamy and membership retention. However, they are residentially and occupationally integrated, unlike Old Order Anabaptists and ultra-Orthodox Jews, so lose more members to assimilation. Despite some outmigration and loss to intermarriage, the Laestadian population in the community of Larsmö has doubled in thirty years, and now stands at 40 per cent. On current trends, it will form a two-thirds majority of the town in a generation.[9]

The situation among Holland's Orthodox Calvinists reflects a milder version of the same dynamic. The fertility advantage of Calvinists is not as pronounced as among ultra-Orthodox Jews or Laestadians, but its effects are amplified by Calvinists' larger share of the total population. Among women born during 1945–9, Calvinist TFR was 3, compared with 2.3 for other Protestants, 1.9 for Catholics and 1.7 for seculars. This, along with greater resistance to the appeal of secularism, is responsible for recent growth.

In 1829, the Dutch split roughly 60:40 between Protestants and Catholics. Beginning in the 1920s, and especially since the 1960s, the mainstream Dutch Reformed (Protestant) Church experienced membership free fall to the point where just 14 per cent of the Dutch population affiliate with it, down from 49 per cent in 1889. When we consider 'active' members who attend at least once a month, the figure falls to 5 per cent of the Dutch total. Catholics still formed 32 per cent of the population in 1999, and were long accused of trying to 'outbreed' Protestants. However, secularisation and demographic transition have battered them more heavily than other groups, and active Catholics now make up a paltry 8 per cent of the population.

Contrast this with the Orthodox Calvinists, who seceded from the Dutch Reformed Church in 1886. In 1889, they constituted 8 per cent of the population. Today, despite many decades of Dutch secularisation, they remain at roughly the same share – 7 per cent – of the total. Unlike other denominations, most Calvinists are regular church attenders, and there are now as many active Calvinists as active members of the Dutch Reformed Church.[10] Calvinists are disproportionately distributed in a string of communities, the 'Bible Belt', stretching from Zeeland in the south-west to Friesland and Overijssel in north-central Holland. The belt's tentative origins lie in the seventeenth century, among Protestant communities on the front line of the war against Spanish Catholic forces in Flanders. Today, these communities are religiously and demographically distinct. Urk, a southern village that was isolated from the mainland until a land reclamation project in 1941, has the youngest population in the Netherlands.

Drive just ninety minutes from liberal Amsterdam to the town of Staphorst and you find a different world. Nearly 80 per cent of residents choose not to have television. On a Sunday, buses remain parked and the local pool closes. A quarter of women wear traditional costume: knee-high black socks tied up with rubber bands, a calf-length skirt, apron, shawl and bonnet, with black shoes or wooden clogs. Most of the rest dress conservatively. Half the town's youngsters move directly from their parents' home into marriage, and many vote for the SGP, a conservative Christian party opposed to euthanasia, gay marriage, brothels and women holding office. It wins about 5 per cent of the vote and holds two to three seats in the Dutch legislature.[11] Their ethos is carried to some degree by the wider religious population. Across all faith in Holland, those without children tend to leave church as they enter adulthood, but those with children remain in the pews. Among Dutch aged thirty-six to thirty-nine, nearly 20 per cent of those with children attend church at least once a month, while the corresponding figure among the childless is only 5 per cent.[12] This religious fertility, together with Calvinist growth and a second demographic transition among other Dutch, is combining to produce a Christian remnant.

A new immigration continent

The quicker, more dramatic side of religious demography is immigration. Current projections suggest that up to a quarter of Western Europeans will be non-white in 2050, rising to 60 per cent – if we include those of mixed race – by 2100.[13] Immigrants to Europe tend to be religious Christians or Muslims, while their host societies are mainly secular. Immigration therefore makes Europe both more colourful and more faithful. No longer can we speak of secular Europeans and a minority of religious immigrants because – in large measure – the immigrants and their children will *be* Europe.

At the epicentre of global southern Christianity stands Pentecostalism, its most exuberant, fastest-growing form.[14] Pentecostals are expressive fundamentalists who believe that individuals can be possessed by the Holy Spirit, hence their predilection for 'speaking in tongues'.

A quarter of the world's Christians are now believed to be Pentecostals, who have grown by converting Catholics in Latin America, animists in Africa and Buddhists, Shintoists and secularists in East Asia.[15] Many have immigrated to Europe. Britain alone has 250,000, mainly immigrants. In France, evangelical Protestants, largely Pentecostal, have swelled from 50,000 to 400,000 inside fifty years, chiefly through African immigration.

Catholicism and mainline Protestantism also benefit. In Denmark, immigrants fill the once ailing Catholic churches and have prompted a demand for more. In Ireland, Poles and Lithuanians are replacing the increasingly secular young Irish at Mass. The Global South is also the sole engine of Christianity for established Protestant denominations such as Anglicanism, symbolised by the appointment of Ugandan-born John Sentamu as Archbishop of York in 2005. This is a direct consequence of population explosion in the global South and, to a lesser extent, secularism in Europe. As the centre of gravity of global Christianity shifts to the tropics, it alters the balance of power between liberal-minded European clerics and more traditionalist African Christians on issues such as gay rights and the ordination of women. This in turn shapes the position of the churches in Europe. In Britain, a tenth of all Christians attending Sunday services are now of African or West Indian origin, rising to 44 per cent in London. If we add other non-whites, the London figure rises to 58 per cent, which of course excludes the more than a million East European immigrant Londoners, who make up a significant share of the 'white' attendance total. Thanks largely to immigration and high immigrant fertility, Christian attendance in 'secular' London barely budged between 1989 and 2005, while it plummeted 40 per cent in the rest of the country.[16]

The rise of Islam in Europe

While religious demography has slowed the pace of Christian decline in Europe, it has positively kickstarted European Islam. At the end of the Second World War, there were virtually no Muslims in Western Europe. Today there are 15 million, and they make up 2 to 6 per cent of the population of most West European countries. The first Muslims arrived in response to employers' demands for cheap factory labour in the wake of the Second World War. In France, North Africans, many from the Kabyle Berber region of Algeria, had been employed in manufacturing since the 1920s. Others arrived in the period up to and immediately after Algerian independence in 1962.[17]

In Germany, most *Gastarbeiter*, or guest workers, came from Turkey, beginning in the 1950s. Moroccans and Turks predominated in Belgium and Holland. Most Turks in Europe hail from small villages in central Turkey or along the Black Sea coast, relatively religious parts of the country. They sprang from the lowest rung of Turkey's socioeconomic ladder, possessing very little education.[18] This resulted in a disproportionately religious inflow. Scandinavian Muslims migrated more recently, largely as refugees. As a result, they reflect the conflicts of the Muslim world: Bosnians, Kurds, Iraqis, Afghans and Somalis. In Britain, the Muslim population is largely South Asian, with a near-majority, 43 per cent, of Pakistani origin and 16 per cent Bengali. Of British Pakistanis, 70 per cent hail from the rural Mirpur district of Pakistani Kashmir. The first wave was brought to Britain to work in textile mills in the English midlands.[19]

In most European countries, the influx of workers was poorly planned, a response to acute crises rather than long-term structural trends. As the sun set on Europe's heavy industrial sector, many of the newcomers lost their jobs. But instead of duly heading home as their hosts naively expected, many stayed on. Even without jobs, they enjoyed a far higher quality of life than could be had back home. The initial migrants, disproportionately male, were followed by their wives and extended families, and occasionally by asylum seekers from their home countries who could rely on ethnic support networks. The second generation, raised with higher expectations, often succumbed to unemployment and despair, with a disproportionate number turning to crime and drug abuse while becoming overrepresented at three to eight times the national rate in the prison population. While there, some found an outlet for their energies in radical Islam.[20]

Like African-Americans in decaying northern cities such as Detroit or Camden, New Jersey, Muslim European areas of settlement – poor, high-rise suburbs or industrial towns – often evolved into ghettoes. In France, *bidonvilles*, or shanty towns, ringed major cities such as Paris and housed hundreds of thousands of poor North African, Spanish, Portuguese and native French families after the war. Each ethnic group had its local services. Some *bidonvilles* persisted into the 1960s, but all were eventually bulldozed to make way for new public housing projects, which, as in the rest of Europe, sprang up like dandelions between the 1950s and 70s.

In France, vertical *cités de transit* were inspired by the functional modernist vision of Le Corbusier. Planners believed that light, airy and streamlined structures were progressive, healthy and rational. The lived reality was something else. Major banlieues, or high-rise suburbs, such as Saint-Denis and Aubervilliers outside Paris, were cut off from the city's Métro system, throwing yet another obstacle in the way of those seeking to work. The cheaply built structures rapidly aged, and now over 80 per cent of the tower blocks suffer from water damage, broken elevators, insulation problems and other defects. Mailboxes are often pilfered, and thus fall out of use. Gangs hang around building entrances, sometimes controlling the elevators. In many banlieues, local markets have closed up shop because of crime and neglect. In an acknowledgement of failure, hundreds of buildings have been demolished: since 1989, 300,000 more apartments have been phased out than built.

Not all residents are ethnic minorities, and most are non-Muslim. Even in Paris, there is a significant white working-class minority in the banlieues. At one time, white residents predominated, and sometimes intimidated or attacked foreigners. In the 'murderous summer' of 1973, over fifteen Algerian workers were killed in racist attacks around Marseilles. An even more insidious form of racist violence was inflicted by white residents shooting North African children playing in the court-yards below with .22 calibre rifles. In the month of July 1983 alone, seven shootings occurred, claiming the lives of a fifteen-year-old boy and a nine-year-old girl in Paris banlieues.

Today, an increasing proportion of white banlieue residents are elderly. This is partly due to 'white flight', but non-whites also try to leave such places. More significant, therefore, is that the supply of new residents is almost exclusively non-white, so areas become progressively dominated by ethnic minorities over time. If anything, local authorities try to discriminate in favour of non-Muslim Asians such as the

Vietnamese, using unofficial quotas. Despite such clandestine efforts, certain banlieues like Aubervilliers have become dominated by Muslims, and concentrations in individual blocks are often higher. The contrast between young minority populations and elderly white residents of adjoining low-density neighbourhoods can be stark. In the Paris suburb of Montfermeil, the mainly North African schoolchildren dub the local white neighbourhood of detached homes *la ville des vieux*, the old people's city. Christopher Caldwell views this demographic disparity as a civilisational metaphor, juxtaposing a vital Islam against an ailing Europe.[21]

Eurabia?: The demography of European Islam

'Europe,' quipped leading Princeton Islamic scholar Bernard Lewis to the Hamburg daily *Die Welt*, 'will have a Muslim majority by the end of the twenty-first century at the very latest.' Lewis's comments generated shock waves and raised the curtain on a new debate over whether Europe will become 'Eurabia'. Citing Lewis, Frits Bolkestein, an outspoken Dutch conservative and former European Union competition commissioner, caused an uproar when he told his audience on the third anniversary of 9/11 that 'Current trends allow only one conclusion ... Europe is being Islamicised.' Bolkestein warned that admitting 83 million Muslim Turks into the EU would hasten the Islamisation of Europe. Picking up on Bolkestein's remarks, Austria's outgoing EU commissioner for agriculture warned his fellow European commissioners against Turkey's accession. Turkey's bid makes strategic and economic sense, but popular fears that it will open the floodgates to large-scale Muslim immigration have kicked the idea into the long grass. Even academics have joined the fray. French demographer Jean-Claude Chesnais, for instance, speaks of his country's 'rapid Islamisation'.[22]

Conservative thinkers frame the issue in civilisational terms. American Catholic theologian George Weigel predicts a Muslim Europe by the turn of the twenty-second century. Europe's below-replacement fertility rate, he writes, is merely one manifestation of a profound moral malaise brought on by an atheistic humanism that couldn't care less about the survival of Western civilisation. 'When an insecure, malleable, relativistic culture meets a culture that is anchored, confident, and strengthened by common doctrines,' adds Christopher Caldwell, 'it is generally the former that changes to suit the latter.' Niall Ferguson confesses to an epiphany in the presence of Oxford's rising new Centre for Islamic Studies, complete with minaret and prayer hall. Viewing it as an omen of Western decline, he cites Edward Gibbon's eighteenth-century speculations about Europe's future. If the Moors rather than Charles Martel had triumphed at Poitiers in 732, 'Perhaps the interpretation of the Koran would now be taught in the schools of Oxford, and her pulpits might demonstrate to a circumcised people the sanctity and truth of the revelation of Mahomet.' [23]

Ferguson, Caldwell and Weigel's observations are generally scholarly. The cover of Egyptian-Jewish writer Bat Ye'or's *Eurabia: The Euro-Arab Axis* (2005) takes fewer prisoners. It shows Europe stained a Muslim green and labelled 'Land of Dhimmitude', a reference to non-Muslims' *dhimmi* status in Muslim empires whereby they submitted to a humiliating subordination to avoid slavery or death. Canadian journalist Mark Steyn's incendiary rhetoric goes further: 'As a point of fact, Mohammed is: a) the most popular baby boy's name in much of the Western world; b) the most common name for terrorists and murderers; c) the name of the revered Prophet of the West's fastest-growing religion. It's at the intersection of these statistics – religious, demographic, terrorist – that a dark future awaits.' These ideas are gaining popular traction. A widely circulated Internet parody of Europe in 2015 relabels Britain 'North Pakistan', France as the 'Islamic Republic of New Algeria', Germany as 'New Turkey', Belgium as 'Belgistan' and Spain as 'the Moorish Emirate of Iberia'. [24]

The Eurabia thesis gains credibility from the optimistic dreams of its Muslim proponents. Muammar Qadaffi glows over Islam's impending peaceful conquest of Europe, 'The 50+ million Muslims [of Europe] will turn it into a Muslim continent within a few decades.' He speaks in the fine tradition set out by his fellow Arab nationalist dictator Houari Boumedienne of Algeria, who in 1974 gushed before the UN, 'One day, millions of men will leave the Southern Hemisphere to go to the Northern Hemisphere. And they will not go there as friends. Because they will go there to conquer it. And they will conquer it with their sons. The wombs of our women will give us victory.' Jihadist Omar Bakri, speaking after the Madrid bombings, told a Lisbon newspaper that one day he expected to see the Muslim crescent flying over No. 10 Downing Street, the British prime minister's residence.[25] Norwegian jihadist Mullah Krekar concurred. 'The number of Muslims is expanding like mosquitoes,' he crowed, blithely unaware of the unflattering double-meaning of his words. Even non-violent Islamists have joined the fray. Al-Jazeera's Salafist agony aunt Yusuf Al-Qaradhawi once boasted, 'Islam will return to Europe as a conqueror and victor' and 'the conquest this time will not be by the sword but by preaching and ideology.'

How accurate are such fears? Let's evaluate some of these claims. In 2009, the seven-minute YouTube video 'Muslim Demographics' became a smash hit, watched more than 10 million times in the space of two months between May and July. Set to dramatic music, using flags and maps to illustrate its points, the video begins with a reasonably accurate statistical portrayal of Europe's low native birth rates. It then veers completely off the rails, claiming that French Muslims have a TFR of 8.1 against the French average of 1.8. French native TFR is indeed 1.8, but French Muslim TFR hovers between 2.8 and 3.3. The video then claims that 30 per cent of French children under twenty are Muslim, when the actual figure is 5.7 per cent.[26]

Though the mainstream media and most commentators correctly panned the video, they can only comment on the veracity of contemporary statistics, because *no one has performed accurate projections*. This was reflected in the comments of those who agreed that the statistics were inflated but bemoaned the lack of any alternative projections coming from the media. In the words of one reader who wrote to the BBC: 'Having read the [BBC rebuttal] article, I'm still none the wiser as far as what is really happening … in that regard, I'd say your article has failed to "debunk" fears provoked by the video. If anything, the article's weakness has reinforced my fears.'[27]

Though demographic projections are the most accurate in the social sciences, only three West European countries collect official data on religion. Moreover, no demographers have performed projections of Europe's religious composition akin to those of the US Census Bureau for America's racial composition in 2020, 2050 and 2100. To rectify this oversight, I teamed up with demographers at the International Institute for Applied Systems Analysis (IIASA) near Vienna, who run the world-leading World Population Program and have developed their own software for projecting the size of groups (educational, religious, ethnic, attitudinal) within countries. Projections must take into account each religion's age structure, fertility rate, immigration rate (by age and sex) and gains and losses to other faiths, including non-religion. Results will be presented later in the chapter, but first, let's take a demographic view at today's European Islam.

Europe's Muslim population today

The current size of Europe's Muslim population is about 15 million, just over 3 per cent of the European Union total. In most West European countries, Muslims form between 2 and 6 per cent of the population. The most up-to-date profile of European Islam is provided in Figure 1 below, though I can only speak with precision for eight of these countries (UK, France, Spain, Sweden, Netherlands, Britain, Austria and Switzerland), since I have been involved with the project which has collected these data from surveys and censuses.

While fertility, immigration and net conversion can fluctuate, much of the future is already legible from the age structure of religious groups. The sharp end of demographically driven social change is first experienced in the public schools and maternity wards of hospitals, because immigrant populations are often younger and more fertile than aging natives. In Britain in 2001, 8.5 per cent were foreign-born, but fully one in five births were to foreign-born mothers. The percentage of Muslims under the age of sixteen is 4.7, but just 0.6 over the age of sixty-five. In Austria in 2001, one of the other two European countries that collects census data on religion, Muslims formed 8 per cent of the under-ten population but only 0.2 per cent of those over seventy.[28] National trends are magnified in the case of urban areas in immigrant receiving regions. For instance, one in five UK births is to a foreign-born mother, but in Greater London the proportion rises to one in two. In Paris, the proportion of foreign-born mothers is a third and in Copenhagen a fifth.

The disparity in what demographers call the 'lowest-low' fertility countries is breathtaking: Italy's foreign-born population stood at a little over 5 per cent in 2004, yet in Rome, a study by La Sapienza University found that 15 per cent of mothers giving birth were foreign-born. In

Figure 1 **Estimated proportion of Muslims in European countries, *c.* 2000–08, %[30]**

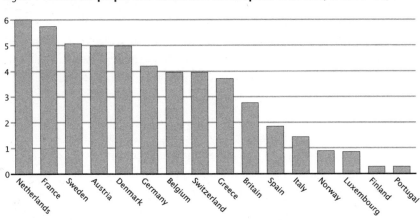

Turin, immigrants account for 25 per cent of births but just 0.2 per cent of deaths.[30] In Moscow, the Russian character of the city belies rapid ethnic change as the country's plunging working-age population combines with an oil-fueled demand for workers to change the makeup of the young population. In 2008, the city's statistical office released figures showing that 30 per cent of newborns in the city were born to mothers originating outside Russia. This almost certainly underestimates the proportion of non-Russian babies, since most illegal immigrants do not register their births. Most are from impoverished Muslim ex-Soviet republics in Central Asia. Caucasian Muslims are also prominent.[31]

Immigration

Since the mid 1980s, roughly a million people have entered Western Europe every year. A third arrive illegally. In most West European countries, the intake is roughly half non-European, of whom perhaps half are estimated to be Muslim. This means that only about a quarter of the current immigrant inflow into the EU is Muslim. This proportion may, however, increase as the supply of Eastern European immigrants dries up due to rising prosperity and the demographic implosion of ex-communist lands. In 2006, about 8 per cent of European Union citizens were foreign-born. A quarter to a half are African and Asian, of which a slight majority are probably Muslim.[32]

All told, perhaps a quarter of a million Muslims arrive in the EU each year, which represents 0.5 per cent of the EU's population. This may not sound like much until we remember that Hispanic immigrants to the United States arrived at the rate of roughly 1 per cent of the US population a year for several decades and have greatly transformed the ethnic landscape. And this in a country with a far higher native TFR than the European Union.

Fertility

Relatively high birth rates are an important factor in European Muslim population growth and would power change even in the absence of immigration. The Muslim total fertility rate in Austria in 1981, for instance, was 3.09 children per woman, against a population average of 1.67. In 1991, the ratio was 2.77 to 1.51. In 2001 it stood at 2.34 to 1.32. Thus even as Muslim fertility declined, the continued plunge in the fertility rate of the dominant Austro-German ethnic group has maintained differentials. Native Austrian fertility has risen slightly in the past eight years to around 1.4, so Muslim fertility should begin to converge with that of other Austrians. This is what has happened in much of the rest of Europe, because birth rates in Muslim home countries have been falling while native TFRs have inched up over the past few years.[33]

Though most Muslim countries have TFRs above 3 and slowing demographic transitions due to Islamist resistance, a number of important European source countries now have low fertility. These include Iran, Turkey, Algeria and Tunisia – all near or below replacement – and Morocco (2.59), but exclude Pakistan (3.6) and Somalia (6.52). These home country transitions affect the diaspora. In Germany, Turkish immigrant TFR declined from 4.4 births per woman in 1970 to 2.4 in 1996. In England and Wales, Pakistani and Bangladeshi immigrant TFR dropped from 9.3 to 4.9 between 1971 and 1996; in Belgium, Moroccan-born TFR fell from 5.72 to 3.91 between 1981 and 1996. On the one hand, Muslim fertility is about three times as high as that of natives in Britain and Norway, largely due to the Pakistani and Somali nature of the inflows. On the other hand, Iranian immigrant fertility is at or below that of natives in all countries, and Turkish nationals in Holland, be they immigrant or native born, have fertility that is falling towards that of the host population. All indications are that Turkish fertility will approach that of natives in most European countries in a generation or two.[34]

Approach, but perhaps never converge. Why? One startling statistic is that the TFR of immigrant populations of North African and Turkish descent is often *higher* in Europe than at home. This is especially true of Turks and Moroccans in Belgium and is probably related to the deprived rural source regions from which most immigrants come. Socioeconomic differences will fade, but not those driven by religion. Religious women of all faiths have higher fertility rates than their non-religious cousins. Among Muslims in Europe this is especially true: *religious* Muslims are nearly 40 per cent more likely to have three or more children than *non-religious* Muslims. This holds even when researchers control for age, marital status, income and education. Muslim women tend to be more religious than those of other faiths, and will therefore have a somewhat higher fertility rate, though much less so than previously.[35] The key fertility gap, however, will be that dividing the religious from the non-religious of all faiths.

Secularisation

European minority surveys show that most immigrants are more religious than their West European hosts.[36] Secularisation can transform Muslims into secular Europeans, but there is little indication of a fall in Muslim devotion. Europe-wide social surveys such as the EVS and ESS tend to undercount Muslims, but pooling together Muslim respondents from all countries across Europe we get a respectable sample, and this shows that roughly a quarter of Muslims attend mosque on a weekly basis. Young Muslims are as likely as older Muslims to regularly attend. This presents a sharp contrast to European Catholicism, where older generations attend at high levels while younger generations stay away in droves. Protestant attendance across age groups is as flat as Islam, but just 5 per cent are weekly attenders, a mere fifth of the Muslim level. In England, more Muslims attend mosque on a weekly basis than those attending Church of England services – and a growing proportion of Anglican communicants are non-white.[37]

Data from two large UK studies of ethnic minorities in the 2001–3 period confirm that Muslims do an exemplary job of passing their faith on to their children. In 2001, 71.4 per cent of British-born Muslims said their Muslim identity was important to them, considerably *more* than the 64.7 per cent of foreign-born Muslims who answered likewise. Among Bengalis and Pakistanis, 97 per cent of both native and foreign-born respondents identified themselves as Muslim, providing further evidence that the second generation is not abandoning their religious affiliation. A 2003 survey found a modest amount of secularism: 80 per cent of second-generation Bengalis and Pakistanis claimed that they 'practised' their religion, somewhat less than the 88 per cent rate for the immigrant generation. But compare this with the rapid secularisation of African and Caribbean Christians: 73 per cent of the foreign-born practised their religion, while just 43 per cent of the British-born generation did. For whites, 42 per cent of the foreign-born, mainly East Europeans, claimed to practise their faith, while 23 per cent of British-born – almost all of British descent – responded in the same manner.[38]

In the 2001 Census, the proportion of Bangladeshis and Pakistanis who said they had no religion was only half a per cent against 11.3 per cent for black Caribbeans. Between the immigrant and second genera-tion, the proportion of Pakistanis and Bangladeshis with no religion barely budges, from 0.32 to a mere 0.68 per cent.[39] A recent Dutch study confirms these results: the proportion citing 'no religion' among second-generation Turkish (4.8 per cent) and Moroccan (3.1 per cent) Dutch respondents is far lower than the general population and differs little from the first generation, though attendance exhibits modest decline. Statistical modelling indicates that being second generation does not erode the religious identity of Muslims and has only a modest secula-rising effect on mosque attendance. European Muslims, it seems, have found the magic formula for resisting secular trends.[40]

French Muslim exceptionalism?

The great exception to these trends are French Muslims, specifically those of Algerian origin. Sixty per cent of second-generation French people with at least one Algerian parent say they have no religion.[41] Why? In the 1999–2000 World Values Survey, Algeria had the lowest proportion of self-identified 'religious' respondents (55 per cent) of any Muslim coun-try, by far the lowest in the Middle East.[42] This is inaccurate, reflecting political identities rather than religious practice, but it does demonstrate something important. Berbers from the Kabyle region in Algeria have a strong tradition of identifying themselves with privatised Islam and the French language against the Arabo-Islamic ideology of the state.

French colonialists and native Berber intellectuals both propagated the idea that the Berbers were cultivators – more like Europeans than nomadic Arabs. They were considered to be of European ethnic origin, less religious and more individualistic than the Arabs. 'Beneath the Muslim peel,' wrote one French observer, 'one finds a Christian seed. We recognise that the Kabyle people, partly autochthonous, partly German in origin, previous entirely Christian, did not completely transform [into Muslims].' During the Algerian War of Independence, Kabyles joined the struggle, but did so as socialists or secular nationalists. In the 1980s, they rose up against the Arab-dominated regime and were violently crushed. In the 1990s, they were disproportionately targeted by the Islamic militants of the GIA. Many Kabyles in France continue to agitate for independence. One young Parisian Kabyle, Yunis, vividly recalls his first boyhood trip from Kabylia to Algiers. 'When I finally got to Algiers, I asked an old man I met on the street directions to the stadium. He hit me for speaking in Kabyle. I then asked a police officer, who threatened me with his baton.'[43]

Some 60 per cent of Franco-Algerians are of Kabyle origin. In addition, many non-Kabyle Algerians who arrived in France did so because they were loyal to France in the independence war. Some were pro-French *harkis* who fought for the French and had to flee to avoid the thousands of reprisals and killings which befell those that remained behind. We see similar loyalty among Indonesians in Holland and Ugandan Asians in Britain, though these are very small parts of their respective Muslim populations. French Algerians have also spawned an inner-city 'Beur' youth culture, complete with rap groups and African-American-style slang and dress.

Sports provides an alternative to traditional religion, and many French Muslims are avid soccer fans. In 1998, the polyglot French national football team won the World Cup, led by superstar Zinedine Zidane, a Marseille Kabyle. In the stadium and spilling out into the streets, supporters chanted his nickname, 'Zizou'. His image was projected onto the Arc de Triomphe and he was captured singing the Marseillaise, the French national anthem. Nike and other sportswear companies exploited this success with the message that pluralism was superior to both Islamic religious zealotry and white racism.[44] These unique factors may account for Algerians' greater propensity to assimilate, the lack of religious mobilisation surrounding the Banlieue Riots of 2005, the limited degree of recent French homegrown terrorism or the fact that a slim majority of French Muslims supported the headscarf ban in state schools. Indeed, as Jonathan Paris points out in *Foreign Affairs*, while 81 per cent of British Muslims said they were Muslim first and British second, just 46 per cent of French Muslims privileged Islam over their national identity.[45]

The role of intermarriage

There is an organic link between intermarriage and secularisation. In Europe, marrying someone with no religion or even a different religion tends to lead one to rear secular children.[46] If we look across Germany, Belgium, Holland, Britain and France, intermarriage rates are lowest among Muslim ethnic groups, averaging just 8 per cent. The Muslim second generation exhibits only a slightly higher level of outmarriage than their immigrant parents: an increase from 6 to 10.5 per cent. Algerian French men account for much of this increase: half married out in 1992, bucking the Muslim trend. Compare the low average Muslim intermarriage figure with that for West Indians: 26 per cent marry out in the first generation and 53 per cent in the second.[47] In Europe, religion appears to pose a larger barrier to mixing than race.

In Britain, where we have good census data, intermarriage between Muslims and non-Muslims remains rare: 92 per cent of Muslims marry within the faith. Muslim ethnic groups are among the most endogamous in the country: roughly 90 per cent of Bangladeshis and Pakistanis marry in, compared with just 49 per cent of black Caribbeans, 62 per cent of Chinese and 65 per cent of black Africans. The percentage of people in the UK who have Bangladeshi or Pakistani mothers and report their ethnicity as identical to their mother's is 92 to 93. By contrast, 30 per cent of those born to Caribbean mothers and 27 per cent of those born to Chinese mothers now claim a mixed or new ethnic identity. This cannot be explained by the recency of arrival since two-thirds of black Africans and 71 per cent of Chinese are immigrants, compared with the more established Pakistanis (45 per cent immigrants) and Bangladeshis (53 per cent).[48]

Still, ethnic habits rather than Islam may be the overriding driver of these trends. Given the smaller numbers of British Hindus and Sikhs, we would expect them to have higher intermarriage rates than Muslims. However, British Hindus are almost (90 per cent) as endogamous as Muslims, while Sikhs (93 per cent) are more so. These South Asian groups prefer to marry whites than each other. In 2001, just 0.3 per cent of Muslims were married to Hindus or Sikhs, compared with 5.7 per cent who wed Christians and 1.5 per cent who chose a person of no religion.

The ethnic nature of marriage shows up in the rarity of intra-Muslim intermarriage. Of more than 12,000 marriages in our British sample involving a Pakistani or a Bengali, there were a mere 25 Pakistani-Bengali couples.[49] Radical Islamist groups such as Hizb-ut-Tahrir provide one of the few settings in which inter-ethnic marriage occurs, suggesting that Islam only overrides ethnic loyalties in the white heat of the most intensely Islamist environments.[50] In short, British Muslims who marry out prefer whites. Their offspring overwhelmingly do as well: just 7 per cent of the children of part-Asian mothers identify themselves as Asian, with the rest splitting evenly between white and 'mixed'.[51]

Ethnicity, then, is the main barrier to assimilation for most Muslim groups, because endogamy is the norm in South Asia and the Middle East. Sub-Saharan African Muslims come from a more 'loose-bounded' region, and probably mix more, but are underrepresented in Europe. In general, South Asian endogamy, be it Muslim, Sikh or Hindu, prevents assimilation, while black Caribbeans' creolised homeland prepares them for it. The Muslim resistance to assimilation gains strength because Turkish, Pakistani and Moroccan children, in particular, are pressured to marry spouses from the home country or even the home village. Often these marriages are arranged, and sometimes involve cousins. In Holland, from 1988 to 2002, 71 per cent of second-generation Turks and 59 per cent of second-generation Moroccans chose a spouse from the home country. Trends appear to be similar in Belgium, the only other case where we have good data. Only France is an exception, with just 17 per cent of second-generation Algerian-origin men (but fully 54 per cent of second-generation Algerian-origin women) opting to find a spouse in Algeria.

Some argue that restrictive immigration laws since the 1970s ramp up the pressure on European Muslims to seek spouses abroad in order to enable friends and relatives to immigrate here. This is especially true for Muslim women, who are more subject to patriarchal constraints.[52] Others reply that targeted measures such as Dutch, German and Danish laws which raise the minimum permissible age of foreign spouses and mandate language proficiency and waiting periods have successfully reduced arranged-marriage migration. Danish law is especially stringent: citizens under the age of twenty-four who marry non-EU spouses cannot even live in Denmark. This may impair Danish–Swiss or Danish–American liaisons, but its results disproportionately affect the local Muslim population: the proportion of Danes of non-European background marrying foreigners declined from 63 to 38 per cent between 2002 and 2005.[53]

Those who claim European Muslims will soon resemble American Hispanics in their pace of integration are mistaken.[54] American Hispanics are more similar to the rapidly assimilating European blacks because both originate in hybridised homelands. A small and growing portion of Muslims are certainly intermarrying and a trickle are secularising, but the pace of change is slow. One also has to factor in the power of Islam as a supra-ethnic, civilisational identity. Recall that secularisation theory recognises that religion can revive when it serves as a prop of identity. Second-generation Muslims are detached from their ethnic roots but also feel spurned by the white majorities in their nation states. This condition of existential purgatory makes the option of Muslim identity more enticing. One may not feel very Pakistani or English, but one can be a *Muslim*. You don't even have to be religious to cheer for Team Islam. The British Pakistani young men who daub 'Hamas rules OK' graffiti on the walls of their Yorkshire slums are indulging in an Islamic machismo no different from the gangsta-clad rioters of the banlieues who chanted 'Allah Akbar' to police. These are boundary-marking identity games with little connection to the obligations of Islam or abstruse debates about sharia.[55] Identity practices are relatively costless, and you can indulge them without embracing the discipline of Islamic practice.

This is not irrelevant to religious revival. Identity politics stimulates spiritual curiosity and strengthens communal norms of piety that might otherwise crumble. Historically, we find this among the relatively religious Poles, Bretons, Basques, Northern Irish Nationalists and others who consider the Catholic religion a key element of their identity. The revival of Islam in the Muslim world – manifested in the wearing of the headscarf and rise of Islamist organisations – makes Islam hip for Europe's nominal Muslims. They feel part of a growing worldwide movement, the umma, or community of believers. Once a vague abstraction, the umma, remarks the always perceptive Aziz Al-Azmeh, has been reinvented as a political and territorial 'nation' knit together by cyberspace, Islamist NGOs and globalisation.[56]

Global communications allow Al-Jazeera and other transnational Islamic cultural products to enter European living rooms. Islamist websites proliferate, many translated into European tongues. The umma even has a political vision. The message that Islam should supersede national and ethnic attachments may ring hollow in the Middle East where nations and sects are locked in competition, but it strikes a chord with Europe's deracinated Muslims.[57] Thirty-one per cent of British Muslims claim a stronger connection with Muslims in other countries than with their fellow Britons, and the figures are much higher among those aged eighteen to twenty-four.[58] For Muslim theologians such as Tariq Ramadan, this ethnic uprooting offers European Muslims a better chance to realise true Islam than their parochial brethren in the Muslim world. He proffers a 'Euro-Islam' which is at once purer and better adapted to modernity. European Muslims who seek to cut loose from backward ethnic traditions such as arranged marriage may even gravitate to Salafi fundamentalism because it derides these as human innovations.[59]

Social exclusion does not explain differences in minority-group integration: Afro-Caribbeans are just as economically deprived as Muslims. But poverty further impedes integration and heightens alienation. In the period 1980–2001, the unemployment rate among Turkish and Moroccan immigrant men in Belgium was 33 per cent, far above that for Italian immigrants (14 per cent) or natives (5.3 per cent). In the Netherlands, roughly a quarter of Turkish and Moroccan immigrant men were unemployed, compared with just over 3 per cent for natives. The picture for Turkish and Moroccan women was even worse: 45 per cent of Moroccan women in Belgium and France were unemployed, compared with 10–12 per cent among their native counterparts. While Turkish and Moroccan men lagged a few percentage points behind Western European natives in terms of labour force participation, the Turkish and Moroccan female participation rate was just half that of native women.[60]

In Britain, 30 per cent of Muslim men are economically inactive, nearly twice the rate of Christian men. Even of those who are in work, 40 per cent perform low-paid service jobs, more than double the Christian rate. Meanwhile, Muslim women are more than twice as economically inactive (68 per cent) as other British women. Inflexible labour markets in continental Europe and racial discrimination in all countries are only part of the problem. Traditional Muslim gender roles mean that in Britain, only a quarter of inactive young Muslim women even *want* to work.[61]

More encouraging is that economic performance rises dramatically the longer an immigrant is in the country, the higher their education and the better their language skills. Most Muslim newcomers to Europe spring from the poorest, least-educated sectors of their homelands, unlike North American Muslim immigrants, who are largely well educated.[62] Even so, their children are doing considerably better. In Britain, Muslim youngsters now outperform natives in both high school and university. Upward educational mobility has been most dramatic for Pakistani Muslims, and this will result in significant economic mobility, at least for men. The gap may not close entirely, however, since Muslim Indians, who vastly surpass British whites in terms of educational qualifications, still experience lower income levels.[63] In France, studies find that even with the same level of education, Muslim youth are twice as likely to be unemployed as non-Muslims. Research using fake résumés shows that having a Muslim surname or address in a banlieue worsens one's employment prospects.

Similar discrimination impairs the ability of Muslims to leave their high-rise ghettoes in Swedish and German cities, locking in deprivation. In Britain, half of Pakistanis and Bengalis live in the most depressed 10 per cent of British wards, where the unemployed are often in the majority. These include segregated former mill towns such as Oldham and Burnley in the British North West, where white–Muslim riots broke out in June 2001. The Cantle Report into the riots pinned much of the blame on the 'parallel lives' led by whites and Muslims there. As a Muslim respondent quoted in the report remarked, 'You are the only white person I shall meet today.' In view of these developments, Commission for Racial Equality chairman Trevor Phillips, himself an Afro-Caribbean immigrant and once a cheerleader for difference, turned against multiculturalism. In 2005, he warned that Britain was 'sleepwalking into segregation'. Yet it is not clear how ghettoes can be dispersed. Muslim demography reproduces them even though upwardly mobile Muslims try to escape their clutches. This in turn impedes intermarriage and integration for the most vulnerable, who are in turn most susceptible to radicalism.[64] Thus while there are encouraging signs of upward mobility, a significant proportion of European Muslims continue to live in ethnic slums, islands of desperation in a sea of prosperity.

The future of Islam in Europe

The authors of the YouTube hit 'Muslim Demographics', in common with other prophets of Eurabia, warn of a Muslim majority in Europe by 2050. Now that we have a grip on the size, age structure, immigration, fertility, intermarriage and secularisation of European Muslims, we are in a position to project their likely population share. Figure 2 shows the numbers that my IIASA colleagues project for eight West European countries. Only two, Austria and Switzerland, have currently been projected to 2050, but their trajectory gives us a good sense of what we might expect for other countries. These projections assume no Muslim secularisation, current rates of immigration and that Muslim fertility rates will converge with that of the native population by 2050. While it is reasonable to assume that some Muslims will become secular, it is also likely that Muslim fertility rates will not converge completely to host society levels, so the projections are not systematically biased up or down.

Notice that Muslim populations in 2050 are projected to fall well shy of a majority, but that the curve of increase bends upward over time, causing the speed of Islamisation to accelerate beyond 2030. This means that most large Western European countries will be between 10 and 15 per cent Muslim in 2050, though Sweden may approach 20–25 per cent,

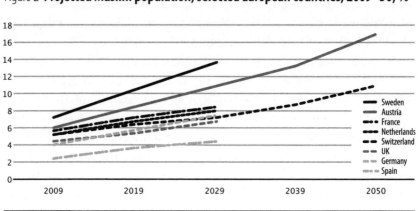

Figure 2 **Projected Muslim population, selected European countries, 2009–50, %**[65]

while countries such as Spain whose inflow is more Latin American will be little more Islamic than they are today.

While Europe will fall well short of Eurabia in 2050, there will be significant changes by 2100. In Austria, if fertility rates between Muslims and others do not converge, the country will be 36 per cent Muslim by century's end, with Muslims in a slight majority among those aged under fourteen. Muslim TFR seems likely to converge towards that of other groups, but even if the gap closes by 2030, Austria would still be more than a fifth Muslim by the turn of the century. In Switzerland, projections based on current fertility differentials and migration flows show that roughly a quarter of Swiss will be Muslim in 2100, rising to nearly 40 per cent of those under the age of fourteen. In the more likely scenario of fertility convergence by 2030, stability will be achieved at a much lower figure of around 10 per cent Muslim.[66]

Needless to say, in the unlikely event that Europe adopts Singapore/ Kuwaiti-style immigration control, most of this growth will not take place. Zero immigration would – in the presence of converging Muslim fertility – stabilise the continent's Muslim component in the 2030s at somewhere between 5 and 10 per cent. Holland is planning to erect an ethnic 'dyke' around Rotterdam by restricting refugee and immigrant settlement into the 'majority minority' city. Meanwhile it has deported thousands of asylum seekers from the country and slashed immigration.

These could be the first steps towards a 'Fortress Europe'.[67] Of course this would also mean that Europe would begin to age and decline at an accelerating rate. In a zero-immigration Austria, for instance, the population would decline from 8.6 to 6.8 million between now and 2050, with the slide gathering pace after mid-century.[68]

In fact, to maintain the size of their working-age population, the fifteen pre-accession EU countries need to bring in 1.5 million immigrants a year, roughly four times current levels. To maintain the same ratio between those of working age (fifteen to sixty-four) and those over sixty-five, about 13.5 million are needed each year, fifty times the current intake.[69] European governments will try to restrict immigration, attract non-Muslim immigrants, raise native fertility and facilitate Muslim secularisation and intermarriage. But even if nothing changes, Islam will fall well short of a European majority – even in 2100 – largely because of Muslim–Christian fertility convergence and the growth of other religious groups.[70]

More important than ethnic change, therefore, is that the fertility gap *within* Christian and Muslim ethnic groups between religious conservatives and secularists will not fade. This will power an erosion of secularism and moderate religion. In both Austria and Switzerland, projections reveal that the non-religious populations will be well past their peak in 2100. From a high of 22 per cent in 2060, the secular total will fall to 19 per cent in Austria in 2100 and sink more quickly thereafter. Swiss patterns are similar, with a secular peak of 24 per cent in 2075.[71] These projections greatly understate the change because they do not disaggregate the 'religious' population by theology and intensity. Within the religious population, the more devout and fundamentalist of all faiths will be increasing their demographic clout, edging out both moderates and seculars.

Why does it matter?

The principal reason that most Europeans worry about the growing Muslim population has less to do with sharia and jihad than old-fashioned ethnic nationalism – the wish to see the dominant ethnic majority remain congruent with the nation state. We shouldn't exhibit the presentist myopia that views Muslim immigration as a greater challenge because Islam is more exotic or conservative than Catholicism. Imagine that France was on its way to becoming a German-speaking country owing to a seemingly bottomless supply of Teutonic immigrants who simultaneously refuse to give up their language and identity. Does anybody doubt that this would lead to as much angst as the prospect of a Muslim-majority France? Given European history, the hysteria might be far worse.

Catalonia has the largest Muslim component in Spain, in part because many Catalan nationalists prefer Muslim immigrants who are willing to speak Catalan to Spaniards who refuse to. In 2008, the immigration issue flared in Spain, but the chief complaint focused on Ecuadorian and other Latin Americans rather than the smaller Muslim population, which in any case was not connected with the Madrid bombings.[72] In other words, fear of exotic strangers is not necessarily more intense than Freud's 'narcissism of minor differences' which drove the slaughter in Nazi Germany, Rwanda and the former Yugoslavia. Indeed, if we turn back the page of European history we find a fear of Catholic fertility and Papal conspiracy. Most of this was the product of ethnic anxieties among majorities concerned that they would be bred into submission.

Europe has long been a continent of emigration, and its foreign-born tended to come from other European countries and make up less than 1 per cent of national populations.[73] There were some exceptions, however. In France, the influx of Orthodox Jews in large numbers from Eastern Europe after the Russian pogroms of 1882 interacted with ingrained anti-Semitic traditions to produce tensions which culminated in the Dreyfus affair of the late 1890s. In Germany, Jewish immigrants flocked to Berlin, and in Austria, they headed for Vienna. These social democratic, more Jewish cities were fiercely denounced by Hitler, and used as a foil in his rise to power. In Britain, the 1905 Aliens Act was designed to control the influx of Jews, but in much of the country, Catholics were deemed the primary challenge. Scotland was just 1.6 per cent Catholic in 1790, but this share rose steadily as poor Irish immigrants poured into industrial central Scotland. By 1851, Catholics formed 4.6 per cent of the population, rising to 11.4 per cent in 1914 and over 20 per cent by 1970. More religious than Protestant Scots, Catholics made up over a third of the population in much of Glasgow and a majority in certain Greater Glasgow industrial towns such as Coatbridge.[74]

The swelling Irish Catholic population around Liverpool also provoked a powerful Protestant backlash and was the central issue for the Protestant working class, who, as in central Scotland, voted Tory despite their economic interests. Meanwhile, in Scotland, the Irish Catholic threat was perceived to be so serious that the Church of Scotland asked the British government to curtail this 'menace to the Scottish race'. During the interwar period, sectarian populist movements such as Protestant Action and the Scottish Protestant League won a third of the vote by campaigning against public funding for Catholic schools, dubbed 'Rome on the Rates'.[75] Traces of this era remain. While researching my previous book at the headquarters of the Scottish Orange Order in Glasgow, I stumbled across titles like 'All Roads Lead to Rome' alleging various Vatican plots. Popular fear of Catholicism, however, like today's fear of Islam, is principally caused not by fear of religious doctrines but by the rapid growth of an ethnic minority which is deemed to be unmeltable.

This, rather than a defence of Enlightenment values, is the principal reason for the rise of the Far Right in Europe. The behaviour of Muslims matters less to most Europeans than Muslims' disruptive growth potential and resistance to European attempts to digest them. If they were demographically moribund and small, Muslims would arouse little worry – regardless of the odd bomb or burqa. If Europe faced large-scale Latin American immigration, as in Arizona, or parts of Spain, it would be worrying mainly about Hispanics, not Muslims. That said, violent jihadism and illiberalism *do* reinforce European anxieties and provide a liberal justification for policy change which matters for European elites. Let us consider each in turn.

Jihad in Europe: religion re-enters the public sphere

Islamic terrorism in Europe has grown noticeably since the early 1990s. Its spread was initially an extension of Islamist campaigns in the Muslim world. Until the early 1990s, Islamic militant groups repressed by the authoritarian regimes of the Middle East were allowed to operate freely in Europe. They exploited the liberal asylum provisions of West European countries to establish residence and raise support for the jihad.[76] When communism was the West's principal bogeyman, Salafi-jihadists were still considered harmless crazies who could usefully resist the Reds. A tacit understanding between the Islamists and European security services offered militants a safe exile if they desisted from attacking European targets.

Khomeini, for example, lived in Paris prior to the 1979 Revolution, as did leading Algerian Islamists before 1994. London, dubbed 'Londonistan' by detractors, looked the other way until 2003–4. London's radical imams were hardly an appendage to the struggle back home. The power of the fatwas they penned controlled swords in Algeria: in 1996, Abu Hamza and Abu Qatada, along with Abu Musab and Ayman al-Zawahiri of Gamaat Islami – who later became bin Laden's second in command – were among the many jihadis who rubbed shoulders in the city.[77] All went on to become Al Qaeda stars.

In 1995, Paris was hit by a series of terrorist attacks as punishment for its support of the Algerian government during the civil war. This was followed by a long lull, which was only punctured in 2004 when Al Qaeda redefined Europe as a *dar-al-Harb*, a 'land of war', where 'defensive' jihad must be waged to comply with Muslim law.[78] The first notes of the new Islamist sonata were played by the Moroccan Jamal Zougam and his confederates in Madrid on 11 March 2004. Ten coordinated blasts on the city's train network between 6.45 and 7.40 in the morning claimed the lives of 191 and injured 2,057. The event scarred the Spanish psyche and, like 9/11, transformed the nation's sense of reality. The next day, 11 million people, a quarter of Spain's population, marched in solidarity to condemn the attack. Three days later, conservative Spanish prime minister José María Aznar, who in backing the unpopular war in Iraq incurred the wrath of Al Qaeda, lost the election. Islamist terrorists were widely credited with swaying the outcome of the contest. Spanish politics would never be the same again.[79]

Britain was the other West European power to support the US-led coalition's 'War on Terror' in Iraq and Afghanistan. This, combined with London's apparent complicity in upholding the Palestinian status quo, was the ostensible reason behind the 7/7 London bombings of 2005. Significantly, unlike Madrid a year earlier, these were suicide attacks. Second, and more ominously, they were carried out by homegrown terrorists, including a convert. It took a concerted propaganda effort on the part of Islamist recruiters to channel the disparate grievances of the four young British bombers into jihad.

European cells have carried out attacks in Madrid, Paris, London, Milan, Berlin, Amsterdam, Rome and Porto.[80] But successful attacks are only the tip of the Euro-jihadist iceberg. In Holland, Islamists have made several attempts to assassinate politicians. In France in 2001, they tried to attack the American embassy before being caught by French police. In Britain, major failed attempts include the London fertiliser plot of 2005, the transatlantic airline plot of 2006 and London and Glasgow airport attacks of June 2007.[81] Roughly 200 mosques, around 3 per cent of the European total, are estimated to be militant. As in Finsbury Park, extremist elements take them over by slowly sidelining and intimidating calmer voices. Philip Jenkins points out that a few hundred committed militants – the maximum strength of the IRA during its zenith – is enough to wreak havoc. Yet in Britain alone, 2,000 Islamists in 200 networks are under surveillance, with perhaps 1,000 deemed potential jihadis. The country faces thirty known plots and countless others that have yet to be uncovered.[82]

Islamism and Liberalism

'It was the coolness of his manner, the composure of a person who knew precisely what he was doing, that struck those who saw Mohammed Bouyeri, a twenty-six-year-old Moroccan-Dutchman in a gray raincoat and prayer hat, blast the filmmaker Theo Van Gogh off his bicycle,' writes Ian Buruma. Though Van Gogh begged for mercy, Bouyeri shot him several more times, slit his throat with a machete and left his weapon planted in Van Gogh's chest. He then pulled out a smaller knife and pinned a note to Van Gogh's body.

The note was directed to Ayaan Hirsi Ali, a Somali-Dutch critic of Islam who wrote the film *Submission*, which Van Gogh produced. The provocative movie dramatised the abuse of women in Islam by projecting Qur'anic quotations on to the naked bodies of several young women. Van Gogh was murdered on 2 November 2004. Many Dutch considered this the last straw and reacted by staging street protests. Others went further. There were forty-seven cases of violent attacks – including arson – on mosques and Muslim schools. In retaliation, Muslims attacked churches in thirteen separate incidents.

Van Gogh's flamboyant style and open lampooning of Islam made him a hate figure among Dutch Muslims, especially Islamists. He especially enjoyed riling militant fundamentalists. In June 2003, he called Abou Jahjah, of the European–Arab League, a 'pimp of the Prophet' after Jahjah arrived in a theatre surrounded by fierce bodyguards and refused to take part in a debate Van Gogh was moderating. Outside the theatre, some of Jahjah's supporters yelled that they would 'get that fat pig [Van Gogh] and cut him open', while Jahjah's bodyguards threatened event organisers.[83] In the year following Van Gogh's assassination, Geert Wilders, an anti-Islamist politician, went into hiding and Ayaan Hirsi Ali relocated to the United States.

This reinforced a pattern of Islamist extremists threatening anyone who dared to publicly ridicule Islam. The opening shot in this war was the fatwa issued by Ayatollah Khomeini in 1989, calling for the murder of British-Indian author Salman Rushdie. This came in the wake of large protests by British Muslims against his book *The Satanic Verses*, some of whom called for Rushdie's execution.[84] Street actions like this convinced the European public that Islamists do not understand free speech. If the concept does not involve tolerating views one disagrees with, then it becomes meaningless.

Van Gogh's murder was followed, a year later, by the Danish Cartoons Controversy of September 2005. The cartoons, published in Denmark's *Jyllands-Posten* newspaper, were relatively benign portrayals of the Prophet, offensive only because of the fundamentalist injunction against a human depicting the Prophet. While there were local Danish Muslim protests, it took the global entrepreneurialism of Danish Islamist Abu Laban to whip up the Muslim world. In order to achieve the desired effect, he appended three incendiary images to the cartoons, including that of a man wearing a pig snout, purportedly a picture of Muhammad. As a result, protests erupted across the Middle East. Danish embassies were burned in Lebanon, Syria and Iran and attacked in Egypt. Attempts were made to boycott Danish goods and Muslim leaders called for a meeting with the Danish prime minister.

On a more mundane level, Islamist threats helped to silence discussion of subjects such as Muslim conversion to Christianity and historical criticism of the Qur'an, notably the fact that it could not have been written in pure Arabic as fundamentalists claim. When Sarah Maple, a Muslim artist of mixed South Asian–English heritage displayed her Muslim-themed work at the SaLon Gallery in Notting Hill, London, the gallery's windows were smashed and she received death threats. Paintings such as *Cherry Bakewell Anyone?* (2006) – featured nothing more sinister than a portrait of herself wearing a hijab and holding a cherry tart. Radical Islam was having none of this, expressing its perceived veto on her right to express herself.[85]

Critics claim that Islamist threats effectively stifle criticism of Islam, and even produce self-censorship among those who might otherwise do so. While other religions are open to ridicule or scrutiny, Islam is not, and this constitutes a double-standard.[86] Just as galling to European sensitivities is the response of mainstream politicians, many of whom fell over themselves to respond to the new threats by reviving disused or discarded blasphemy laws while bending to Islamist requests. The work of anti-Muslim polemicist Oriana Fallaci and even that of fiction writer Michel Houllebecq were targeted for censorship.[87] For many Europeans, banning free speech to soothe the sensitivities of irrational zealots seemed a step in the wrong direction.

The sharia debate becomes especially poignant in view of the widespread abuse of women in many Muslim countries, a phenomenon chronicled by successive UN Arab Human Development reports. Unsurprisingly, some of this cultural baggage has arrived in Europe. The issue of female genital mutilation has aroused controversy in a number of European countries, notably Sweden. In Britain in 2007, a scandal ensued when it was discovered that public money had been used to fund dozens of 'hymen replacement operations' to restore Muslim women's virginity. Honour killings and the gang-raping of supposedly 'loose' women in Muslim ghettoes by local Islamist thugs raise hackles. Both revolve around the idea that Muslim women should be chaste and refrain from dating Western men or adopting Western sexual mores or face the consequences. In Germany, some forty-five honour killings took place in the 2000–2005 period alone, including that of Hatun Sürücü, slain by her brothers in broad daylight for 'dishonouring' her family. Her crime: dating a German and raising a child on her own.[88] Honour killings reflect Kurdish and Pakistani ethnic customs rather than Islamic law, but sharia was perceived as offering carte blanche to abusers because of its sexist take on marriage, divorce, virginity, women's testimony and domestic violence.

European Muslims are less supportive of all aspects of sharia and domestic abuse than Muslims elsewhere. However, support for sharia is not absent in Europe – worse, it appears to be rising among the new generation. Comparing British Muslims aged sixteen to twenty-four with those over fifty-five, a 2006 poll discovered that 37 per cent of youth would prefer to live under sharia compared with just 17 per cent of those over fifty-five. Thirty-seven per cent of 16- to 24-year-olds would opt to send their children to Islamic schools, versus just 19 per cent among their elders; 31 per cent of those in the younger group believe that conversion should be punished by death, against 19 per cent among the older group; and 74 per cent of youth prefer women to wear the hijab (headscarf), while only 28 per cent of elders do.[89]

Sharia might be interpreted as a harmless badge of Muslim pride, which people support in principle, but not in practice. There is some evidence for this: a recent survey of women in Turkey's (Islamist) Welfare Party found that while 95 per cent supported sharia, the vast majority also opposed legal changes which would implement its specific precepts.[90] A less sanguine view is that Muslim identity politics leads to a punctilious adherence to doctrine. Gilles Kepel writes that when Salafist organisations reach a critical mass in deprived French neighbourhoods, their men begin to enforce Islamist norms on local women. The women in turn start to agitate to wear the headscarf in local schools.[91]

In 2004, France and five German state governments banned the wearing of the headscarf in public schools. This capped a lengthy process of hand-wringing over the issue. In France, controversy dates from 1989, when three Muslim girls were expelled from school in a Paris banlieue for refusing to remove their headscarves. The High Court subsequently ruled that expulsions could be justified if the wearing of a symbol was deemed a political or proselytising act that might interfere with the 'progress of teaching'. This edict was rarely enforced, but public pressure mounted, calling for stronger enforcement of the ban to defend not only education, but the values of the republic. The hijab had now become a symbolic issue in which the French state would brook no compromise.[92] Despite four major demonstrations in which veiled demonstrators protested that their human rights were being violated, the French government went ahead with the ban. This was widely supported. Even a slim majority (52 per cent) of French Muslims supported it.[93]

Though only France and some German states banned the headscarf, the issue was increasingly politicised throughout Western Europe. Banks, cleaning companies, department stores, food chains, day-care centres and hospitals refused to hire hijab-clad women.[94] In 2006, British Labour MP Jack Straw, a former foreign secretary who represents a constituency with a significant Muslim population, made headlines when he called the headscarf 'a visible statement of separation and of difference' and asked women who wore the veil to remove it when visiting his constituency office.[95]

Criticism of the hijab remains controversial, since it can be interpreted as both an individual choice or a coercive community norm and there is no easy way of determining the wearer's motivation. As one moderate Dutch Muslim cleverly put it, 'It is a crime to force a woman to wear a headscarf, and it is a crime to prevent her from wearing it.'[96] While hijabs expose the face and can even be fashionable, the burqa, which completely covers the face, provides a clear affront to European sensibilities. In September 2009, French president Nicolas Sarkozy took the bold step of openly blasting the burqa as a symbol of oppression. 'In our country, we cannot accept that women be prisoners behind a screen, cut off from all social life, deprived of all identity,' he declared to an applauding crowd of lawmakers. 'The burqa is ... a sign of debasement ... It will not be welcome on the territory of the French Republic.' The Dutch went further, banning the burqa in public places via an act of parliament.[97]

The demise of multiculturalism

Sarkozy's tough response to the Banlieue Riots of 2005, which burned for over three weeks and consumed nearly 9,000 vehicles, helped him to win office. As interior minister, he pledged to a mother at one riot scene that he would deal with the 'riff-raff' who were behind the trouble. His ascent reflects a major shift in European attitudes that has been building since the mid 1990s. I once saw Britain's racial-equality czar Trevor Phillips refer to multiculturalism as a 'meaningless word'. He is correct insofar as popular deployment of the term has rendered it a completely malleable concept. Proponents trade on the fact that many people support the idea of having a mixture of people and cultures in one place. Opponents claim it supports a world of multiple ghettoes.

Strictly speaking, multiculturalism is not about ethnic geography, but rather the policy used to manage diversity. You can have a melting-pot policy in a very diverse country such as the USA, or a multicultural policy in largely homogeneous Norway. Properly construed, multiculturalism supports ethnic and religious groups having rights against the state which can sometimes supersede those of individual citizens. The Quebecois, to take a Canadian example, have a collective right to compel businesses in their province to erect signs in French, regardless of Anglo individuals' right to freedom of expression; in Britain, some argue that Muslims should have a right to adjudicate their own disputes according to sharia even if this violates the civil rights of Muslim individuals, and so forth.

There is an important difference between a multiculturalism of means and one of ends. Sometimes group rights are justified on the basis that they will ultimately lead to integration. President Sarkozy is using affirmative action to increase the participation of Muslims in French public life and combat Muslim unemployment. This is an example of using multicultural tools to achieve integrationist ends. The same goes for attempts to increase minority representation in the British police, military or parliament. These measures, if temporary, may promote integration. However, multiculturalism can become an end in itself. Many of its standard-bearers desire a country where groups maintain themselves in perpetuity, acquiring political power, parallel institutions and even self-government.

On this view, rather than *e pluribus unum* (from the many, one), there is a desire for, in Al Gore's words, 'from the one, many'. The logical end point of this system is a politics of ethnic power-sharing where group loyalties trump individual choice. For instance, in Northern Ireland and Lebanon, the constitution and electoral systems guarantee each ethnic bloc a fixed share of political power and a veto on new legislation. When politics is organised communally, it becomes difficult to cross the tribal aisle or be a floating voter.

This doesn't mean multiculturalism is always a bad idea. It is required in societies like Lebanon and Northern Ireland, where minorities are indigenous 'sons of the soil' and therefore have a right to self-determination that would be slighted under a majoritarian system.[98] Without multicultural arrangements, restive native minorities might resort to violence to achieve independence. Minorities such as Northern Ireland's Catholics want a guarantee they will not simply be outvoted by the Protestant majority every election – which would invariably happen because voters rarely opt for parties of the other ethnic stripe. Minorities also want to be protected from the dominant culture, which they fear could assimilate their group the way the English absorbed the Cornish.

On the other hand, immigrant groups such as the Turks in Germany, whose ancestral homelands lie elsewhere, make no such claims. How extraordinary therefore that multiculturalism is propounded in their name. To explain this, we need to look beyond minorities – most of whom did not agitate for multiculturalism – to the majority culture. The defining moment was the 1960s, when the Afro-American Civil Rights struggle inspired an epochal shift in the Western Left. As the class struggle lost its allure, ethnic minorities replaced white working-class men as the objects of sympathy. Darker-hued immigrants became the chosen agents of radical social transformation, while uneducated white males elbowed aside capitalists as the primary bugbear of the Left. Relieved, business, which had long opposed nationalism for impeding the free movement of goods, capital and labour, joined the party. The result was a 'celebration of difference' by both radical artists and cosmopolitan multinationals like Benetton, in which growing diversity forever effaces the white monoculture.

The cosmopolitan version of multiculturalism, popular among liberal intellectuals and the global economic elite, wants to have its cake and eat it too. Cultural diversity is great – especially if it can be packaged and consumed, but ethnic endogamy, sexism and homophobia are multiculturalism's embarrassing country cousins. Multicultural political philosophers such as my fellow Canadians Will Kymlicka and Charles Taylor square this circle by convincing themselves that ethnicity is always in flux. Today a group is fixated on race and religion, but tomorrow they will forget these obsessions and signify their difference through more inclusive, liberal symbols such as food and music. Ethnic groups 'wish to be cosmopolitan,' says Kymlicka. Their symbolic content is 'constantly forming and dissolving,' adds Chandran Kukathas.[99] Perhaps British Pakistanis will get over Islam while Quebecois console themselves with maple syrup as a fillip for their lost French language.

Those who take the contradictions between cosmopolitanism and ethnicity more seriously recognise that the end point of cosmopolitan interaction is a 'multiculture' without groups. This vision is utterly repugnant to conservative associations like the Muslim Council of Britain (MCB) which desire a Britain of clearly defined communities.[100] For them, a nation's identity, if such a thing exists, consists of groups' overlapping interests – which is likely to be rather minimal in the case of, say, the MCB, gays and the Board of Deputies of British Jews. The MCB gravitates to the communitarian ideas of Taylor, who rejects the republican notion that the state should be neutral in matters of religion and ethnicity. Instead of these remaining private matters, he claims that religion and ethnicity deserve official 'recognition' because they are important to people's self-esteem. Will Kymlicka adds that public recognition is necessary because the majority culture receives de facto recognition so minorities invariably suffer second-class status.[101]

The problem is that ethnic and religious groups often contain a sizeable conservative wing. Recognition of fundamentalists grates against individual rights and the recognition demanded by the majority. Ethnic and religious fundamentalists defend outrageous symbols like the burqa, proscriptions against driving on the Sabbath, or sharia law – *precisely because* they challenge the liberal status quo. These are typically sacralised and depicted as non-negotiable. The logic of multiculturalism therefore easily leads to a trampling of basic rights. A French court, for example, permitted a Muslim man to annul his marriage because his wife was discovered not to be a virgin on their wedding night. The British pensions department maintained a policy of recognising polygamy by providing benefits for 'additional spouses'.[102] In Montreal, the management of a YMCA installed frosted windows at the behest of a local Orthodox Jewish congregation to prevent others peering in. Sensitive to Muslim demands, another local YMCA obeyed requests to clear a swimming pool of men so that pious Muslim women could enter.[103]

With incidents like these, the conflict between group and individual rights can no longer be theorised away. When the state gives in to such demands from self-appointed 'community leaders', the majority of all faiths get annoyed. To be fair to multicultural theorists, even Kymlicka and Taylor, in their recent work, specify that minorities must respect non-negotiable liberal norms. For Kymlicka, this is especially imperative for immigrant-origin minorities who do not have historic territorial claims.[104]

High theory is often influenced by events on the ground, and these forced a major rethink among liberal intellectuals in the 1990s. The tripling of support for the Far Right from the mid 1980s in many Western European countries showed that the white working, rural and petit-bourgeois masses did not see a place for themselves in multiculturalism, except as its despised 'other'. The central plank of the Far Right message was ethnic nationalism, which called for a defence of the 'native' ethnic majority against rootless elites and growing immigrant minorities. However, agitation against multiculturalism and 'reverse discrimination' struck a chord as well and attracted some who might not have considered voting for the radical Right.[105]

Centre-right parties began to form governments with the Far Right, edging out the mainstream Left in countries as diverse as Norway, Italy and Austria.[106] To head off this challenge, Centre-Left parties began to call for a renewal of national identity, albeit in inclusive, 'civic' form. Territory, history, values and institutions could be adopted by anyone, regardless of bloodline. The French in particular could offer a rich republican tradition based on the Revolution, high culture and a history of immigrant incorporation. The Dutch government withdrew public funding for ethnic organisations, abolished dual citizenship and scrapped public airtime for multicultural groups.[107] In Britain, immigrants were obliged to swear an oath of national loyalty, demonstrate proficiency in English and take a citizenship test.

Intellectually, the sea change began in continental Europe in the 1990s. Centre-Left French writers such as Alain Finkielkraut, Pierre-André Taguieff and Emmanuel Todd were the first to break ranks. In France, the slogan *droit à la différence* gave way to *droit à la resemblance*. 'What happened to the ascendant differentialism?' asks Rogers Brubaker.

'Two words: Le Pen.' The Far Right's deployment of the language of eth-nic essentialism – 'they can never be like us' – revealed to many centrist intellectuals how politicising cultural differences has dire consequences.

In Germany, the Left no longer agitated for non-citizens to enjoy rights while remaining apart. Instead, they encouraged immigrants to integrate into a common citizenship.[108] Postmodernism, a post-Marxist trend which voiced a relativist critique of the Enlightenment in psyche-delic lingo, was finally exposed – after a quarter century – as the fraud it always was. Even angry intellectuals realised how irresponsible it was to preach that all ideas are created equal. For in the end, postmodernist multiculturalism has no standard by which to elevate gender equality over sharia. Even in the softest subjects, such as sociology, critical realism challenged postmodernism's formerly dominant position.[109]

In Britain, one senses the Parekh report of 2000 as the last gasp of the old order. Bhikhu Parekh, a genial and bright Labour peer of Bangladeshi origin, chaired a report on community relations which contained much good sense but also reproduced some of the shibboleths of the academic New Left. The report called for Britain to officially commit itself to mul-ticulturalism. This would legally define society as a collection of groups, not merely individual citizens.[110] While this is understandable for the his-toric Scots and Welsh, whose political aspirations and memories are in Britain, it is bizarre for immigrant groups like the Jews or Pakistanis, most of whom simply want to be left alone. The report's statement that Brit-ish nationalism was inherently racist was uncontroversial among the pro-fessoriate, but this time, Tony Blair's hitherto pro-multiculturalist New Labour administration pushed back. Gone was talk of 'Cool Britannia' and celebrating differences. Responding to grassroots annoyance, Blair's home secretary David Blunkett and foreign secretary Jack Straw advanced ever more robust defences of Britishness and even Englishness.[111]

A growing chorus of left-leaning writers and officials lambasted multiculturalism as divisive. Some, like Kenan Malik, Stuart Hall and Trevor Phillips, were non-white. Phillips, Head of the Commission for Racial Equality, emerged as one of multiculturalism's most forceful crit-ics. After 2004, his high-profile agency demanded that funds only be handed out for anti-racism or integrated activities and not to parochial ethnic associations that promoted an agenda of difference. In taking this stand, he clashed with socialist London mayor 'Red Ken' Livingstone – part of a frosty relationship which dates back to 1999, when the unlikely duo ran on a joint mayoral ticket.[112]

Some in the British republic of letters stepped beyond integration policy to question cultural pluralism. In a controversial intervention, David Goodhart, editor of *Prospect*, a leading intellectual magazine in the country, boldly asked his largely Centre-Left readers in 2004, 'Is Britain Too Diverse?' Drawing on research which found more ethnically diverse parts of the United States to be less supportive of social provision, Goodhart warned that growing diversity could erode the sense of communal obligation needed to persuade middle-class Britons to share their wealth.

After all, he argued, if universal need rather than shared nationality is the rationale behind the welfare state, the malnourished of the Third World are much more valid claimants on the middle-class purse than low-income Brits. The subtext of Goodhart's argument was that the task of integrating minorities into the nation must go beyond the obligations of citizenship. Integration also requires a deeper melting of some of Britain's growing diversity. For Goodhart, British society has to choose between higher levels of diversity with a minimum commonweal, as in America, or greater homogeneity in a more caring society, as in Europe.[113]

Islam played only a bit part in all this drama. The main headache for centrist parties and intellectuals was the rising profile of immigration, asylum and national identity. Still, Islamism added fuel to the fire and the Far Right seized upon Islamophobia to broaden its electoral appeal. Islamist threats to free speech and gender equality became banner issues in Holland, Denmark, Sweden and Germany. Notable was the fact that gay and feminist figures were in the forefront of the new nationalism. Pim Fortuyn, assassinated in 2002 by an animal rights activist, is a paradigm case. A charismatic, openly homosexual politician, he combined a robust defence of secular liberties with anti-Islamist Dutch nationalism. Likewise, Bruce Bawer, gay author of *While Europe Slept* (2006), urged Europe to respond more robustly to the Islamic threat in its midst.[114]

Other liberal minorities changed their minds too. European Jews increasingly voiced concerns about multiculturalism. This followed a rise in anti-Semitic incidents largely perpetrated by European Muslims frustrated at both local Jewish success and Israel's hardline policies towards the Palestinians.[115] In addition to secular Jewish intellectuals such as Alain Finkielkraut, Jewish critics included mainstream community leaders like Britain's chief rabbi Jonathan Sacks. Sacks urges a shift from rights-based to responsibility-based citizenship, and is openly critical of the trend towards difference.[116]

Liberal criticism of multiculturalism was vital. It helped to relax the elite consensus which had conflated multiculturalism with diversity and anti-multiculturalism with white racism. To a large extent this consensus still operates in Canada and the United States, and one now observes a marked difference in discussions of multiculturalism between the two sides of the Atlantic. In Europe, you cannot legitimately oppose Islam as a foreign religion, but you can fault it for being illiberal. The Dutch government was among the first to take its cue from the new mood of liberal integrationism. It introduced a citizenship video for prospective immigrants which featured two expressive homosexuals kissing and emphasised women's freedom as a core national value.

France's ban on headscarves in public schools, largely inspired by nationalism, was also legitimated by the need to regulate conservative religious subgroups who restrict women's freedom. At the margins of the new integrationism one could find a less noble Islamophobia. In her bestselling *The Rage and the Pride* (2002), Italian journalist Oriana Fallaci ridiculed pious Muslims as 'the gentlemen who, instead of contributing to the progress of humanity, spend their time with their behinds in the air, praying five times a day'.[117] More tragically, there occurred a rise in Islamophobic attacks. In Britain alone, there were 200 reported incidents and 65 violent attacks on Muslims in the immediate wake of the London bombings, including a fatal stabbing where attackers repeatedly screamed 'Taliban' at their victim.[118]

Jihadi violence slowly climbed up the scale of European government priorities. September 11, Iraq and Afghanistan thereby elevated the security factor in the integration conversation. In the words of British Labour MP Tony Wright, 'Before September 11 it [multiculturalism] looked like a bad idea, now it looks like a mad idea.'[119] The Madrid and London bombings sent security concerns to the top of governments' agendas. In an attempt to manage rising security threats, they entered the business of regulating religion. This practical multiculturalism muddied the separation of religion and state, demonstrating how the demographic rise of Islam in Europe has called a halt to post-1789 secularising trends. Muslim states generally do not tolerate dissent. Therefore citizens of Muslim-majority countries such as Egypt often express their public selves through Islam. Religious associations and mosques are the anchor of civil society, not secular parties and unions. Only at mosque can citizens escape the heavy hand of state repression.

These modalities travelled with the immigrants to Europe. During the heyday of multiculturalism, Muslim organisations sometimes received government funding to carry on their activities, consistent with the 'celebrate the differences' spirit of the times. More often, European governments were content to sit back and let foreign funders and their imams run the show. Saudi, Algerian and Turkish governments poured money in to fund new mosques and jockeyed for influence. Homeland conflicts were replayed on European soil. The Algerian government, for example, sponsored the moderate Paris Mosque and its extended network of sister mosques, supplying imams with government-approved ideas. Islamists preached their own counter-message through alternative mosques affiliated to the more Moroccan, Muslim Brotherhood-dominated UOIF (Union des Organisations Islamiques de France).

Often these were supported by Saudi or other Middle Eastern Islamist funds.[120] In Germany, the Turkish government appoints imams for the DITIB (Diyanet İsleri Türk Islam Birliği) network of mosques, the oldest Turkish religious association which accompanied the original *Gastarbeiter*. Their adversaries are Milli Görüs, affiliated to moderate Islamist parties such as Refah and AKP, who have had a presence in Germany since 1960. More radical are Süleymanci and Nurcu, two newer associations with Muslim Brotherhood links that service the Salafist sector of society. Both are banned in Turkey. Finally, there is a revolutionary Caliphate State movement, similar to Britain's Hizb-ut-Tahrir. The Muslim Brotherhood, Saudi-inspired Muslim World League, Pakistani Jamaat-e-Islami and Jamaat Tabligh are also active throughout Europe. European-dominated Islamist groups such as Hizb-ut-Tahrir and the Antwerp-based Arab European League (AEL) are attractive because they preach in European languages that local Muslims understand and are less weighed down by homeland baggage.[121]

European governments feel the heat of the anti-multiculturalist backlash from the mass public, but are pushed back towards multiculturalism by the imperatives of security. Many northern European countries have long practised a form of governance known as corporatism. In this model, groups like trade unions and churches meet directly with government officials. Grafting Muslims onto this framework was the logical thing to do. The danger here is that these organisations may not reflect the views of those whom they claim to represent, leading to a policy stitch-up by elites in smoke-filled rooms which exaggerates parochial concerns at the expense of national ones. This is one reason why corporatism is frowned upon in Britain and France.

Yet what is remarkable is the degree to which Britain and France have followed Germany, Holland and Scandinavia in recognising Muslim leaders and entering into corporatist relationships with them. In 1989, France created its Conseil Français du Culte Musulman (CFCM); in 1992, Spain followed with its Comisión Islámica; in 1998, Belgium with its Exécutif Musulman; in 2000, special councils for Islam/state relations were created in seven German Länder, and in 2002, the British government gave its blessing to the new Muslim Council of Britain (MCB). An Italian body followed in 2003. This is not the imams-in-government model we find in the Muslim world, but it is a step in that direction.[122]

In all countries, officials sought a European Islam to reduce the role of foreign imams and open up a direct channel between potentially alienated Muslims and the government. The outcome of such maneouvring remains uncertain. Foreign imams can be more moderate than home-grown ones. Government-sponsored mosques, as in the Muslim world, often enjoy less legitimacy than independent ones. To recover their popularity among the people, government-approved Islamic quangos may tack well to the right of most Muslims, ignoring the secular minority altogether. This certainly seems true of the MCB in Britain and CFCM in France.[123] Still, governments have been so keen to avoid radicalism that they are willing to risk antagonising majorities by extending the hand of recognition to groups with repugnant beliefs, such as the Salafists.

The British government, for instance, hoped Salafism would provide the certainty and direction that jihadism offers to alienated Muslim youth. Sometimes they were right: in a number of instances, Salafism helped pull young jihadis back from the brink of suicide terrorism and deradicalise them.[124] Though Britain's security services have tentatively begun to step away from this engagement, it shows how the practical need to deal with security challenges often necessitates multiculturalism. Like Sarkozy's affirmative action programmes, this is an expedient multiculturalism of means. But it risks institutionalising a place for official Islam in the constitution of states, an expansion of *pluribus* at the expense of *unum* which may prove difficult to revoke.

Political effects

Europe's changing religious composition won't affect political power for decades because the median voter tends to be considerably older than the average European Muslim. Candidates require a sense of familiarity with the new society that usually only comes from native birth or long-term residence. On the other hand, Europe's Muslims are heavily concentrated in important urban areas. When immigrant groups predominate locally, as with Cubans in Miami or the Irish in Boston, they can dominate local politics. If these locales are nationally important, minority groups can wield disproportionate power at national level. Hispanics, for instance, are a major presence in several large, hotly contested states such as California, so can deliver a significant number of electoral college votes in the state by state, 'winner-takes-all' American system. This means that elites of both parties make great efforts to win Hispanic support and back their policy concerns – such as an amnesty for illegal immigrants – even when these are opposed by most voters.

In much of Europe, the electoral system is based on proportional representation, so numbers translate directly into political influence. This permits a minority to jockey for position in coalition politics. Sometimes the Muslim minority can act as kingmaker, as when the votes of several hundred thousand Turkish Germans provided incumbent chancellor Gerhard Schröder with his narrow margin of victory in 2002.[125] What is more likely is that Europe's conservative Muslims will exercise indirect influence over specific policy areas through implied violence.

Rightly or wrongly, a fear of their young, inner-city 'Muslim street' may dampen European leaders' willingness to support the foreign policies of the United States and Israel or artists' freedom of expression.

Studies of non-European immigrants in Europe suggest they vote for left-wing parties but have more conservative social attitudes than others.[126] This certainly seems the Muslim pattern. Might this offer conservative parties an opening, prompting them to alter their appeal from ethnic nationalism to moral traditionalism? The Republican Party in the United States did precisely that, successively sidelining Protestant nationalism to pursue conservative white Catholics, and white nationalism to court religious Hispanics. Late in his second term, George W. Bush tried to introduce an amnesty for illegal immigrants and largely avoided taking a strong position against bilingual (Spanish-English) education. The Religious Right, specifically the Christian Coalition, joined Bush by promoting a generally pro-immigrant message that embraced both Hispanics and religious Muslims.[127]

Thus far there is little indication of a shift in the conservative value axis in Europe because the native Religious Right is weak outside Ireland and Poland while conservative religious minorities are still small. The anti-immigrant vote has therefore been far more valuable than the immigrant vote. From Italy to Norway, Switzerland to Belgium, the Far Right in Western Europe has trebled its performance since the late 1980s, forcing centrist parties to appeal to ethnic anxieties. Even in Britain, where the Far Right is a contender only in local elections, successive Tory Party platforms in the 1990s and 2000s stressed their toughness on immigration and multiculturalism. Ethnic nationalism in Europe is explicitly non-religious, decrying the Muslim 'other' but seeking to unite white secularists and Christians. This is reflected in the rise to prominence of secular nationalists such as Pim Fortuyn or Nicolas Sarkozy as well as the overtly secular platforms of Far Right parties. Contrast this with the tepid, failed attempt by the British Tories to shift the late-term abortion period from twenty-four to twenty weeks, or the absence of a 'Religious Right' within the party. In effect, for the European Right, ethno-nationalist concerns trump moral-religious ones.

Yet change may be in the air as a 'religious' minority of Muslims, immigrant Christians and conservative white Christians emerge. The

American population is currently a third, and its electorate a fifth, non-white. In Europe, these proportions are far lower, with non-white voters accounting for less than 5 per cent of the electorate. As religiously motivated minorities grow, European conservative parties could sound the alarm, strengthening their current emphasis on ethno-nationalism by promising tighter immigration controls. This would see members of dominant white majorities closing ranks and acting tribally. However, if the American case is anything to go by, majority ethnic unity will prove episodic and elusive because ideological differences are so ingrained among whites. European liberals, socialists and the university-educated middle class will prove difficult for ethno-nationalists to mobilise. As a result, immigrant growth may not generate a concomitant rise in the anti-immigrant vote. The electoral calculus would then shift to favour immigrants over anti-immigrants.

Today in Flanders, left-wing parties that get immigrant votes do not openly court them for fear of alienating anti-immigrant voters.[128] But their strategy changes where minorities are thicker on the ground. For instance, at national level, the Belgian socialist party (PS) downplays its immigrant and Muslim vote. In Brussels, where the proportion of non-Europeans in the electorate is roughly a quarter, it woos them.[129] In 2006, for instance, the Brussels PS went out of its way to appoint the first Muslim deputy mayor, Faouzia Hariche, a woman of North African origin. Indeed, more than 20 per cent of the city's councillors were Muslim, largely socialists. It was a similar story in Antwerp, where the socialist share leapt from 19 to 35 per cent on the strength of the Muslim vote. The anti-immigrant Vlaams Belang (VB) increased its share of Antwerp's white vote, but stagnated overall because of the decline of whites in the city's population.

In the longer term, ethno-religious change brings political change. As Filip Dewinter, the VB leader in Antwerp, commented, 'I am a realist. The number of potential voters for our party is declining year by year ... Currently a quarter of the population are immigrants. These people do not vote for us. Every year 4,000 indigenous Antwerpians move out and 5,000 immigrants move in.' Less noticed was the impressive effort of the centre-right Christian Democrats to recruit Muslim candidates. This may signal the rise of an ecumenical 'culture wars'-style conservatism in the city. In the Brussels borough of Sint-Joost-ten-Node, where ironically the party headquarters of the VB is located, four out of five Christian Democrat councillors were non-European in 2006, a higher proportion than among the socialists. In Antwerp, a third of Christian Democrat councillors were non-European, equal to the socialists.[130] Clearly, in a more diverse environment, the taint of courting the immigrant vote pales beside the need to compete for their support. This redefines the axis of politics.

Over time, might we see the cultural cleavage in Europe shift from ethnicity to religiosity? At present, the Left has a virtual lock on the Muslim vote in Brussels and in Europe more generally. This stems from its progressive views on the welfare state, pro-Muslim foreign policy and liberal take on immigration. However, pious non-Europeans are uncomfortable with socialists' secular mores and repelled by their coalition of gays, feminists and secular humanists. Thus there is an opportunity for conservative parties to win back this constituency. An American 'culture wars' strategy would see conservative parties wooing traditionalist minorities by stressing religious and family values while downplaying anti-immigrant themes. Such a coalition could be built upon a combination of urban religious minorities and religious whites. White Christians remain a political force. Though the proportion of religious voters in Europe declined in the late twentieth century, an individual's degree of religiosity remains one of the strongest predictors of how ideologically right-wing they are, and how likely they are to back established conservative parties.[131]

On the face of it, the idea of conservative Muslims and Christians of all races joining hands seems absurd. But we shouldn't forget that the Republicans managed this feat in the United States before 9/11. It becomes conceivable because politics is local. When Christians and Muslims largely inhabit separate constituencies, party machines can insulate them from each other while mobilising both against a common opponent. This is the essence of resource mobilisation theory, which argues that strong movements permit diversity across local branches to dissipate internal tensions.[132]

In Britain, for instance, the Labour Party allows conservative Muslims to dominate some Labour constituencies while feminists, gays or white male trade unionists rule other fiefs. The party prevents these glaring contradictions from tearing it apart by devolving divisive policy debates to the local level. Unity at party level coalesces around more general themes such as economic policy. The Tories could do likewise with Christians, Muslims and Orthodox Jews. In the proportional representation systems of continental Europe, Muslim parties may spring up, in which case ecumenism could be established through coalition politics. After all, green parties have recently forged once-unthinkable coalitions with conservative parties in Ireland and Germany. In Lebanon, Christians and Sunni Muslims, once bitter rivals, are now political bedfellows.

The ghosts in Europe's closet predispose its elites to downplay ethnic nationalism. The anti-nationalist legacy of the Second World War, expressed most fervently after 1968, has made it difficult for ethnic majorities in the West to use the language of race. All societies, as Freud noted, require taboos, and in the West, moral restrictions have crystallised along anti-racist lines. Conservative parties which stress religious traditionalism may be disliked by media elites, but they cannot be smeared as morally noxious.

Indeed, multiculturalism explicitly defends conservative religion against a 'hegemonic grand narrative' of Western secularism, as demonstrated by finger-wagging Anglo-Saxon liberal commentary on the hijab controversies in France and Quebec. 'Political correctness' is stronger in North America than in Europe, hence the more rapid relinquishing of race and immigration by American conservatives compared with their European counterparts. Yet the European Right must also beware the stick of political correctness lest it appear nasty. It, too, knows that it is easier to trumpet a morally than a racially conservative message. When the carrot of the minority vote becomes more attractive, the ideological appeal of moral traditionalism will grow. At a key tipping point, secular liberals will replace non-whites as the conservative bogeyman, with Christians and Muslims joining forces to oppose secular Europeans. The main fissure in European politics will then shift from ethnicity to religion.

The decline of European secularism

Is Muslim–Christian comity so far-fetched? The rise of Islam offers interesting possibilities for Europe's committed Christians. Together, immigrant Christianity and Islam are bringing religion back to Europe and raising Christian hopes for an end to decades of gloom.[133] A sociologist colleague of mine who teaches at the inner-city London Metropolitan University recounts how she is probably the only secularist in classes largely populated by devout Muslims and evangelical Afro-Caribbean Christians. One of my Muslim students adds that his pocket of London's deprived, immigrant East End sprouts mosques and evangelical churches in equal measure. Such tales will become more common as Europe's ethnic composition changes.

Islam and Christianity may not seem like natural bedfellows, but in most European countries, believers of all faiths feel like an embattled minority in the face of secularism. This was the message of Pope John Paul II, who, as we saw earlier, reached out to Muslim and evangelical Protestant groups to combat UN family planning and gender equality initiatives. Prince Charles, who will one day become King of Britain, preaches the same message. He wishes to see the British constitution amended so that his title is not 'Defender of the [Christian] Faith' but 'Defender of Faith'.[134] As I write, I see an email in my inbox from something called the 'CI Dialogue Foundation', whose executive is chaired by the Grand Mufti of Egypt, includes the Archbishop of London, ex-British PM Tony Blair, as well as the Orthodox Patriarch of Jerusalem and representatives from other faiths. This is laudable insofar as it advances interfaith peace, but as Blair states in the circular, there is also a religious agenda: 'There are few more important tasks today than locating a proper place for religion in the affairs of the world, drawing on its wisdom to help solve the world's problems.'[135]

Pope Benedict's attempt to bridge the secular–Christian divide by upbraiding Islam in his Regensburg speech and breaking bread with the secular Jürgen Habermas is an exception to business-as-usual.[136] But it seems more of a stretch than the ecumenical pro-faith message of John Paul II, Tony Blair and Prince Charles. Their voices are moderate, but fundamentalists can piggyback on the interfaith message and utilise their networks, as we saw with the anti-family planning activities of the World Congress of Families.[137]

The religious also find common ground at national level. Beneath the froth of the Islam-in-Europe debate, one detects the outlines of a shared Christian-Muslim 'religious' interest. European Muslims have positive views of Christians.[138] Many feel a sense of commonality. Tariq Ramadan speaks of Islam contributing to Europe's rediscovery of spirituality, with Islam as 'revelator rather than ... aggressor'.[139] Practising Christians in turn lend support to many Muslim religious and moral positions. When British Conservative Party leader Michael Howard expressed his wish to scale back the term limit for abortion from twenty-four to twenty weeks in 2005, he received unanimous support from Anglican, Catholic, Jewish and Muslim religious leaders.[140]

The Muslim Council of Britain has also worked with Catholic groups to maintain the right to reject gay adoptees and keep the teaching of gay rights out of religious schools.[141] A similar coalition came together in Britain over the issue of protecting religion from defamation. A religious hate law, approved by Prime Minister Tony Blair, a committed Catholic, would have proscribed virtually any intemperate speech against Muslims. In 2006, it only failed to pass the House of Commons by one vote.[142] In a reprise of the issue, Church of England Archbishop Rowan Williams and his MCB counterpart Sir Iqbal Sacranie urged more robust legislation against religious hate speech than the watered-down 2006 bill.[143]

Williams continued to court controversy when he suggested in a speech to leading lawyers that Britain should permit some aspects of sharia law to operate. In his view, the Orthodox Jewish and Catholic adoption agencies' de facto opt-out of accepting gay parents pointed in this direction. In Williams's words, the 'principle that there is only one law for everybody is an important pillar of our social identity ... but I think it is a misunderstanding to suppose that means people don't have other affiliations, other loyalties which shape and dictate how they behave in society and that the law needs to take some account of that.'[144] A similar meeting of the minds occurs over the issue of publicly funded faith schools, with Christian, Jewish and Muslim leaders singing in unison. Currently, there are over 4,600 Anglican, 2,000 Catholic and 35 Jewish schools in Britain, but just 9 Muslim ones.[145] Despite secularist worries over the implications of public funds for faith schools, the status quo is in no great danger and we should expect growth in the Muslim school sector.

The multicultural ethos, which remains current among many left-liberal intellectuals, encourages a publicly assertive religious lobby. Charles Taylor, a committed Catholic and the doyen of multiculturalism theory, contends that religious commitments are integral to individuals' identities. To impugn these identities is to demean the individuals who hold them. Moreover, he argues, religious identities should not be kept private but should be publicly recognised as important components of society alongside secular institutions.[146] At conferences on religion or multiculturalism, 'sensitivity' and respect for religion – even conservative religion – is the watchword.

On this, academic multiculturalists find themselves in the odd company of evangelical Christians. One should never underestimate the sentiments of many of Europe's evangelicals, who resent secularism far more than Islam. Several years ago, I had the opportunity to attend a debate in London hosted by a conservative Muslim society, in which men and women sat on opposite sides of the hall. The principal speaker was a fiery Islamist of Afro-Caribbean origin who harangued the British over their permissive social mores and ostensibly anti-Muslim foreign policy. During question time, one of the few non-Muslims in the audience identified himself as an evangelical Christian and urged 'young Muslims' to 'get off their backsides' and start voting, to enhance the voice of those upholding traditional religious values.

All told, there is plenty of meeting of the minds between Europe's conservative Christians and Muslims. True, we will continue to see inter-ethnic conflict as the main axis of cultural politics. The rise of 'culture wars' conflict *within* ethnic groups between secular liberals and 'values voters' will prove a longer term development. As we move towards mid-century, however, Europe may soon begin to follow the American pattern. Diverse cities will lead the way. The sustained demographic increase of strong religion ensures that the European Right's path of least resistance will lie in moral conservatism. Religious fundamentalism will slowly reclaim a political field left vacant by the retreat of the great secular religions, which no longer excite Western Europeans. Liberty, equality and rationality once drove back religion because they were married to an enchanting vision of the future. Today, their only residues are the social taboos that constrain secular nationalism, Europe's sole serious alternative to religious politics.

6

'A SCHOLAR SOCIETY':
THE HAREDISATION OF
THE JEWISH WORLD

'[T]he Jews are like everyone else, only more so' – Eliot Cohen[1]

Nowhere is the religiosity–fertility nexus as stark as in Israel and the Jewish diaspora.

On 8 February 2007, Israeli economist Dan Ben David wrote in *Ha'aretz*:

> It is difficult to overstate the pace at which Israeli society is changing. In 1960, 15 percent of primary-school pupils studied in either the ultra-Orthodox or the Arab-sector school systems (these are today's adults). In 1980, this rate reached 27 percent, and last year it was 46 percent.[2]

The trends sketched by Ben David have radical implications in a society founded by secular Zionists. Both Israeli Arabs – those living within pre-1967 Israel rather than the West Bank and Gaza – and the ultra-Orthodox were opponents of the Zionist project of creating a Jewish State. They do not serve in the military and have unemployment rates of over 50 per cent.[3] Arab growth has received the most attention from Israeli and Western commentators. However, the Arab share of Israeli births has been declining in recent years.[4] In addition, Israeli Arabs are politically contained by restrictive laws and practices which limit their access to land, government funding and the military. Ultra-Orthodox Jews, by contrast, have much higher fertility rates than Israeli Arabs, with no signs of decline. Few of them emigrate and they have access to the nation's power centre.

Origins

Who exactly are the ultra-Orthodox, or Haredi, Jews? This is not as simple a question as it may seem. In fact, much of what we think of as ultra-Orthodoxy – in terms of dress, social closure and institutions – arose in the modern period and reached full flower only recently. Traditional Judaism emphasised the study and recitation of the Hebrew Bible (Torah) and mastery of traditional commentary and Halachic laws (Talmud). Proficient religious scholars were highly prized, and acquired elite status in the community. Religion was organically linked to the ethnic community. As in traditional Islam and Christianity, austere strands of thought would surface periodically. But religious leaders were also community leaders who felt responsible for the fate of the entire Jewish community, regardless of observance.[5]

Secular concerns pressed hard on the embattled communities of diaspora Jews, which curbed puritanical appetites. The need to trade with Gentiles, for instance, or to bend rules on kosher meat to sell it to them, overpowered strict interpretations of the text. Religious leaders therefore used the full range of scriptural resources and traditions, which allowed for *kullah,* or leniency of interpretation. Religious fundamentalists who sought out the most stringent passages of the Torah and Talmud were smacked down by the communally minded rabbinic authorities. The noted Halachic arbitrator of Germany and Austria, Rabbi Jacob Reischer (d. 1733), expressed this well when he branded certain fundamentalist local rabbis 'innovators' because of their economically crippling decrees on kosher meat. Such men were reprimanded for deviating from the ways of the rabbinic elites, carriers of the traditions of their more lenient forefathers. In this way, ethnicity and custom trumped textual literalism.[6] Fundamentalism could only emerge when modern processes broke the link between community and religion.

The story of ultra-Orthodoxy is not one of enduring tradition, but of modern innovation. It begins with the eighteenth-century

Enlightenment. Enlightenment ideas of liberty and reason led to Jewish emancipation: a gradual removal of restrictions on where Jews could live and the professions they could pursue. The French Revolution, for example, and its Declaration of the Rights of Man, offered Jews full citizenship as individuals. The quid pro quo was Jewish assimilation, for it was expected that just as French Christians would slough off their Catholicism, Jews would join in forging the revolutionary French nation and transcend their faith. 'We must refuse everything to the Jews as a nation,' declared a delegate to the French National Assembly, but 'accord everything to Jews as individuals'. As Jews left the confines of their ghettoes, most moved in the direction of the Enlightenment. Religious practice declined and even those who remained in the synagogue moved into closer harmony with Enlightenment ideals.

At the same time the dissolution of traditional Jewish communal authority empowered those who sought to return to religious fundamentals. Secularism and liberal Judaism created a pluralistic environment which created Orthodoxy as a new option within a differentiated Jewishness. External persecution could not be relied upon to maintain group boundaries and conformity. Religious Jews could no longer take Judaism for granted as the inheritance of ages past. Instead, they had to fight to preserve Orthodoxy. Freed from communal rabbinic authority, they could now define this as strictly as they pleased. Soon, they erected symbolic boundaries such as black hats and a Yiddish-only language policy to mark out 'true' Orthodox Jews from those who had strayed from the 'truth'.[7]

German rabbi Moses Sofer was one of the first to lead the charge against secular trends in West European Jewry. He argued that separation from the wider society was necessary in order to preserve the true faith. The new ultra-Orthodoxy also drew strength from modern innovations. Chaim Volozhin, for instance, revolutionised yeshiva study in 1802 by creating a centralised, rationalised and formalised centre for Talmudic study in Lithuania. Most yeshivas had been local and communal affairs, but Volozhin was a meritocratic mass institution which drew pupils from a wide geographical area. This development is analogous to the new Islamic universities and Bible colleges which came to form the backbone of modern Islamic and Protestant fundamentalism. From institutions like Volozhin, ultra-Orthodoxy could begin its cultural *reconquista*.[8]

As in Islam, the faith of the urban, upper-class ultra-Orthodox was more scholarly and textual while that of the rural and lower classes was more expressive. This produced a division between the scriptural-ist 'Lithuanian' and more emotional Hasidic tradition, with its miracle-workers.[9] Yet these variants could all agree on the threat which Jewish assimilation posed to the faith, and sought to defend the Torah, the Talmud, and its associated ritual practices from erosion. On the one hand, much of the fight had been lost in Western Europe. On the other, prejudice and repression kept East European Jews traditionally Ortho-dox. In Habsburg central Europe, the boundary between emancipation and traditionalism was more contested, which explains the Hungarian origins of ultra-Orthodoxy.[10] As the nineteenth century turned into the twentieth, emancipation penetrated into Orthodoxy's Eastern European redoubts. In Poland and Russia, Jews were permitted to leave the Pale of Settlement and settle in the less segregated newer cities and towns, where they tended to lose their Orthodoxy.[11]

Alarmed, ultra-Orthodox leaders convened a conference of Ger-man, Lithuanian, Polish and Hungarian rabbis at Katowice, Poland, in 1912. This launched the Agudat Israel ('Union of Israel') movement, which later spawned an Israeli religious party of the same name. In Rus-sia, Agudat Israel had little success, especially after the establishment of the openly secular Soviet Union in 1917 where Jewish communists zeal-ously suppressed Orthodoxy. In Poland, it fared better, winning a third of the Jewish vote in 1927, but was clearly a rearguard movement. In Israel as well, the Orthodox had once predominated, but waves of Zion-ist settlers from Europe increased the number of Jews attending secular schools from under 20 per cent in 1918 to nearly two-thirds by 1940.[12] By 1939, things looked bleak for ultra-Orthodoxy and were about to get considerably worse.

Highest on Agudat Israel's Haredi agenda was its opposition to Zionism and socialism, two movements with immense appeal to young Jews. Among the modern ideas which emancipated Jews absorbed, none was more influential than that of national self-determination, the belief that each people should possess their own state. Beginning in the late nineteenth century, Jewish nationalists known as Zionists began to make the case for a Jewish state – not in the hereafter but in the here and now. The most famous was Theodor Herzl, whose book *Judenstaat*, or Jewish State (1896), envisioned a new Jewish nation state along secular lines. Many Zionists were socialist or liberal atheists. Others were privately religious, but favoured liberal Jewish sects such as Conservative and Reform. All believed in the separation of religion from the state. The secular Zionist concept of community, like that of their French Revolutionary and German Romantic progenitors, was the nation state. Shared ancestry, territory and politics held the key to Zionism, not religious authority. Zionists savaged the otherworldly eschatology of Haredi rabbis, who decreed that Jewish exile was punishment for Jews' sins – a form of tough love from God that served as proof of Jewish chosenness. The Haredim preferred to wait for the Messiah to deliver the Promised Land to the Jews and opposed any attempt to establish a Jewish home on earth.[13]

In pre-1948 Palestine, secular Zionists contrasted their active settlement of the land, economic dynamism and political power with the slothful passivity of both the Haredim and local Arabs. This angle of critique was loudest on the 'Revisionist' right of the Zionist spectrum. Ze'ev Jabotinsky, a Russian-born Zionist influenced by Mussolini, charged Orthodoxy with suffocating the martial impulses that made ancient Israel great. This disease was incubated through a millennium of powerless exile. The pallid ghetto Jew, focused on Torah study, compared unfavourably with action-oriented ancient Israelite heroes such as Judas Maccabeus. Left-wing Labor Zionists shared Jabotinsky's criticism of the 'landless', homeless Jew, and recommended a return to the land, ushering in the kibbutz movement. In both cases, Zionists sought to overthrow the Orthodox *ancien régime* so that Jews could become a 'normal' people once again, rooted in a homeland.

In return, many Haredi clergy considered Zionism idolatrous. They opposed it because the return of the Jews to the Promised Land was supposed to occur through divine, rather than human, intervention. Human intercession – in the form of Zionism – ran counter to God's Plan. In the words of the Talmud, 'Whoever comes up to [prematurely settle] the land of Israel transgresses the positive commandment which says, "Unto Babylon shall they be carried and there should remain until the day I think of them, says the Lord"' (Jeremiah 22:2).[14] While the secular Zionists pioneered Hebrew as the new language of state, the ultra-Orthodox clung to Yiddish, the dialect of German spoken in the *shtetls* (Jewish ghettoes) of Eastern Europe. Zionists romanticised the militarily powerful ethnic kingdoms of ancient Israel while the Haredim idealised the *shtetl* of the seventeenth and eighteenth centuries, transforming the broad-brimmed hats and dress common to the Poland of that day into a Haredi boundary marker. Today, different schools of Haredim can be identified by their subtle variations in costume.

The Haredi movement began to achieve social penetration in the 1920s, setting up separate schools, courts, rabbinic authorities and other institutions in Europe, America and Palestine. But it was soon blind-sided by the defining moment of modern Jewish consciousness, the Holocaust. The Holocaust affected all European Jews, but none were hit as hard as the Orthodox. Their unwillingness to emigrate to the United States – where their rabbis feared they would be lost to secularism – or to Israel, owing to a distaste for Zionism, left them trapped to face annihilation. Polish Jewry, the heart of Orthodox Judaism, was virtually wiped out, eliminating the centuries-old, Yiddish-speaking culture and institutions of the *shtetl*.

In the assessment of one Orthodox writer at the end of the war:

> In Poland ... about thirty thousand Jews remained ... the proportion of observant Jews among them was totally negligible, since it was those who spoke fluent Polish and were able to pass themselves off as Poles who were saved. In the labor camps it was the master craftsmen and the most robust who survived [and many Orthodox yeshiva boys or elderly rabbinic sages belonged to neither category] ... religious Jewry in Poland and the Baltic states was effectively annihilated ... in Slovakia ... [the Jews] excelled in piousness and the pure belief in the sages [and were] nearly wiped out ... in Romania ... the Holocaust had singled out Orthodox Jewry in particular. One hundred and forty thousand Jews from Carpathian Russia, all of them followers of popular Hasidim, were deported to the crematoria ...[15]

Paradoxically, the seeds of renaissance were sown in the moment of greatest Haredi weakness. Those who survived the Holocaust turned more forcefully against modern assimilation. They felt acute guilt that they were spared, and channelled this into a desire to rebuild.[16] Some, like Hasidic rabbi Joel Moshe Teitelbaum, blamed Zionism for luring 'the majority of the Jewish people into awful heresy … And so it is no wonder that the Lord lashed out in anger'.[17] The Jewish diaspora, few of whom were ultra-Orthodox, waxed nostalgically about their lost Yiddish Orthodox past, opening their coffers to establish yeshivas and other Haredi institutions. In Israel, a similar metamorphosis had taken place. Before the 1920s, Arabs were an object of romantic affection for some Zionists while the Haredim were feared and reviled for their anti-Zionism. By 1948, the tables had turned completely. Secular Zionists no longer feared the Haredim, and Arabs now became the principal 'other' for secular Jews.[18]

With their religious infrastructure in flames, the Haredim in Israel were forced to beg cap-in-hand to the Israeli state. The founders of the new Jewish state considered the Haredim a fading relic, but they worried that anti-Zionist Haredi agitators would sway the Great Powers towards the Arab side in the delicate negotiations over whether to create a Jewish state. This was no idle threat. Haredi radicals represented by Rabbi Amram Blau's Neturei Karta ('Guardians of the City') sent ambassadors around the world to lobby strenuously against the creation of Israel. Blau's group later refused to recognise Israel and helped to organise the 1950 'Sabbath Riots' in which Haredim pelted motorists driving through the ultra-Orthodox Jerusalem neighbourhood of Meah Sharim on the Sabbath.[19]

Yet Blau's brand of rejectionism was unpopular even among Haredi Jews. Chastened by the experience of the 1929 Jaffa riots and the Holocaust, most Haredim were willing to work with the new state – to reform it rather than resist it. Government jobs for Haredi elites in the Israeli religious ministry didn't hurt either. While continuing to oppose secular control of state institutions, Agudat Israel joined the government of Israel's first prime minister David Ben-Gurion. In return, Ben-Gurion promised 'not a theocracy' but that the Sabbath would be the official day of rest in the country. Kitchens in schools, museums and other public buildings would be kosher; all state-sanctioned marriages would be consecrated by Haredi rabbis, and the Haredim would be granted full autonomy over their own education.[20] In making peace with the new state, the Agudat leadership inaugurated the tradition of religious parties entering Israeli politics.

The Zionist leadership legitimated religious actors in other ways. They recognised that theirs was, after all, a *Jewish* state, and thus could not be entirely divorced from the Jewish religion. The new state's flag bore the Star of David, a religious symbol, and while the Haredim were seen as backward, their strict observance of Halachic law served as the religious conscience of the Zionist leadership. This phenomenon can be seen elsewhere, as in Northern Ireland, where many Ulster Protestants scorn Ian Paisley's fundamentalist Free Presbyterian Church, but vote for his Democratic Unionist Party in part because they concede that the Free Presbyterians provide the moral compass for Protestant Ulster.[21] Thus in a recent poll, 77 per cent of Israeli Jewish respondents admitted they do not observe religious law, yet 50 per cent still believed that the state should 'definitely' or 'probably' ensure that Jewish religious traditions are maintained in public life.[22]

The rise of a Haredi 'scholar society'

The Haredi world, in both Israel and the diaspora, is largely self-contained, with rules governing all aspects of daily life. The Haredim live in separate communities that have little contact with the secular Jewish world. Where this is impossible, they colonise discrete apartment blocks to keep secularism at bay. Their dress – black hats, sidelocks, beards and coats for men; shaved heads and wigs for women – marks them out as different. Rabbis, drawing on strict interpretations of religious texts, shape the character of their communities. Religious laws govern food, clothing and codes of behaviour. Men are required to pray three times a day in groups of ten, focusing their lives inward to the community. Strict gender roles consign women to the home, where child-rearing is the main function. The education of women is derided, even when not actively discouraged. Yiddish, a language incomprehensible to many other Israeli Jews, is often spoken. These practices help to sharpen the boundary between Haredim and other Jews.[23]

Like other conservative religious movements, the Haredim have mobilised strongly against secularism, their 'other'. Rejection of the secular world is expressed in prohibitions on television, movies, books, music, the Internet and other temporal pursuits. Haredi education focuses on Jewish law, avoiding secular subjects such as science, history and literature. Non-observant Jews are castigated for living meaningless lives while Haredim are taught that their lives bring them closer to God and a higher truth. The Haredim are chosen, their task to redeem those Jews who have drifted from the truth. In a myriad of ways, the Haredim have constructed a parallel world, mobilised against secularism, which limits exit and promotes internal population growth.[24]

'Strict church' theory tells us that demanding religious denominations are harder to leave than liberal churches. They tend to be the focus of an individual's social and economic ties, even their identity and worldview. A break with a strict church is thus much more disorienting and costly than leaving a liberal faith.[25] The same holds for Judaism. When a secular Jew leaves Reform Judaism for non-religion, chances are he already has an alternative network of friends and is at ease with the impersonal support structures of modern life. The loss of religion therefore only affects one aspect of his life. In the Haredi case, a departing individual is leaving behind an entire world, belief system, identity and support structure for something completely alien. In the words of one defector:

> When I made a telephone call on [a Jewish holiday] I felt as though I was tearing apart one of my vital organs. I felt as though I was foolishly opening the door to hell and sending myself into a wilderness where hope for survival was grim. I felt as though I was standing on the tallest bridge and I was jumping off to a sea filled with sharks and deadly fish. I felt as though I was separating myself from a group I had grown to love, which raised and supported me.[26]

Here, departure from the group leads not only to fear, but to a complete rupture of the person's identity and sense of self. This explains the low rate of defection from Haredi communities.[27]

Separatism
Haredim believe they are preserving a time-hallowed way of life, but as previously noted many elements of the Haredi world are of recent

vintage. The new innovations reflect the difference between Haredi fundamentalism and the more rounded, flexible Orthodox Judaism of the *shtetl*. Traditionally, only a small number of young men in any traditional Jewish community were yeshiva students. In today's Israel, the majority are. Most young Jewish men of the ghetto worked, but now only a minority of Israeli Haredim do. Residential and educational segregation between the Orthodox and other Jews used to be less marked and distinctions of dress less distinct.[28]

No longer. The Haredi settlement of Bnai Brak, near Tel Aviv, is one of two original epicentres of ultra-Orthodoxy. Founded in 1924 by Polish Hasidim, it actually became less doctrinaire in its practice in the decades before 1948 and was a mixed area. Only after the purposeful construction of yeshivas in the 1950s did it begin to attract ultra-Orthodox settlers from around Israel and the world and repel non-Haredim to become the 'City of Torah' by the 1960s. The same was true in organisational terms. As late as the 1950s, there was talk of a rapprochement between the ultra-Orthodox and more modern-minded Orthodox and Conservative Jews. This only became unthinkable when the ultra-Orthodox strove to separate themselves.[29]

The Haredi economy and social structure began to sharply diverge from that of other Israeli Jews around the same time. In pre-war Eastern Europe, only a small elite studied in yeshiva, with most gainfully employed. This is also true of contemporary Europe and North America, where most Haredim work. In Montreal in the 1990s, for instance, just 6 per cent of Haredi men over the age of twenty-five attended yeshiva full-time.[30] In England, the proportion of students among men in the Haredi-dominated Jewish communities of Hackney, in London, and Salford, near Manchester, was less than 7 per cent.[31] In Israel, by contrast, the share of Haredi men aged twenty-five to fifty-four in yeshiva reached 41 per cent by 1980, increasing dramatically to 60 per cent by 1996. The percentage of Israeli children with a father in yeshiva more than doubled during this period.[32] What had been created was an unprecedented Haredi Utopia, the 'scholar society'.

How was this achieved? We have seen that a radical ultra-Orthodox elite, mobilised against secularism, sprang up in Europe in the early nineteenth century and began to institutionalise its vision after 1912.

Two political events – the Russian Revolution and the Holocaust – set this project back. But in Israel, a more propitious environment allowed the vision to flourish. The first gift came from Ben-Gurion: an exemption for a specified number of yeshiva students from the army. Set at 400 in 1948, this was more than enough to cover the number demanded by Haredi leaders. Few could imagine that this figure would swell more than a hundredfold in fifty years owing to both Haredi population explosion and their growing predilection for encouraging male yeshiva study. In the early years of the state, though, their population share was small and had been declining due to secular immigration. Why not toss them a few crumbs? Uri Avneri, a left-leaning journalist who served in the Knesset with Ben-Gurion remarked, 'We [Avneri and Ben-Gurion] both felt that it was acceptable to give the religious what they wanted because they were in any case dying off. It never occurred to either of us that this primitivism would survive for another generation.'[33]

In the early 1950s, the Haredim established a raft of separate institutions independent of the state, including rabbinic authorities, a comprehensive network of yeshivas and a mutual benefit system. The latter enabled young men to study and raise large families without working. This infrastructure floated on a sea of government money: the state picked up 70 per cent of the tab for Haredi yeshiva schooling while the generous new Israeli welfare state freed up Haredi resources. These could now be directed to Haredi-only 'club goods' such as interest-free loans, childcare and insurance. Generous donations from diaspora Jews, swelled by German reparations payments and memories of the Holocaust, further enhanced Haredi institutional capacity. The growth helped to fund Haredi kindergartens, ritual baths, prayer houses and, crucially, *kollelim*, Talmudic schools for married men which enabled prolonged periods of adult study. These innovations sunk deep roots in Haredi society by the 1960s to the point where they began to be seen as time-hallowed.[34]

Haredi political acumen greased the wheels of growth. Despite the concessions it wrung from Ben-Gurion in 1948, Haredi political clout was initially puny. The Zionist Labor party governed the country for almost thirty unbroken years, and implemented its modernising vision. This included a 1952 measure drafting women into the military, which it passed over Agudat Israel's protests. Haredi representatives promptly left Ben-Gurion's government. Nonetheless, funding for Haredi schools and welfare kept flowing. Agudat Israel offered unofficial support to the government in exchange for continued draft exemptions and yeshiva funding.[35] In the 1950s and 60s, the Haredim consolidated themselves, quietly separating from the wider society. Apart from the noisy anti-Zionists of Neturei Karta, they kept a low profile.

Behind the scenes, though, growth was causing problems. The burgeoning Haredi population was pressing against the military exemptions and financial limits that had once appeared so generous.[36] As a result, in 1977, the Haredim dramatically re-entered politics to safeguard their privileges. They joined the Likud right-wing coalition which unseated Labor for the first time in the nation's history, riding a wave of anti-government dissatisfaction which began to crest after the 1973 Yom Kippur War. In the finely balanced post-77 Knesset, Haredi swing votes became pivotal, anointing the ultra-Orthodox as kingmakers. The Haredim cared little about foreign policy, and could therefore sell their votes to the highest bidder to advance their domestic agenda. So began a golden age of Haredi politics. Their first concrete pay-off for joining Menachem Begin's Likud coalition was an epochal lifting of the cap placed on Haredi military exemptions: deferments soared from 800 in 1977 to 20,000 inside a decade.[37]

Haredi fragmentation: unity in diversity

In 1990, secular journalist Amnon Levy's novel *The Haredim* rocketed up the Israeli best-seller lists to inaugurate a new genre, the Haredi exposé. The book opens with a dramatic description of 'ultra-Orthodox thugs trashing the synagogue of a rival ultra-Orthodox clique, beating their opponents to a pulp and sending their octogenarian rabbi to the hospital.'[38] This graphically illustrates that while Haredi elites successfully pursued their dream of a scholar society, they did so as a fractious, faction-ridden rabble. A key guiding figure in the early days was Rabbi Abraham Yeshayahu Karlitz (1878–1953), or Hazon Ish. His disciples formed an elite within Israeli Haredim. Rabbi Elazar Menachem Man 'Rav' Shach was one of Ish's key epigones.[39] The Ish-Shach stream represents the upper-class, scripturalist 'Lithuanian' branch of Ashkenazi, or European Jewish, ultra-Orthodoxy.

The traditionally lower-class, mystical Hasidic current was led by Rebbe Menachem Mendel Schneerson. He captained the Lubavitcher movement, overseeing impressive growth between 1950 and his death in 1994. Shach and Schneerson were bitter rivals whose quarrels made front-page news, and subdivisions within their movements multiplied. Even within this configuration, Haredim coalesced behind specific charismatic rebbes, sparking vituperative turf wars and attempts to poach each other's students. Population growth and battles over government largesse interacted with the decentralised Haredi institutions, leading to schism and conflict. Ecumenical Haredi movements such as Young Agudat Israel, the Agudat Israel Party and the Council of Torah Sages failed or were riven with schisms, while individual rebbes competed among each other for followers.[40]

A political spat with the Hasidim led the 'Lithuanian' Shach to break with Agudat Israel and form the Shas and Degel Ha'Tora parties in 1988. Four years later, after the 1992 elections, the Oriental Jewish rabbi Ovadia Yosef emerged as the spiritual leader of Shas, breaking with his Ashkenazi mentor Shach. Yosef and other Sephardic (Middle Eastern origin) rabbis had been firmly under the thumb of their Ashkenazi Haredi leaders since their arrival from Middle Eastern countries in the 1950s and 60s.

Sephardic, or Oriental, Jews were prevented from running their own yeshivas and forced to adopt Ashkenazi prayer styles and dress, while Ashkenazi rabbi matchmakers ensured that only poor or handicapped Ashkenazi yeshiva students married Oriental Jewish women. Secular Israeli newspapers made a fuss of this, but the Sephardic Haredi accepted this state of affairs without complaint, considering Shach their spiritual leader. But the Sephardim were growing out of their subservience. One of their own, Ovadia Yosef, gradually prised spiritual authority away from the Ashkenazi Shach, causing Shas to spin out of Shach's control. In response, Shach and his supporters turned to bully tactics. Shas leaders were harassed and beaten at synagogues. Ashkenazi Haredim even published fake death and accident notices for Shas leaders and notified their families, sending ambulances to their homes. Shas retaliated in kind, escalating the conflict.[41]

Some mistake division for weakness, but Haredi fragmentation has not affected growth. Time and again, Israeli commentators witnessed Haredi infighting, predicted the demise of the ultra-Orthodox and wound up eating their words.[42] Why? The simple answer is that diversity can lead to strength. This is as true of Judaism as it is of evangelical Protestantism and Islamism. This is not primarily because diversity offers a greater array of religious choice for Haredi individuals, allowing for the internal venting of dissent.[43] Rather, it stems from the shared goal to which competitors allude. When antagonists refer to common aims, such as religious purity, and seek to outdo each other in zeal, this advances those aims.[44] We see this in ethnic politics in divided societies, where splinter groups such as the Catholic Sinn Féin or Protestant DUP in Northern Ireland, the Hindu BJP in India or the Sinhala-Only movement in Sri Lanka 'outbid' more moderate mainstream parties as defenders of their group's interest.[45] Competing rebbes hammer away at the same images of the Haredi self and secular other using the idiom of ultra-Orthodoxy, which reinforces group identity.

Identity is critical to religious vitality in the contemporary world, but is often ignored by sociologists of religion. The leading 'sect-to-church' theory of religion predicts that fundamentalist sects tend toward moderation because upwardly mobile fundamentalists try to reduce cultural tension with the surrounding society. In pursuit of mainstream respectability and useful connections, bourgeois fundamentalists lead a breakaway 'sect-to-church' movement towards social normality.[46] This may have characterised the Methodists and Baptists, but in the Haredi world, as in the Islamist one, moderating 'church' movements are rare.

Also, what counts as moderation? True, Agudat Israel agreed to participate in politics and recognise Israel in 1948, a kind of 'moderation' of Haredi zeal. Yet the boundary between the Haredim and the rest of Israeli society persisted. The same is true of the Muslim Brotherhood, despite moderating on the question of violence, the Mormons, though they gave way over polygamy, and Southern Baptists, regardless of the fact they don't speak in tongues. What matters, therefore, are the broader stories of identity which reinforce group boundaries, papering over internal schism. When boundaries are strong, internal competition is channelled into fundamentalism.

Identity politics and boundaries have intensified in the modern age because of improved surveillance, record-keeping and communications – what British sociologist Anthony Giddens terms 'reflexivity'.[47] Most nationalist movements, for instance, date from the nineteenth or twentieth centuries. Before this period, the Irish, Poles, Kurds or Somalis had no standardised language, no means of real-time communication, no agreement on myths and symbols, and no mental maps of their territory. Modernity brought better roads, rail, literacy, newspapers, censuses, maps, dictionaries, organisations and mass education.[48] This connects leaders to potential followers. Radio, television and the Internet sharpen the awareness of the ethnic self and the 'others' against which 'we' define ourselves. Ethnic organisations improve their reach and their ability to enumerate, organise and monitor 'their' people. Lo and behold, identities become more fixed and social movements flourish.

National borders, citizenship and passports have really only solidified over the past century.[49] Ethnic boundaries hardened alongside those of nations, except where an explicit commitment to liberalism emerged. Intermarrying or changing identity beneath society's radar became more difficult.[50] In Northern Ireland, for instance, mixed marriage used to be more common – consider the IRA's Gerry Adams, who has an English surname, or the Protestant leader Terence O' Neill, with his Irish surname. Even members of the ultra-Protestant Orange Order married Catholics in the early nineteenth century, a deed which today leads to automatic expulsion.[51] In India, identities used to be more fluid, permitting low-caste Hindus to convert en masse to Christianity or Islam. Today, this kind of conversion is much more heavily policed. All told, identity groups are better mobilised, their boundaries less permeable.

The same hardening of boundaries can be found with religious sects such as the Haredim. Like ethnic groups and nation states, they established new institutions to link insiders and exclude outsiders. Pioneering elites such as Rabbi Volozhin in Vilnius got the ball rolling. But it took modern processes – urbanisation, newspapers, rapid travel and international fundraising networks – to knit elites and masses together in common purpose. Today, Haredi global networks, media, yeshivas and Israeli politics amplify the average Haredi's awareness of their community and its conflict with the secular 'other'. The message is constantly reinforced, in real time, while dense sets of new Haredi institutions – parties, yeshivas, kollels, media – spin webs that keep stray sheep within the flock. Increasingly, these lines of communication and surveillance link Haredim with individual charismatic rebbes, even when the rebbe and follower live on different continents.[52]

Naturally this only works when the key dividing lines in society prevent moderates from reaching out across tribal battle lines. Electoral competition would lead to the demise of ethnic extremism if moderate Catholics voted for moderate Protestant parties in Northern Ireland, moderate Tamils for moderate Sinhalese parties in Sri Lanka, moderate Haredim for Kadima in Israel, and vice versa. This is precisely what happens in 'normal' polities such as Britain and the United States, where major parties are forced to appeal to the interests of the nation and not to their narrow group, and must therefore fight over swing voters at the centre.[53]

When dominant lines of cleavage fade, moderates on both sides can come together. For example, the ecumenical movement in American Protestantism originally sought to bring Protestants of all denominations together to meet the 'threat' of Catholicism. But these bridge-building ecumenicals wound up drifting towards accommodation with Catholics after 1905 because their journey beyond their denominations led many to surmount their Protestant identity. Some eventually became interfaith cosmopolitans who questioned Christian exclusivism.[54]

In divided societies, on the other hand, even moderates stay loyal to their group, making transgression unthinkable. This transforms the effects of competition: antagonists drive each other to the extremes rather than the middle. The moderate Ulster Unionist Party in Northern Ireland, for instance, was tempted to compromise with the Catholic minority until outflanked by breakaway movements like Paisley's DUP.[55] In Israel, Haredim vote for Haredi parties and seculars avoid them like the plague. This segments electoral competition, fuelling extremism rather than a drift to the centre.

The demography of ultra-Orthodox Jewry

In 2007, two government reports made headlines in Israel. The first, compiled by the Israeli Bureau of Statistics for the Ministry of Education, discovered that a third of Jewish primary-school pupils will be studying in Haredi classrooms by 2012. If one adds modern Orthodox Jews, this brings the 'religious' total among Jews to half. This represents a Haredi increase from a few percentage points in 1960 to 12 per cent in 1992 and 27 per cent in 2007. What a different picture from the surging, self-confident secular school system of the first six decades of the twentieth century. Factor in the Israeli Arabs, and one is left with an Israeli primary-school system in which the descendants of the original secular Zionists are a minority of just 41 per cent. These are tomorrow's Israelis.[56]

Many are aware that the ultra-Orthodox have large families, but the scale is monumental. Few modern populations have so blatantly bucked the demographic transition. Between 1950 and 1980, Jewish immigrants from high-fertility Muslim countries reduced their TFR from over 6 to just over 3 children per woman, only slightly above the Jewish average. Israeli Arab TFR fell from 8.5 in 1950 to around 4 by the late 1980s. But Haredi fertility remained stuck in a time warp, at 6.49 children per woman in 1980–82. This subsequently *rose* to 7.61 during 1990–96 and has remained at that level ever since. During the same period, the TFR of other Jews declined from 2.61 to 2.27.[57] Since modern Orthodox Jews are included in the non-Haredi figures and have an intermediate level of fertility between the Haredim and secular Jews, it may be that secular Israeli fertility is below replacement level.[58] This means that secular Jewish women bear little more than a quarter of the children produced by their Haredi counterparts.

Meanwhile, migration trends have turned decisively against secular Jewry. Apart from the Oriental Jewish wave of the 1950s and 60s, most immigrants to Israel have been secular. Zionists took secular immigration for granted as the cornerstone of their vision. Today, that dream is over. A look at the immigration figures reveals a steady decline since the 1950s as the relative economic attractiveness of Israel has waned. By the late 1980s, Israeli emigrants outnumbered immigrants.

The collapse of the Soviet Union handed secular Zionists a windfall of 765,000 largely secular immigrants in the 1990s, but there were flies in the ointment. Over 100,000 of the newcomers were non-Jews, many with an eye to re-emigrating to the West.[59] In 2007, the previous pattern reasserted itself: more Jews left Israel than entered it. Janglo. net, a popular Israeli English-language website, did a thriving business as many emigrants advertised their moving sales. Barring a European or American *Kristallnacht*, there are simply no other pockets of secular Jews to draw upon. In Russia, Jews are demographically dwindling, with high rates of mixed marriage. In Europe and North America, intermarriage is also high. For instance, nearly half of American Jews now marry non-Jews, and they have the lowest fertility rate – 1.43 – of any major American ethno-religious group.[60]

To add insult to injury, migration trends have shifted in favour of Orthodoxy. This is so for three reasons. First, Jews with more marketable skills tend to leave Israel, and these are overwhelmingly secular. A third of Holland's 30,000 Jews are Israeli immigrants, for example, and the American high-tech sector is a well-known employer of Israeli expatriates.[61] Second, secular Jews in the diaspora are more likely than the Orthodox to intermarry with non-Jews, assimilate and thus disappear as a source of emigrants. Third, many Jews who choose to immigrate to Israel do so for religious reasons.[62] This dynamic is almost certain to deepen over time, accelerating the decline of secularism in Israel. Yaakov Wise of the University of Manchester and Sergio Della Pergola of Hebrew University in Jerusalem estimate that Haredi Jews will double their share of the Israeli population to an impressive 17 per cent by 2020, reaching a majority of the Israeli Jewish total in the decades after 2050.[63]

Today, just 2.3 per cent of Israelis over the age of eighty are Haredi, against 16 per cent of Israelis under ten. The figures rise when we exclude Arabs from the Israeli total: even if Haredi fertility miraculously converges with that of other Israelis by 2030, the population momentum stored up in its young population will increase the Haredi share of Israeli Jewry from 13.7 today to over 23 per cent by 2030.[64] Around 2050, secularists will dip below 50 per cent of Israel's Jews, reflecting the make-up of today's under-ten Jewish population. Haredim would be poised to form an outright majority of Israeli Jews soon after, raising the spectre of theocracy, an option favoured by two-thirds of Haredim.[65]

Haredi geography
The Haredi footprint is not evenly distributed across Israeli society. From the 1950s, the ultra-Orthodox quietly built their segregated worlds in a small number of communities such as Bnai Brak and Meah Sharim.

Secular outmigration by people who could not bear the growing social conformity of dress and Sabbath observance was matched by religious in-migration of those who feared their children would be sullied by secular neighbourhoods. As the 1970s turned into the 1980s, demand rapidly outstripped supply and Bnai Brak and Meah Sharim became extremely expensive and overcrowded.

A major source of new affordable housing for young Haredi families were purpose-built Haredi towns such as Kiryat Sefer and Beitar, many in the Occupied Territories. These accommodated 80 per cent of the overflow from traditional Haredi areas, but even this did not suffice. The Haredi rank and file were thus forced to look to traditionally non-Haredi areas. Greater Jerusalem was most directly affected, and also bordered some of the Haredi new towns in the Territories. The mass of the Haredi populace were not keen on living in secular surroundings, but some Hasidic elites considered this incursion into the secular world to be part of a proselytising mission. Established secular residents responded by accusing the newcomers of targeting particular areas for takeover. A residents' coalition in the northern Tel Aviv suburb of Ramat Aviv characterised Haredi strategy as follows:

A. Establishing a beachhead in the neighbourhood, which is to say, inhabiting a limited number of houses (at relatively high prices).

B. In this stage, they submit requests to establish 'appropriate' institutions for the Haredi population that has moved to the neighbourhood, including: Haredi kindergartens, Haredi elementary schools, a *kollel*, additional Orthodox synagogues, and more. The establishment of such institutions encourages the entry of more Haredi population to the neighbourhood.

C. The Haredi population, which has established itself in the neighbourhood, begins to demand 'sensitivity to its feelings' from the secular neighbours. Examples that we have run into of such demands were: Not to listen to music on Shabbat, (for women) to dress 'modestly', and at a later stage, even to close off roads and to vandalise vehicles that drive on Shabbat. At the same time, they begin to carry out mass 'kabbalot Shabbat' ceremonies, Haredi rallies, demonstrations in front of stores that sell unkosher food, posting offensive and threatening announcements, and spray-painting anti-secular graffiti.

D. In the final stage, as a result of the aggression, generally two processes take place: First, secular people who are fed up with the mistreatment begin to leave. Second, as a result of this and in parallel, the value of apartments drops, which allows more Haredi families to buy the empty apartments.[66]

Secular Israelis are hardly powerless in these situations. Access to land in Israel is tightly controlled by municipalities and the state, initially to facilitate the seizure of formerly Arab land.[67] The flipside of this is that locals can use democratic municipal pressure to prevent permits being issued for religious buildings, thereby making their communities less attractive to Haredim. These were precisely the tactics used by residents of the new satellite city of Modiin. Its first municipal elections in 1996 witnessed an all-out campaign by anti-Haredi parties under the banner 'Free City of Modiin', who warned of the ultra-Orthodox threat to property values and the community's way of life. The alarmist campaign succeeded and anti-Haredi parties won a majority on the town council, establishing a 'secular atmosphere' in Modiin.[68]

Needless to say, such tactics are much more difficult for secular residents to apply in the 'politically correct' environment of North America or even Western Europe. In the Outremont section of Montreal, for example, Haredi Jews have succeeded in nearly all their sensitivity requests, from cordoning off city streets on the Sabbath to mandating kosher-only food during Passover in a hospital with an 80 per cent non-Jewish clientele.[69] Residents who dislike such changes must either put up with it or leave the area.

The emerging Haredi vote

Demography moves like a silent wave, first hitting maternity wards and schools, then military recruitment, affecting the median voter only several decades later. Effects are telescoped onto certain locales, often in urban areas. The Haredisation of Jerusalem, for example, is a function of both demography and the internal movement of Haredim into Jerusalem and adjacent parts of the Occupied Territories. Already, nearly half of Jerusalem's under-five Jewish population lives in districts with an ultra-Orthodox voting pattern.[70] As the Haredi youth bulge enters the electorate, it is flexing its political muscles. In 2003, Uri Lupolianski became the city's first Haredi mayor. He succeeded because of both Haredi demography *and* their strong internal cohesion, which allows them to unite squarely behind their leaders: 90 per cent of Jerusalem's Haredi electorate voted, nearly all plumping for Lupolianski while just 32 per cent of other Jews bothered to cast a ballot.[71]

In the 2008 mayoral contest, secularists counterattacked, but their turnout remained poor and Haredi candidate Meir Porush only lost by a whisker, 52–48. Moreover, secular mayor Nir Barkat agreed to broaden his coalition to include an ultra-Orthodox faction. Evidently the Haredi electorate cannot be silenced, even in defeat.[72] Given prevailing demographic trends, the eventual Haredi dominance of the Jerusalem mayor's office is as certain as was the ascent of the Irish in the municipal politics of Boston, New York and Chicago in the late nineteenth century. Secular Jewish rights and privileges are protected by the state, but the ultra-Orthodox 'capture' of Jerusalem is a powerful symbolic statement on the national scene. Greater Jerusalem is emerging as an Orthodox milieu, the capital of Israel's religious alter ego. Its atmosphere contrasts sharply with the secular, Mediterranean ambience of Tel-Aviv, and the two poles are growing further apart.[73] The gap between red and blue America pales by comparison.

Events in Jerusalem are sending shock waves to other parts of the country. One reason for the successful anti-Haredi mobilisation in Modiin, for instance, was the presence of a substantial group of secular 'refugees' from pious Jerusalem.[74] Though the Haredim have a smaller national presence than in Jerusalem, they have proven adept at leveraging their still small demographic presence into outsized political clout. Between 1977 and 2003, Israeli elections pitted left-leaning Labor against rightist Likud. Haredi parties played their hand well, offering their votes to the highest bidder between Labor and Likud to retain their religious privileges in the face of mounting secular resentment.

The key to their success was their agnosticism on the issue of 'land for peace' with the Palestinians. Haredi parties do not sacralise the land of ancient Israel (i.e. the West Bank) as religious Zionists do. Instead, they privilege Jewish religious purity. They thereby spice their religious absolutism with territorial flexibility, making them ideal coalition partners in a state where politics revolves around how much territory to trade for peace. It is said that when Israel makes peace with the Arabs, the next conflict will pit Jew against Jew. But until that day dawns, the religious-secular axis will remain subordinate to the 'hawk–dove' dimension.[75] Israeli coalition leaders of both stripes have been only too pleased to accede to the puritanical demands of Haredi parties in exchange for their support. For their part, Haredi parties have been happy to back Labor doves and Likudnik hawks alike.

The combined vote of Haredi parties has steadily risen in recent years, from six seats in 1984 to eighteen in 2009, representing 15 per cent of the Knesset. When we add the vote for the modern Orthodox parties, including the National Religious Party (NRP), Jewish Home and National Union, we find religious parties garnering fully twenty-seven seats in 2009, 22.5 per cent of the legislature. This represents an important step change over the period between 1949 and the 1990s, when religious parties generally won thirteen to eighteen seats. In a democracy, especially one based on proportional representation, numbers are readily translated into power. Already, the demographic expansion of the Haredim, and to a lesser extent the modern Orthodox, is changing Israeli politics. This will continue in the years to come, when the composition of the Knesset will reflect the demographic balance of power we already see in the nation's primary schools.

What might this mean in policy terms? The key aims of the ultra-Orthodox parties are to preserve the Haredi school system, pay baby bonuses for large families, exempt yeshiva students from military service and fund their studies, alter the Law of Return to only admit those Jews who qualify as Jewish under religious law, maintain the status quo with regard to the Sabbath and kosher public spaces, and finally to enshrine Orthodoxy as the sole recognised religious authority in Israel. This preserves Haredi rabbis' exclusive right to solemnise marriages, secure burial plots, perform conversions and otherwise officiate over most of the key turning points in one's private life.[76] The Haredi concept of Jewishness casts aspersions on secular, Reform and Conservative Jews and stands in the way of basic demands such as the right to civil – as opposed to religious – marriage. Few feel this slight as keenly as the 800,000 ex-Soviet citizens who came to settle in Israel after the collapse of communism. Haredi initiatives cramp their ability to be recognised as Jews, officially marry, bury their dead or sponsor relatives to immigrate.

Locally, Haredim have won the right to seal their local streets off to Saturday (Sabbath) traffic. More recently, they have staged protests to expand restrictions to major thoroughfares such as Jerusalem's Bar Ilan Street, whose central section contains apartment blocks inhabited primarily by Haredim. Motorists who drive on the Sabbath may find their cars stoned, while non-Haredim who fail to observe the Sabbath or dress conservatively are abused in Haredi-dominated streets. In 1994, a Bar-Ilan Street demonstration brought 150,000 Haredim out in protest. In 1995, Haredi stones led to a child being injured in a passing automobile. Subsequently, the city agreed to close the street for parts of Friday and Saturday and to consider constructing an expensive tunnel to avoid Haredi areas.[77] The mobilising capacity of the Haredim is impressive: in 1999, Menachem Porush, a Haredi MK, organised a rally of between a quarter and a half million Haredim to protest against a series of Israeli High Court rulings that were deemed anti-Haredi. 'We will undermine the legitimacy of the Supreme Court,' announced Porush to the enthusiastic crowd, the largest ever gathering in Israel's history.[78]

Haredim are also accused of using their tight-knit, mobilised cohesiveness as an instrument of market power. The growing and well-organised Haredi population represents an enormous and well-defined market segment. If offended, it can kick a sizeable dent in a company's bottom line and transfer its custom to a competitor. One vehicle for Haredi market power is kosher certification. The Badatz (Tribunal of Justice) label, controlled by a Haredi rabbinic authority, is viewed by the Haredi consumer as the gold standard. Badatz charges a 4 per cent commission to all factories which it certifies, a cost passed on to all Jewish consumers, Haredi or otherwise. Haredi watchdog organisations can even bring powerful corporations to heel. For instance, one group threatened to persuade Badatz to repeal the kosher certification for Vita, a major food producer, if it did not fire its human resources manager Eduardo

Campos, a Jehovah's Witness. The company tried to pay Campos to leave and he was only reinstated after a highly public media campaign.[79]

A similar high-profile case was that of Ronit Penso, the forty-year-old female head chef at the Jerusalem Hilton. Considered a rising star, she cooked for the Clintons during their presidential visit. On 3 September 1999, she was summoned to the hotel personnel manager and fired. Her crime: using a pot dedicated to milk products to cook rice that would be served with meat. This transgressed the biblical injunction against cooking a kid in the milk of its mother. In fact, Penso had done nothing of the kind but had made the mistake of crossing swords with her rabbinic supervisor, a religious functionary hired to advise chefs on the fine points of kosher. This hardly endeared her to the man, who resented the meteoric rise of a secular woman to the position of head chef.[80]

Haredi authorities are not shy about using their power to regulate Israel's cultural climate. A yoghurt company with a product line which featured a dinosaur logo was asked to remove the offensive symbol since it led Haredi children to raise 'awkward' questions to their parents about the absence of dinosaurs in the Bible. The firm complied immediately. Large companies were just as quick to bow to religious pressure. For instance, in 1999, a Haredi watchdog group entitled the 'National Committee for the Prevention of Obscene Advertising in the Holy Land' compelled Israeli media giant Maxi-Media to pull a series of ads for the Disney film *Tarzan*. These had portrayed the cartoon character in a loincloth, but were quickly replaced with a figure pictured from the waist up.

Pepsi aggravated Haredi sympathies for a different reason. The company aired a commercial tracing the ascent of man from chimpanzee through Neanderthal to a boy on a skateboard guzzling a Pepsi. The implicit endorsement of the theory of evolution prompted a Haredi consumer group to threaten to boycott Pepsi and pull its kosher certification for all drinks produced by Tempo, its local distributor. This led to a climbdown by the company. The same fate befell a Pepsi-sponsored Michael Jackson concert slated for a Saturday. Pepsi duly withdrew its support after Haredim complained about Sabbath desecration.[81]

In consumer behaviour, as in the voting booth, the ultra-Orthodox were able to readily parlay their social cohesion into enhanced clout.

When it comes to consumer markets characterised by a small number of big players, such as media and wholesale distribution, no major player is willing to give an edge to the competition by sacrificing the Haredi market without a commensurate gain in secular customers. This reflects an asymmetry of social glue between secular and ultra-Orthodox Jews. Haredim are unified behind their leaders and willing to forego superior products boycotted by their leaders. By comparison, secular consumers are disorganised and more apt to free-ride on the sacrifices of others. This enables companies to placate Haredi consumers without risking secular retribution.

The demography of Arab and Jew

In most societies, a fast-growing minority with values antithetical to the majority creates fresh divisions in national politics. In the United States, Catholic immigration became an issue in the 1840s, with northern Protestants tending to vote Republican and Catholics Democratic. In the Ivory Coast, rapid Muslim minority growth set the scene for majority repression.[82] Yet fate can intervene. The Civil War took the steam out of American anti-Catholic politics for a quarter-century.[83] So too in Israel, where the first (1987–93) and second (post-2000) Palestinian intifadas concentrated secular Israeli minds on the Arab ethnic threat. Next to the thousands killed in the intifadas, the Haredi mountain looked more like a molehill.

Israeli demographic worries fixate squarely on Arabs rather than on Haredi Jews. In the 1990s, government projections suggested Jews would be a minority of the population of Israel–Palestine by 2010, rendering the conquest of 'Greater Israel' a pyrrhic victory. This helped convince Ariel Sharon and his security advisers to withdraw from Gaza and begin the construction of a security wall in 2004.[84] Once a settlement hawk, Sharon realised that a smaller Jewish state was better than an Arab-dominated Israel.

Avigdor Lieberman, leader of the secular right-wing Yisrael Beitenu (Israel Our Home) Party who was made foreign minister in 2009, is even more explicit about the ethno-demographic threat. He wants to take Sharon's implicit strategy to its logical conclusion by trading Arab-majority patches of land within Israel's 1967 borders to the new Palestinian state in exchange for Jewish-majority settlements in the West Bank. Israeli Arabs are to be disenfranchised by loyalty oaths. This explains why Lieberman supports the two-state solution in spite of his tough talk on territorial concessions. For the first time since the dawn of Jewish settlement, territorial expansion is being sacrificed to demographic survival.[85] What's more, when the focus shifts inward to Israel's ethnic demography, Haredi growth may be deemed an asset in the battle with the Arabs for demographic supremacy. After all, the Haredim are the reason that Jews are now winning the demographic race against the Arabs in Israel's delivery rooms.[86]

The secular counterreaction

Arab demography has been at the forefront of Zionist concerns, occluding the sensational rise of the Haredim. But Haredi expansion began to be a simmering issue in the late 1980s, and can burst on to the national agenda under certain conditions.[87] The 1993 Oslo Accords provided a pause in the ethnic conflict between Arab and Jew which intimated that peace was at hand. This created an opening for anti-Haredi sentiment to surface. The pivotal issues were Haredi military deferments and welfare dependency. Since its inception, Israel has demanded all Jews serve in the Israeli Defense Forces (IDF) for a period of at least three years between the ages of eighteen and thirty-five. However, Haredis' otherworldly pacifism, anti-Zionism and commitment to Talmudic study inclines them against military service.

As a small, disgruntled element within the new State of Israel, the Haredi lobbied for, and received, an exemption from military service. The exemptions were capped, but this cap was lifted by Menachem Begin in 1977 in exchange for Haredi political support. As noted, deferment shot up, from 800 in 1977 to 20,000 a decade later. As of 2007, the number excused stood at 55,000, or 11 per cent of the eligible eighteen-year-old cohort of young Israeli Jews.[88] This is predicted to rise to 23 per cent by 2019 and close to a third by the late 2020s as today's primary-schoolers hit draft age.

Haredi exemptions are matched by those given to Israeli Arabs, who do not serve in the IDF. An Israeli military manpower report now places the combined proportion of exempted eighteen-year-olds – Arabs,

Haredim and seculars exempted for health or education reasons – at 23 per cent of the target population. In the long run, this could become a security problem. In the near term, it grates on secular Jews, who risk the lives of their children to defend the state and contribute three of their prime years of life to national service while Haredi men skirt this sacrifice.[89]

A second irritant for non-Haredi Jews is the ultra-Orthodox drain on the economy. The state provides Haredi yeshiva students with stipends to fund their religious studies. These typically last from the age of eighteen to forty. By 1998, some 70,000 students declared their sole occupation as that of Torah student, drawing a total of 500 million NIS in stipends. The Haredim reply that government subsidies are augmented by contributions from American Jewish donors. In fact, the lion's share of a yeshiva student's 1,000 to 4,000 NIS annual stipend now comes from private overseas donors.[90]

But direct government support for yeshiva study is only part of the problem. The larger issue is the exceedingly low employment – and hence tax-paying – rate among Haredim. In 1996, just 40 per cent of Haredi men aged twenty-five to fifty-four worked, and 70 per cent of the income of a typical Haredi family came from government transfers, twice the level of 1980. A third of this growth was through baby bonuses.[91] Secular Israelis also fret over stories of yeshiva students working black (for cash) to avoid tax, or Haredi rabbis exploiting their control of the Ministry of Religious Affairs and burial societies to extract bribes from Israelis seeking a fast-tracked conversion or burial plot.[92]

Since 1984, these grievances have been captured by secular splinter parties such as Ratz, Meretz, Tzomet and Shinui. They regularly displayed posters of angry Haredi mobs and vowed to beat them back. The secular media joined in the fray, cranking out a steady stream of anti-Haredi cartoons and exposés. The most popular featured a tide of black-hatted Haredim overwhelming secular Israelis, or suggested that lascivious desires lurked just beneath the veneer of sanctimonious Orthodoxy.

Furthermore, Haredim were regularly likened to parasites on the body politic. A 1985 leftist cartoon featured a 'greasy Haredi, his gut hanging in rolls over the dinner table, clutching in one chubby fist a goblet of wine, while the other hand holds to his mouth a miniature secular

Jew, whose blood he is sucking daintily, pinky extended'.[93] In 1999, television personality Tommy Lapid took the reins of Shinui and embarked on an aggressively anti-religious campaign. This proved a lightning rod for rising secular resentment. Lapid took the bold step of refusing to enter any coalition that contained a religious party. In 1999, Shinui won six seats. Four years later, its support shot up to fifteen seats, representing 12.3 per cent of the vote.

In Tel-Aviv nightclubs, patrons would regularly shout their approval. 'Fuck them [Haredim], Tommy,' yelled one, as the Shinui leader passed through a club during a campaign.[94] Shinui's strong showing enabled it to enter into Sharon's right-wing coalition in 2003. Significantly, Haredi parties were excluded from government for the first time since 1977. Shinui gained the Interior Ministry and promptly used its position to close down the Religious Affairs Ministry. The government slashed funding to yeshivas by close to half and reduced child benefits.

However, Sharon's coalition could not hold and he was compelled to bring the Haredi United Torah Judaism (UTJ) on board in 2004 to retain his majority. Lapid was placated until Sharon submitted a budget more favourable to Haredi interests in December 2004. Shinui voted against it, and was subsequently replaced by Labor in Sharon's coalition. During 2005, Shinui splintered into squabbling factions. Despite running television commercials showing armies of Haredim vanishing into the sky with a Shinui vote, it posted a pathetic sixth of a per cent of the popular vote in 2006 and abstained in 2009.

The implosion of Shinui is partly attributable to the ongoing Arab–Israeli conflict, but its concerns have not disappeared. In 2008, the centrist Kadima Party of Tzipi Livni failed to come to terms with Haredi parties, who demanded a reinstatement of child benefits for families with more than four children.[95] Another beneficiary of Shinui's demise is Avigdor Lieberman, leader of the right-wing Yisrael Beitenu party. Yisrael Beitenu won an unprecedented 9 per cent of the vote in 2006, the year Shinui collapsed, and in 2009 placed third, ahead of Labor, with nearly 12 per cent of the poll. Lieberman's success was built upon the anti-Haredi grievances of its Soviet-immigrant base and the support of secular-nationalist Israelis. Like Shinui, the party seeks to implement civil marriages and end Haredi moralising. However, as part of a coalition deal with Likud's Benjamin Netanyahu, Lieberman downplayed his secularist aims in order to placate the concerns of Shas and the UTJ.

Haredi integration

In our treatment of the Mormons, we saw how the wider society can constrain the most troublesome aspects of minority group behaviour, such as polygamy and theocracy. In Israel, government pressure, group conflict and secular resentment are driving the state to act. Haredi integration into mainstream Israeli society is beginning to take place. A growing number of Haredi women are employed in clerical and back-office work. In the years since the 2003 welfare cuts, the proportion of Haredi men in work has increased by several per cent. Some seminaries now offer IT and other practical skills courses.[96]

This reflects trends among American Haredim, most of whom work and have influenced their Israeli counterparts. So long as courses are strictly vocational and do not impart a critical worldview, they are tolerated by American Haredi rabbis. Back-office work such as filing medical records helps to insulate Haredi women from the prying eyes of men. The men typically work as computer programmers or electronics salesmen. Jobs and training must be narrowly focused, sex segregated and located in Haredi areas, if possible. Rebbes frown upon the idea of work as 'career' since this competes with the paramount value of Talmudic study. Working in humdrum jobs to fund family and community, however, seems kosher.[97] Haredi women reinforce this proclivity since they prefer scholarly to worldly success when seeking a mate. Scholarship, not money, drives the ultra-Orthodox status system and marriage market.

Changes are also afoot on the military front. In 1999, the IDF and a group of Haredi rabbis helped to create the Nahal Haredi battalion. Their website fuses religious with nationalist commitment:

> Nahal Haredi was founded on the premise that physical strength alone is not enough – the spirit of Torah and Mitzvot must underlie all that is achieved. The Nahal provides religious men who seek to contribute to Israel's military defense with a framework for personal and professional achievement that in every way promotes a Torah-true lifestyle.[98]

Nahal Haredi has increased from a small unit of thirty in 1999 to a full, thousand-strong battalion, seeing action in several theatres. Its 2,000th recruit, in 2007, was Itamar Grilus, an eighteen-year-old Haredi from Jerusalem. 'I believe that the best way to defend the land of Israel is by sitting and learning Torah,' remarked Grilus. 'But someone who doesn't sit all day and learn needs to contribute in the second and more physical [way].' There is also an elite unit, dubbed Israel's first 'glatt kosher commandos', complete with velvet yarmulkes and sidelocks. Rabbi Zvi Klebanow, director of the Nahal Haredi Organisation, expressed his view that the elite fighters 'are a pride for Israel by demonstrating their ability to maintain a Haredi lifestyle while at the same time serving their country'.[99]

Though the 2,000 Nahal Haredi inductees pale beside the 55,000 Haredim who defer their service, the growth of this battalion may be a portent of successful integration. Military service provides a path to employment in Israel, thus a survey found that over 90 per cent of Nahal Haredi graduates were employed, many in sectors ranging from high tech and engineering to the prison service.[100] These are small but significant steps towards integration, but there are important limits: Nahal Haredi is housed in male-only barracks which observe kosher rules and is therefore segregated from the bulk of the secular, mixed-gender IDF. There is also little military pressure for more Haredi recruits since many IDF commanders view them as troublesome to integrate, accepting them only out of a sense of duty.[101]

On the other side, many Haredi rabbis bitterly oppose Nahal Haredi, so its recruits tend to be drawn from the less scholarly, and thus less respectable, margins of Haredi society.[102] A more promising avenue for Haredi community service is the ZAKA units, which specialise in collecting and cataloguing body parts in the wake of suicide attacks. This requires Haredi volunteers to use motorcycles and modern technology in coordination with the emergency services, but is justified by the proprietary role of Haredi rabbis in death and burial. This 'death work' wins the Haredim the rare praise of the wider Israeli public.[103]

The recent flurry of integrationist initiatives comes in the wake of government cutbacks that have led to tighter Haredi finances, forcing Haredi rabbis to grudgingly modify their ideal of the scholar society at the edges. There is also pressure from a different quarter: the large new generation of young Haredim. Many are attracted by the heroic image of the military and yearn to serve in the army. For example, police and army uniforms are two of the most popular costumes worn by Haredi boys during the annual Purim festivals, which allow for ritual expressions of transgression. Haredi action videos such as *Soldiers Without Uniforms* portray Haredi men studying but also excelling in combat.[104] In opinion polls, Haredim are consistently among the most hawkish of Israelis. Anti-Zionist Haredi parties with connections to the Palestinians such as Neturei Karta find their posters torn down almost as soon as they go up.[105]

Population expansion feeds these political shifts. Haredi migration to East Jerusalem and new towns in the Occupied Territories gives them a powerful stake in the Israeli state and familiarity with firearms. Though Haredi leaders remain in control of their flock, their legitimacy increasingly depends on taking a hawkish stand on foreign policy. This may narrow their room to make political deals. In 2009, Haredi political leaders insisted on the indivisibility of Jerusalem in talks with Tzipi Livni, Kadima party leader. This, along with unrealistic demands for child benefits, scuttled the possibility of the religious parties joining Kadima in coalition rather than Netanyahu's Likud. Next time, Kadima may have to compromise with the rising Haredim. In effect, Haredi growth is nudging the central tendency of Israeli politics to the right.

The modern Orthodox and religious violence

The newly hawkish Haredim join other powerful currents on the Religious Right. The modern Orthodox are important because they furnish the shock troops of religious Zionism. The modern Orthodox can be identified by their knitted skullcaps, which mark them out as less distinct than Haredim. On religious issues, they are more flexible than Haredim. They believe that religion can be compartmentalised, allowing secular concerns to predominate in functional spheres of life such as the economy and military. Custom frequently overrides Halachic law.[106] They fully participate in the economic and military sectors of society. Less alienated from the Zionist state, they take a more inclusive view of 'who is a Jew' than the Haredim. They try to bridge the gap between this world and the next, balancing between Haredi and mainstream Jewish life. Unsurprisingly, their fertility rates stand midway between the extremes of the Haredim and secular Jews. They are also disproportionately represented among European and American immigrants. Middling fertility and steady immigration will enable the modern Orthodox to remain roughly 18 per cent of the school-age population in the face of Haredi growth and secular decline.

Though less explosive in demographic terms, the modern Orthodox are a large element, currently twice the size of the Haredim. They have lent their weight to a number of political parties, notably the National Religious Party (NRP), which has sided with right-wing coalitions since 1977. Paradoxically, the religious moderation of the modern Orthodox creates a 'secular' opening for them to sacralise the land and state of Israel. The result is religious nationalism, which can take extreme forms, as with the Settler movement. The modern Orthodox consider the creation of Israel and its expansion into the holy land of the West Bank as divinely significant. When separated, Orthodox Judaism and secular Zionism are powerful forces. Fused, they energise each other to produce a potent cocktail.

The religious and nationalist strands of Judaism were first entwined in the persona of Rabbi Abraham Isaac Kook, the godfather of modern Orthodoxy. Born in Russian Courland, in what is now Estonia, in 1865, Kook sought to reconcile the two solitudes of Orthodox Judaism and secular Zionism. He foresaw that Zionism, in leading to an ingathering of the Jews after 2,000 years of exile, was a prelude to the messianic redemption of world Jewry. The sacrifices of Jewish settlers – even if secular – would hasten this redemption. In 1904, Kook moved to Palestine, where he became the leader of the religious Zionist movement and helped to build bridges between secular and religious Jews as Chief Rabbi of Palestine.

Religious Zionism consists principally of a modern Orthodox branch, but also encompasses an ultra-Orthodox wing, Hardal. Hardal, influenced by the teachings of Rabbi Kook's son, Zvi Yehuda, is extremely hawkish on foreign policy, with many of its adherents living in the Occupied Territories and supporting the idea of a Greater, biblical Israel which includes the West Bank and Gaza. It demonstrates how strict adherence to Halachic law does not always preclude activist political commitments. The Settler movement, notably the Gush Emunim (Community of the Faithful), draws strongly on the religious Zionism of the elder and younger Kooks. It was a central actor driving the expansion of settlements in the Occupied Territories after 1967 – a policy the Labor government and defense minister Moshe Dayan opposed. The NRP, like the Haredi parties, used its position in successive coalitions to its advantage. In contrast to the Haredim, however, the modern Orthodox have won the accolades of secular nationalist Israelis. Polls in the late 1980s show that between a fifth and a half of all Israelis support Gush aims.[107]

The militant Gush Emunim Underground is the extremist fringe of the movement. During 1979–84, Underground members mounted a series of attacks on Palestinian civilians to retaliate against PLO terrorism. Baruch Goldstein's daytime gun and grenade attack on the Islamic College of Hebron killed three and injured thirty-three. Members also detonated two car bombs which maimed Nablus Mayor Bassam Shaka'a and Ramallah Mayor Karim Khalaf. These actions were endorsed by many within the wider Settler movement. The case of Yigal Amir nicely exemplifies the potential connection between Orthodoxy and religious violence. On 4 November 1995, Amir, together with his brother Hasai and another accomplice, Dror Adani, assassinated Yitzhak Rabin, the popular Israeli Labor prime minister.

Winner of the 1994 Nobel Peace Prize for his role in signing the Oslo Accords, which recognised Palestinian control of parts of the West Bank and Gaza, Rabin was widely reviled by religious Zionists. Amir typified their attitude. Born into a modern Orthodox family of Yemeni descent, he attended a Haredi elementary school and yeshiva before entering the Israeli defence forces as a Hesder student. Hesder programmes combine Talmudic study – focusing on passages which underline the sacredness of the land of Israel – with military service. An ascetic environment prevails and secular Jews are considered an impure 'other' whose influence the Hesder students must resist. As one exponent explains it, Hesder helps to reconcile the potentially conflicting spiritual and patriotic duties of religious Zionists:

> The defense of Israel is an ethical and halakhic imperative – be it

because, as we believe, the birth of the state was a momentous historical event and its preservation of great spiritual significance or because, even failing that, the physical survival of its three million plus Jewish inhabitants is at stake.[108]

Hesder graduates are everything that draft-exempt Haredim are not: they have distinguished themselves in battle, and are known for both their effectiveness and ferocity. During the First Lebanon War (1982–5), Hesder students continued to fight and defeat their opponents after their secular comrades had capitulated. Less admirable is their zeal for treating Palestinians harshly, which they displayed in abundance during the first intifada of the late 1980s. Their willingness to perform crackdowns with gusto has marked them as the units of choice for commanders seeking to wreak havoc on rebellious Palestinians.[109]

Fundamentalism in the diaspora

The diaspora is the historic source of immigrants to Israel. It provides most of the funding for both Haredi yeshivas and modern Orthodox settlements. Has demographic change affected the diasporic half of world Jewry? The answer is provided by the *Tribune*, the principal organ of Britain's Haredi community, which recently boasted, 'We will be the majority by 2050.' The paper's claims are founded on census-based research by historian Yaakov Wise of the University of Manchester. Though his methodology is disputed by some scholars, Wise found that Haredim constitute 17 per cent of the UK's Jewish population but account for three-quarters of all British Jewish births. The high Haredi fertility rate has even managed to counteract the long-term decline in the wider UK Jewish population. Within British Jewry, the effect is overwhelming. In Manchester, a third of Jews are already Haredi, up from a quarter just ten years ago.[110]

Trends in continental Europe are more difficult to discern, but point in the same direction. Among Europe-wide Jewish women who have completed their fertility (those over forty-five), the average number of children ever born to women who describe themselves as 'religious' is around three. Among those who describe themselves as 'not religious' this figure drops to 1.8, while atheist women bear less than 1.5. This pattern seems even stronger among a rising generation of Jewish women who have yet to complete their fertility (aged eighteen to forty-four). Religious women in this age bracket are already close to the replacement level, while the non-religious are at just 1.2 and atheist women have borne a mere 0.7 children.[111] The fertility gap between Haredi and non-Haredi European Jews undoubtedly surpasses that between the merely 'religious' and the rest.

The divergent population trajectories of Haredi and secular diaspora Jews is accentuated by secular Jews' extremely low fertility rates and greater propensity to marry out. Consider Britain, where census data on religion enables us to pinpoint relevant trends. The story of British Jews is really that of two communities: a demographically vibrant, economically deprived ultra-Orthodox group; and an aging, economically successful majority of secular/moderate Jews. The latter are much more likely to assimilate and intermarry, hastening their decline. One can graphically see this in the youthful age pyramid of the Jewish community of Salford, near Manchester, with its wide base of young people converging sharply to a small apex of elderly. This contrasts with the top-heavy population pyramid of the Leeds Jewish community, which is more similar to the Anglo-Jewish average. Salford's Jews are primarily, though not exclusively, ultra-Orthodox, while Leeds has very few Haredim.[112]

In the United States, the General Social Surveys of 2000–2006 show that Jews have the lowest fertility rate of eleven ethno-religious groups: 1.43 children per woman. As in Europe, small families combine with high intermarriage and few converts to reduce the Jewish proportion of the population. Among those born after 1945, there are now more Mormons than Jews, and Muslims will overtake them by 2025, perhaps heralding a historic sea change in American foreign policy, with its traditional support for the state of Israel.[113] The decline of American Jewry, however, masks an opposing trend: the rise of the Orthodox – especially the Haredim. American Haredim have lower fertility than their Israeli cousins, but far higher rates than secular Jews. For instance, the average family size in ultra-Orthodox New York State villages such as Kiryas Joel and New Square is 6.6, against a statewide average of 2.63 in 2002.

Haredi and modern Orthodox membership retention is also on the rise. The 2000 National Jewish Population Survey (NJPS) found that half of all Americans who were raised Orthodox – some Haredi, most modern – had left Orthodoxy.[114] But many of these were only nominally Orthodox, choosing the label more as a badge of identity than a reflection of ideology. Indeed, until the 1960s, Orthodox Jews were on the defensive. Joseph Lookstein, an Orthodox rabbi, even called upon Orthodox Jews in the 1950s to jettison the term 'Orthodox' since it had archaic connotations which would repel Jewish youth.[115]

Since the 1960s, however, the tide has swiftly turned. A more muscular Orthodoxy drove many nominals towards liberal synagogues or secularism. Those who remained Orthodox were in turn 'out-Orthodoxed' by their kids. This came about as modern Orthodox parents sent their children to new private Jewish day schools where they were taught by Haredi rabbis. What a contrast from the American public education their parents received, in which Jewish education was supplemental rather than central. The use of Haredim as teachers was the outcome of a default process in which the modern Orthodox avoided the rabbinate in pursuit of secular professions.[116] Their legacy is that the proportion of defectors among young Orthodox is lower. The 2002 NJPS found that for Orthodox Jews aged 18 to 29, two-thirds who were raised Orthodox remained Orthodox. This is more than twice the retention rate of those 30–44, and four times that of the 45- to 64-year-old Orthodox. Intermarriage with non-Jews was virtually non-existent. Haredi retention is undoubtedly higher. This runs counter to the trend among Conservative and Reform Jews, where the young tend to defect more than their elders.[117]

Like the Amish and evangelical Protestants, modernity provides fundamentalist groups with more carrots and sticks to retain their youth. In the low-fertility Jewish environment of the diaspora, the Haredim are poised for explosive growth. Professor Joshua Comenetz of the University of Florida estimates that the Haredi minority increased their share of the American Jewish total from 7.2 to 9.4 per cent during 2000–2006 alone. At this rate, they will constitute the majority of American Jews in 2050.[118]

Together with the modern Orthodox, Haredim make up 23 per cent of the American Jews who belong to a synagogue and 38 per cent of their children.[119] Forty per cent of American synagogues are now Orthodox, rising to 57 per cent in the greater New York region. The market for kosher food doubled between 1997 and 2002 to $6.5 billion and is expanding at the rate of 10–15 per cent a year.[120] The change can be vividly seen in Greater New York, where a majority of American ultra-Orthodox Jews live. The small Hasidic settlement of Kiryas Joel, in Orange County, New York, for example, tripled in population from 6,000 to 18,000 between 1990 and 2006.[121] Some of this was due to in-migration, but this cannot explain why the median age of the population in Kiryas Joel and New Square is just fourteen.[122]

Numbers increasingly bring power. Where once the ultra-Ortho-dox sought to secede from mainstream diaspora Jewish organisations, in the future they will be in a position to take them over. Orthodox Jews are increasingly acquiring positions of leadership in leading Ameri-can organisations, such as the Conference of Presidents of Major Jew-ish Organizations, the American Jewish Committee and the Memorial Foundation for Jewish Culture. Haredi lobbyists like Agudat Israel and the Lubavitchers are becoming a presence on Capitol Hill. As in Israel, Haredim wield local power by voting en bloc, in accord with the wishes of their rebbes. This has helped them to win influence in local munici-palities such as Williamsburg or in Crown Heights, in Brooklyn, where they bore the brunt of African-American anti-Haredi riots in 1991. In state elections, Kiryas Joel's bloc voters can swing congressional races.[123]

Nationally, Haredim 'have been in the Oval office in every adminis-tration since Jimmy Carter's' and national politicians such as Bill Clinton find it prudent to pose with rebbes and don the yarmulke.[124] Orthodox Jews are especially significant because they are more likely than other Jews to vote Republican. In 2004, 70 per cent backed Bush while just 30 per cent favoured Kerry, an inversion of the national pattern, where Jews preferred Kerry 75:25 over Bush.[125] This is mainly because of Republican support for faith-based schools and initiatives, and traditionalist moral values. For some Orthodox Jews, the affinity between Christian and Jew-ish Zionism matters. Republican support for more muscular pro-Israeli foreign policies doesn't hurt either. A curious feature of the 2008 election is that Jews were the only major ethno-religious group to resist the swing to Obama. Twenty-seven per cent backed Bush in 2004, increasing to 29 per cent who supported McCain in 2008. This may signal the beginning of a historic Jewish realignment towards the Republicans caused by the Orthodoxisation of American Jewry.[126]

Orthodox hegemony in the diaspora will shape debates in Israel. For instance, roughly half of young American Jews now marry those of other faiths. This sparked a debate in the Jewish community over how best to keep these 'part-Jewish' Jews within the fold. Reform and Conservative Judaism relaxed traditional Jewish matrilineal descent rules to enable those with Jewish fathers but non-Jewish mothers (such as myself) to be Jews. However, the American Haredim have resisted these initiatives because they stray from Halachic orthodoxy – much as they have in Israel when discussing 'who can be a Jew'. This constrains who can emigrate to Israel under the provisions of the Law of Return. Given the weak Israeli economy and a restricted definition of Jewish eligibility, Israel's future immigrants will be far more Orthodox than ever before. One again, this redounds in favour of religious Jews over their secular adversaries.

The triumph of Orthodoxy

Nowhere is demographic sacralisation as advanced as in Israel and the diaspora. The fertility gap between secular and religious is greater than elsewhere, and will usher in revolutionary change in the next few decades. Practically speaking, the demography of Israeli Jewry will make peace harder to achieve. Young Haredim admire religious nationalists and have little time for the anti-Israeli quietism of their grandparents. The fast-expanding Haredim have become more hawkish as their population has overflowed into the Occupied Territories.

The modern Orthodox, who form the backbone of religious Zionism and Gush Emunim radicalism, are holding their own. Only secular Jews are shrinking, beset by low fertility and adverse migration trends. In the second half of this century, they will come to resemble Lebanon's Christians, a group that played the leading role in establishing the country, but has since shrunk from a majority to just a quarter of the population because of low fertility and emigration. The idea of an Orthodox Israel would have turned the stomachs of the country's Labor Zionist pioneers. Nonetheless, the question is not *if* the country will become

Orthodox, but *when*. The window for peace with the Palestinians is closing, if it has not closed already. Yet ironically, if an Arab–Israeli peace
deal is miraculously struck, this will only serve to pit Jew against Jew in
a struggle for the soul of Israel.

7

SHALL THE RELIGIOUS INHERIT THE EARTH?

The classical view of history is that it moves in cycles. This is influenced by a religious sensibility: there is a 'time for every season'; civilisations rise and fall like everything else in nature. Thomas Cole's magnificent, room-sized *Course of Empire* canvases at the Smithsonian in Washington graphically portray this epic. Civilisations emerge when youthful and vigorous and enjoy an efflorescence. But they eventually succumb to hubris and begin to decline, falling victim to more disciplined challengers. I vividly recall thumbing through my father's set of Arnold Toynbee's Civilisations series, with its green and purple textboxes, heavy clay-enriched paper and evocative illustrations. Toynbee held that a cultural 'schism in the soul' was the first intimation that a society had lost its way.[1] The sickness might be concealed for some time, but would inevitably expose itself in the material realm of the economy and war. Cole's painting *Course of Empire: Destruction* shows grand classical temples being ransacked and pillaged. A classy maiden plunges to her death. A great statue is decapitated. Others prefer the motif of plants growing around ruined monuments: high culture being reclaimed and rejuvenated by rude nature.

Classical scholars from Polybius and Cicero onwards contrasted the social cohesion, moral virtue and youthful vitality of tribal invaders with the individualism and decadence of high civilisation. Polybius, though Greek, warned that Roman youth were being corrupted by a seductive

Hellenic culture. There was more. 'In our time all Greece was visited by a dearth of children and a general decay of population,' he lamented around 140 BC, as Greece was yielding to Roman domination. 'This evil grew upon us rapidly, and without attracting attention, by our men becoming perverted to a passion for show and money and the pleasures of an idle life.' Medieval Arab theorist Ibn Khaldun even claimed that invading nomads were periodically necessary to renew the demographic and moral basis of Muslim civilisation. Some, looking at Venice, sensed a connection between its thousands of nightly balls and eventual political implosion. Whether Romans displaced Greeks, Germanic barbarians sacked Rome or Turks and Mongols conquered Arabs, the pattern seemed distressingly similar.

At a time when most children died at birth, a civilisation's commitment to pronatalism furnished the demographic bedrock for its native military. Falling short in this department meant having to depend on allies and mercenaries, who might turn their guns on their paymasters. Native fertility could only be maintained through the ascetic denial of worldly consumption and freedom in favour of communal reproduction. 'Once a society grows cosmopolitan, fast-paced, and filled with new ideas, new peoples, and new luxuries ... [the] connection to one's ancestors begins to fade, and with it, any sense of the necessity of reproduction,' argues Philip Longman of the centrist New America Foundation. 'When the ordinary thought of a highly cultivated people begins to regard "having children" as a question of pro's and con's,' Oswald Spengler, the German historian and philosopher, once observed, 'the great turning point has come.'[2]

Such interpretations have fallen out of favour among many historians as the circular, seasonal approach to time of the pre-modern era has been replaced by a linear or disaggregated view of history.[3] Many hold that something has irrevocably changed since the Enlightenment. Demographic and moral theories of decline are labelled post hoc conservative fantasies, disguising the real, material causes of civilisational decline: new technologies, shifting resource supplies and modes of production; plagues, ecological collapses and other chance events; shifting alliances and political innovations, and so forth.[4] Liberal theorists now believe that Enlightened civilisations can control their own destiny.

Bertrand Russell, who penned his ideas a few streets away from me here in Bloosmbury, straddled the two perspectives. At the end of the Second World War he wrote:

> Social cohesion is a necessity and mankind has never yet succeeded in enforcing social cohesion by merely rational arguments. Every community is exposed to two opposite dangers; ossification through too much discipline and reverence for tradition, on the one hand; on the other hand, dissolution, or subjection to foreign conquest, through the growth of an individualism and personal independence that makes cooperation impossible. In general, important civilisations start with a rigid and superstitious system, gradually relaxed, and leading, at a certain stage, to a period of brilliant genius ... as the evil unfolds it leads to anarchy, thence, inevitably, to a new tyranny, producing a new synthesis secured by a new system of dogma. The doctrine of liberalism is an attempt to escape from this endless oscillation ... to secure a social order not based on irrational dogma ... Whether this can succeed only the future can determine.[5]

Russell, a card-carrying member of the bohemian 'Bloomsbury Set', was an atheistic libertine, but a realist. His hope was that the political genius of liberal democracy could surmount the contradictions between cohesive narrowness and individualistic weakness. Talcott Parsons preferred an analogy with life on earth, which evolves from simple to more complex, 'higher' organisms. As a Yankee liberal who lived through the Second World War, Parsons named liberal institutions, markets and democracy as the most advanced institutions known to man.[6] Francis Fukuyama was more specific: modern technology produces sophisticated economies and weapons systems. Since open, liberal societies are more technologically advanced, they are inoculated from the challenges posed by cohesive but backward 'barbarians at the gates'.[7]

Karl Marx and Friedrich Hegel take an intermediate position: history has a direction, but the path isn't straight. History's dialectic is caused by an antithesis which contradicts society's central thesis, leading to conflict. This produces a synthesis which allows for a more complex, higher stage of civilisation to emerge. In the long run, humanity passes through successive stages onward and upward, from primitive hunting and gathering through feudalism, capitalism, and, for Marx, socialism. This is an optimistic view, but a conflictual one. In the long run we will be fine, but in the short run we could be entering a phase of greater conflict and collapse before the new order emerges. This model seems to capture the current conflict between secularism and its fundamentalist antithesis.

Different dialectical thinkers cherished their own mechanisms of system collapse which would herald the rise of a new order. Marx thought capitalist society would implode of its own contradictions. Businesses would exploit the proletariat, absorbing the entire labour supply, and subsequently compete each other into penury. The collapse of profits and immiseration of the workers would spark revolution, leading to socialism. It didn't happen. Capitalism withstood communism and survived numerous booms and busts. Despite childish predictions of capitalist collapse in the wake of the Asian, dot.com and global financial crises, the system has proven shock-proof. Others agree, but maintain that cultural rather than economic collapse will bring liberal capitalism to its knees. Daniel Bell flagged the contradiction between capitalism's need for disciplined production and its promotion of instant gratification. He warned that the individualist ethos of modern consumerism would corrode the system from within, producing a 'great instauration' of religion to renew social cohesion and economic productivity.[8] However, modern liberal societies have withstood the breakdown of the family, consumerism and rising crime rates without degenerating into anarchy.

It is less clear that the reigning liberal-capitalist 'end of history' model can surmount its demographic contradictions. Demographically powerful groups don't require superior technology to conquer their adversaries. The change, as in Israel, takes place peacefully over generations. Around the world, secular individuals are in the forefront of the shift to below-replacement fertility rates which have swept the West and East Asia and, on UN projections, will encompass the entire planet by 2085. As the sea of humanity drains away, it will expose resistant fundamentalist wellsprings – the future of our species. Already we see early signs of this in the resistance of all devout populations to population decline. Old Order Anabaptists, Mormons, Haredi Jews, Laestadian Lutherans, Salafi Islamists and Quiverfull Protestants are rapidly increasing their share of a shrinking pie. These endogenous growth sects segregate themselves from modern society while encouraging large families, benefiting from both a fertility premium over others and a strong capacity to retain and transmit membership to their children. They are the archetype, but radical change can also come from slower-growing large groups such as mainstream Christian charismatics, Protestant fundamentalists or Islamists, all of whom are on the rise against demographically moribund seculars and moderates. As the growth of early Christianity shows, compound effects mean that even a small demographic advantage can lead to big changes over several generations.

Secularisation mainly erodes unconscious religion: the taken-for-granted, moderate faiths that trade on being mainstream and established. This explains the rapid decline of religion in Europe and, increasingly, the United States. On the other hand, religious fundamentalists have mobilised against secularism and moderate faith, self-consciously warning their members of its influence. Pronatalism and segregation, the core features of endogenous growth sects, are catching on: we already see conservative Christian theologians advocating these strategies. Mainstream fundamentalist Christians have above-replacement fertility rates and the most theologically zealous are considerably more fecund than average. Regular attenders of more moderate denominations have a fertility advantage over seculars but tend to be less effective at passing on their faith to their children. On the other hand, fundamentalists, combining both high retention and fertility rates, are the demographic equivalent of a coiled spring, whose energy has only recently become apparent.

Religious fundamentalism tends to flare for three reasons: insecurity, identity and demography. Insecurity, or what Adrian Wooldridge and John Micklethwait dub 'the dislocations of modernity', are only powerful motives in developing countries where people remain open to 'enchanted' responses to their condition.[9] In such societies, rural populations are uprooting and moving to the cities in droves. Many are poor, and some have experienced violent conflict. This provides tinder for religious revival. In Europe, only a small number of isolated or vulnerable individuals, freed from secular peer pressure, come to faith this way. Some make up the volatile ranks of cults such as the Jehovah's Witnesses, which suffer rapid membership turnover.

Identity dynamics are also important in explaining religious resurgence in the developing world. When much of the world is poor and religious while the wealthy are mostly secular, religion becomes a symbol of resistance, something most apparent in the global Islamic revival. Muslim morality is contrasted with Western licentiousness. The religion grows inadvertently through population explosion among the poor. Once again, the demographic revolution of our time increases the power of fundamentalism by boosting the ranks of the devout. We have a long way to go before all regions of the planet complete their demographic transitions – resulting in a population surge whose scale dwarfs that of the West's milder explosion of 1750–1950. By the time the transition runs its course in the twenty-second century, the secular nations of the planet will account for a much smaller share of the world's population than they do today. And this assumes the West will remain as secular as it is now, which is unlikely.

The wide disparity – economic and demographic – between the West, East Asia and 'the Rest' is interacting with globalisation to bring the demographic revolution on to Western city streets. The fact that most immigrants are culturally and racially, as well as religiously, different from the majority associates religion with ethnic difference. This produces ethno-religious self-consciousness, which insulates religion from decline. This is especially true of Islam, which acts as a potent marker of ethnic identity, even for lapsed Muslims. Declaring oneself a 'Muslim' in Europe makes a modern statement which can pave the way for deeper spiritual commitment. Ethnicity and religion play off each other to resist secular assimilation.

The 'browning' of the West is injecting a fresh infusion of religious blood into secular society of the kind that has allowed immigrant London to buck Britain's secularising trend. The success of religion in urban Europe – where secularisation is most intense – demonstrates the power of religious demography. While white Christians suffer ridicule from the secular majority, European Muslims in ethnic neighbourhoods gain community approval for their beliefs. The children of nominal Muslims therefore take a more positive view of religion than their Christian counterparts.

In the near term, identity-driven religion, borne by the Third World poor, brought north on the backs of immigrants and spread by their relatively large number of children, will be the most important source of religious vitality in Europe. However, immigrant Christian and Muslim birth rates are falling. Intermarriage, secularisation and assimilation will steadily melt non-white Christians and work away at the edges of the moderate Muslim majority. Muslims will not take over Europe, but will stabilise at somewhere around a fifth of the West European population in 2100. At the same time, native Europeans are becoming more resistant to the charms of secularism, with white Christianity retrenching into a charismatic and fundamentalist core. In a generation or two, most white Europeans who wish to become secular will have done so: religion is no longer declining in the most godless parts of the continent such as France, the Czech Republic and Scandinavia. With input from immigrant Christians and Muslims, religion will begin to grow again. At some point between 2020 and 2070, demography will reverse aggregate religious decline in European societies which have been in train for decades or even centuries. Interfaith structures could incubate a shared social conservatism uniting conservative Muslims with Christians, Jews and others. This could mesh with the incorporation of minorities into mainstream parties to set the stage for a new era of religious politics, an unprecedented European desecularisation.

Slowly but surely, ethnic enmities will be cross-cut by an American-style 'culture wars' cleavage which distinguishes moral conservatives of all faiths from secular liberals. Beyond 2050, European and Israeli fundamentalist growth may increasingly follow the American pattern, where the central tendency is towards *intra*-ethnic politics. In our age of migration, ethnic conflict is very powerful, and it is difficult to see beyond it. But in liberal societies, things change when minorities breach a threshold beyond which their ballots count for more than anti-immigrant votes. As the experience of the United States and some of Europe's most diverse cities shows, moral politics is both more acceptable and more lucrative for conservative parties than white nationalism.

Religious conservatism has the same demographic advantages in the Muslim world, though these are currently being obscured by the socially driven upheavals of the Islamic revival. According to Second Demographic Transition theory, the growth of cities and conquering of infant mortality remove the material incentives for women to bear large numbers of children. Prior to modern medicine, both the secular and religious had to have large families, and value choices had less impact on total fertility rates. The religious fertility premium only begins to increase when seculars are free to exercise their demographic preferences and contraceptives become widely available. Religious fundamentalists maintain high fertility as others transition to lower TFRs, opening up a demographic divide. Seculars and moderates marry later than fundamentalists and are more apt to choose smaller families. Values come to strongly condition growth rates.

In the Sunni Muslim world, Islamists are slowly losing the battle against family planning clinics to determined authoritarian regimes, just as they have lost their struggle for Islamic revolution. Their future strategy may involve pronatalism 'from below' to grow their own. Such words are already on the lips of their leaders, from Turkey to Iran and Pakistan. In the freest and most modern Muslim contexts, Islamists have an impressive fertility advantage over other Muslims. Fundamentalists' fertility advantage over the non-religious will persist into the foreseeable future, unlike the ethnic fertility gap between Muslims and Christians, which will go the way of Catholic–Protestant differences. At the same time, like all fundamentalists, Islamists have self-consciously mobilised against secularism to ensure that boundaries between themselves and the profane world remain vigilantly policed. The combination of higher fertility and superior retention rates produces the endogenous growth of strong religion in all Abrahamic societies.

The growth of religious fundamentalism shapes patterns of political violence. Salafi-jihadists will continue to occupy centre stage, despite their current setbacks in the Muslim world. Religious Zionists will resist attempts to dismantle settlements and make territorial concessions to the Palestinians. Christian fundamentalists are currently the least violent, notwithstanding Uganda's Lord's Resistance Army. But American fundamentalists will continue to support religious Zionism and a messianic foreign policy, which may indirectly lead to conflict. Occasionally, they will spawn an anti-abortion terrorist. This means our world will be more dangerous than if we all morphed into Fukuyaman 'last men', but not necessarily more so than if the great secular creeds of the twentieth century were to rise again.

To be fair, religious traditions contain important restraining forces which may set limits to violence. In South West Africa in the late nineteenth century, German missionaries lobbied against settler genocide against the Herero, and in Northern Ireland, Catholic clergy largely opposed the message of the Marxist IRA while Protestant ministers discouraged their flock from joining secular loyalist paramilitaries. Today, Saudi Salafists are helping to deradicalise many potential jihadists, even though many jihadis spring, unofficially, from their ranks. Islamists like Hamas, the Muslim Brotherhood and Hezbollah, are strong supporters of democracy. Those such as Tony Blair who call for us to use faith-based solutions to resolve conflicts are on to something.

Religious violence is therefore less of a worry than the fundamentalist threat to basic liberties. Their ascent will cast a pall over freedom of expression, science, sumptuary liberty and minority rights. This is strikingly evident in much of the Muslim world, where rulers have co-opted the Islamist social agenda to head off the threat of revolution. The imposition of sharia places restrictions on liquor, television, female attire and expressive freedom. Often secularists, liberals, converts and minorities live in fear of their life. In the Jewish world, restrictions on dress, food and mobility are only imposed in Haredi neighbourhoods, but will spread as Haredi power increases. The ultra-Orthodox also control Israeli burial and marriage, censor advertising and seek to determine who counts as a Jew. In American Christendom, restrictions are milder: dry counties in Utah and the South or Sunday closing are as ascetic as it gets. Even so, fundamentalist pressure is nipping at abortion rights, gay rights, family planning and the science curriculum. Atheists are unelectable and 'god talk' pervades many political campaigns.

Religion, human nature and ideology

Taking a step back from it all, one might ask: what does the demographic rise of religious fundamentalism tell us about our cultural condition at the dawn of the third millennium? Some might conclude that we are seeing evolution playing out before our very eyes. Evolution works through fertility and mortality differences. Given certain environmental pressures, those with adaptive traits are naturally selected to have more surviving children than those without them. Religious belief could be one such trait. It might operate at the level of our genes. A number of twin studies suggest that, regardless of upbringing, twins tend to strongly resemble each other in their religious behaviour. The conclusion is that religiosity is partly inherited.[10] The problem with genetic theories of religion, however, is that they have a hard time explaining changes in religiosity over time and place. Unless, that is, we presume that Danes lack religious genes or somehow have undergone mutation since 1850!

Another possibility is that religion is a self-replicating cultural trait, or meme, which helps individuals to compete in the game of cultural evolution. Its DNA is encoded in its holy texts, priesthoods and rituals. Those possessing the religious meme will gradually displace seculars the way monotheists replaced animists. Throughout human history, people have been almost universally religious, unlike our closest relatives, the chimpanzees. Some argue that religious rituals and a belief in the supernatural helped humans to cooperate. We thereby gained the upper hand over other species and humans who did not adopt religion. Talcott Parsons adds that religion is an 'evolutionary universal' of human progress – a stage all developing societies must pass through – because it legitimates power and the social order. Without it, anarchy ensues.[11] Like our other emotions, existential curiosity and a desire for meaning, transcendence and community may be an evolved part of human nature. Cognitive neuroscience may one day identify the precise mechanisms in the brain that produce a state of nirvana or intensity when stimulated by religious thoughts and rituals.[12]

The question this begs is why we are not all Hutterites. One answer is that we are on our way there. Another is that a fast-reproducing strategy does not always win out. There is now an extensive literature on the evolutionary origins of religion, and it shows that there are two routes to evolutionary success, 'r' and 'K' strategies.[13] An r-strategy is to have lots of children and invest very little in each. Bacteria and rabbits use this approach very effectively. Birth and death rates are high and those with lower fertility die out. Another option is to run with a K-strategy: bear fewer children but invest a lot in each to ensure they have low mortality. Elephants and humans do this quite well. Scientists find that in times of change, as with a forest fire, the r-strategy does best. In burnt-over areas, fast-growing plants such as weeds have the advantage.

Once vegetation matures and plants have to compete with each other for resources, K-strategies take over. This favours larger plants and animals. Sometimes we find a combination of strategies, as with trees that grow large but spread many seeds.

The analogy does not translate seamlessly into human behaviour. Even Hutterites have very few children by rodent standards, and the Amish and Haredim inhabit well-populated, competitive environments. Endogenous growth sects invest considerably in their children's religious education, often at the expense of themselves. Retention is high. So they use both K- and r-strategies. Much therefore depends on selection pressures obtaining in a particular situation. A Hutterite r-strategy would doubtless be optimal in the aftermath of a nuclear holocaust or if we had new planets to colonise. It would be of little use in a world of intolerant high-tech powers such as Nazi Germany. Had my grandfather been an Orthodox Jew instead of a sceptical, mobile, assimilated Jewish chemist, I would probably not be sitting here. So context matters. What is true now may not hold for all time. All of which suggests that fundamentalist religiosity may be on the rise because it successfully exploits a social niche characterised by liberal toleration and demographic transition. As the Nazis showed, secular persecution can bring fundamentalist growth to an abrupt halt.

There is another possibility which may offer a more optimistic scenario: symbiosis. Consider an equilibrium in which religious pronatalism is counterbalanced by low secular fertility, where religious defections to the secular population precisely offset the religious fertility advantage. Fundamentalists produce the excess children who resolve the demographic contradictions of secular individualism. The largest groups of religious fundamentalists – Islamists, evangelical Protestants, conservative Catholics – have only a modest fertility advantage over others. An increase in defections to secularism is all that is needed to maintain a steady state.

Perhaps the rise of fundamentalism is no bad thing. In our glitzy consumer world of status competition and hedonism, you have to admire the restraint of world-denying fundamentalists. (Here I speak of real fundamentalists, not America's soft neo-evangelicals with their prosperity gospel!) There is unquestionably an optimum degree of hedonism, sexual permissiveness and freedom beyond which we no longer derive added value. I would rather this point be determined by reflective choice than theological fiat, but maybe fundamentalism can replenish the social fibre and demographic capital that seculars expend. This is also the liberal ideal. Let a thousand lifestyles bloom. Fundamentalists can happily do their thing without affecting secular hegemony in culture, science and education. The open society will endure as we remain perfectly free to consume and express ourselves. Fundamentalists could even be a source of new cultural experiences and ideas as liberal cosmopolites 'slum it' by soaking up the piety of Meah Sharim, Riyadh, Provo or Nashville.

Sound too good to be true? It probably is. Dry atheism, even with the leaven of humanism and modern art, can never compete with the rich emotions evoked by religion. This was recognised by the German-Jewish Marxist Ernst Bloch, who asked, 'Why is it ... that this remote language [of the ancient Bible] is never boring?' He warned that myths bore a truth that atheistic communism ignored at its peril, and implored the movement not to abandon its Utopian eschatology in favour of dry historical materialism: 'Man must be able to see the Kingdom of heavenly freedom as his ... Utopia.' [14] Secularism, shorn of ideology, cannot inspire a commitment to generations past and sacrifices for those yet to come. The spread of liberal democracy is not, contra John Gray, a genuine secular faith. It only animates a small number of internationally minded neoconservatives and Wilsonian liberals. It promises no radical change in the lives of most Western people. Neoconservatism's power sprang not from liberal-democracy's own myths, symbols and rituals but from its association with Christian Zionism and American nationalism, genuine emotive creeds.[15]

Ideologies can inspire a sense of trans-generational commitment. But the so-called 'secular religions' of socialism and anarchism, which fired the emotions of some as recently as the 1980s, are exhausted. Political parties in the West have abandoned ideology and moved towards incrementalism and managerialism. The Green movement is a partial exception, but lacks a cultural and political vision that can mobilise large numbers of ordinary people. Could secular individualism be its problem? As James Lovelock, founder of Gaia theory, laments, Greens have failed to stir the mass altruism and collective sacrifice that curbing emissions require. He looks to a nationalist-style emotional outpouring to bring the sacrifices needed to save the planet.[16] Romantic nationalism is perhaps the only realistic alternative to religion, but lost credibility after the excesses of fascism. It has since been subjected to relentless assault. The Islamic revival strikingly demonstrates how religious fundamentalism has rushed into the void left by secular nationalism.

Among some left-wing elites, the radical cultural transformation of society from relatively mono-ethnic nation states into beehives of multi-cultural 'transgression' is a form of chiliastic ideology, but this utopia barely extends beyond bohemian enclaves and university districts. It does, however, dovetail with the casual attitude of many to far-reaching demographic change, with their disenchanted 'here for a good time not a long time' approach. If one is nonplussed about society being demographically transformed by non-Western cultures, surely it is no great leap to throw one's hands up at the demographic encroachment of religion.

Still, one might argue, reports of secularism's demise are greatly exaggerated. All of today's fast-growing religious sects are minorities, many of which, like the Laestadians, are very small. As they grow in confidence, they will lose their siege mentality and their high fertility. Growth will produce splits and moderating 'sect-to-church' movements. A taste of power will bring pragmatic moderation and a hunger for the goods of this world rather than those of the next. As more powerful fundamentalist movements collide with competing fundamentalisms rather than secularism, they will begin to join hands with secular allies rather than religious ones.

This rosy scenario will eventually take place, but only when fundamentalist religion decisively buries the ghost of secularism which created it, defined it and has haunted it for the past two centuries. Until that point, secularism will continue to provide the 'other' against which fundamentalist religions valiantly struggle. This focus will unite the movement across lines of sect and even civilisation. Secularism will revive, but only when it becomes marginal. Ironically, secular success breeds its fundamentalist contradiction by driving out moderate religion. Until a new synthesis is found that can recapture some of the soulful elements provided by fundamentalism, demographically turbo-charged piety will continue to flourish.

The demographic challenge of strong religion raises searching questions that strike at the heart of liberalism. Liberty, according to Isaiah Berlin, can take negative or positive form. Negative liberty consists of value-neutral procedures and institutions. People can do as they please as long as they don't violate the freedoms of others. Positive liberalism refers to an ideal about what one ought to do with one's liberty.[17] Most liberals emphasise that the good life consists of being an autonomous individual, making free choices and developing one's potential. Multicultural liberals counter that individualism is no more valid than choosing to identify with communal traditions. They claim that society should not privilege autonomy over community, and urge us to tolerate or even 'respect' fundamentalist groups.

Liberals are aware that tolerating illiberal groups is risky. In John Rawls's words, 'justice does not require that men stand idly by while others destroy the basis of their existence.' However, Rawls urges liberals to tolerate the intolerant unless they pose a threat to the institutions of liberty.[18] The problem arises when illiberal groups such as religious fundamentalists demographically increase to the point where they are able to threaten the freedom of others. This is principally true in Muslim societies and Israel. But even in Europe, Islamic extremists such as Mohammed Bouyeri can effectively silence critics of Islam and restrict the liberty of Muslim women. In the United States, Christian fundamentalists may respect liberal institutions, but if given a chance, the neo-Calvinists among them would constrain the freedom of women, hedonists and gays and challenge the hegemony of secular education and science.

Liberals could crack down by curtailing the freedom of illiberal groups, just as the American government did when it banned polygamy and theocracy in Utah. But it is difficult to justify prohibiting democratically chosen conservative policies on abortion, pornography, gay marriage, Creationism, driving on the Sabbath, and so forth. Furthermore, as Karen Armstrong notes, repression can radicalise fundamentalists, as in Nasser's Egypt and the Shah's Iran.[19] In these cases, the best remedy for those wishing to defend Enlightenment ideals is to win over fundamentalists to their point of view. There is fragmentary evidence that Hutterites, for example, can be wooed to neo-evangelicalism, and thence into mainstream society.[20] Israel is currently trying to integrate the Haredim into the economy and military in the hope that birth rates will fall, and it is worth making the effort to do so. Another option is to incentivise seculars to have more children or encourage secular immigration.

But unless this is matched by a concomitant decline in religious fertility, it raises an ecological problem. The earth's growing population is combining with economic development to produce unsustainable levels of carbon emissions. In the present climate, a falling global population may be exactly what the doctor ordered – at least until we find the technological fix required to meet our energy needs while cooling the planet. Populations can sustain a period of decline: oddly, steady decline will eventually produce a younger, more stable population. This will occur after 2050, when we, the generations born during the demographic transition, die off. This will remove the bulge from the top of the population pyramid leaving a more even age structure. In the long term, population decline is suicidal, but it is far from disastrous over the span of a century or two. A population footrace between seculars and fundamentalists that fuels environmental catastrophe is a much greater threat to human existence.

According to Andrew Watkinson of the Tyndall Centre for Climate Change Research, three-quarters of climate change is caused by population growth. This was recently recognised by the UN Population Fund in its 2009 report, *The State of World Population*. Coming just a month before the Copenhagen conference on climate change, the report broke fresh ground in challenging its decades-long reticence about broaching the population–environment link. 'Fear of appearing supportive of population control has until recently held back any mention of "population" in the climate debate,' the report admits. Negotiators, notably the EU, have tentatively suggested that it should be discussed at the summit. The UN report also hints that family planning could be the most effective green policy of all. UN projections suggest that world population will rise from 6.8 billion today to between 8 and 10.5 billion at midcentury. If fertility cuts reduce world population by a billion in 2050, this would achieve the same effect as the daunting task of constructing all new buildings to the highest energy-efficiency standards or replacing all coal-fired power plants with wind turbines. One study found that, dollar-for-dollar, investing in family planning and women's education reduces emissions as much or more than investing in nuclear power or wind energy.[21]

The stakes are especially high in the developed world, where fundamentalist growth and religious immigration are most pronounced. The typical citizen of the developed world emits as much as thirty times the carbon of those in the poorest countries. In November 2009, Alex Renton called for a reduction in rich world population to combat climate change. 'Are condoms not the greenest technology of all?' he dared ask. This resulted in a campaign against his 'war on the human race', orchestrated by American religious conservatives, which attracted nearly 10,000 Google hits. 'Alex Renton has declared war on mankind, in general, and Western man, in particular,' charged blogger Reverend James Heiser of Salem Lutheran Church in Malone, Texas.[22]

Though Renton rightly draws our attention to rich world population growth as a vehicle of climate change, his call for those in the developed world to have fewer children is not realistic given the developed world's below-replacement TFR. Moreover, what Renton and the UNFPA report deliberately fail to mention are the taboos of immigration and religious fertility. Without (largely religious) immigration and the impact of religious fertility, the American population would be closer to 300 million in 2050 instead of its projected 400–500 million. Western Europe's population would be falling instead of soaring. Immigration is more visible, since it transports people from the low-emitting global South to the energy-hungry North. However, most immigrants are moderate in their religious orientation and their fertility rates fall rapidly after their arrival. Domestic religious fertility, on the other hand, is resistant to decline and will eventually produce unsustainable carbon growth.

Seculars and moderates can encourage the fastest-growing fundamentalists to integrate, pointing out that high fertility is a political act which, for the sake of harmony, should be moderated. All the same, we must be prepared for the possibility that religious demography cannot be killed with kindness. Israel will reach the breaking point around 2050. This may explain their use of policy sticks alongside carrots, such as Haredi work placement. Policies can remain liberal as long as they do not explicitly discriminate against a group. For instance, Danish spousal migration restrictions affect all citizens, not just Muslims, so do not contravene liberal principles. Limiting child benefits to the first three children is another example of a neutral policy that might lower Haredi birth rates – though I have my doubts. Removing military exemptions and instituting workfare are more drastic possibilities. Secular Jews need to expend political capital now to address these matters before Shas and UTJ foreclose this option for ever. This may not be enough, but more drastic policies such as gerrymandering or disenfranchising the Haredim from power would contradict the very principles that many seculars defend.

At some point, secular Jews in Israel may face a stark choice: make the best of it as a minority or try to organise for separation. The minority strategy is no disaster. Deists such as Thomas Jefferson made common cause with sectarian religious groups to separate church from state. In Europe, seculars and moderates may one day act as a swing vote between literalist Muslims and Christians. What seculars would do in Muslim, Jewish or Christian majority countries is less clear. Separatism is a possibility, but is difficult without a territorial base. Many of its benefits could, however, be achieved through power sharing. These might include constitutional guarantees for secular schools and media, as well as exemptions from liquor control and censorship laws of the kind foreigners enjoy in many Muslim countries.

The rationality of faith?

That we are even having this conversation tells us we need to revisit the old Enlightenment story of reason conquering superstition. I am at least a third-generation secularist. A family story concerns the local rabbi of Prostejov, Czechoslovakia, who paid a visit to my grandfather's home. He asked for a copy of his Bible, at which point my grandfather replied, 'I don't have a Bible.' 'You don't have a Bible,' gasped the rabbi. 'NO, I DON'T HAVE A BIBLE!' responded my grandfather with irritation, a perfect product of the Jewish Enlightenment. My mother was raised Catholic but has long since abandoned religion. My wife and her father were non-believers. I even notice that my children are repeating the mischievous 'I don't believe in God' mantras in their Church of England-run public school that I once trotted out when I attended Catholic school for a year.

Having said this, and notwithstanding the New Atheists, one has to admit that religion is more rational than unbelief. The root of the word rational is *ratio*, in which we weigh up a number of alternatives, calculate a ratio of how well each satisfies our end, and decide accordingly. As a utilitarian, I believe that the maximisation of collective happiness is the proper end of humanity, and on that score, religion seems more rational than irreligion. A growing body of research suggests that the religious live longer and are happier than sceptics. Noted British economist Richard Layard, a pioneer in the field, writes, 'One of the most robust findings of happiness research [is that] people who believe in God are happier. At the individual level one cannot be sure whether belief causes happiness or happiness causes belief. But since the relation also exists at the national level, we can be sure that to some extent belief causes happiness.' [23]

It is less clear that one's religion is good for other people. Some argue that religion has prosocial effects, stimulating philanthropy and greater male responsibility.[24] On the other hand, secular Scandinavia is a model of progress while the pious Middle East and Africa are mired in poverty. Human development in a country increases as religiosity falls. This could be a legacy of the link between religion and scientific progress, with more secular societies achieving better social outcomes than more religious ones. It might be a spurious correlation caused by the unique history of Europe and East Asia in relation to the rest of the world – in which case the relationship will disappear as pious India, Latin America and the Muslim world develop. As a utilitarian, I would need to weigh up the effects of religion on collective happiness against its benign impact on my individual wellbeing before deciding which way to cast my vote.

Lest I be accused of deserting my secular inheritance, I should say that I applaud Richard Dawkins when he writes, 'As long as we accept the principle that religious faith must be respected simply because it is religious faith, it is hard to withhold respect from the faith of Osama bin Laden and the suicide bombers. The alternative ... is to abandon the principle of automatic respect for religious faith.' His lampooning of certain madrasa students as 'demented parrots' is masterful. When he cites Bertrand Russell's 'open windows of science' and speaks of a world unburdened by religious superstitions, one feels a great sense of liberation. I can even concur with his advocacy of a rational humanist ethics, though I have doubts about whether this will work in the most dysfunctional corners of society. But where Dawkins is least convincing is in his assertion that God's consoling role can be supplanted by science, art, humanism or a 'love of life in this world'. Dawkins expresses his thrill 'to be alive at a time when humanity is pushing against the limits of understanding'. Perhaps because I have always been underwhelmed by Carl Sagan's 'billions and billions', I can't see how scientific wonder gets us any closer to filling the God gap.[25]

Dawkins is correct that even if religion were essential to human wellbeing this wouldn't make it true. Sam Harris insists that those like Blaise Pascal who pragmatically believe in God offer us no more than an epistemological Ponzi scheme.[26] Yet we could say the same about free will and the Self. From a scientific perspective, both are illusions – indeed, the idea of free will has its roots in monotheism, which places humanity at the centre of the world.[27] Since our every act is a result of physical, chemical, biological, psychological and social structures, we aren't free. Self-consciousness may be just a useful evolutionary adaptation. Be that as it may, none of us are going to abandon our subjectivity any time soon. More than that, we will continue to indulge in the habit of narrating our life as a story in which we overestimate our good points and understate the bad. The more sceptical, realistic approach is actually considered psychologically unhealthy and results in depression. No wonder atheists such as Daniel Dennett consider it so vital to reconcile scientific materialism with free will. [28] There are limits to this process: an inflated sense of our own importance will make us overbearing and self-centred. The same seems true for religion. Beliefs, like fire, warm us when taken in moderation, but are antisocial if pushed to an extreme. Perhaps religion has too many malign social effects for us to indulge in it.

There may be another way forward. There is a strong utilitarian case for reason and scientific truth: wilful ignorance opens up a Pandora's box which leads to Jehovah's Witnesses refusing blood transfusions and Socrates being sentenced to death. This means that Creationism, or claims that a man lived to 969 and our planet was founded in 4004 BC, should remain minority views. But luckily, if we restrict ourselves to dogmas that do not violate empirical evidence, beliefs can run free without affecting progress. Scientific laws and mathematical formulae tend to reach logical paradoxes when taken to infinity. Scientific truth requires empirical evidence, which can never be infinite. So a moderate faith that combines a belief in God with an allegorical approach to holy texts poses no threat to the Enlightenment – even if it becomes the norm. As Charles Taylor and Karen Armstrong note, fundamentalists who challenge science by taking their holy texts literally are actually applying a scientific sensibility to traditions that were meant to be approached through art, ritual, allegory and contemplation. Ironically, Taylor treats fundamentalism as one in a long series of 'secularising' steps which began when the monotheisms of the Axial Age first poured cold water on our belief in the spirit world.[29]

Human happiness should be sacralised. Religion's problems would instantly evaporate if all holy books began with, 'And the Lord decreed that His highest purpose is the wellbeing of mankind and that everything in this Book must be interpreted in that light.' The more sentient of animals could also be afforded some worth in this scheme. The common good could be viewed as a divine signal, around which all else should pivot. This does not necessarily point in a secular direction. The poetic, mythical stories of religion may be more effective in inculcating morality than secular methods. Regular attendance at worship and belief in God may improve societies. Or perhaps they may cause more harm than good. But whatever the case, a lively debate would emerge between secularists and the religious that would be anchored in scientific evidence.

The fact that religious researchers such as those based at the Institute for Studies of Religion at Baylor University are trying to make the case for religion or faith-based policy in secular terms – citing improved health and social capital, reduced crime and the like – is a positive development. Whether they are scientifically correct is beside the point. They may be wrong, but their arguments are potentially falsifiable, whereas those of the anti-abortionists (and, one might add, most pro-choicers) – who make no argument about pleasure, pain or psychological effects – are not. This is akin to Sam Harris's 'science of good and evil', harnessing scientific progress for our moral advancement.[30] However, contra Harris, this would not, in principle, rule out a religious society. Full-orbed biblical inerrancy will be marginalised, but parts of scripture may come through unscathed. There is probably no utilitarian limit to fundamentalism about the Golden Rule.

Yet all this seems a vain hope. Moderate faith is being squeezed by both secularism and fundamentalism, its contradiction. Furthermore, the titanic struggle between secularism and fundamentalism takes place on a battlefield tilted in favour of faith. We inhabit a period of ideological exhaustion. The great secular religions, with their utopian dreams, have lost their allure. Relativism and managerialism rise in their stead. At the same time, we are entering a period of unprecedented demographic upheaval. It will be a century or more before the world completes its demographic transition. There is still too much smoke in the air for us to pick out the peaks and valleys of the emerging social order. This much seems certain: without an ideology to inspire social cohesion, fundamentalism cannot be stopped. The religious shall inherit the earth.

NOTES

Introduction

1. Wattenberg, Ben, *Fewer: How the New Demography of Depopulation Will Shape Our Future* (Chicago: Ivan R. Dee, 2004).

2. Skirbekk, V., 'Fertility Trends by Social Status', *Demographic Research* 18:5 (2008), pp. 145–80.

3. Gray, John, *Al Qaeda and What It Means to Be Modern* (London: Faber & Faber, 2003).

4. Zuckerman, Phil, *Society Without God: What the Least Religious Nations Can Tell Us about Contentment* (New York and London: NYU Press, 2008), pp. 4–5.

5. Norris, Pippa, and Ronald Inglehart, *Sacred and Secular: Religion and Politics Worldwide* (Cambridge: Cambridge University Press, 2004), pp. 62–6.

6. Berger, Peter L., *The Sacred Canopy: Elements of a Sociological Theory of Religion* (Garden City, N.Y.: Doubleday, 1967).

7. Fukuyama, Francis, *The End of History and the Last Man* (Hamish Hamilton: London, 1992).

8. Taylor, Charles, *Sources of the Self: The Making of the Modern Identity* (Cambridge: Cambridge University Press, 1989), p. 494.

9. Voas, D., 'The Rise and Fall of Fuzzy Fidelity in Europe', *European Sociological Review* 25:2 (2009), p. 166.

10. Taylor, Charles, 'Secularization Theory: Science or Ideology?', working paper (2009); quoted in Gray, *Al Qaeda and What It Means to Be Modern*, pp. 104–5.

11. Stark, R., and Roger Finke, *Acts of Faith: Explaining the Human Side of Religion* (Berkeley: University of California Press, 2000), p. 79.

12. Norris and Inglehart, *Sacred and Secular*, pp. 4–5.

13. Taylor, Charles, *A Secular Age* (Cambridge, Mass.: Belknap Press of Harvard University Press, 2007).

14. Norris and Inglehart. *Sacred and Secular*, pp. 5, 54.

15. Bruce, Steve, *God Is Dead* (Oxford: Blackwell, 2002), p. 31; Martin, David, *A General Theory of Secularization* (1978; Aldershot: Gregg Revivals, 1993), pp. 77–80.

16. Wise, Yaakov, 'Majority of Jews Will Be Ultra-Orthodox by 2050', University of Manchester press release, 23 July 2007. These figures are a matter of some dispute, however, especially in the case of Britain. See Graham, David, and Daniel Vulkan, 'Population Trends among Britain's Strictly Orthodox Jews' (London: Board of Deputies of British Jews, 2008), http://www.boardofdeputies.org.uk/file/StrictlyOrthodox.pdf.

17. Stark, Rodney, *The Rise of Christianity: A Sociologist Reconsiders History* (Princeton, N.J.: Princeton University Press, 1996); Hout, M., A. Greeley and M. Wilde, 'The Demographic Imperative in Religious Change in the United States', *American Journal of Sociology* 107: 2 (2001), pp. 468–500.

18. Gray, *Al Qaeda and What It Means to Be Modern*, p. 3.

19. Smith, Adam, *An Inquiry into the Nature and Causes of the Wealth of Nations* (1776; 2nd edn, Chicago: Encyclopædia Britannica, Inc., 1990), book 1, ch. 8.

20. Dawkins, Richard, *The God Delusion* (Boston: Houghton Mifflin, 2006), pp. 190, 199–201; Wilson, David Sloan, *Darwin's Cathedral: Evolution, Religion and the Nature of Society* (Chicago and London: University of Chicago Press, 2002), pp. 138–43.

21. See, for instance, van de Kaa, Dirk, 'Europe's Second Demographic Transition', *Population Bulletin* 42:1 (1987), pp. 1–57; Lesthaeghe, R., and J. Surkyn, 'When History Moves On: The Foundations and Diffusion of a Second Demographic Transition', in *International Family Change: Ideational Perspectives*, ed. R. Jayakody, A. Thornton and W. Axinn (Mahwah, N.J.: Lawrence Erlbaum Associates, 2007).

22. Koenig, Laura B., Matt McGue, Robert F. Krueger and Thomas J. Bouchard Jr, 'Genetic and Environmental Influences on Religiousness: Findings for Retrospective and Current Religiousness Ratings', *Journal of Personality* 73:2 (2005), pp. 471–88.

23. Blume, Michael, 'The Reproductive Benefits of Religious Affiliation', in *The Biological Evolution of Religious Mind and Behavior*, ed. E. Voland and W. Schiefenhövel (New York: Springer-Verlag, 2009), p. 125.

24. Glausiusz, Josie, 'Discover Dialogue: Anthropologist Scott Atran. "It's not a new phenomenon, and natural selection may play a role in producing it"', *Discover Magazine*, 1 October 2003.

25. Dawkins, *The God Delusion*, p. 198.

26. Longman, Philip, *The Empty Cradle: How Falling Birthrates Threaten World Prosperity and What to Do About It* (New York: Basic Books, 2004), pp. 168–9.

1. The Crisis of Secularism

1. Beattie, Tina, *The New Atheists: The Twilight of Reason and the War on Religion* (Maryknoll, N.Y.: Orbis Books, 2007).

2. Berger, *The Sacred Canopy*; Mathewes, Charles, 'An interview with Peter Berger', *Hedgehog Review*, Spring-Summer 2006, p. 151.

3. For instance, see Berger, Peter L., *The Desecularization of the World: Resurgent Religion and World Politics* (Washington, D.C. and Grand Rapids, Mich.: Ethics and Public Policy Center and W. B. Eerdmans Pub. Co., 1999); Shah, Tim, Monica Toft and Daniel Philpott, *God's Century* (forthcoming); Micklethwait, John, and Adrian Wooldridge, *God Is Back: How the Global Revival of Faith Is Changing the World* (New York: Penguin Press, 2009).

4. Bruce, *God is Dead*; Norris and Inglehart, *Sacred and Secular*; Paul, Gregory, and Phil Zuckerman, 'Why the Gods Are Not Winning', *Edge* (2007).

5. Dennett, Daniel Clement, *Breaking the Spell: religion as a natural phenomenon* (New York: Viking, 2006).

6. Day, Abby, 'Believing in Belonging: An Ethnography of Young People's Constructions of Belief', *Culture and Religion* 10:3 (2009); Caldwell, Christopher, *Reflections on the Revolution in Europe: Immigration, Islam, and the West*, 1st edn (New York: Doubleday, 2009), p. 142.

7. Taylor, 'Secularization Theory: Science or Ideology?'; 'Public Religions Revisited', in *Religion: Beyond the Concept*, ed. H. de Vries (New York: Fordham University Press, 2008).

8. Mannheim Eurobarometer Trend File, 1970–2002.

9. Gledhill, Ruth, 'Thousands of churches face closure in ten years', *The Times*, 10 February 2007.

10. European Values Survey, 1981, 1990, 1999–2000; Mannheim Eurobarometer Trend File; Norris and Inglehart, *Sacred and Secular*, p. 74.

11. Froese, Paul, *The Plot to Kill God: Findings from the Soviet Experiment in Secularization* (Berkeley: University of California Press, 2008), pp. 78, 81.

12. Davie, Grace, *Religion in Britain Since 1945: Believing Without Belonging* (Oxford: Blackwell, 1994); Stark and Finke, *Acts of Faith*, pp. 230–32; Davie,

G., 'Vicarious Religion: A Methodological Challenge', *Everyday Religion*, January 2006, pp. 21–37.

13. Calculated from European Social Survey 2004; Bruce, *God Is Dead*; Voas, D., 'Religion in Europe: One Theme, Many Variations?', working paper, Cathie Marsh Centre for Census and Survey Research, (2004).

14. Norris and Inglehart, *Sacred and Secular*, p. 90.

15. European Values Survey, 1999–2000; Kaufmann, Eric, 'Human Development and the Demography of Secularisation in Global Perspective', *Interdisciplinary Journal of Research on Religion* 4 (2008).

16. Huntington, S., *Who Are We? The Cultural Core of American National Identity* (New York and London: Simon & Schuster, 2005); Lipset, Seymour Martin, *American Exceptionalism: A Double-Edged Sword* (New York: W. W. Norton, 1996).

17. Handy, Robert T., 'The Religious Depression, 1925–35', *Church History* (March 1960), p. 5; Stark, Rodney, *What Americans Really Believe: New Findings from the Baylor Surveys of Religion* (Waco, Tex.: Baylor University Press, 2008), p. 12.

18. Clark, Warren, and Grant Schellenberg, 'Who's Religious', *Canadian Social Trends (Statistics Canada)* (Summer 2006), p. 4.

19. Gerson, Michael, 'Editorial: A Faith for the Nones', *Washington Post*, 8 May 2009; private conversation with Robert Putnam, Harvard University, May 2009.

20. Hout, M., and C. Fischer, 'Why More Americans Have No Religious Preference', *American Sociological Review* 67:2 (2002), p. 174.

21. Private conversation with Paul Froese, Arlington, Va., April 2009.

22. Martin, *A General Theory of Secularization*.

23. World Values Survey 1999–2000. Though their pattern of religious decline differs in some respects from Europe because of the recent upsurge of Pentecostalism in these countries and the tendency for religion to flourish among higher income individuals there.

24. Bruce, *God Is Dead*, p. 37.

25. Bell, Daniel, *The Coming of Post-Industrial Society: A Venture in Social Forecasting* (New York: Basic Books, 1973), p. 115.

26. Putnam, Robert D., *Bowling Alone: The Collapse and Revival of American Community* (New York: Simon & Schuster, 2000).

27. Martin, *A General Theory of Secularization*, pp. 87, 254–60.

28. Chua, Amy, *Day of Empire: How Hyperpowers Rise to Global Dominance –and Why They Fall*, 1st edn (New York: Doubleday, 2007); Bruce, Steve, *A House Divided: Protestantism, Schism and Secularization* (London: Routledge, 1990), pp. 98–9.

29. Micklethwait and Wooldridge, *God Is Back*, pp. 42–3.

30. Taylor, *A Secular Age*, p. 361.

31. Larson, Edward J., and Larry Witham, 'Leading Scientists Still Reject God', *Nature* 394:6691 (1998), p. 313.

32. See especially Bell, Daniel, *The Cultural Contradictions of Capitalism* (1976; New York: Harper Collins, 1996).

33. Taylor, 'Secularization Theory: Science or Ideology?'.

34. Heelas, Paul, *The Spiritual Revolution: Why Religion Is Giving Way to Spirituality* (Malden, Mass.: Blackwell, 2005); Houtmann, Dirk, and Stefan Aupers, 'The Spiritual Turn and the Decline of Tradition: The Spread of Post-Christian Spirituality in 14 Western Countries, 1981–2000', *Journal for the Scientific Study of Religion* 46:3 (2007), pp. 305–320; Bainbridge, William Sims, and Rodney Stark, *The Future of Religion: Secularization, Revival and Cult Formation* (Berkeley-Los Angeles: University of California Press, 1985), p. 293.

35. Francis, Fukuyama, *The End of History and the Last Man* (London: Hamish Hamilton, 1992), pp. 306–7.

36. Putnam, *Bowling Alone*.

37. Gans, Herbert J., 'Symbolic Ethnicity and Symbolic Religiosity: Towards a Comparison of Ethnic and Religious Acculturation', *Ethnic & Racial Studies* 17:4 (1994), pp. 577–92.

38. Bellah, Robert N., *Habits of the Heart*, 2nd edn (London and Berkeley: University of California Press, 1996), pp. 221, 228.

39. Bell, *Cultural Contradictions*; Taylor, Charles, *The Ethics of Authenticity* (Cambridge, Mass.: Harvard University Press, 1992); Taylor, *A Secular Age*, pp. 567–73.

40. Roof, Wade Clark, and William McKinney, *American Mainline Religion, Its Changing Shape and Future* (New Brunswick: Rutgers University Press, 1987), p. 236; Pew Forum on Religion and Public Life, 'Faith in Flux: Changes in Religious Affiliation in the U.S.' (Washington, D.C., 2009).

41. Inglehart, Ronald, *Culture Shift in Advanced Industrial Society* (Princeton, N.J.: Princeton University Press, 1990).

42. Stark, Rodney, and Laurence R. Iannaccone, 'A Supply-Side Reinterpretation of the "Secularization" of Europe', *Journal for the Scientific Study of Religion* 33:3 (1994), pp. 230–52.

43. McCleary, R, and R. Barro, 2006. 'Religion and Political Economy in an International Panel', *Journal for the Scientific Study of Religion* 45:2 (2006), pp. 149–75.

44. Gray, John, *Black Mass: Apocalyptic Religion and the Death of Utopia* (London: Penguin, 2007).

45. Bell, *The Cultural Contradictions of Capitalism*.

46. Honoré, Carl, *In Praise of Slow: How a Worldwide Movement Is Challenging the Cult of Speed* (London: Orion, 2004).

47. Bell, *The Cultural Contradictions of Capitalism*; Giddens, Anthony, *Modernity and Self-Identity* (Cambridge: Polity Press, 1991); Bellah, *Habits of the Heart*.

48. http://www.bereavementadvice.org/uploads/img46249391e63ea1.pdf., emphasis added.

49. Froese, *The Plot to Kill God*.

50. Taylor, *A Secular Age*, pp. 272–94.

51. Xing, Jun, *Baptized in the Fire of Revolution: The American Social Gospel and the YMCA in China 1919–37* (Cranbury, N.J. and London: Associated University Presses, 1996), p. 72.

52. Kraut, Benny, 1989. 'A Wary Collaboration: Jews, Catholics, and the Protestant Goodwill Movement', in *Between the Times: The Travail of the Protestant Establishment in America, 1900–1960*, ed. W. R. Hutchison (Cambridge and New York: Cambridge University Press), p. 202.

53. Dinges, William, and James Hitchcock, 'Roman Catholic Traditionalism', in *The Fundamentalism Project*, ed. M. E. Marty and R. S. Appleby (Chicago: University of Chicago Press, 1991), pp. 83–4.

54. Zubaida, S., *Law and Power in the Islamic World* (London and New York: I. B. Tauris, 2003), pp. 142–6.

55. Though this has divided the Anglican community.

56. Connor, W., *Ethnonationalism: The Quest For Understanding* (Princeton, N.J.: Princeton University Press, 1994).

57. Novak, Michael, *The Rise of the Unmeltable Ethnics: Politics and Culture in the Seventies* (New York: Macmillan, 1972).

58. Silber, Michael K., 'The Emergence of Ultra-Orthodoxy: The Invention of a Tradition', in *The Uses of Tradition*, ed. J. Wertheimer (Cambridge, Mass. and London: Harvard University Press, 1992), pp. 59–60.

59. Sivan, Emmanuel, 'The Enclave Culture', in *Strong Religion: The Rise of Fundamentalisms around the World*, ed. G. A. Almond, R. Scott Appleby and Emmanuel Sivan (Chicago: University of Chicago Press, 2003), pp. 12–17, 41, 44.

60. Stark, Rodney, and William Sims Bainbridge, *A Theory of Religion* (New York: P. Lang, 1987), ch. 5.

61. Berman, E., 'Sect, Subsidy, and Sacrifice: An Economist's View of Ultra-Orthodox Jews', *Quarterly Journal of Economics* 115:3 (2000), pp. 905–53.

62. Sivan, 'The Enclave Culture'.

63. Reiff, Mark A., 'The Attack on Liberalism', in *Law and Philosophy*, ed. M. Freeman and R. Harrison (Oxford: Oxford University Press, 2007), p. 208.

64. Almond, Gabriel A., Emmanuel Sivan and R. Scott Appleby, 'Fundamentalism: Genus and Species', in *Fundamentalisms Comprehended*, ed. M. E. Marty, R. S. Appleby and American Academy of Arts and Sciences (Chicago: University of Chicago Press, 1995), p. 410.

65. Gellner, Ernest, *Nations and Nationalism* (Oxford: Blackwell, 1983); Anderson, Benedict, *Imagined Communities: Reflections on the Origin and Spread of Nationalism* (London: Verso, 1983).

66. Smith, A. D., *The Ethnic Origins of Nations* (Oxford: Blackwell, 1986).

67. Wimmer, Andreas, *Nationalist Exclusion and Ethnic Conflict* (Cambridge: Cambridge University Press, 2002).

68. Stadler, Nurit, *Yeshiva Fundamentalism: Piety, Gender, and Resistance in the Ultra-Orthodox World* (New York: New York University Press, 2009), p. 38.

69. Ammerman, Nancy, 'North American Protestant Fundamentalism', in *Fundamentalisms Observed, The Fundamentalism Project*, ed. M. E. Marty, R. Scott Appleby (Chicago: University of Chicago Press, 1991), pp. 1–65.

70. Micklethwait and Wooldridge, *God Is Back*, ch. 6.

71. Clerics in Karbala and Najaf, in Iraq, have traditionally enjoyed a higher status than those in Qom, and this was not entirely affected by the Iranian Revolution.

72. Phillips, R., 1998. 'The "Secularization" of Utah and Religious Competition', *Journal for the Scientific Study of Religion* 38:1 (1998), p. 74.

73. Stark, *What Americans Really Believe*, pp. 19, 22.

74. Dawkins, *The God Delusion*, pp. 305–7.

75. Stark and Neilson, *The Rise of Mormonism*, pp. 141–6. Stark's estimate of 3.8 per cent for Buddhists is probably too low, as the figure is closer to 6 per cent.

76. Stark, Rodney, 1996. *The Rise of Christianity: A Sociologist Reconsiders History* (Princeton, N.J.: Princeton University Press, 1996).

77. Stark and Neilson, *The Rise of Mormonism*, p. 136.

78. See discussion at: http://www.exmormon.org/mormon/mormon411.htm.

79. Mauss, Armand L., 1994. *The Angel and the Beehive: The Mormon Struggle with Assimilation* (Urbana: University of Illinois Press, 1994), pp. 57–8.

80. Ibid., p. 13.

81. 'Largest Latter-day Saint Communities (Mormon/Church of Jesus Christ Statistics)', http://www.adherents.com/largecom/com_lds.html; Sherkat, Darren E., 'Tracking the Restructuring of American Religion: Religious Affiliation and Patterns of Religious Mobility, 1973–1998', *Social Forces* 79:4 (2001), pp. 1459–93; Mauss, *The Angle and the Beehive*, p. 87.

82. Stark and Neilson, *The Rise of Mormonism*, pp. 88–9.

83. Heaton, T. B., 'How Does Religion Influence Fertility: The Case of the Mormons', *Journal for the Scientific Study of Religion* 25:2 (1986), pp. 253–6.

84. Heaton, T. B., 'Religious Influences on Mormon Fertility – Cross-National Comparisons', *Review of Religious Research* 30:4 (1989), pp. 401–11.

85. Phillips, 'The "Secularization" of Utah,' pp. 75–7; Mauss, *The Angel and the Beehive*, p. 49.

86. Green, John C., Lyman A. Kellstedt, Corwin E. Smidt and James Guth, 'How the Faithful Voted: Religious Communities and the Presidential Vote', in *A Matter of Faith: Religion in the 2004 Presidential Election*, ed. D. E. Campbell (Washington, D.C.: Brookings Institution Press, 2007), p. 28.

87. Kraybill, D, and C. Bowman, *On the Backroad to Heaven: Old Order Hutterites, Mennonites, Amish and Brethren* (Baltimore, Md.: The Johns Hopkins University Press, 2001), pp. 49–53; Peter, Karl A., *The Dynamics of Hutterite Society: An Analytical Approach* (Edmonton: University of Alberta Press, 1987).

88. Robinson, G. M., and J. Wreford Watson, *A Social Geography of Canada*, rev. edn (Toronto: Dundurn Press, 1991), pp. 349–55.

89. *Census of Canada*, 1981 and 2001.

90. Donnermeyer, J. F., and Elizabeth Cooksey, 'The Demographic Foundations of Amish Society', paper presented at the Rural Sociological Society, Sacramento, Ca., 11–15 August 2004, p. 12.

91. Kraybill and Bowman, *On the Backroad to Heaven*, p. 134.

92. Peter, Karl A., Edward Boldt, Ian Whittaker and Lance Roberts, 'The Dynamics of Religious Defection among Hutterites', *Journal for the Scientific Study of Religion* 21:4 (1983), pp. 327–37.

93. Donnermeyer and Cooksey, 'The Demographic Foundations of Amish Society', pp. 6–8.

94. Blume, M., 'Von Hayek and the Amish fertility', in *Evolution and Religion: The Natural Selection of God*, ed. U. Frey and E. Voland (Marburg: Tectum, 2010); Kraybill and Bowman, *On the Backroad to Heaven*, p. 49.

95. The Old Order Mennonites provide an exception to the ruling on beards, and Old German Baptist Brethren, the most liberal Old Order group, use English.

96. Kraybill and Bowman, *On the Backroad to Heaven*, pp. 110, 135, 220–21.

97. Ibid., pp. 187–8.

98. Ibid., pp. 221–7.

99. Ibid., p. 220; Kraybill, *The Amish and the State*, 2nd edn (Baltimore, Md.: The Johns Hopkins University Press, 2003).

100. Driedger, Leo, *Mennonites in the Global Village* (Toronto and Buffalo: University of Toronto Press, 2000), pp. 8–9.

101. Johnson, T., and B. Grim, *World Religion Database* (Leiden and Boston: Brill, 2009).

102. Regional Economic Development Initiative for Northwest Alberta, http://www.rediregion.ca/quickfacts/index.php.

103. Johnson and Grim, *World Religion Database*.

104. Haandrikman, K., and T. Sobotka, 'The Dutch Bible Belt: A Demographic Perspective', working paper (2003), University of Groningen, Population Research Centre.

105. Joyce, Kathryn, *Quiverfull: Inside the Christian Patriarchy Movement* (Boston: Beacon Press, 2009), p. 179.

106. Sivan, 'The Enclave Culture', p. 33.

107. Stark, R., 'How New Religions Succeed: A Theoretical Model', in *The Future of New Religious Movements*, ed. D. G. Bromley and P. E. Hammond (Macon, Ga.: Mercer University Press, 1987), p. 11.

108. Sosis, Richard, 'Why Aren't We All Hutterites?'. *Human Nature* 14:2 (2003), p. 113.

109. Bainbridge and Stark, *The Future of Religion*, pp. 347–8.

110. Sosis, R., and E. R. Bressler, 'Cooperation and Commune Longevity: A Test of the Costly Signaling Theory of Religion', *Cross-Cultural Research* 37:2 (2003), pp. 211–39.

111. Chase, Stacey, 'The Last Ones Standing', *Boston Globe*, 23 July 2006.

112. Unisa, Sayeed, R. B. Bhagat and T. K. Roy, 'Demographic Predicament of Parsis in India', paper delivered at IUSSP International Population Conference, Marrakech, 2009; Fariboz, Arian, 'In Decline: Zoroastrians in Iran', www.NewAgeIslam.com, 15 August 2009; Ryan, Sally, 'Zoroastrians Keep the Faith, and Keep Dwindling', *New York Times*, 6 September 2006.

113. Bainbridge and Stark, *The Future of Religion*, pp. 449–50; Wilson, Bryan R., *The Social Dimensions of Sectarianism: Sects and New Religious Movements in Contemporary Society* (Oxford and New York: Oxford University Press, 1990), p. 240.

114. Bainbridge, William Sims, *Across the Secular Abyss: From Faith to Wisdom* (Lanham, Md.: Lexington Books, 2007), pp. 80–82.

115. Bainbridge and Stark, *The Future of Religion*.

116. Bainbridge and Stark, *A Theory of Religion*.

117. Hout, M., A. Greeley and M. Wilde, 'The Demographic Imperative in Religious Change in the United States', *American Journal of Sociology* 107:2 (2001), p. 486.

118. Mauss, *The Angel and the Beehive*, pp. 72–100.

119. Merrill, R., J. Lyon and W. Jensen, 'Lack of a Secularizing Influence of Education on Religious Activity and Parity Among Mormons', *Journal for the Scientific Study of Religion* 42:1 (2003), pp. 113–24.

120. Kraybill and Bowman, *On the Backroad to Heaven*, p. 102.

121. Wolfe, Alan, *The Transformation of American Religion: How We Actually Live Our Faith* (New York: Free Press, 2003).

122. See, for instance, Norris and Inglehart, *Sacred and Secular*.

123. Ibid., p. 23.

2. *The Hidden Hand of History: Demography and Society*

1. Skirbekk, V., 'Fertility Trends by Social Status', *Demographic Research* 18:5 (2008), pp. 145–80. This does not take away from the fact that at certain moments in history – such as during the cultural efflorescence of Greek, Roman, Arab and Venetian civilisation – the elite may have opted for smaller families, foreshadowing present trends.

2. Darwin, Charles Galton, *The Next Million Years* (London: R. Hart Davis, 1952), pp. 200–201. The book itself is unremarkable, however, and marred by a somewhat inchoate, eugenically tinged worldview.

3. Jackson, Richard, and Neil Howe, 'Global Aging and Global Security in the 21st Century', in *Political Demography: Identity, Conflict and Institutions*, ed. J. A. Goldstone, Eric Kaufmann and Monica Duffy Toft (forthcoming, 2010).

4. Goldstone, Jack A., *Revolution and Rebellion in the Early Modern World*. (Berkeley: University of California Press, 1991); Heinsohn, Gunnar, *Söhne und Weltmacht: Terror im Aufstieg und Fall der Nationen* (Zurich: Orell Füssli, 2006).

5. Cavalli-Sforza, L. L., *Genes, Peoples and Languages* (Stanford, Ca.: University of California Press, 2001); Diamond, J., *Guns, Germs, and Steel: The Fates of Human Societies* (New York and London: W. W. Norton, 1997).

6. Demeny, P, and G. McNicoll (eds.), *The Political Economy of Global Population Change, 1950–2050* (New York: Population Council, 2006), p. 2.

7. Van de Walle, E., 'Alone in Europe: The French Fertility Decline until 1850', in *Historical Studies of Changing Fertility*, ed. C. Tilly (Princeton, N.J.: Princeton University Press, 1978).

8. Huss, Marie-Monique, 'Pronatalism in the Inter-War Period in France', *Journal of Contemporary History* 25:1 (1990), p. 39.

9. Ibid.

10. King, L., 'Demographic Trends, Pronatalism, and Nationalist Ideologies in the late Twentieth Century', *Ethnic and Racial Studies* 25:3 (2002), pp. 367–89; Jackson and Howe, *Global Aging and Global Security*.

11. Winnie, Trista, 'China May Eliminate One-Child Policy', *Common Census Blog*, 29 February 2008; Jackson, Richard, Neil Howe, and Center for Strategic and International Studies, *The Graying of the Great Powers: Demography and Geopolitics in the 21st Century* (Washington, D.C.: Center for Strategic and International Studies, 2008), pp. 171–88.

12. Easterlin, Richard A., 'The Conflict between Aspiration and Resources', *Population and Development Review* 2 (1976), pp. 418–25.

13. There is some evidence of a marginal increase in TFR in the wealthiest countries, but this does not correct for the effects of fertility postponement. Much of the recent rise is probably the result of older women having children later in life rather than any broad-based increase in TFR. See Myrskyla, M., H. P. Kohler and F. C. Billari, 'Advances in Development Reverse Fertility Declines', *Nature* 460: 7256 (2009), pp. 741–3; Goldstein, Joshua, T. Sobotka, and Arva Jasilioniene, 'The end of "lowest-low" fertility?', *Population and Development Review* 35(4): 663–99 (2009).

14. Lutz, Wolfgang, V Skirbekk and Maria Testa, 'The Low Fertility Trap Hypothesis: Forces That May Lead to Further Postponement and Fewer Births in Europe', paper presented at conference on Political Demography: Ethnic, National and Religious Dimensions, LSE, London, 2006.

15. Ibid.

16. Caldwell, Christopher, *Reflections on the Revolution in Europe: Immigration, Islam, and the West*, 1st edn (New York: Doubleday, 2009), p. 16.

17. Wattenberg, Ben, *Fewer: How the New Demography of Depopulation will Shape our Future* (Chicago: Ivan R. Dee, 2004); United Nations Department of Economic and Social Affairs, Population Division Homepage: World Population Prospects, 2006 Revision Database.

18. Lesthaeghe, R., 'Second Demographic Transition', in *Encyclopedia of Sociology*, ed. G. Ritzer (Oxford: Blackwell, 2007).

19. Bellah, *Habits of the Heart*.

20. Abrahams, Edward, *The Lyrical Left: Randolph Bourne, Alfred Stieglitz and the Origins of Cultural Radicalism in America* (Charlottesville: University Press of Virginia, 1986); Siegel, J., *Bohemian Paris* (New York: Viking, 1986).

21. Caplow, Theodore, Howard M. Bahr, John Modell and Bruce A. Chadwick, *Recent Social Trends in the United States, 1960–1990* (Montreal & Kingston: McGill-Queens University Press, 1994), p. 313.

22. Bell, Daniel, *The Coming of Post-Industrial Society: A Venture in Social Forecasting* (New York: Basic Books, 1973), p. 115; Campbell, Colin, *The Romantic Ethic and the Spirit of Modern Consumerism* (Oxford: Basil Blackwell, 1987), p. 201; Brooks, D., *Bobos in Paradise: The New Upper Class and How They Got There* (New York: Simon & Schuster, 2001).

23. Ibid., pp. 42–3, 478; Delli Carpini, Michael X., *Stability and Change in American Politics: The Coming of Age of the Generation of the 1960s* (New York: New York University Press, 1986), p. 29; Inglehart, Ronald, *Culture Shift in Advanced Industrial Society* (Princeton, NJ: Princeton University Press, 1990).

24. Mayer, William G., *The Changing American Mind: How and Why American Public Opinion Changed between 1960 and 1988* (Ann Arbor: University of Michigan Press, 1992), p. 18; Putnam, Robert D., *Bowling Alone: The Collapse and Revival of American Community* (New York: Simon & Schuster, 2000), p. 352; Jennings, M. Kent and Richard G. Niemi, *Generations and Politics: A Panel Study of Young Adults and their Parents* (Princeton, N.J.: Princeton University Press, 1981), pp. 100, 160, 261, 267–9.

25. Inglehart, *Culture Shift*, pp. 74–5, 252, 262.

26. Bell, *The Cultural Contradictions of Capitalism*, p. 54.

27. Putnam, *Bowling Alone*; Thornton, Arland, and Linda Young-DeMarco, 'Four Decades of Trends in Attitudes toward Family Issues in the United States: The 1960s through the 1990s', *Journal of Marriage and the Family* 63:4 (2001), pp. 1009–37.

28. Caplow et al., *Recent Social Trends*, pp. 46–50.

29. Shoumatoff, Alex, *The Mountain of Names: A History of the Human Family* (New York: Vintage Books, 1985), p. 190.

30. Inglehart, *Culture Shift*, p. 198.

31. Ibid., pp. 199, 202–3, 240. Thornton and Young-Demarco, 'Four Decades of Trends in Attitudes'.

32. Lesthaeghe, R., and J Surkyn, 'When History Moves on: The Foundations and Diffusion of a Second Demographic Transition', in *International Family Change: Ideational Perspectives*, ed. R. Jayakody, A. Thornton and W. Axinn (Mahwah, N.J.: Lawrence Erlbaum Associates, 2007); van de Kaa, Dirk, 'Europe's Second Demographic Transition', *Population Bulletin* 42:1 (1987), pp.1–57.

33. Ibid.

34. Caldwell, John C., and Thomas Schindelmayer, 'Explanations of the Fertility Crisis in Modern Societies: A Search for Commonalities', *Population Studies* 57:3 (2003), pp. 241–63.

35. Baizan, Pau, 'Do Childcare Arrangements Matter for Fertility Decisions? The Effects of Men's Involvement in Childcare, and of Formal and Informal Options', European Population Conference, Liverpool, UK, 2006.

36. Goldberg, Michelle, *The Means of Reproduction: Sex, Power, Population and the Future of the World* (New York: Penguin Press, 2009), p. 222.

37. Berman, E, L. Iannaccone and G. Ragusa, 'From Empty Pews to Empty Cradles: Fertility Decline Among European Catholics', National Bureau of

Economic Research working paper (2005), http://papers.nber.org/papers. html; Berghammer, C, D. Philipov and T. Sobotka, 2006. 'Religiosity and Demographic Events: A Comparative Study of European Countries', paper delivered at European Population Conference, Liverpool, UK, 2006; Regnier-Loilier, Arnaud, and France Prioux, 'Does Religious Practice Influence Fertility Behaviour in France?', European Population Conference, Barcelona, 2008.

38. Lesthaeghe and Surkyn, 'When History Moves on'.

39. Norris, Pippa, and Ronald Inglehart, *Sacred and Secular: Religion and Politics Worldwide* (Cambridge: Cambridge University Press, 2004), p. 23.

40. Eberstadt, Mary, 'How the West Really Lost God', *Policy Review* 143 (June–July 2007).

41. Demeny and McNicoll, *The Political Economy of Global Population Change*, p. 256; UN Department of Economic and Social Affairs, Population Division Homepage.

42. Goldstone, Jack, 'A Theory of Political Demography: Human and Institutional Reproduction', in *Political Demography: Identity, Conflict and Institutions*, ed. J. A. Goldstone, Eric Kaufmann and Monica Duffy Toft (forthcoming, 2010).

43. Demeny and McNicoll, *The Political Economy of Global Population Change*, p. 257.

44. Quoted in McNicoll, G., 'Population Weights in the International Order', *Population and Development Review* 25:3 (1999), pp. 411–42.

45. Mearsheimer, John J., *The Tragedy of Great Power Politics*, 1st edn (New York: W. W. Norton, 2001), p. 55.

46. Nye, Joseph S., *Soft power: The Means to Success in World Politics*, 1st edn (New York: Public Affairs, 2004).

47. Goldstone, Jack, 'The New Population Bomb: The Four Megatrends That Will Change the World', *Foreign Affairs* 1:89 (2010); Heinsohn, *Söhne und Weltmacht*.

48. Urdal, Henrik, 'A Clash of Generations? Youth Bulges and Political Violence', *International Studies Quarterly* 50 (2006), pp. 607–29.

49. Haas, Mark, 2010. 'America's Golden Years?: U.S. Security in an Aging World', in *Political Demography*, ed. Goldstone et al.

50. Goldstone, 'The New Population Bomb'; Jackson and Howe, *The Graying of the Great Powers*. This in spite of the fact that fertility rates have come down, more so in the Middle East than sub-Saharan Africa, and especially in Iran, Turkey and the Maghreb. Even so, population momentum will mask the shift for several decades.

51. Durch, William J., 'Keepers of the Gates: National Militaries in an Age of International Population Movement', in *Demography and National Security*, ed. M. Wiener and S. S. Russell (New York and Oxford: Berghahn Books, 2001), p. 144; Economic and Social Research Council, *Global Migration Factsheet 2007* [cited 4 October 2007]. Available from http://www.esrc.ac.uk/ESRCInfoCentre/facts/international/migration.aspx?ComponentId=15051&SourcePageId=14912.

52. Caldwell, *Reflections*, pp. 66–7.

53. United Nations, Economic and Social Development, *Estimated number of international migrants at mid-year (2006), United Nations, World Migrant Stock* [cited 15 October 2007. Available from http://www.un.org/esa/; United States Census Bureau, 'State and County Quick Facts', 2006. Set against the backdrop of rising global population, the numbers are less dramatic, but still suggest that the effect of post-1960 globalisation is real: the proportion of the world made up of immigrant stock increased from 2.5 per cent in 1960 to 3 per cent in 2006.

54. United States Census Bureau, 'State and County Quick Facts', 2006.

55. Coleman, David, 2006. 'Immigration and Ethnic Change in Low-Fertility Countries: A Third Demographic Transition', *Population and Development Review*, 32:3 (September 2006), pp. 401–46.

56. Wimmer, Andreas, *Nationalist Exclusion and Ethnic Conflict: Shadows of Modernity* (Cambridge, Cambridge University Press, 2002), esp. ch. 3.

57. Horowitz, D., *Ethnic Groups in Conflict* (Berkeley: University of California Press, 1985), pp. 194–6.

58. Alesina, Alberto, Reza Baqir and William Easterly, 'Public Goods and Ethnic Divisions', *Quarterly Journal of Economics* 114 (November 1999), pp. 1243–84; Putnam, Robert, 'E Pluribus Unum: Diversity and Community in the Twenty-first Century', *Scandinavian Political Studies* 30:2 (2007), pp. 137–74.

59. Chua, A., *World on Fire: How Exporting Free Market Democracy Breeds Ethnic Violence and Global Instability* (London: Heinemann, 2003); Shoup, Brian, 'Dollars Versus Sense: The Nation-Building Logics of Ethnically-Based Redistribution', presented at the American Political Science Association, 3–6 September 2009, Toronto.

60. Kaufmann, Eric, *The Rise and Fall of Anglo-America: The Decline of Dominant Ethnicity in the United States* (Cambridge, Mass.: Harvard University Press, 2004); Cornelius, Wayne A., Philip L. Martin and James Hollifield (eds.), *Controlling Immigration: A Global Perspective* (Stanford: Stanford University Press, 1994).

61. Patterson, H., and E. Kaufmann, *Unionism and Orangeism in Northern Ireland Since 1945* (Manchester: Manchester University Press, 2007).

62. Kaufmann, Eric, *The Orange Order: A Contemporary Northern Irish History* (Oxford: Oxford University Press, 2007), pp. 151, 291.

63. In terms of urbanisation, education, income, occupation and demographic behaviour.

64. Fargues, P., 'Protracted National Conflict and Fertility Change: Palestinians and Israelis in the twentieth century', *Population and Development Review* 26:3 (2000), pp. 441–82.

65. Conversation with Ehud Eiran, former assistant to Prime Minister Ehud Barak's foreign policy advisor.

66. Cincotta, Richard, and Eric Kaufmann, 'The Changing Face of Israel', *Foreign Policy* (June 2009).

67. Morland, Paul, 'Defusing the Demographic Scare', *Ha'aretz*, 2 June 2009.

68. Slack, J. A, and R. Doyon, 2001. 'Population Dynamics and Susceptibility for Ethnic Conflict: The Case of Bosnia and Herzegovina', *Journal of Peace Research* 38:2 (2001), pp. 139–61.

69. Toft, Monica, 'Differential Demographic Growth in Multinational States: The Case of Israel's Two-Front War', *Review of International Affairs* (Fall 2002), p. 81.

70. Hussain, Wasbir, 'The Muslim Factor in Assam Politics', *Institute of Peace and Conflict Studies* (2005).

71. Wiener, Myron, 'The Political Demography of Assam's Anti-Immigrant Movement', *Population and Development Review* 9:2 (1983), pp. 279–92.

72. Bhat, P. N. Mari, and A. J. Francis Xavier, 'The Role of Religion in Fertility Decline: The Case of Indian Muslims', *Economic & Political Weekly* 40:5 (2005), p. 399.

73. Marshall-Fratani, Ruth, 'The War of "Who Is Who": Autochthony, Nationalism, and Citizenship in the Ivoirian Crisis', *African Studies Review* 49:2 (2006), pp. 9–43.

74. Green, Elliott, 2010. 'Demographic Change and Conflict in Contemporary Africa', in *Political Demography*, ed. Goldstone et al.

75. Fearon, James, and D. Laitin, 'Sons of the Soil, Immigrants and Civil War', working paper, 2009.

76. Coleman, 'Immigration and Ethnic Change', pp. 402–3.

77. Sandmeyer, Elmer Clarence, *The Anti-Chinese Movement in California* (Urbana: University of Illinois Press, 1939).

78. Kaufmann, *The Rise and Fall of Anglo-America*, p. 238.

79. Edmonston, Barry, and James P. Smith, *The New Americans: Economic, Demographic and Fiscal Effects of Immigration* (Washington, D.C.: National Research Council, 1997); Coleman, David, 'The Changing Face of Europe', in *Political Demography*, ed. Goldstone et al.

80. Norris, Pippa, 'The "New Cleavage" Thesis and the Social Basis of Radical Right Support', paper presented at the American Political Science Association, Washington, D.C., 2005.

81. Kaufmann, E. P., 'Dominant Ethnicity: From Background to Foreground', in *Rethinking Ethnicity: Majority Groups and Dominant Minorities*, ed. E. Kaufmann (London: Routledge, 2004).

82. Gratton, Brian, 'Demography and Immigration Restriction in United States History', in *Political Demography*, ed. Goldstone et al.

83. Kaufmann, *The Rise and Fall of Anglo-America*.

84. Simon, Rita J., and Susan H. Alexander, *The Ambivalent Welcome: Print Media, Public Opinion and Immigration* (Westport: Praeger Publishers, 1993).

85. Adams, Michael, 2003. *Fire and Ice: The United States, Canada and the Myth of Converging Values* (Toronto: Penguin Canada, 2003).

86. Huntington, S., *Who Are We? The Cultural Core of American National Identity* (New York and London: Simon & Schuster, 2004); Lind, Michael, *The Next American Nation: The New Nationalism and the Fourth American Revolution* (New York: The Free Press, 2004).

87. Gellner, Ernest, *Nations and Nationalism* (Oxford: Blackwell, 1983).

88. Bouchard, Gerard, and Charles Taylor, *Building the Future: A Time for Reconciliation* (Quebec: Gouvernement de Quebec, 2008).

89. Some argue that it transformed the gene pool as well. See Weale, M., Deborah A. Weiss, Rolf F. Jager, Neil Bradman and Mark G. Thomas, 'Y Chromosome Evidence for Anglo-Saxon Mass Migration', *Molecular Biology and Evolution* 19 (2002), pp. 1008–21.

90. Diamond, *Guns, Germs and Steel*.

3. 'A Full Quiver': Fertility and the Rise of American Fundamentalism

1. 'Falwell Apologizes to Gays, Feminists, Lesbians', www. CNN.com, 14 September 2001, http://archives.cnn.com/2001/US/09/14/Falwell.apology/.

2. Berger, *The Sacred Canopy*.

3. Fischer, D. H., *Albion's Seed: Four British Folkways in America*, (New York: Oxford University Press, 1989); Baltzell, E. D., *Puritan Boston and Quaker Philadelphia* (1979; New Brunswick, N.J. and London: Transaction, 1996); Baltzell, E. D., *The Protestant Establishment: Aristocracy and Caste in America* (New York: Random House, 1964); Billington, R. A., *The Genesis of the Frontier Thesis: A Study in Historical Creativity* (San Marino, Ca.: Huntington, 1971).

4. Zelinsky, Wilbur, 1973. *The Cultural Geography of the United States* (Englewood Cliffs, N.J.: Prentice-Hall, 1973), p. 13.

5. Micklethwait and Wooldridge, *God Is back*, pp. 58–68.

6. Sosis, R., and E. R. Bressler, 'Cooperation and Commune Longevity: A Test of the Costly Signaling Theory of Religion', *Cross-Cultural Research* 37:2 (2003), pp. 211–39; Stark and Neilson, *The Rise of Mormonism*, p. 44.

7. Gusfield, Joseph R., *Symbolic Crusade: Status Politics and the American Temperance Movement* (Urbana: University of Illinois Press, 1963).

8. Kaufmann, *The Rise and Fall of Anglo-America*, pp. 116–17; Hutchison, *Between the Times*.

9. Higham, John, 'Ethnicity and American Protestants: Collective Identity in the Mainstream,' in *New Directions in American Religious History*, ed. H. Stout and D. G. Hart (New York and Oxford: Oxford University Press, 1997).

10. Ammerman, Nancy, 1991. 'North American Protestant Fundamentalism', in *Fundamentalisms observed, The Fundamentalism project*, ed. Marty et al., pp. 1–65; Northcott, Michael S., *An Angel Directs the Storm: Apocalyptic Religion and American Empire* (London and New York: I. B. Tauris, 2004), p. 59; Greeley, Andrew M., and Michael Hout, 2006. *The Truth about Conservative Christians: What They Think and What They Believe* (Chicago: University of Chicago Press), pp. 16–17.

11. Micklethwait and Wooldridge, *God Is Back*, p. 89; Ammerman, 'North American Protestant Fundamentalism', p. 6; Northcott, *An Angel Directs the Storm*, pp. 59, 62–3; Greeley and Hout, *The Truth about Conservative Christians*, pp. 16–17.

12. Ammerman, 'North American Protestant Fundamentalism', pp. 21–34.

13. Micklethwait and Wooldridge, *God Is Back*, pp. 171–9.

14. Stark and Bainbridge, *A Theory of Religion*; Gellner, E., *Muslim Society* (Cambridge: Cambridge University Press, 1981).

15. Noll, Mark A., 'The Eclipse of Old Hostilities between and the Potential for New Strife among Catholics and Protestants Since Vatican II', in *Uncivil Religion: Interreligious Hostility in America*, ed. R. N. Bellah and F. Greenspahn (NY: Crossroad Publishing, 1987), pp. 88, 90.

16. Joyce, pp. 195–6.

17. Wolfe, *The Transformation of American Religion*, pp. 28, 31, 135.

18. Wolfe, A., 'Dieting for Jesus', *Prospect* (January 2005).

19. Martin, David, *Pentecostalism: The World Their Parish* (Oxford: Blackwell, 2001); Wolfe, *The Transformation of American* Religion, p. 33.

20. Berger, Peter L., 'Max Weber is Alive and Well, and Living in Guatemala: The Protestant Ethic Today', paper delivered at the Religion and Politics Seminar, Weatherhead Center, Harvard University, 17 November 2008.

21. Micklethwait and Wooldridge, *God Is Back*, p. 183.

22. Thumma, Scott, Dave Travis, and Leadership Network (Dallas Tex.), *Beyond Megachurch Myths: What We Can Learn from America's Largest Churches*, 1st edn (San Francisco, Ca.: Jossey-Bass, 2007); Elzinga, Ken, and Colin Page, 'Congregational Economies of Scale and the Megachurch: An Application of the Stigler Survivor Technique', paper delivered at the Association for the Study of Religion, Economics, and Culture conference, Arlington, Va., 2–5 April 2009.

23. Greeley and Hout, *The Truth about Conservative Christians*, p. 130.

24. Ibid., pp. 100–139.

25. Guth, James, Lyman A. Kellstedt, Corwin E. Smidt, and John C. Green, 'Religious Influences in the 2004 Presidential Election', *Presidential Studies Quarterly* 36:2 (2006), pp. 223–42; Greeley and Hout, *The Truth about Conservative Christians*, p. 123.

26. Ammerman, 'North American Protestant Fundamentalism', p. 49; Joyce, *Quiverfull*, p. 25.

27. Jackson, Kenneth T., *The Ku Klux Klan in the City, 1915–1930* (New York: Oxford University Press, 1967).

28. Noll, 'The Eclipse of Hostilities', p. 87.

29. Voskuil, Dennis N., 1989. 'Reaching Out: Mainline Protestantism and the Media', in *Between the Times*, ed. Hutchison.

30. Greeley and Hout, *The Truth about Conservative Christians*, pp. 108–9; Bainbridge, William Sims, *The Sociology of Religious Movements* (New York: Routledge, 1997), pp. 47–55.

31. Underwood, Kenneth Wilson, *Protestant and Catholic: Religious and Social Interaction in an Industrial Community* (Boston: Beacon Press, 1957), pp. 3–21.

32. Joyce, *Quiverfull*, pp. 150–51.

33. Bruce, Steve, *Comparative Protestant Politics* (Oxford: Oxford University Press, 1998), p. 148.

34. McAdam, Doug, John McCarthy and Meyer Zald (eds.), *Comparative Perspectives on Social Movements* (New York: Cambridge University Press, 1996).

35. Bruce, *Comparative Protestant Politics*, pp. 161–3.

36. Lamare, James W., Jerry L. Polinard and Robert D. Wrinkle, 'Texas: Religion and Politics in God's Country', in *The Christian Right in American Politics: Marching to the Millennium*, ed. J. C. Green, M. J. Rozell and C. Wilcox (Washington, D.C.: Georgetown University Press, 2003), p. 72.

37. Green et al., *The Christian Right in American Politics*.

38. Wells, John W., and David B. Cohen, 'George W Bush, the Christian Right and the New Vital Center of American Politics', in *Religion and the Bush*

Presidency, ed. M. J. Rozell and G. Whitney (New York: Palgrave Macmillan, 2007), pp. 129–54.

39. Northcott, *An Angel Directs the Storm*, pp. 61–3.

40. Barker, D. C., J. Hurwitz and T. L. Nelson, 'Of Crusades and Culture Wars: "Messianic" militarism and political conflict in the United States', *Journal of Politics* 70:2 (2008), pp. 307–22; Guth, James, 'Religion and American Attitudes on Foreign Policy', paper presented at the International Studies Association, New York, 15 February 2009.

41. Phillips, Kevin P., *American Theocracy: The Peril and Politics of Radical Religion, Oil, and Borrowed Money in the 21st Century* (New York: Viking, 2006).

42. Mearsheimer, John J., and Stephen M. Walt, *The Israel Lobby and U.S. Foreign Policy*, 1st edn (New York: Farrar, Straus & Giroux, 2007).

43. Green et al., *The Christian Right in American Politics*.

44. Hout, M., A. Greeley and M. Wilde, 'The Demographic Imperative in Religious Change in the United States', *American Journal of Sociology* 107:2 (2001), pp. 468–500.

45. Greeley and Hout, *The Truth about Conservative Christians*, pp. 111–12.

46. Skirbekk, V, A. Goujon and Eric Kaufmann, *Secularism, Fundamentalism or Catholicism?*, *Journal for the Scientific Study of Religion*, forthcoming (see note 60, p. 308).

47. Mearsheimer and Walt, *The Israel Lobby and U.S. Foreign Policy*.

48. Lerner, Robert, Althea K. Nagai and Stanley Rothman, *American Elites* (New Haven and London: Yale University Press, 1996).

49. Herberg, Will, *Protestant, Catholic, Jew: An Essay in American Religious Sociology* (Garden City, N.Y.: Country Life Press, 1955).

50. Interview with Robert Putnam, Harvard University, May 2009.

51. Stark, Rodney, 2008. *What Americans Really Believe*, pp. 141–2; Putnam interview.

52. Joyce, *Quiverfull*, pp. 134–5.

53. Ibid., pp. 133, 218, 229.

54. Ibid., pp. 77, 110.

55. Ibid., p. 218.

56. Ibid., p. 179.

57. Longman, Philip, 'The Return of Patriarchy', *Foreign Policy* (March/April 2006).

58. Hackett, Conrad, *Religion and Fertility in the United States: The Influence of Affiliation, Region, and Congregation*, PhD Dissertation, University of Texas, Austin, 2008, pp. 12–17.

59. Lesthaeghe, R., and L. Neidert, 'The Second Demographic Transition in the United States: Exception or Textbook Example?', *Population and Development Review* 32:4 (2006), pp. 669–98.

60. Brooks, Arthur, 'The Fertility Gap: Liberal Politics Will Prove Fruitless as Long as Liberals Refuse to Multiply', *Wall Street Journal*, 22 August 2006; Steyn, M., 'It's the Demography, Stupid: The Real Reason the West Is in Danger of Extinction', *New Criterion*, January 2006; Lind, Michael, 'Red-State Sneer', *Prospect* (January 2005); Longman, Philip, 'The Liberal Baby Bust', *USA Today*, 13 March 2006.

61. Ammerman, 'North American Protestant Fundamentalism', pp. 47–50.

62. Bainbridge, *Across the Secular Abyss*, pp. 73–4; Stark, *The Rise of Christianity.*

63. Hackett, *Religion and Fertility in the United States*, pp. 37–42.

64. Heilman, Samuel C., *Sliding to the Right: The Contest for the Future of American Jewish Orthodoxy* (Berkeley: University of California Press, 2006), pp. 6, 224.

65. Abramowitz, Alan I. and Kyle L. Saunders, 'Exploring the Bases of Partisanship in the American Electorate: Social Identity vs. Ideology', *Political Research Quarterly* 59:2 (2006), p. 178.

66. American National Election Study (ANES) cumulative data file 1948–2004 (http://www.electionstudies.org/); Abramowitz, A. I., and K. L. Saunders, 'Ideological Realignment in the US Electorate', *Journal of Politics* 60:3 (1998), pp. 634–52.

67. Mayer, *The Changing American Mind.*

68. Box-Steffensmeier, Janet M., and Suzanna De Boef, 'Macropartisanship and Macroideology in the Sophisticated Electorate', *The Journal of Politics* 63:1 (2001), pp. 232–48.

69. Bishop, Bill, and Robert G. Cushing, *The Big Sort: Why the Clustering of Like-minded America Is Tearing Us Apart* (Boston: Houghton Mifflin, 2008).

70. Knoll, B. R., '"And Who Is My Neighbor?" Religion and Immigration Policy Attitudes', *Journal for the Scientific Study of Religion* 48:2 (2009), pp. 313–31.

71. Leal, David L., 'Latinos and Religion', in *A Matter of Faith*, ed. Campbell, pp. 202–23.

72. Rozell, Mark J., and Clyde Wilcox, 2003. 'Virginia: Birthplace of the Christian Right', in *The Christian Right in American Politics*, ed. Green et al., p. 53.

73. McConnell, Scott, 'Review of Chris Caldwell, Reflections on the Revolution in Europe', *Mondoweiss.net* (2009).

74. Christian Coalition, 1997, www.cc.org, accessed 1998; Reed, Ralph, 'Remarks to the Anti-Defamation League', Christian Coalition, 1995, www.cc.org, accessed 1998.

75. Leege, David, 'From Event to Theory: A Summary Analysis', in *A Matter of Faith*, ed. Campbell, p. 264; Soper, J. Christopher and J. Fetzer, 2003. 'The Christian Right in California: Dimming Fortunes in the Golden State', in *The Christian Right in American Politics*, ed. Green et al., pp. 209–30.

76. Wuthnow, Robert, *The Struggle for America's Soul: Evangelicals, Liberals and Secularism* (Grand Rapids, Mich: Eerdmans, 1989); Hunter, James, *Culture Wars: The Struggle to Define America* (New York: Basic Books, 1991).

77. Guth et al., 'Religious Influences in the 2004 Presidential Election'.

78. Noll, 'The Eclipse of Old Hostilities', p. 90; Wilson, J. Matthew, 2007. 'The Changing Catholic Voter: Comparing Responses to John Kennedy in 1960 and John Kerry in 2004', in *A Matter of Faith*, ed. Campbell, pp. 164–80.

79. Green, John C., Lyman A. Kellstedt, Corwin E. Smidt and James Guth, 'How the Faithful Voted: Religious Communities and the Presidential Vote', in *A Matter of Faith*, ed. Campbell, p. 28; Guth et al., 'Religious Influences in the 2004 Presidential Election'; Mark, Jonathan, 'Only the Orthodox Jews Go Big for Bush', *Jewish Week*, 22 October 2004; VandeHei, Jim, 'Future of Orthodox Jewish Vote Has Implications for GOP: Small but Growing Group Receptive to Republican Ideas', *Washington Post*, 3 August 2006; Smidt, Corwin, 'Religion and Election Day: Voting Patterns', in Smidt, Corwin, Kevin den Dulk, Bryan Froehle, James Penning, Stephen Monsma and Douglas Koopman, *The Disappearing God Gap?: Religion in the 2008 Presidential Election* (Oxford: Oxford University Press, 2010) – from tables presented at the American Political Science Association, Toronto, 3–6 September 2009.

80. Carty, R. Kenneth, 2002. 'The Politics of Tecumseh Corners: Canadian Political Parties as Franchise Organizations', *Canadian Journal of Political Science* 35:4 (2002), pp. 723–46.

81. Joyce, *Quiverfull*, p. 195; Goldberg, *The Means of Reproduction*, pp. 155–7, 163.

82. Goldberg, *The Means of Reproduction*, p. 164; Joyce, *Quiverfull*, pp. 197–200.

83. Goldberg, *The Means of Reproduction*, pp. 95–8.

84. Ibid., pp. 18, 162–3.

85. Ibid., pp. 15–16, 110.

86. Ibid., pp. 96–7, 106–7, 169.

87. Ibid., pp. 3, 161, 227, 233.

88. Urdal, H., 'Youth Bulges and Violence', in *Political Demography*, ed. Goldstone et al.; Cincotta, Richard, 'The Youth Bulge Effect: Does a Large Proportion of Young Adults Deter the Rise of Liberal Democracy?', in *Political Demography*, ed. Goldstone et al.

89. Juergensmeyer, Mark, 2001. *Terror in the Mind of God* (Berkeley: University of California Press, 2001), pp. 20, 29–30.

90. Sullum, Jacob, 'Why is Killing Abortionists Like George Tiller So Wrong?' *Opposing Views*, 1 June 2009; Allen, Bob, 'Former SBC officer Says Tiller Murder Answer to Prayer', *Associated Baptist Press*, 2 June 2009; National Abortion Federation Violence Statistics, accessed 27 July 2009; Juergensmeyer, *Terror in the Mind of God*, p. 30.

91. Bowers, Chris, 'The End of Bubba Dominance', *The Nation*, 1–8 September 2008; Texeira, Ruy, *Red, Blue, and Purple America: The Future of Election Demographics* (Washington, D.C.: Brookings Institution Press, 2008), p. 21.

92. Wells and Cohen, 'George W Bush, the Christian Right and the new Vital Center of American Politics'.

93. Wald, Kenneth D., and Richard K. Scher, 2003. 'A Necessary Annoyance: The Christian Right and the Development of Party Politics in Florida', in *The Christian Right in American politics*, ed. Green et al., p. 96.

94. 'California Votes for Prop 8', *Wall Street Journal (Online)*, 5 November 2008; 'Prop 8 Passes', *Los Angeles Times*, 5 November 2008.

95. Thumma et al., *Beyond Megachurch Myths*, pp. 134–47; Micklethwait and Wooldridge, *God Is Back*, p. 208.

4. The Demography of Islamism in the Muslim World

1. Johnson and Grim, *World Religion Database*, 2009.

2. Jenkins, Philip, *God's Continent: Christianity, Islam, and Europe's religious crisis* (Oxford and New York: Oxford University Press, 2007), pp. 8, 21; Fargues, P., 'Protracted National Conflict and Fertility Change: Palestinians and Israelis in the Twentieth Century', *Population and Development Review* 26:3 (2000), pp. 441–82.

3. Moulasha, K., and G. R. Rao, 'Religion-Specific Differentials in Fertility and Family Planning', *Economic and Political Weekly* 34:42–43 (1999), pp. 3047–3051; Morgan, S. P., S. Stash, H. L. Smith and K. O. Mason, 'Muslim and Non-Muslim Differences in Female Autonomy and Fertility: Evidence from four Asian Countries', *Population and Development Review* 28:3 (2002), pp. 515–38; Goldscheider, Calvin, *Population, Modernization and Social Structure* (Boston: Little, Brown, 1971); Jones, Gavin, 'A Demographic Perspective on the Muslim World', *Journal of Population Research* 23:2 (2006), pp. 251–2; Fargues, P., 2001. 'Demographic Islamization: Non-Muslims in Muslim Countries' *SAIS Review* XXI:2 (2001), pp. 103–16.

4. Karim, Mehtab, 'Islamic Teachings on Reproductive Health', in *Islam, the State and Population*, ed. G. Jones and M. Karim (London: Hurst & Co., 2005), pp. 45–9.

5. Caldwell, J. C., 'Mass Education as a Determinant of the Timing of Fertility Decline', *Population and Development Review* 6:2 (1980), pp. 225–55.
6. Bakar, O., 'Islam on reproduction', in W. Reich (ed.), *The Ethics of Sex and Genetics* (New York: Macmillan Reference, 1998).
7. Karim, 'Islamic Teachings on Reproductive Health', pp. 52–3.
8. RCPRHE, 'Pakistan: Debating Islam and Family Planning', in *The Religious Consultation on Population, Reproductive Health & Ethics*, 2005, http://www.religiousconsultation.org/News_Tracker/debating_Islam_and_family_planning.htm.
9. Jenkins, *God's Continent*, p. 21.
10. Jones, 'A Demographic Perspective on the Muslim World', p. 255; Leahy, Elizabeth, 'Age Structure and Development: Global and National Analysis through a Policy Lens', in *Political Demography*, ed. Goldstone et al.
11. Aghajanian, A., 'Population-Change in Iran, 1966–86 – a Stalled Demographic-Transition', *Population and Development Review* 17:4 (1991), pp. 709, 713.
12. Hoodfar, H., and S. Assadpour, 'The Politics of Population Policy in the Islamic Republic of Iran', *Studies in Family Planning* 31:1 (2000), pp. 19–34.
13. Abbasi-Shavazi, Mohammad Jalal, Meimanat Hossein-Chavoshi, Peter S. McDonald and Philip Morgan, 'Family Change and Continuity in the Islamic Republic of Iran: Birth Control Use Before the First Pregnancy', working paper, Duke University, 2007.
14. Mehryar, A. H., 'Shi'ite Teachings, Pragmatism and Fertility Change in Iran', in *Islam, the State and Population*, ed. G. Jones and M. Karim (London: Hurst & Co., 2005), p. 155.
15. Cincotta, Richard, 'Prospects for Ahmadinejad's Call for More Rapid Population Growth in Iran', working paper, National Intelligence Council, 2006.
16. Karim, 'Islamic Teachings on Reproductive Health', pp. 50–51; Hakim, Abdul, 'Fertility Trends and their Determinants in Pakistan', in *Islam, the State and Population*, ed. Jones and Karim, pp. 238–40.
17. Akin to the Wahhabis of Arabia, the Deobandis are a fundamental theological movement which arose in 1867 seeking to purify Islam of heterodox and foreign influence.
18. Kepel, G., *Jihad: the Trial of Political Islam* (London: I. B. Tauris, 2002) p. 101.
19. RCPRHE, 'Pakistan: Debating Islam and Family Planning'.
20. Cleland, J., and L. Lush, 'Population and Policies in Bangladesh, Pakistan', *Forum for Applied Research and Public Policy* 12 (1997), pp. 46–50.

21. Private conversation with Mehtab Karim, Pew Forum for Religious Research, Washington, 24 October 2008.

22. Blackwell, Tom, 'Death for Birth Control: Taliban Targets Kandahar Health-care Workers', *National Post*, 3 November 2008.

23. King, L., 'Demographic Trends, Pronatalism, and Nationalist Ideologies in the late Twentieth Century', *Ethnic and Racial Studies* 25:3 (2002), p. 386.

24. Fargues, 'Protracted Nationalist Conflict and Fertility Change', pp. 469–73; *CIA World Factbook* 2008, https://www.cia.gov/library/publications/the-world-factbook/.

25. Kulczycki, Andrzej, 'Recent Fertility Changes in the Arab States: In Search of Population Policy', paper read at the Population Association of America, 2004.

26. Rashad, Hoda, and Eltigani E. Eltigani, 'Explaining Fertility Decline in Egypt', in *Islam, the State and Population*, ed. Jones and Karim, pp. 188–9; Abbasi-Shavazi, Mohammad Jalal, 2005. 'The Rise and Fall of Fertility in Post-Revolutionary Pakistan', in *Islam, the State and Population*, ed. Jones and Karim, pp. 216–19; Winckler, Onn, *Arab Political Demography, Sussex Studies in Demographic Developments and Socioeconomic Policies in the Middle East and North Africa* (Brighton, UK, and Portland, Oreg.: Sussex Academic Press, 2005), pp. 140–41, 145.

27. Longman, *The Empty Cradle*, p. 9.

28. Caldwell, Christopher, 'The East in the West', *New York Times Magazine*, 25 September 2005.

29. Solak, Ferrah, and Attila Hancioglu, 'Islam and Reproductive Health Policies in Turkey', in *Islam, the State and Population*, ed. Jones and Karim, pp. 116–17.

30. Berman, Eli, and A. Stepanyan, 'Fertility and Education in Radical Islamic Sects: Evidence from Asia and Africa' *NBER working paper*, 2003.

31. Abbasi-Shavazi et al., 'Family Change and Continuity in the Islamic Republic of Iran'.

32. Yavuz, Sutay, 'Fertility Transition and the Progression to Third Birth in Turkey', MPIDR working paper, 2005. Also personal calculations with data from Turkish Statistical Institute.

33. Personal calculations from World Values Survey, 4th Wave (1999–2000) and 5th Wave (2005–8).

34. Westoff and Frejka, 'Religiousness and Fertility among European Muslims'; Gilles Kepel, private conversation, 1 October 2009.

35. Personal calculations from Moaddel, Mansoor, Stuart Karabenick and Arland Thornton, *Youth, Emotional Energy, and Political Violence: The Cases*

of Egypt and Saudi Arabia Survey, Association of Religion Data Archives (ARDA), 2005.

36. Norris and Inglehart, *Sacred and Secular*; Kaufmann, 'Human Development and the Demography of Secularisation in Global Perspective'.

37. Quoted in von Drehle, David, 'A Lesson In Hate: How an Egyptian Student Came to Study 1950s America and Left Determined to Wage Holy War', *Smithsonian Magazine*, February 2006.

38. Lewis, Bernard, 2003. *The Crisis of Islam: Holy War and Unholy Terror* (New York: Modern Library, 2003), p. 61.

39. Gellner, *Muslim Society*, pp. 75–90; Zubaida, *Law and Power in the Islamic World*, pp. 74–6.

40. Cole, *Colonialism and Revolution in the Middle East*, ch. 4; Zubaida, *Law and Power in the Islamic World*, pp. 121–42.

41. 'Allah and Opium', *Time*, 9 January 1933.

42. Smith, Anthony, *National Identity* (London: Penguin, 1991), p. 104.

43. Armstrong, Harold Courtenay, *Grey Wolf, Mustafa Kemal* (London: A. Barker, 1932), p. 241

44. Armstrong, Karen, *The Battle for God: Fundamentalism in Judaism, Christianity and Islam* (London: HarperCollins, 2000), p. 227.

45. Zubaida, Sami, 'Islam and Nationalism: Continuities and Contradictions', *Nations & Nationalism* 10:4 (2004), pp. 407–20.

46. Gellner, *Muslim Society*, pp. 66, 78, 117.

47. Zubaida, *Law and Power in the Islamic World*, pp. 103–4.

48. Ibid., pp. 142–4.

49. Goldberg, Ellis, 'Smashing Idols and the State: The Protestant Ethic and Egyptian Sunni Radicalism', *Comparative Studies in Society and History* 33 (1991).

50. Munson, Ziad, 'Islamic Mobilization: Social Movement Theory and the Egyptian Muslim Brotherhood', *The Sociological Quarterly* 42:4 (2001), p. 501.

51. Hroch, Miroslav, *Social Preconditions of National Revival in Europe*, (Cambridge: Cambridge University Press, 1988), pp. 173–4.

52. Munson, *Islamic Mobilization*.

53. Kepel, *Jihad*, pp. 137–42; Halliday, Fred, 'The Iranian Revolution: Uneven Development and Religious Populism', in *State and Ideology in the Middle East and Pakistan*, ed. F. Halliday and H. Alavi (Basingstoke: Macmillan, 1988), pp. 40, 48; F. Hameed, Faissal, 'The Electoral Failure of Islamic Revivalism: The Ideology and Practice of the Jamâ'at-I Islami of Pakistan, 1947–1977', unpublished paper.

54. Levitt, Matthew, and Washington Institute for Near East Policy, *Hamas: Politics, Charity, and Terrorism in the Service of Jihad* (New Haven: Yale University Press, 2006); Sivan, 'The Enclave Culture', in *Strong Religion*, ed. Almond et al.; Kepel, *Jihad*, pp. 44–5.

55. Kepel, *Jihad*, p. 53.

56. Ibid., pp. 36–7; Sivan, 'Enclave Culture', pp. 41, 44–5.

57. Kepel, *Jihad*, p. 52.

58. Gaffney, P. D., 'Popular Islam', *Annals of the American Academy of Political and Social Science* 524 (1992), pp. 47–8.

59. Cincotta, Richard, 'The Youth Bulge Effect: Does a Large Proportion of Young Adults Deter the Rise of Liberal Democracy?', in *Political Demography*, ed. Goldstone et al.

60. Kepel, *Jihad*, p. 66.

61. Gaffney, 'Popular Islam', pp. 50–51.

62. Kepel, *Jihad*, pp. 114, 364; Halliday, 'The Iranian Revolution', p. 49.

63. Kepel, *Jihad*, pp. 116–17.

64. Ibid., pp. 127–30.

65. Ibid., pp. 134–5, 184.

66. Finke, Roger, and Rodney Stark, *The Churching of America, 1776–2005: Winners and Losers in Our Religious Economy*, 2nd edn (New Brunswick, N.J.: Rutgers University Press, 2005).

67. Micklethwait and Wooldridge, *God Is Back*, pp. 269–70.

68. Miguel, Edward, Paul Gertler and David Levine, 'Did Industrialization Destroy Social Capital in Indonesia?', NBER working paper, 2002, p. 21.

69. Wickham, Carrie R., *Mobilizing Islam, Religion, Activism and Political Change in Egypt* (New York: Columbia University Press, 2002), pp. 60–61, 92, 98, 106–7, 110–11, 127; Slackman, Michael, 'Marriage Delayed, Altering Mideast', *International Herald Tribune*, 18 February 2008.

70. Rinaldo, Rachel, 'Pious Islam and Women's Activism in Indonesia', Michigan State University Women in Development Working Paper Series # 291, 2008.

71. Kaufmann, Eric, and Henry Patterson, 'The Dynamics of Intra-Party Support for the Good Friday Agreement in the Ulster Unionist Party', *Political Studies* 54:3 (2006), pp. 509–32.

72. Froese, Paul, *The Plot to Kill God*.

73. Commins, David Dean, *The Wahhabi Mission and Saudi Arabia* (London and New York: I. B. Tauris, 2006).

74. Toft, Monica, 'Getting Religion? The Puzzling Case of Islam and ????', *International Security* 31:4 (2007), pp. 97–131.

75. Toft, 'Getting Religion', pp. 112–17.

76. Philpott, D., 'Explaining the Political Ambivalence of Religion', *American Political Science Review* 101:3 (2007), p. 520.

77. For an account, see Kepel, *Jihad*; Kepel, Gilles, 2004. *The War for Muslim Minds: Islam and the West* (Cambridge, Mass.: Belknap Press of Harvard University Press, 2004); Esposito, John L., *Unholy War: Terror in the Name of Islam* (New York: Oxford University Press, 2002); Juergensmeyer, *Terror in the Mind of God*.

78. Appleby, F. Scott, 'Analyzing Religious Trends – An Overview', paper for INR-NIC Global Religious Trends: Implications for the United States conference, Washington, D.C, 2008.

79. World Values Survey 1999–2000; Ramsay et al., 'Public Opinion in the Islamic World on Terrorism'; ARDA Youth, Emotional Energy and Political Violence survey.

80. ARDA Youth, Emotional Energy, and Political Violence survey; Tessler, M., and A. Jamal, 'Attitudes in the Arab World', *Journal of Democracy* 19:1 (2008), pp. 102–3.

81. Pape, Robert, *Dying to Win: The Strategic Logic of Suicide Terrorism* (New York: Random House, 2005), pp. 270–77; Robbins, M. D. H., 2009. 'What Accounts for the Success or Failure of Islamist Parties in the Arab World?', Harvard Dubai Initiative Seminar, Cambridge, Mass., 11 May 2009.

82. Gray, *Black Mass*, p. 207.

83. Kepel, *Jihad*, p. 154.

84. Ibid., p. 170.

85. Ibid., p. 183.

86. Kepel, *Jihad*, pp. 229, 235; Hussein, Shakira, 'The War on Terror and the 'Rescue' of Muslim Women', in *Islam in World Politics*, ed. N. Lahoud and A. Johns (Abingdon and New York: Routledge, 2005), p. 93.

87. Kepel, *Jihad*, pp. 282, 287, 336, 348.

88. Ibid., pp. 48–9, 82, 91–2, 96, 101, 348, 352.

89. Gurpinar, Aysu Gelgec, *Women in the Twentieth Century: Modernity, Feminism, and Islam in Turkey*, Masters dissertation, University of Texas at Arlington, 2006.

90. Kepel, *Jihad*, pp. 212–13; Halliday, Fred, *Two Hours that Shook the World: September 11, 2001, Causes and Consequences* (London: Saqi, 2002), pp. 162–5.

91. UNDP, *The Arab Human Development Report 2009: Challenges to Human Security in the Arab Countries* (New York: United Nations Development Programme, Regional Bureau for Arab States, 2009), pp. 79–89.

92. Zubaida, *Law and Power in the Islamic World*, p. 223; 'Sudan's Dress Code Row: A Martyr to Her Trousers', *Economist*, 6 August 2009; 'Analysts Say Malaysian Islamic Party Wins Big with Gentler Image', www.

channelnewsasia.com, 9 March 2008; Ayoob, Mohammed, 'The Many Faces of Political Islam', Belfer Center seminar, Harvard University, 22 October 2008.

93. Gusfield, *Symbolic Crusade.*
94. Zubaida, 'Islam and Nationalism'; Kepel, *Jihad,* pp. 250–51.

5. Sacralisation by Stealth: Religion Returns to Europe

1. Wainwright, Martin, 'Obituary: Benedetta Ciaccia', *Guardian,* 9 December 2005.
2. Rai, Milan, *7/7 : The London Bombings, Islam and the Iraq War* (London and Ann Arbor, Mich.: Pluto Press, 2006), pp. 25–50.
3. Johnson and Grim, *World Religion Database,* 2009; Jenkins, *God's Continent,* pp. 61–2, 75.
4. Adsera, A., 'Marital Fertility and Religion: Recent Changes in Spain', IZA Discussion Paper 1399 (University of Chicago: Population Research Center, 2004), p. 23; Berghammer et al., 'Religiosity and Demographic Events'.
5. Regnier-Loilier et al., 'Does Religious Practice Influence Fertility Behaviour in France?'.
6. Kaufmann, 'Human Development and the Demography of Secularisation in Global Perspective'.
7. *European Values Surveys* 1981, 1990, 1997.
8. Wise, Yaakov, 'Britain's Jewish Population on the Rise: Britain's Jewish population is on the increase for the first time since the Second World War, according to new research' *Telegraph Online,* 20 May 2008. The figures are disputed by others. See Graham, David, and Daniel Vulkan, 'Population Trends among Britain's Strictly Orthodox Jews' (London: Board of Deputies of British Jews, 2008); Graham, David, Marlena Schmool and Stanley Waterman, 'Jews in Britain: A Snapshot from the 2001 Census' (London: Institute of Jewish Policy Research, 2007). Wise claims that the JPR/Board of Deputies figures, which place the Haredim at 10–12 per cent of the population and closer to 35–40 per cent of births, inflate the number of non-Orthodox Jews by including non-Jews in their denominator. While the Haredi numbers are lower when set against the population of ethnic Jews (including secular or part-Jews), the question is whether the relevant unit of consciousness is the wider ethnic group or the narrower – active Jewish – population used by Wise.
9. Finnas, F., 'Fertility in Larsmö – the Effect of Laestadianism', *Population Studies – a Journal of Demography* 45:2 (1991), pp. 339–51.

10. Haandrikman, K., and T. Sobotka, 'The Dutch Bible Belt: A Demographic Perspective', working paper, University of Groningen, Population Research Centre, 2003.
11. Haandrikman and Sobotka, 'The Dutch Bible Belt'; Le Roux, Mariette, 'Calvinists Thrive in Dutch Bible Belt', *Jakarta Globe*, 2 September 2009.
12. Berghammer, C., 'Causality between Religiosity and Childbearing: Evidence from a Dutch Panel Study', paper presented at IUSSP conference, 2009.
13. Coleman and Scherbov, 'Immigration and Ethnic Change in Low-Fertility Countries'.
14. Jenkins, *God's Continent*, pp. 58–67, 167.
15. Martin, *Pentecostalism*.
16. Ibid.; Jenkins, *God's Continent*, pp. 58, 92–6; Johnson and Grim, *World Religion Database*; 'A New Jerusalem', *Economist*, 21 September 2006.
17. Silverstein, Paul A., *Algeria in France: Transpolitics, race, and nation*, New Anthropologies of Europe (Bloomington: Indiana University Press, 2004).
18. Crul, Maurice, and Hans Vermeulen, 'Immigration, Education, and the Turkish Second Generation in Five European Nations: A Comparative Study', in *Immigration and the Transformation of Europe*, ed. C. Parsons and T. M. Smeeding (Cambridge: Cambridge University Press, 2006), pp. 238–9.
19. Rai, 7/7, p. 72.
20. Caldwell, *Reflections*, p. 136; Khosrokhavar, Farhad, *L'islam dans les prisons*, Voix et regards (Paris: Balland, 2004).
21. Silverstein, *Algeria in France*, pp. 92–7, 159–60; Caldwell, *Reflections*, p. 16.
22. Caldwell, Christopher, 'Islamic Europe', *Weekly Standard*, 25 September 2004.
23. Weigel, George, *The Cube and the Cathedral: Europe, America, and Politics without God* (New York: Basic Books, 2005); Caldwell, *Reflections*, p. 394; Ferguson, Niall, 'Eurabia?' *Hoover Digest*, 4 April 2004.
24. Jenkins, *God's Continent*, p. 6; Steyn, Mark, *America Alone: The End of the World as We Know it* (Washington, D.C., and Lanham, Md.: Regnery, 2006), p. 65.
25. Ibid., p. 197.
26. Héran, François, and Gilles Pison, 'Two Children Per Woman in France in 2006: Are Immigrants to Blame?', *Population and Societies* 432 (March 2007), p. 2; Westoff, C. F., and T. Frejka, 'Religiousness and Fertility among European Muslims', *Population and Development Review* 33:4 (2007), pp. 785–809; Vegard Skirbekk, Bilal Barakat, Anne Goujon, Samir KC, Eric Kaufmann, Erling Lundevaller and Marcin Stonawski,'Pew Forum Muslim Religious Demography Report: Albania, Bosnia and Herzegovina, France,

Germany, Netherlands, Spain, Sweden and United Kingdom', forthcoming spring 2010.

27. Knight, Richard, 'Debunking a YouTube hit', *BBC Online*, 9 August 2009.

28. UK Census 2001, 'Ethnic Group by Age', table 4.8; Goujon, A., V. Skirbekk and K. Fliegenschnee, 'New Times, Old Beliefs: Investigating the Future of Religions in Austria and Switzerland', paper presented at the Joint Eurostat/UNECE Work Session on Demographic Projections, Bucharest 10–12 October 2007 (Luxembourg: Office for Official Publications of the European Communities); Caldwell, *Reflections*, p. 18.

29. Maréchal, B., *A Guidebook on Islam and Muslims in the Wide Contemporary Europe* (Louvain-la-Neuve: Academia Bruylant, 2002); Westoff and Frejka, 'Religiousness and Fertility among European Muslims', Mapping the Global Muslim Population, Pew Research Center's Forum on Religion and Public Life, 2009, Pew Research Center http://pewforum.org/ p. 32.

30. Office of National Statistics 2006; www.wantedinrome.com, 'Immigrants: Foreign Babies in Rome, 30 November 2006.

31. Goble, Paul, 2008. 'Nearly One-third of Moscow Newborns Are Children of Migrants', *Window on Eurasia*, from Kavkaz Center Russian Events, accessed 4 December 2008.

32. Pedersen, Peder J., Mariola Pytlikova and Nina Smith, 2006. 'Migration into OECD Countries, 1990–2000', in *Immigration and the Transformation of Europe*, ed. Parsons and Smeeding, pp. 56–7; Barbone, Luca, Misha Bontch-Osmolovsky and Salman Zaidi, 'The Foreign-born Population in the European Union and Its Contribution to National Tax and Benefit Systems – Some Insights from Recent Household Survey Data,' World Bank Policy Research working paper 4899 (2009).

33. Myrskyla, M., H. P. Kohler and F. C. Billari, 2009. 'Advances in Development Reverse Fertility Declines', *Nature* 460:7256 (2009), pp. 741–3.

34. Westoff and Frejka, 'Religiousness and Fertility among European Muslims'.

35. Ibid.; Courbage, Y., 'Migrants in Europe: Demographic Characteristics and Socio-Economic Conditions', INED Working Paper (Paris), 2007.

36. Van Tubergen, Frank, 2006. 'Religious Affiliation and Attendance among Immigrants in Eight Western Countries: Individual and Contextual Effects', *Journal for the Scientific Study of Religion* 45:1 (2006), pp. 1–22.

37. European Values Survey, 1999–2000; European Social Survey, 2004; 'UK Mosque Goers to Double Church Attendance: Study', www.Islamonline.net, 4 September 2005.

38. Office for National Statistics and Home Office, *Communities Group, Home Office Citizenship Survey, 2003*, UK Data Archive Study #5367 (2005).

39. UK Census 2001, table 4.11, 'Religion by ethnic group and country of birth'.

40. Phalet, K., and Frea Haker, 'Moslim in Nederland, Diversiteit en Verandering in Religieuze Betrokkenheid: Turken en Marokkanen in Nederland 1998–2002', in *SCP-werkdocument 106b*, Sociaal en Cultureel Planbureau, Utrecht, & Ercomer-ICS, Universiteit Utrecht (2004), pp. 17–22.
41. Amiraux, Valérie, 'L'Islam en France', in *Encyclopaedia Universalis France* (Paris, 2004).
42. The question reads 'Are you a religious person? 1 – Religious, 2 – Not religious, 3 – Atheist.'
43. Silverstein, *Algeria in France*, pp. 36, 54, 70–72.
44. Ibid., pp. 124–7.
45. Paris, J., 'Europe and Its Muslims', *Foreign Affairs* 86:1 (2007), pp. 182–4.
46. Voas, D., 'Intermarriage and the Demography of Secularisation', *British Journal of Sociology* 54:1 (2003), pp. 83–108.
47. Lucassen, Leo, and Charlotte Laarman, 'Immigration, Intermarriage and the Changing Face of Europe in the Post War Period', *The History of the Family* 14:1 (2009).
48. Office for National Statistics, ONS Longitudinal Survey, 2001; Labour Force Surveys (UK), 1990–2001.
49. Ibid.
50. Private conversation with Shiraz Maher, February 2008
51. Labour Force Surveys, 1990–2001.
52. Lucassen and Laarman, 'Immigration, Intermarriage and the Changing Face of Europe'; Klausen, Jytte, *The Islamic Challenge: Politics and Religion in Western Europe* (Oxford and New York: Oxford University Press, 2005), p. 188.
53. Caldwell, *Reflections*, p. 230.
54. Zolberg, A. R., and L. L. Woon, 'Why Islam is Like Spanish: Cultural Incorporation in Europe and the United States', *Politics & Society* 27:1 (1999), pp. 5–38.
55. Rai, *7/7*, p. 97.
56. Al-Azmeh, Aziz, 'Afterword', in *Islam in Europe: Diversity, Identity and Influence*, ed. Aziz Al-Azmeh and Effie Fokas (Cambridge: Cambridge University Press, 2007), p. 210.
57. Cesari, Jocelyne, 'Muslim Identities in Europe: The Snare of Exceptionalism', in *Islam in Europe*, ed. Al-Azmeh and Fokas, pp. 58, 62–4.
58. Mirza, Munir, Abi Senthilkumaran and Zein Ja'far, *Living Apart Together: British Muslims and the Paradox of Multiculturalism* (London: Policy Exchange, 2007), p. 38.

59. Klausen, *The Islamic Challenge*, pp. 100–102; Ramadan, Tariq, 'Europeanization of Islam or Islamization of Europe,' in *Islam, Europe's Second Religion: The New Social, Cultural, and Political Landscape*, ed. S. Hunter (Westport, Conn.: Praeger, 2002), pp. 211–13; Caldwell, *Reflections*, p. 219.

60. Van Tubergen, Frank, *Immigrant Integration: A Cross-national Study* (New York: LFB Scholarly Pub., 2006), pp. 77–82.

61. Mirza et al., *Living Apart Together*, pp. 68–9.

62. Pew Forum on Religion and Public Life, *Muslim Americans: Middle Class and Mostly Mainstream* (Washington, D.C., 2007).

63. Samad, Yunas, 'Muslim Youth in Britain: Ethnic to Religious Identity', for conference on Muslim Youth in Europe: Typologies of religious belonging and sociocultural dynamics, Edoardo Agnelli Centre for Comparative Religious Studies, Turin, 2004.

64. Cesari, 'Muslim Identities in Europe', pp. 59–60; Caldwell, *Reflections*, pp. 128–9; Mirza, *Living Apart Together*, p. 68.

65. Skirbekk et al., 'Pew Forum Muslim Religious Demography Report'; Goujon et al., 'New Times, Old Beliefs'.

66. Goujon, Anne, projections with Austrian and Swiss census data, unpublished.

67. Shore, Zachary, 'Muslim Europe's Dilemma and Muslim Europe's Choice', in *Is There Still a West?: The Future of the Atlantic Alliance*, ed. W. A. Hay and H. Sicherman (Columbia: University of Missouri Press, 2007), pp. 42–3.

68. Coleman and Scherbov, 'Immigration and Ethnic Change in Low-Fertility Countries'.

69. Parsons, Craig, and Timothy M. Smeeding, 'What's Unique about Immigration in Europe', in *Immigration and the Transformation of Europe*, ed. Parsons and Smeeding, p. 16.

70. Largely Hindus, Buddhists and other Eastern religions.

71. Goujon, Anne, projections with Austrian and Swiss census data, unpublished.

72. Bezunartea, Patricia, José Manuel López and Laura Tedesco, 'Muslims in Spain and Islamic Religious Radicalism', in *Ethno-religious Conflict in Europe: Typologies of Radicalisation among Europe's Muslim Nations*, ed. M. Emerson (Brussels: Center for European Policy Studies, 2009), pp. 140–41.

73. Baycroft, T., and M. Hewitson, *What Is a Nation? Europe, 1789–1914* (Oxford: Oxford University Press, 2006), p. 328.

74. Brown, Callum G., *The Social History of Religion in Scotland since 1730: Christianity and Society in the Modern World* (London and New York: Methuen, 1987), pp. 71–6.

75. Bruce, Steve, 'Comparing Scotland and Northern Ireland', pp. 135–42, in *Scotland's Shame?: Bigotry and Sectarianism in Modern Scotland*, ed. T. M. Devine (Edinburgh: Mainstream, 2000), p. 139.

76. Vidino, Lorenzo, and Steven Emerson, *Al Qaeda in Europe: The New Battleground of International Jihad* (Amherst, N.Y.: Prometheus Books, 2006), pp. 52–3.

77. Kepel, *Jihad*, pp. 220, 269–70.

78. Kepel, *The War for Muslim Minds*, p. 255.

79. Bezunartea et al., 'Muslims in Spain', p. 147.

80. Vidino, *Al Qaeda in Europe*, p. 81.

81. Briggs et al., 'Radicalisation among Muslims in the UK', pp. 116–21; Veldhuis, Tinka, and Edwin Bakker, 2009. 'Muslims in the Netherlands: Tensions and Violent Conflict', in *Ethno-religious Conflict in Europe*, ed. Emerson, p. 97.

82. Jenkins, *God's Continent*, p. 214; Briggs, Rachel, and Jonathan Birdwell, 'Radicalisation among Muslims in the UK', in *Ethno-religious Conflict in Europe*, ed. Emerson, p. 113.

83. Buruma, Ian, *Murder in Amsterdam* (New York: Atlantic Books, 2006), pp. 2, 100.

84. Rai, *7/7*, p. 75; Caldwell, *Reflections*, p. 253.

85. 'Muslim artist gets death threats', *BBC Online*, 31 October 2008.

86. Caldwell, *Reflections*, pp. 253–6.

87. Jenkins, *God's Continent*, pp. 240–45.

88. Caldwell, *Reflections*, pp. 213–18.

89. Mirza et al., *Living Apart Together*, p. 41.

90. Ayoob, Mohammed, 'The Many Faces of Political Islam', Belfer Center seminar, Harvard University, 22 October 2008.

91. Kepel, *War for Muslim Minds*, p. 251.

92. Silverstein, *Algeria in France*, pp. 139–42.

93. Kepel, *The War for Muslim Minds*, p. 246.

94. Klausen, *The Islamic Challenge*, p. 171.

95. 'Straw's veil comments spark anger', *BBC Online*, 5 October 2006.

96. Klausen, *The Islamic Challenge*, p. 91.

97. Keaten, Jamey, 'Sarkozy: Burqas Are "Not Welcome" in France', *Huffington Post*, 22 June 2009; Meer, Nasar, and T Modood, 'The Multicultural State We're in: Muslims, "Multiculture" and the "Civic Re-balancing" of British Multiculturalism', *Political Studies* 57:3 (2009), p. 474.

98. Fearon, James, and D Laitin, 'Sons of the Soil, Immigrants and Civil War', working paper, 2009.

99. Kymlicka, Will (ed.), *The Rights of Minority Cultures* (Oxford: Oxford University Press, 1995), p. 8; Kukathas, Chandran, 'Are There Any Cultural Rights?', in *The Rights of Minority Cultures*, ed. Kymlicka, pp. 232–4.

100. Meer and Modood, 'The Multicultural State We're in', pp. 488–9.

101. Taylor, Charles, *Multiculturalism and the Politics of Recognition: An Essay, with commentary by Amy Gutmann, editor … [et al.]* (Princeton, N.J.: Princeton University Press, 1992); Kymlicka, Will, *Finding Our Way: Rethinking Ethnocultural Relations in Canada* (Oxford and New York: Oxford University Press, 1998), p. 27.

102. Caldwell, *Reflections*, p. 87.

103. Bouchard and Taylor, *Building the Future*, pp. 53–4.

104. Kymlicka, *Finding Our Way*, p. 39.

105. Mudde, Cas, *Populist Radical Right Parties in Europe* (Cambridge, UK, and New York: Cambridge University Press, 2007).

106. Bale, T., 'Cinderella and Her Ugly Sisters: The Mainstream and Extreme Right in Europe's Bipolarising Party Systems', *West European Politics* 26:3 (2003), pp. 67–90.

107. Entzinger, Han, 'The Parallel Decline of Multiculturalism and the Welfare State in the Netherlands', in *Multiculturalism and the Welfare State: Recognition and Redistribution in Contemporary Democracies*, ed. W. Kymlicka and K. G. Banting (Oxford and New York: Oxford University Press, 2006).

108. Brubaker, R., 'The Return of Assimilation? Changing Perspectives on Immigration and Its Sequels in France, Germany and the United States', *Ethnic and Racial Studies* 24:4 (2001), pp. 536–78.

109. Bhaskar, Roy, *Reclaiming Reality: A Critical Introduction to Contemporary Philosophy* (London and New York: Verso, 1989).

110. Parekh, Bhikhu, *The Future of Multi-Ethnic Britain: The Report of the Commission on the Future of Multi-Ethnic Britain* (London: Profile Books, 2000).

111. Blunkett, Sir David, 'New Challenges for Race Equality and Community Cohesion in the 21st Century', Institute of Public Policy Research, 7 July 2005, http://www.ippr.org.uk.

112. Meer and Modood, 'The Multicultural State We're in'.

113. Goodhart, D., 'Is Britain Too Diverse?' *Prospect* (February 2004); Goodhart, D., *Progressive Nationalism: Citizenship and the Left* (London: Demos, 2006), p.72.

114. Buruma, *Murder in Amsterdam*, p. 67; Jenkins, *God's Continent*, p. 12.

115. Caldwell, *Reflections*, pp. 259–61.

116. Sacks, Jonathan, *The Home We Build Together: Recreating Society* (London and New York: Continuum, 2007).

117. Quoted in Caldwell, *Reflections*, p. 94.

118. Meer and Modood, 'The Multicultural State We're in', p. 482.

119. Ibid., p. 481.

120. Klausen, *The Islamic Challenge*, p. 37; Laurence, Jonathan, 'Managing Transnational Islam: Muslims and the State in Western Europe', in *Immigration and the Transformation of Europe*, ed. Parsons and Smeeding, pp. 265–6.

121. Schiffauer, Werner, 2007. 'From Exile to Diaspora: The Development of Transnational Islam in Europe', in *Islam in Europe*, ed. Al-Azmeh and Fokas, pp. 73–4, 87; Klausen, *The Islamic Challenge*, pp. 37–44.

122. Laurence, 'Managing Transnational Islam', pp. 267–9.

123. Ibid., p. 269; Caldwell, *Reflections*, p. 200.

124. Conversation with Peter Neumann, ICSR, King's College, 1 October 2009.

125. Caldwell, *Reflections*, p. 251.

126. Dancygier, R., and E. Saunders, 'A New Electorate? Comparing Preferences and Partisanship between Immigrants and Natives', *American Journal of Political Science* (October 2006), pp. 964–81.

127. Kaufmann, *The Rise and Fall of Anglo-America*, p. 281. Barack Obama has generally avoided the immigration issue, viewing it as a third rail of politics that could detract from his more pressing policy priorities.

128. Erk, Jan, 'Red, White and Orange: Dominant Nationalism in France and the Netherlands Compared', in *Dominant Nationalism, Dominant Ethnicity*, ed. André Lecours and G. Nootens (New York: Peter Lang, 2009).

129. Jacobs, D., M. Martiniello and A. Rea, 'Changing Patterns of Political Participation of Immigrant-origin Citizens in the Brussels Capital Region: The October 2000 elections', *Journal of International Migration and Integration* 3:2 (2002), pp. 201–21.

130. Belien, Paul, 'Turning Red: Immigrants Tip the Balance in Belgian Local Elections', *Canada Free Press*, 10 October 2006.

131. Minkenberg, Michael, 'Party Politics, Religion and Elections in Western Democracies', paper for International Studies Association, San Francisco, Ca. (2008); Kaufmann, Eric, 'Religiosity, Ideology and Voting in Western Europe, 1981, 1990: research note' (2007), www.sneps.net/RD/RD1.htm.

132. McAdam, Doug, John McCarthy, and Meyer Zald (eds.), *Comparative Perspectives on Social Movements* (New York: Cambridge University Press, 1996); Carty, R. Kenneth, 'The Politics of Tecumseh Corners: Canadian Political Parties as Franchise Organizations', *Canadian Journal of Political Science* 35:4 (2002), pp. 723–46.

133. Kaufmann, Eric, 'Breeding for God: Religion Returns to Europe', *Prospect* 128 (19 November 2006).

134. Pierce, Andrew, 'Prince Charles to be Known as Defender of Faith', *Daily Telegraph*, 13 November 2008.
135. Schatz, Roland, 'CI Foundation Annual Dialogue Report', 2009.
136. Caldwell, *Reflections*, pp. 183, 271.
137. Goldberg, Michelle, *The Means of Reproduction*, pp. 155–64.
138. Ibid.
139. Ramadan, 'Europeanization of Islam or Islamization of Europe', p. 218.
140. Sennott, Richard, 'Abortion is Suddenly an Issue in British Election', *International Herald Tribune*, 24 March 2005.
141. Klausen, *The Islamic Challenge*, pp. 73–4.
142. Jenkins, *God's Continent*, p. 244.
143. Gledhill, Ruth, 'Archbishop of Canterbury Calls for New Law to Punish "Thoughtless or Cruel" words', *The Times*, 29 January 2008.
144. BBC News, 'Shari'a law in UK is "unavoidable" ', 7 February 2007.
145. BBC News, 'Archbishop defends faith schools', 29 October 2006.
146. Taylor, *Multiculturalism and the Politics of Recognition*.

6. 'A Scholar Society': The Haredisation of the Jewish World

1. Cohen, E. E., *Commentary on the American Scene: Portraits of Jewish Life in America* (New York: Knopf, 1953), introduction.
2. Ben David, D., 'The Moment of Truth', *Ha'aretz*, 8 February 2007.
3. Ibid.
4. Morland, Paul, 'Defusing the Demographic Scare', *Ha'aretz*, 2 June 2009.
5. Liebman, C. S., and E. Don-Yehiya, *Religion and Politics in Israel* (Bloomington: Indiana University Press, 1984), ch. 8.
6. Kirschenbaum, A., 'Fundamentalism: A Jewish Traditional Perspective', in *Jewish Fundamentalism in Comparative Perspective: Religion, Ideology and the Crisis of Modernity*, ed. L. J. Silberstein (New York and London: New York University Press, 1993), pp. 197–202.
7. Heilman, S. C., *Sliding to the Right: The Contest for the Future of American Jewish Orthodoxy* (Berkeley: University of California Press, 2006), p. 159.
8. Stadler, N., *Yeshiva Fundamentalism: Piety, Gender, and Resistance in the Ultra-Orthodox World* (New York: New York University Press, 2009), pp. 9, 38.
9. Demant, P. R., *Jewish Fundamentalism in Israel: Implications for the Mideast Conflict* (Jerusalem: IPCRI, 1994), pp. 4–5.
10. Silber, M. K., 'The Emergence of Ultra-Orthodoxy: The Invention of a Tradition', in *The Uses of Tradition*, ed. J. Wertheimer (Cambridge, Mass. and London: Harvard University Press, 1992), pp. 23–84.

11. Goldstein, Y., *Jewish History in Modern Times* (Brighton, UK and Portland, Oreg.: Sussex Academic Press, 1995), pp. 52–63.

12. Ibid., p. 70.

13. Reform Jews also believed in a universalist, non-national concept of Jewishness, but abandoned this soon after the creation of the state of Israel.

14. Heilman, S. C., 'The Religious Battle for Israel', *Christian Century* (1995).

15. Quoted in Heilman, *Sliding to the Right*, pp. 20–21.

16. Ibid., pp. 28–31.

17. Armstrong, Karen, *The Battle for God: Fundamentalism in Judaism, Christianity and Islam* (London: HarperCollins, 2000), pp. 202–3.

18. Efron, N. J., *Real Jews: Secular versus Ultra-Orthodox and the Struggle for Jewish Identity in Israel* (New York, Basic Books, 2003), p. 261.

19. Ibid., pp. 37–9.

20. Ibid., p. 44.

21. Bruce, S., *The Edge of the Union: The Ulster Loyalist Political Vision* (Oxford: Oxford University Press, 1994).

22. Arian, A., *Politics in Israel: The Second Republic* (Washington, D.C.: CQ Press, 2005), p. 152.

23. Davidman, L. and A. L. Greil, 'Characters in Search of a Script: The Exit Narratives of Formerly Ultra-Orthodox Jews', *Journal for the Scientific Study of Religion* 46:2 (2007), pp. 201–16.

24. Ibid.

25. Iannaccone, L., 'Why Strict Churches Are Strong', *American Journal of Sociology* 99 (1994), pp. 1180–1211.

26. Quoted in Davidman and Greil, 'Characters in Search of a Script', p. 201.

27. Greenberg, D., and E. Witztum, *Sanity and Sanctity: Mental Health Work among the Ultra-Orthodox in Jerusalem* (New Haven: Yale University Press, 2001).

28. Friedman, M., (1992). 'The Lost Kiddush Cup: Changes in Ashkenzic Haredi Culture, a Tradition in Crisis', in *The Uses of Tradition*, ed. Wertheimer, pp. 175–86.

29. Kirschenbaum, 'Fundamentalism', pp. 188, 195.

30. Berman, 'Sect, Subsidy and Sacrifice: An Economist's View of Ultra-Orthodox Jews', *Quarterly Journal of Economics* 155: 3, p. 920.

31. Graham, D., M. Schmool et al., *Jews in Britain: A Snapshot from the 2001 Census* (London: Institute for Jewish Policy Research, 2007), p. 90. Using Schmool et al.'s data, 37.7 per cent of Salford's Jews over the age of twenty-five and 47.1 per cent of Hackney Jews over the age of twenty-five were economically inactive, as against 30.5 per cent in the Jewish population of England and Wales as a whole. Most of the inactive are retired, but

Hackney and Salford Jews have the highest proportion of the economically inactive, and the lowest proportion of retirees among the inactive, of all major UK wards. Of the inactive, 7 per cent in both wards were students. Assuming that all students over the age of twenty-five are men, and that none are postgraduates or mature students in secular institutions, arrive at a maximum of 7 per cent. In fact this is probably a considerable overestimate.

32. Berman, 'Sect, Subsidy and Sacrifice', p. 913.

33. Quoted in Efron, *Real Jews*, p. 65.

34. Ibid., pp. 47–51; Berman, 'Sect, Subsidy and Sacrifice'.

35. Efron, *Real Jews*, pp. 49–50.

36. Friedman, M., 'The Ultra-Orthodox in Israeli Politics', *Jerusalem Letter Viewpoints* 104 (1990).

37. Efron, *Real Jews*, pp. 65–6.

38. Ibid., p. 248.

39. Shahak, I., and N. Mezvinsky, *Jewish Fundamentalism in Israel* (London and Sterling, Va.: Pluto Press, 1999), p. 50.

40. Friedman, 'The Ultra-Orthodox in Israeli Politics'.

41. Shahak and Mezvinsky, *Jewish Fundamentalism in Israel*, pp. 50–55.

42. Rose, A., 'The Haredim: A Defense', *Azure* 25 (Summer 2006).

43. This is the explanation favoured by 'religious markets' and social movements theorists.

44. Hutchinson, J., *Nations as Zones of Conflict* (London: Sage, 2005).

45. Horowitz, *Ethnic Groups in Conflict*.

46. Bainbridge and Stark, *The Future of Religion*, pp. 161–6.

47. Giddens, A., *The Nation-State and Violence* (1985; Cambridge: Polity Press, 1996).

48. Anderson, *Imagined Communities*.

49. Torpey, J., *The Invention of the Passport: Surveillance, Citizenship and the State* (Cambridge: Cambridge University Press, 2000); Brubaker, R., *Citizenship and Nationhood in France and Germany* (Cambridge, Mass. and London: Harvard University Press, 1992).

50. Wimmer, A., *Nationalist Exclusion and Ethnic Conflict* (Cambridge, Cambridge University Press, 2002).

51. Kennaway, B., *The Orange Order: A Tradition Betrayed* (London, Methuen, 2006).

52. Friedman, 'The Ultra-Orthodox in Israeli Politics'.

53. Horowitz, *Ethnic Groups in Conflict*.

54. Kaufmann, *The Rise and Fall of Anglo-America*, ch. 6.

55. Patterson, H., and E. Kaufmann, *Unionism and Orangeism in Northern Ireland Since 1945* (Manchester: Manchester University Press, 2007).

56. 'Israel's Hidden Crisis', *Jewish Daily Forward*, 3 August 2007.

57. Fargues, P., 'Protracted National Conflict and Fertility Change: Palestinians and Israelis in the Twentieth Century', *Population and Development Review* 26:3 (2000), pp. 441–82; Berman, 'Sect, Subsidy and Sacrifice', pp. 935–7.

58. Sosis, R., and B. J. Ruffle, 'Religious Ritual and Cooperation: Testing for a Relationship on Israeli Religious and Secular Kibbutzim', *Current Anthropology* 44 (2003), pp. 713–22.

59. Fargues, 'Protracted National Conflict and Fertility Change', pp. 453–4.

60. Skirbekk, V., Eric Kaufmann and A. Goujon, 'Secularism, Fundamentalism or Catholicism?', *Journal for the Scientific Study of Religion* (forthcoming); Ament, J., 'American Jewish Religious Denominations', *United Jewish Communities Report Series on the National Jewish Population Survey 2000–01* (2005).

61. Della Pergola, S., *American Jewish Year Book* (Philadelphia [etc.]: American Jewish Committee, 2007), pp. 37–8.

62. Though this is more common among the modern Orthodox than the ultra-Orthodox, some of whom believe that they can better maintain their insularity and holiness in exile than in a Zionist state. See Heilman, *Sliding to the Right*, pp. 297–8.

63. Wise, Y., 'Majority of Jews Will Be Ultra-Orthodox by 2050', University of Manchester press release (2007).

64. Cincotta, R., and E. Kaufmann, 'The Changing Face of Israel', *Foreign Policy* (June 2009).

65. Efron, *Real Jews*, pp. 237–8.

66. Ibid., p. 106.

67. Yiftachel, O., and S. Kedar, 'Landed Power: The Emergence of an Ethnocratic Land Regime in Israel', *Teorya Uvikkoret (Theory and Critique)* 19:1 (2000), pp. 67–100.

68. Efron, *Real Jews*, pp. 120–27.

69. Bouchard and Taylor, *Building the Future*, pp. 48–60.

70. Della Pergola, S., 'Jerusalem's Population, 1995–2020: Demography, Multiculturalism and Urban Policies', *European Journal of Population* 17 (2001), pp. 165–99.

71. 'Israel's Hidden Crisis', *Jewish Daily Forward*.

72. Lis, J., 'Jerusalem's New Secular Mayor Barkat Brings Haredim into Coalition', *Ha'aretz*, 12 October 2008.

73. Avishai, B., 'The Obama Peace Deal', *Prospect* (February 2009).

74. Efron, *Real Jews*, p. 128.

75. Diskin, A., and R. Y. Hazan, 'The Knesset Election in Israel, March 2006', *Electoral Studies* 26:3 (2007), p. 711.

76. Elman, M., 'Does Democracy Tame the Religious Radicals? Lessons from the Case of Israel's SHAS party', conference paper, International Studies Association, New York, 2009.

77. Efron, *Real Jews*, p. 135.

78. Ibid., pp. 212–15.

79. Ibid., pp. 152–3.

80. Ibid., p. 154.

81. Ibid., pp. 142–52.

82. Marshall-Fratani, 'The War of "Who Is Who"', pp. 9–43.

83. Billington, R. A., *The Protestant Crusade, 1800–1860: A Study of the Origins of American Nativism* (New York: Macmillan, 1938).

84. Personal discussion with Ehud Eiran and Monica Toft, Harvard University, 2008–9, who have both interviewed key Israeli officials on this point.

85. Cincotta and Kaufmann, 'The Changing Face of Israel'.

86. Morland, 'Defusing the Demographic Scare'.

87. Friedman, M., 'The Ultra-Orthodox in Israeli Politics'.

88. Druze also serve in the military.

89. 'Israel's Hidden Crisis', *Jewish Daily Forward*.

90. Shapiro, H., 'Haredi Yeshiva Students Work Illegally', *Jerusalem Post*, 19 January 1998.

91. Berman, 'Sect, Subsidy and Sacrifice', pp. 913–15.

92. Shapiro, 'Haredi Yeshiva Students'; Efron, *Real Jews*, pp. 189–91.

93. Ibid., p. 57.

94. Ibid., introduction.

95. 'Livni: We've Made Final Offer to Shas', *Jerusalem Post*, 23 October 2008.

96. Levine, J. J., 'More Haredim Go Back to Work', *Jerusalem Post*, 7 April 2008; City Book Services, 'Globalization of Israeli Economy and Haredi Employment', online document (April 2008).

97. Heilman, *Sliding to the Right*, pp. 150–74.

98. http://www.nahalharedi.org/background_about_nahal_haredi.php.

99. Katz, Y., 'The IDF's First "Glatt Kosher" Commandos', *Jerusalem Post*, 6 April 2008.

100. Katz, Y., 'Over 90% of Nahal Haredi Employed', *Jerusalem Post*, 25 December 2007.

101. Efron, *Real Jews*, p. 68.

102. Rose, 'The Haredim: A Defense'.

103. Stadler, *Yeshiva Fundamentalism*, p. xviii.

104. Ibid., p. 112.

105. Ibid., p. 37.

106. Liebman and Don-Yehiya, *Religion and Politics in Israel*, pp. 122–3.

107. Lustick, I., *For the Land and the Lord: Jewish Fundamentalism in Israel* (New York: Council on Foreign Relations, 1988).
108. Lichtenstein, H. A., 'The Ideology of Hesder: The View from Yeshivat Har Etzion', *Tradition – a Journal of Orthodox Jewish Thought* 19:3 (1981).
109. Shahak and Mezvinsky, *Jewish Fundamentalism in Israel*, pp. 90–95.
110. Wise, 'Majority of Jews will be Ultra-Orthodox by 2050'. Wise's figures are a matter of some dispute among scholars. See note 8 in the previous chapter regarding differences in methodology between Wise and others.
111. European Values Surveys, 1981, 1990, 1995–97 combined sample. Total of 852 Jewish respondents under forty-five, and 419 over forty-five.
112. Graham, Schmool et al., 'Jews in Britain', pp. 40–44.
113. Mearsheimer, J. J., and S. M. Walt, 'The Israel Lobby and U.S. Foreign Policy', *KSG Faculty Research Working Paper Series*, John F. Kennedy School of Government, Harvard University (2006).
114. Ament, 'American Jewish Religious Denominations'.
115. Heilman, *Sliding to the Right*, p. 11.
116. Ibid., pp. 40–60.
117. Ibid., p. 68; Ament, 'American Jewish Religious Denominations', pp. 9–10.
118. Hoover, R., 'As Hasidic Population Grows, Jewish Politics May Shift Right', *University of Florida News* (27 November 2006).
119. Ament, 'American Jewish Religious Denominations', pp. 24–5.
120. Heilman, *Sliding to the Right*, pp. 8–9.
121. Kraushaar, J., 'The Secret Behind a Rocker's Election to Congress: Hasidim', *Jewish Daily Forward* (19 January 2007).
122. Heilman, *Sliding to the Right*, p. 64.
123. Kraushaar, 'The Secret Behind a Rocker's Election'.
124. Heilman, *Sliding to the Right*, p. 7.
125. Ibid., p. 299.
126. Smidt, Corwin, 'Religion and Election Day: Voting Patterns', in *The Disappearing God Gap*, ed. Smidt et al. – from tables presented at the American Political Science Association, Toronto, 3–6 September 2009.

7. Shall the Religious Inherit the Earth?

1. Toynbee, Arnold J., *A Study of History Vol. 5: The Disintegrations of Civilizations (Part One)* (Oxford: Oxford University Press, 1962).
2. Gellner, *Muslim Society*, pp. 46, 77; Jackson, Richard, and Neil Howe, 2010. 'Global Aging and Global Security in the 21st Century', in *Political Demography*, ed, Goldstone et al.; Longman, Philip, 'The Return of Patriarchy' *Foreign Policy* (March/April 2006).
3. Anderson, *Imagined Communities*.

4. McNeill, William Hardy, *The Rise of the West: A History of the Human Community* (Chicago: University of Chicago Press, 1963).

5. Russell, Bertrand, *A History of Western Philosophy* (1946; London: George Allen & Unwin, 1985), p. 22.

6. Parsons, Talcott, 'Evolutionary Universals in Society', *American Sociological Review* (1964), pp. 339–57.

7. Fukuyama, *The End of History and the Last Man.*

8. Bell, *The Cultural Contradictions of Capitalism*, p. 171.

9. Micklethwait and Wooldridge, *God Is Back.*

10. Koenig, Laura B., Matt McGue, Robert F. Krueger and Thomas J. Bouchard Jr, 'Genetic and Environmental Influences on Religiousness: Findings for Retrospective and Current Religiousness Ratings', *Journal of Personality* 73:2 (2005), pp. 471–88.

11. Parsons, 'Evolutionary Universals in Society', pp. 345–6; Wilson, *Darwin's Cathedral*, pp. 138–43.

12. Sosis, 'Why Aren't We All Hutterites?', pp. 91–127.

13. Blume, Michael, 2009. 'The Reproductive Benefits of Religious Affiliation', in *The Biological Evolution of Religious Mind and Behavior*, ed. Voland and Schiefenhövel; Reynolds, Vernon, and Ralph Tanner, *The Social Ecology of Religion* (New York and Oxford: Oxford University Press, 1996).

14. Bloch, Ernst, *Atheism in Christianity* (1972; London: Verso, 2009), pp. 10, 225.

15. Gray, *Al Qaeda and What it Means to Be Modern*; Gray, *Black Mass*, chs 3–5.

16. Lovelock, James, 'Selfish Greens', *Prospect* 99 (June 2004).

17. Berlin, Isaiah, *Two Concepts of Liberty* (Oxford: Clarendon Press, 1958).

18. Reiff, Mark A., 'The Attack on Liberalism', in *Law and Philosophy*, ed. Freeman and Harrison, p. 178.

19. Armstrong, *The Battle for God.*

20. Peter, Karl A., Edward Boldt, Ian Whittaker and Lance Roberts, 'The Dynamics of Religious Defection Among Hutterites', *Journal for the Scientific Study of Religion* 21:4 (1983), pp. 327–37.

21. *State of World Population 2009*, ed. R. Engelman, United Nations Population Fund, pp. 25–6.

22. Renton, Alex, 'The Human Time Bomb', *Prospect* (November 2009); 'A New Hate for the Right', *Prospect* (December 2009); Heiser, James, 'Alex Renton Declares War on the Human Race', www.JBS.org, 28 October 2009.

23. Layard, Richard, *Happiness: Lessons from a New Science* (London: Penguin, 2005), p. 72; see also Brooks, Arthur, *Gross National Happiness: Why Happiness Matters for America and How We Can Get More of it* (New York: Basic Books, 2008).

24. Brooks, Arthur, *Who Really Cares: The Surprising Truth About Compassionate Conservatism – Who Gives, Who Doesn't, and Why it Matters* (New York: Basic Books, 2007); Wilcox, W. Bradford, *Soft Patriarchs and New Men: How Christianity Shapes Fathers and Husbands* (Chicago, Ill.: University of Chicago Press, 2004).
25. Dawkins, *The God Delusion*, pp. 306, 308, 347, 352, 374.
26. Harris, Sam, *The End of Faith: Religion, Terror, and the Future of Reason*, 1st edn (New York: W.W. Norton, 2004), pp. 62–3.
27. Gray, *Black Mass*, p. 266; Taylor, *Sources of the Self*.
28. Elster, Jon, *Nuts and Bolts for the Social Sciences* (Cambridge: Cambridge University Press, 1989); Giddens, *Modernity and Self-Identity*; Gray, *Black Mass*, p. 266.
29. Armstrong, Karen, *The Case for God: What Religion Really Means* (London: Bodley Head, 2009); Taylor, *A Secular Age*.
30. Harris, *The End of Faith*, p. 191.

INDEX